ITALIAN IMPRINTS ON
TWENTIETH-CENTURY ARCHITECTURE

ITALIAN IMPRINTS ON TWENTIETH-CENTURY ARCHITECTURE

Edited by Denise Costanzo and Andrew Leach

BLOOMSBURY VISUAL ARTS

LONDON • NEW YORK • OXFORD • NEW DELHI • SYDNEY

BLOOMSBURY VISUAL ARTS
Bloomsbury Publishing Plc
50 Bedford Square, London, WC1B 3DP, UK
1385 Broadway, New York, NY 10018, USA
29 Earlsfort Terrace, Dublin 2, Ireland

BLOOMSBURY, BLOOMSBURY VISUAL ARTS and the Diana logo are trademarks of
Bloomsbury Publishing Plc

First published in Great Britain 2022

Cover design: Eleanor Rose
Cover image: Eugene Feldman, "St. Mark's Square", lithograph, 1965. Eugenefeldman.com.
Palmer Museum of Art of The Pennsylvania State University, Gift of Rosina Feldman, 2002.80.

A catalogue record for this book is available from the British Library.

A catalog record for this book is available from the Library of Congress.

ISBN: HB: 978-1-3502-5772-6
ePDF: 978-1-3502-5773-3
eBook: 978-1-3502-5774-0

Typeset by RefineCatch Limited, Bungay, Suffolk
Printed and bound in Great Britain

To find out more about our authors and books visit www.bloomsbury.com
and sign up for our newsletters.

ILLUSTRATIONS

Figures

1.1 "The Lesson of Rome," Le Corbusier, *Vers une architecture*, 2nd edn (Paris: G. Cres, 1928 [1923]), 119. © Fondation Le Corbusier/ADAGP Copyright Agency, 2021. 1

2.1 Sigfried Giedion, "Situation of Contemporary Architecture in Italy," in *Cahiers d'art* (1931). Cahiers d'art, Paris. 13

2.2 Irenio Diotallevi, Franco Parescotti, and Giuseppe Pagano, "La civiltà e la casa: note introduttive al progetto di quartiere di città orizzontale, studiato dall'ing. Diotallevi, Marescotti e dall'arch. Pagano," in *Costruzione Casabella* (1948). Collection Jean-Louis Cohen. 15

2.3 Ludovico Quaroni and Mario Ridolfi, with Carlo Aymonino, Mario Fiorentino, Carlo Melograni, et al., Tiburtino housing estate, Rome, 1950. Collection Jean-Louis Cohen. 18

2.4 Ludovico Belgiojoso, Enrico Peressutti, and Ernesto Nathan Rogers, Torre Velasca, Milan, 1957. Mondadori Portfolio/Electa/Sergio Anelli. 21

2.5 Giuseppe Samonà, Luigi Piccinato, et al., INA-Casa housing estate, San Giuliano, Mestre, 1951–6. Collection Jean-Louis Cohen. 23

3.1 A Water-Biennale Park in the North of S. Elena from the *ILA&UD Annual Report* 1 (1997). Alison and Peter Smithson Archive, Frances Loeb Library, Harvard University. 29

3.2 Cover of *Casabella* 359–60 (1971), special issue by the Institute for Architecture and Urban Studies. Mondadori/Electa/Marco Covi. 30

3.3 Arata Isozaki and Akira Asada, Haishi/Mirage City project, 1997. © Arata Isozaki, courtesy of Arata Isozaki & Associates. 33

3.4 Installation view of the exhibition *ISOZAKI Arata: SOLARIS*. Photo: KIOKU Keizo. 34

3.5 Jon Jerde's unbuilt design for Mud Island/Festival City near Memphis, 1998. Courtesy: JERDE. 35

4.1 Vincent Scully, "Michelangelo's Fortification Drawings: A Study in the Reflex Diagonal," in *Perspecta: The Yale Architectural Journal* (1952). Reprinted with the permission of *Perspecta*, Yale School of Architecture. 45

4.2 Student models, "Michelangiolo architetto," special issue of *L'architettura. Cronache e storia* (1964). Fondazione Bruno Zevi, Rome. 47

4.3 Luigi Moretti (models), "Strutture e sequenze di spazi," in *Spazio* 7 (December 1952-April 1953). Archivio Centrale dello Stato, Rome. 47

Illustrations

4.4 Colin Rowe, "The Mathematics of the Ideal Villa: Palladio and Le Corbusier Compared," in *Architectural Review* 101 (March 1947). 50

5.1 Portrait of Carlo Lodoli framed by the banderole "One must unite fabrication and reasoning / And function shall be representation." 56

5.2 Alberto Sartoris, *Gli elementi dell'architettura funzionale* (Milan: Hoepli, 1932). 60

5.3 Aldo Rossi, *L'architettura della città* (Padua: Marsilio, 1966). 63

6.1 The Cathedral of Santa Maria del Fiore, Florence. Photograph by the author. 70

6.2 Palazzo Piccolomini (right), Pienza, designed by Bernardo Rossellino. AKG Images/Erich Lessing. 73

6.3 Palazzo Rucellai, Florence, attributed to Leon Battista Alberti. Photo 1890. AKG Images. 74

6.4 Doorway in the east wall of the garden of the Palazzo Piccolomini, Pienza. Photograph by the author. 75

7.1 Leon Battista Alberti, *De re aedificatoria*, first typeset edition (Florence: Nicolaus Laurentii, Alamanus, 1485). 82

7.2 Leon Battista Alberti, *De re aedificatoria*, manuscript, Codex Ms1, ca. 1485. Hanna Holborn Gray Special Collections Research Center, University of Chicago Library, 173a. 83

7.3 Philibert de l'Orme, "The Bad Architect, the Good Architect," woodcut illustrations, 1567. Source: Philibert de l'Orme, *Le Premier Tome de L'Architecture*, Bibliothèque nationale de France (Paris: F. Morel, 1568), 281r, 283r. 85

7.4 Engineer Michael Jay works on the *B of the Bang* sculpture at the AK Heavy Engineering Factory in Sheffield, northern England, May 25, 2004. Reuters Pictures. Photograph by Ian Hogson. 91

8.1 Carla Marzoli with Francesco Gnecchi-Ruscone, view of *Studi sulle proporzioni*, IX Milan Triennale, Milan, 1951. Courtesy of the Archivio Fotografico, La Triennale di Milano, Milan. 96

8.2 Francesco Gnecchi-Ruscone, Project for *Studi sulle proporzioni*, 1951. Courtesy of Archivio Francesco Gnecchi-Ruscone, CASVA, Milan. 102

8.3 Opening of the exhibition *La città dell'ERP*, November 22, 1950. Courtesy of Archivio Istituto Luce, Rome. 104

8.4 Carla Marzoli with Francesco Gnecchi-Ruscone, view of *Studi sulle proporzioni*, IX Milan Triennale, Milan, 1951. Courtesy of the Archivio Fotografico, La Triennale di Milano, Milan. 105

9.1 "Apartment House, Roma, 1936," in *The Work of Architects Olgyay + Olgyay*, 1944. Courtesy Victor Olgyay. 111

9.2 Olgyay + Olgyay, "House Reversed," Budapest, 1939, in *The Work of Architects Olgyay + Olgyay*, 1944. Courtesy Victor Olgyay. 113

9.3 Olgyay + Olgyay, Stühmer Chocolate Factory outside Budapest, 1941, in *The Work of Architects Olgyay + Olgyay*, 1944. Courtesy Victor Olgyay. 115

9.4   Victor Olgyay at Limone sul Garda, Italy, 1935. Courtesy Victor Olgyay.   119

10.1 and 10.2   Jacob Rueff, The successive stages of the development of the human embryo inside the womb, from *De conceptu et generatione hominis* (Tiguri: Christoffel Froschouer, 1554). Courtesy the Wellcome Institute via Wikimedia Commons.   128

10.3   Hand-made terrazzo floor with aggregate in Rouge Royal marble, Chaumont-Gistoux (Belgium), 2007. Photograph by Lionel Devlieger.   130

10.4   Cones of dripped PU from a Flemish boot factory, as displayed in *Deutschland im Herbst* by Rotor. Kraichtal (Germany), 2008. Photograph by Rotor.   131

10.5   Dismantling by Rotor DC of ceramic floor tiles in the former Institut de Génie Civil (architect Joseph Moutschen), Liège (Belgium), 2014. Photograph © Olivier Beart.   132

11.1   Robert Venturi, the elliptical double-ramp staircase of the Certosa in Padula, 1955. The Architectural Archives, University of Pennsylvania, by the gift of Robert Venturi and Denise Scott Brown.   140

11.2   Robert Venturi, the details of the baroque staircase and the facade of the Basilica of San Paolo Maggiore in Naples framing the view of the lively facade of a residential building, 1955–6. The Architectural Archives, University of Pennsylvania, by the gift of Robert Venturi and Denise Scott Brown.   142

11.3   Robert Venturi, the staircase of Palazzo Sanfelice in Naples and its inhabitants, 1955–6. The Architectural Archives, University of Pennsylvania, by the gift of Robert Venturi and Denise Scott Brown.   143

11.4   Robert Venturi, the main staircase of Palazzo Sanfelice in Naples, 1955–6. The Architectural Archives, University of Pennsylvania, by the gift of Robert Venturi and Denise Scott Brown.   144

12.1   Gio Ponti, "Nuvole nel bicchiere," drawing published in Ponti's book of poems, entitled *Nuvole sono immagini* (Milan: All'Insegna del Pesce d'Oro, 1967), 49. Courtesy Gio Ponti Archives.   151

12.2   Gio Ponti, apartment of Ponti's family in Casa Laporte (via Brin, Milan), 1936. On the wall, Massimo Campigli, *La famiglia dell'architetto*, oil on canvas, 1934. Courtesy Gio Ponti Archives.   153

12.3   Daria Guarnati (right) and Gio Ponti (left) meeting in front of the architect's country house in Civate, a small town in the province of Lecco, early 1950s. Courtesy Gio Ponti Archives.   156

12.4   Portrait of Lisa Licitra Ponti (left) and Enrichetta Ritter (right) working in the editorial office of the magazine *Domus*, located in Ponti's atelier, viale Coni Zugna 10, Milan, ca. 1953. Courtesy Gio Ponti Archives.   159

12.5   Gio Ponti, letter to Anala and Armando Planchard, Milan, April 4, 1978. Courtesy of Archivio Gio Ponti Caracas: Correspondencia.   160

13.1   Marking: Lioz limestone cladding, Centro Cultural de Belém, Lisbon. Photograph © Maria Mitsoula. Reproduced with permission.   170

13.2 and 13.3   Framing: the University of Palermo and the Madonie mountains through "earthwork" walls. Photograph © Chris French. Reproduced with permission.   171

13.4   Marking: prefabricated raked concrete facade panels, University of Palermo. Photograph © Chris French. Reproduced with permission.   172

13.5   Measuring: portal windows in "earthwork" walls, University of Palermo. Photograph © Chris French. Reproduced with permission.   173

14.1   Aldo Rossi, *La città analoga*, 1981. Courtesy MAXXI Museo nazionale delle arti del XXI secolo, Roma, Collezione MAXXI Architettura, Archivio Aldo Rossi. © Eredi Aldo Rossi.   180

14.2   Giorgio de Chirico, *Il grande metafisico*, 1917. © Giorgio De Chirico/SIAE, Copyright Agency, 2021.   181

14.3   Aldo Rossi, San Cataldo cemetery, Modena, 1971. Photograph courtesy Diego Terna.   183

14.4   Aldo Rossi, *Il natale di Diane*, ca. 1990. © Eredi Aldo Rossi, Fondazione Aldo Rossi.   189

15.1   Collage by Lina Bo and Carlo Pagani illustrating the article "Lumen," *Stile* 10 (October 1941). Courtesy Gio Ponti Archives.   193

15.2   Wood furniture by Ditta Fratelli Suemin, featured in "Esposizione di Milano del concorso nazionale per l'ammobiliamento economico indetto dall'Opera Nazionale Dopolavoro," *Domus* 11 (November 1928). © Editoriale Domus SpA.   198

15.3   Gastone Medin, set design for *Due cuori felici*, directed by Baldessari Negroni (1932). Included in Edoardo Persico, "L'arredamento moderno nel cinema," *La Casa bella* 59 (November 1932). Archivio fotografico della Cineteca Nazionale—Centro sperimentale di cinematografia, Rome.   199

15.4   Salvo d'Angelo, Kitchen, featured in the "Exhibition of Colonial Equipment" at the VII Milan Triennale (1940). Archivio della Triennale di Milano. © Triennale Milano—Archivi.   201

16.1   Installation view of the exhibition *Italy: The New Domestic Landscape*, Museum of Modern Art, New York, May 26, 1972 through September 11, 1972. Curatorial Exhibition Files, Exh#1004. Photographer Leonardo LeGrand. © MoMA (acc. no: IN1004.232), digital image © 2022, Museum of Modern Art/Scala, Florence.   208

16.2   Mario Bellini, "Kar-A-Sutra," 1972. Photograph by Studio Castelli. Courtesy Mario Bellini Architects.   209

16.3   Gianni Agnelli (standing) and Gianluigi Gabetti (third from the right) at the FIAT shareholders meeting, 1983. © Centro Storico FIAT, Turin.   212

16.4   Installation view of the exhibition *Italy: The New Domestic Landscape*, Museum of Modern Art, New York, May 26, 1972 through September 11, 1972. Photographer: Leonardo LeGrand. © MoMA (acc. no.: IN1004.81), digital image © 2022, Museum of Modern Art/Scala, Florence.   216

17.1   Funeral of Sun-Yat Sen, Nanjing, June 1, 1929, with Mausoleum in the
        background. Historic Collection/Alamy Stock Photo.   223
17.2   Jianghan Road, Wuhan. Imaginechina Limited/Alamy Stock Photo.   224
17.3 and 17.4   Wang Shu, Youth Center, Haining, completed 1990.
        Photographs © Cole Roskam.   227
18.1   Cover page to Part 3 of Robin Boyd, *The Australian Ugliness* (Melbourne:
        Cheshire, 1960). Drawing by Robin Boyd. © Estate of Robin Boyd,
        courtesy Robin Boyd Foundation.   235
18.2   Vittoriano Viganò, Istituto Marchiondi Spagliardi, Baggio, Milan, 1954–8,
        view of the boarders' block and fire escape seen from the northwest.
        RIBA Collections.   239
18.3   Vittoriano Viganò, Istituto Marchiondi Spagliardi, Baggio, Milan, 1954–8,
        close-up of the fire escape of the boarders' block. RIBA Collections.   239
18.4   Cover of *Casabella continuità* 251 (May 1961), special issue devoted to
        "Fifteen Years of Italian Architecture." Mondadori/Electa/Marco Covi.   240
18.5   Cover of Giancarlo De Carlo, *An Architecture of Participation*, Architecture
        in the Seventies: Melbourne Architectural Papers (South Melbourne,
        Victoria: Royal Australian Institute of Architects Victorian Chapter, 1972).
        Australian Institute of Architects.   244
19.1   Henry Hornbostel, travel sketchbook, page 15, 1893 (Rome). Courtesy of
        Carnegie Mellon University Architecture Archives.   254
19.2   Henry Hornbostel, travel sketchbook, page 16, 1893 (Rome). Courtesy of
        Carnegie Mellon University Architecture Archives.   257
19.3   College of Fine Arts, Carnegie Mellon University, Pittsburgh. The Great
        Hall. Portion of ceiling mural, inlaid floor plan, and plaster cast portal
        framing entrance to the Office of the Dean. Photograph by Pablo Garcia,
        used with permission.   260
19.4   College of Fine Arts, Carnegie Mellon University, Pittsburgh. Detail of
        mural in the Great Hall. Henry Hornbostel, architect; James Monroe
        Hewlett, muralist, 1914–15. Creative Commons CC0 Universal Public
        Domain Dedication.   261
20.1   Roberto Segre, *Gráfica urbana*, Havana, 1969, Graphics Department of the
        Commission on Revolutionary Views. Courtesy Concepción R. Pedrosa
        Morgado de Segre.   269
20.2   Roberto Segre, partial view of the José Martí district complex, Santiago de
        Cuba, 1964–7. Courtesy Concepción R. Pedrosa Morgado de Segre.   270

Plates

1   Installation view of the exhibition *ISOZAKI Arata: SOLARIS*. Photo: KIOKU
       Keizo.

2   Engineer Michael Jay works on the *B of the Bang* sculpture at the AK Heavy
     Engineering Factory in Sheffield, northern England, May 25, 2004. Reuters
     Pictures. Photograph by Ian Hogson.

3   Marking: Lioz limestone cladding, Centro Cultural de Belém, Lisbon.
     Photograph © Maria Mitsoula. Reproduced with permission.

4   College of Fine Arts, Carnegie Mellon University, Pittsburgh. Detail of mural in
     the Great Hall. Henry Hornbostel, architect; James Monroe Hewlett, muralist,
     1914–15. Creative Commons CC0 Universal Public Domain Dedication.

5   Doorway in the east wall of the garden of the Palazzo Piccolomini, Pienza.
     Photograph by Caspar Pearson.

6   Francesco Gnecchi-Ruscone, Project for *Studi sulle proporzioni*, 1951. Courtesy of
     Archivio Francesco Gnecchi-Ruscone, at CASVA, Milan.

7   Robert Venturi, details of the baroque staircase and the facade of the Basilica of
     San Paolo Maggiore in Naples, framing the view of the lively facade of a
     residential building, 1955–6. The Architectural Archives, University of
     Pennsylvania, by the gift of Robert Venturi and Denise Scott Brown.

8   Gio Ponti, letter to Anala and Armando Planchard, Milan, April 4, 1978.
     Courtesy of Archivio Gio Ponti Caracas: Correspondencia.

9   Aldo Rossi, San Cataldo Cemetery, Modena, 1971. Photograph courtesy
     Diego Terna.

10   Wang Shu, Amateur Architecture Studio, Youth Center, Haining, Zhejiang, 1990.
     Photograph courtesy Cole Roskam.

LIST OF CONTRIBUTORS

Giorgia Aquilar is an architect and research fellow at the IUAV University of Venice, postdoctoral scholar at the Bauhaus University Weimar, and lecturer in architectural theory at Berlin International University of Applied Sciences. She was a Humboldt Postdoctoral Researcher and TUM Foundation Fellow at the Technical University of Munich, Honorary Research Fellow at the Bartlett School of Architecture at UCL, and Adjunct Professor at the University of Naples Federico II. She was the 2015-16 A.E. Bye Archival Research Fellow at the Pennsylvania State University and received grants and awards for her scholarly work, including from the Dumbarton Oaks Research Libraries and Collections of Harvard University.

Daniel A. Barber is an Associate Professor of Architecture and Chair of the Ph.D. Program at the University of Pennsylvania's Weitzman School of Design. He researches historical relationships between architecture and global environmental culture, reframing the means and ends of architectural expertise towards a more robust engagement with the climate crisis. Barber's most recent book is *Modern Architecture and Climate: Design before Air Conditioning* (2020). He has held fellowships at the Harvard Center for the Environment, the Princeton Environmental Institute, the Sydney Environmental Institute, and through the Alexander von Humboldt Foundation. Barber edits the *Accumulation* series on *e-flux Architecture* and is a co-founder of *Current*, a platform for the discussion of environmental histories of architecture.

Frank Bauer is a research associate in the Cluster of Excellence "Matters of Activity" at Humboldt University in Berlin. His Ph.D. at Berlin University of the Arts (UdK) engineers instrumental and operative extensions of manufacturing in computational art production. Bauer studied architecture at UdK, with stays at UIC/IIT Chicago, and social science and cultural history at Freiburg, Berlin, and Mainz. Following positions at the Fondation Vasarely and KWY Lisbon, he co-founded Büro Vogel Bauer, a planning agency for fine arts production. Bauer teaches in the Architecture and Design & Computation programs at UdK and the Design for Manufacture MArch at The Bartlett (UCL).

Maristella Casciato, architect and architectural historian, is Senior Curator of Architecture at the Getty Research Institute in Los Angeles (2016-present). She was Mellon Senior Fellow (2010), then Associate Director of Research (2012-15) at the Canadian Centre for Architecture, Montreal. Casciato has taught the history of architecture in Italy and in the United States. Since the late 1990s, she has investigated Pierre Jeanneret and the planning of Chandigarh in post-colonial India, on which she has curated multiple exhibitions and published extensively. Casciato co-curated the 2020 exhibition *Gio Ponti. Amare l'architettura* at the MAXXI Museum in Rome and co-edited the eponymous volume.

Dijia Chen is a doctoral candidate in the University of Virginia's School of Architecture. Her dissertation, "Displaced Display: The Making of Contemporary Chinese Architecture in the Sino-German Exhibitionary Contact Zone," examines the architectural production of the developing world as a form of mediated knowledge under asymmetrical power dynamics. Her research brings together the study of contemporary Chinese architecture, transcultural communication studies, and curatorial studies. Chen's work has appeared in the *Architectural Theory Review*, *Histories of Postwar Architecture*, and *Log*, and has been supported by the American Council of Learned Societies, Visual Resources Association, and the Society of Architectural Historians.

Lorenzo Ciccarelli studied architecture at the Politecnico delle Marche and earned his Ph.D. from Rome Tor Vergata. He is a Research Fellow in the History of Architecture at the University of Florence. His studies consider the international connections of twentieth-century Italian architecture. Ciccarelli is the author of *Renzo Piano before Renzo Piano* (2017) and *Il mito dell'equilibrio* (2019), and has co-edited *Largest Architectural Firms: Design Authorship and Organization Management* (2021). His most recent book is the co-edited collection *Post-War Architecture between Italy and the UK* (2021). Ciccarelli has been a Visiting Fellow at the University of Queensland (2019) and at University College London (2021).

Jean-Louis Cohen trained as an architect and a historian, and has since 1994 held the Sheldon H. Solow Chair for the History of Architecture at New York University's Institute of Fine Arts. He has published more than thirty books, including *Building a New New World: Amerikanizm in Russian Architecture* (2020), *Frank Gehry: Catalogue Raisonné of the Drawings*, vol. 1, *1954–1978* (2020), *Le Corbusier: The Built Work* (2018), *France, Modern Architectures in History* (2015), *Le Corbusier: An Atlas of Modern Landscapes* (2013), *The Future of Architecture since 1889* (2012), *Architecture in Uniform* (2011), and *Le Corbusier and the Mystique of the USSR* (1992).

Denise Costanzo is Associate Professor of Architecture in the Pennsylvania State University's Stuckeman School, where she teaches history and theory. She is the author of *What Architecture Means: Connecting Architecture and Design* (2016), along with essays in volumes on architectural, art, and cultural history from the early modern era to the present. In 2015 she was the Marian and Andrew Heiskell Rome Prize Fellow in Modern Italian Studies at the American Academy in Rome. Her next book is *Modern Architects and the Problem of the Postwar Rome Prize: France, Spain, America and Britain, 1946–1960*.

Lionel Devlieger is a researcher, designer, educator, and exhibition maker. In 2021, he was appointed Chair of Material-Cultural History of Architectural Practice at the Faculty of Engineering and Architecture of Ghent University. He co-founded Rotor, a research and design group focusing on building element salvage and reuse in 2006. Devlieger has also taught architecture at UC Berkeley, TU Delft, Columbia University, the AA School in London, and elsewhere. He has curated and designed, with Rotor, critically acclaimed exhibitions on architecture and material culture. He is the co-author of *Deconstruction et réemploi* (2018), a reference on building component reuse.

Chris French is Lecturer in Architecture and Contemporary Practice at ESALA, University of Edinburgh. He received his Ph.D. in Architecture by Design from the University of Edinburgh in 2015, funded by the AHRC. His research explores the relationship between critical forms of representation and the production of architectural and urban imaginaries, and the intersection of architecture and agricultural and urban landscapes. Central to both interests is design-research and design-practice. French has worked in architectural practice in Scotland and Spain, and is co-founder and editor of the architectural design-research e-journal *Drawing-On*.

Ignacio G. Galán is an architect and historian and Assistant Professor at Barnard College, Columbia University. His scholarship addresses the relationship between architecture, politics, and media, with a particular focus on nationalism, colonialism, and migration. Galán's research has been featured in a number of journals including the *Journal of the Society of Architectural Historians* and exhibitions including the installation *Cinecittá Occupata* for the 2014 Venice Biennale. He has co-edited the volumes *After Belonging* (2016) for the 2016 Oslo Architecture Triennale—which he co-curated—and *Radical Pedagogies* (2022).

Diane Ghirardo is ACSA Distinguished Professor of Architecture at the University of Southern California and a world-renowned architectural historian. Ghirardo's book *Aldo Rossi and the Spirit of Architecture* (2019) is one of many other works on Rossi following her first English translation of his 1966 *Architecture of the City* in 1982. Her books include *Building New Communities: New Deal America and Fascist Italy* (1989); *Out of Site: A Social Criticism of Architecture* (1992); *Architecture After Modernism* (1996), *Dopo il Sogno: Architettura e città nell'America di oggi* (2008); *Italy: Modern Architectures in History* (2013); and *Lucrezia Borgia: Le lettere* (2020).

Philip Goad is Chair of Architecture and Redmond Barry Distinguished Professor in the Faculty of Architecture, Building and Planning at the University of Melbourne. His research interests focus on modernism, architectural criticism, professional networks, and architecture for housing, education, and health after World War II. Goad's most recent books include *Architecture and the Modern Hospital: Nosokomeion to Hygeia* (with Julie Willis and Cameron Logan, 2019), *Bauhaus Diaspora and Beyond: Transforming Education through Art, Design and Architecture* (with Ann Stephen, Andrew McNamara, Harriet Edquist, and Isabel Wünsche, 2019), and *Australia Modern: Architecture, Landscape and Design 1925–1975* (with Hannah Lewi, 2019).

Andrew Leach teaches the history of architecture at the University of Sydney School of Architecture, Design and Planning, where he was appointed Professor of Architecture in 2016. His books include *Manfredo Tafuri* (2007), *What is Architectural History?* (2010),

The Baroque in Architectural Culture, 1880–1980 (2015, edited with Maarten Delbeke and John Macarthur), *Rome* (2016), and *Crisis on Crisis* (2018). In 2018, he was a Wallace Fellow at the Harvard Center for Italian Renaissance Studies, Villa I Tatti; and was the 2019–20 Stuckeman Visiting Professor of Interdisciplinary Design at Penn State University. His next book is called *Unstylish Style*.

Raúl Martínez Martínez is is an architect, historian, and MArch II student at Yale University. He was previously an adjunct lecturer in the Department of Theory and History of Architecture at Universitat Politècnica de Catalunya (where he earned his Ph.D.) and at the Illinois Architecture Study Abroad Program in Barcelona-El Vallès. Specializing in the historiography of modern and postmodern architecture, he has published on the concepts of space and empathy as well as on methods for the analysis of architecture. His work has appeared in the *Journal of the History of Ideas*, the *Journal of Architecture*, *arq: Architectural Research Quarterly*, *Arquitectura Revista*, and elsewhere.

Silvia Micheli studied architecture at the Politecnico di Milano and earned her doctorate at IUAV (Venice). She is a Senior Lecturer in Architecture at the University of Queensland. Her research investigates global architecture and cross-cultural exchanges in the twentieth and twenty-first centuries. She co-edited *Italy/Australia: Postmodern Architecture in Translation* (2018), co-authored *Storia dell'Architettura Italiana 1985–2015* (2013), and co-edited *Italia 60/70. Una Stagione dell'Architettura* (2010). Micheli is currently preparing a book on the work of Paolo Portoghesi, to be published by Bloomsbury. She collaborates with such institutions as the Alvar Aalto Foundation, Centre Pompidou, Vitra Design Museum, MAXXI Museum, and the Seoul Biennale of Architecture and Urbanism.

Daniela Ortiz dos Santos is Assistant Professor at the Goethe University Frankfurt and coordinator of the Center for Critical Studies in Architecture, a research cluster based in Frankfurt that collaborates with the Deutsches Architekturmuseum and the Technical University Darmstadt. She studied architecture in Rio de Janeiro and Buenos Aires and received her doctorate from ETH Zurich. Ortiz dos Santos' research, teaching, and curatorial activities focus on the intersection between transatlantic architectural history and historiography. She is co-editor of *Bauhaus Clouds: Challenges to the Nebula of Architectural Histories and Archives* (forthcoming) and co-curator of the exhibition *gta Films* (gta Institute/ETH Zurich, 2017).

Caspar Pearson is Senior Lecturer in Art History at the Warburg Institute. His work focuses on the art and architecture of the Italian Renaissance, as well as historiography and the afterlives of the Renaissance in later periods. He is particularly interested in images and writings regarding cities, in the relationship between representation and place, and in Renaissance theories of architecture and urbanism. Pearson is the author of *Humanism and the Urban World: Leon Battista Alberti and the Renaissance City* (2011) and the forthcoming *The Chameleon's Eye: Leon Battista Alberti in Perspective*.

Ute Poerschke is Professor of Architecture in the Stuckeman School at the Pennsylvania State University, where she teaches architectural design. She is a co-principal of Friedrich

Poerschke Zwink Architects/Urban Planners and co-editor of *Wolkenkuckucksheim—Cloud-Cuckoo-Land—Воздушныы замок*, a journal of architectural theory published since 1996. She has previously taught in Berlin and Munich. Poerschke's research focuses on functionalism in architecture and the relationship between technology and architecture. Her publications include *Architectural Theory of Modernism: Relating Functions and Forms* (2016) and *Theorie der Architektur. Zeitgenössische Positionen* (co-edited with Sebastian Feldhusen, 2017).

Rosa Sessa is an architect, curator, and researcher in architectural history at the University of Naples Federico II. Her first book, *Robert Venturi e l'Italia: Educazione, viaggi e prime progetti, 1925‑1966* (2020), investigated Italy's influence on Venturi's early work. She has been a visiting scholar at the University of Pennsylvania and at the Technical University of Munich, won a 2021 Fulbright fellowship for her research on women architects and travelers in postwar architectural culture at New York University's Institute of Fine Arts, and an Italian Fellowship at the American Academy in Rome for 2021‑2.

Francesca Torello is an architectural historian and is Special Faculty with the Carnegie Mellon University School of Architecture. She writes on the role of history in architectural education and practice, and is engaged in digital humanities projects that explore architecture's latent virtuality. Torello is currently working on American travel to the Mediterranean between 1870 and 1920, in connection with the study of two "Grand Tour surrogates" from Pittsburgh's Gilded Age: the College of Fine Arts, a beaux-arts building on the Carnegie Mellon campus, and the collection of architectural plaster casts of the Carnegie Museum of Art.

Federica Vannucchi is an architect and architectural historian who teaches global history and theory of architecture, and urban history and analysis at the Pratt Institute, and has also taught at Columbia, Parsons, Yale, and Princeton. Her scholarly interests include the global history of architectural pedagogy, architectural exhibitions, international relations, and political theory. Vannucchi's book manuscript, entitled *A Disciplinary Mechanism: The Milan Triennale, 1964–1973*, concerns the architectural exhibition as a national and international agent of cultural, political, and diplomatic exchange. She holds a Ph.D. in Architecture from Princeton and master's degrees from Yale and the University of Florence.

ACKNOWLEDGMENTS

Many of this volume's authors met together with us on the main campus of Penn State University in mid-January 2020 to discuss "Italian Imprints," traveling from London, Brisbane, Los Angeles, Naples, New York, Berlin, and elsewhere to talk through the legacy of Italy's long-standing centrality to the history and criticism of architecture's long twentieth century. While we were following the news of a troubling new virus, we could not have foreseen that our in-person gathering would be the last such experience any of us would have from then until now, as we dispatch this manuscript to press. In so many respects, the continuing conversations we have enjoyed with our colleagues from around the world, trading ideas through digital media, have sustained us in vital ways as the pandemic took hold and changed so many aspects of work and life. For this we are grateful to all our authors and interlocutors. That our conversations have now turned to the presentation of this book on sales tables at live conferences we might attend in person (or so we are assured, fingers crossed) seems surreal, but this turn of events seems a fitting return to a project that inadvertently spanned a period of global pause.

The underlying infrastructure of this project was the Stuckeman Professorship in Interdisciplinary Design, a visiting position which Andrew held on Denise's nomination in 2019 and 2020. Its agenda has been wrapped around the central question this book explores, and it has been gratifying to see how much this concern, a natural overlap of our areas of interest, has resonated with our colleagues. That we were able to meet in person and pursue our thinking around this question into its published form owes much to the generosity of many entities and individuals. Chief among these are Penn State's Stuckeman School and its current Director, Patricia Kucker, as well as her predecessor Kelleann Foster. We also wish to thank the Department of Architecture and its Head, Mehrdad Hadighi, for crucial support on many fronts. They, along with other colleagues in Architecture—particularly Pep Avilés, Ute Poerschke, and Alexandra Staub—enriched the symposium through their participation. So did valued colleagues in the Department of Art History, including Elizabeth Mansfield, its Head, along with Madhuri Desai and Robin Thomas. It was a clear demonstration of how architectural history provides a vital discursive space that transcends academic silos.

Many other Penn State colleagues provided countless forms of support and creative contributions. Among them are Jamie Behers, Jennifer Howard, Janejira Kalsmith, Karen McNeal, Courtney Wingard, Pam Wertz, and Ranasadat Zarei. Further gratitude is due to the School of Architecture, Design, and Planning at the University of Sydney, which gave Andrew the freedom to accept Penn State's invitation and which offered opportunities to share this work in its development with colleagues and students.

Our hope that our contributors' critical conversation could reach a wider audience found a wonderfully receptive audience at Bloomsbury Press. We thank its editors James

Thompson and Alexander Highfield for their encouraging welcome to this project, and for the many ways they and their expert staff have shepherded this book through to completion. Their anonymous reviewers offered vital direction and suggestions that have made this book stronger, and which make its contents available to a wider audience than we first envisaged. Ronnie Hanna and Merv Honeywood expertly guided the manuscript to its final form. At Penn State, our editorial assistant James (Jimmy) Phillips provided indispensable assistance, helping us transform twenty essays into one coherent manuscript with characteristic ebullience and alacrity. We thank him and all our authors, who shared their own outstanding research and generously welcomed lively exchanges and editorial suggestions.

We extend further gratitude to those who provided illustrations that support and enrich the conversation in the pages ahead. We wish to highlight two especially: the Gio Ponti Archive in Milan, which shared numerous images from a figure who features across several chapters, and the family of Eugene Feldman, whose enigmatic lithograph of the Piazza San Marco in Venice, produced in 1965 and now owned by Penn State's Palmer Museum of Art, graces our cover. This image, sitting next door to the Stuckeman Building, captured perfectly our project's central aim: to highlight the uncanny familiarity of figures in an iconic Italian space, and consider the shadows they cast. It was an ideal image to represent the symposium, and this book which has now resulted.

Finally, we add our deepest thanks to two families. One gamely joined the adventure by crossing two hemispheres, trading a searing summer for snow and sleet; another helped welcome them and others who converged during the Pennsylvania winter. That they now know each other is a delight.

CHAPTER 1
IMPRINTS AND TRACKS
Denise Costanzo and Andrew Leach

Le Corbusier's *Vers une architecture* of 1923 is almost indisputably the twentieth century's most influential publication on architecture. This famous book urges architects to embrace a brave new industrial world of engineers, ocean liners, and airplanes. It reminds them of transcendent formal principles, and culminates with Le Corbusier's vision of architectural "perfection," which he sees in the Athenian Acropolis and (with characteristic modesty) his own work. At the precise midpoint of this sweeping modernist vision is a detour of a chapter called "La leçon de Rome" (see Figure 1.1). The title is written in the singular—"*The* Lesson of Rome"—insisting that there is one crucial truth to be drawn from this storied city; yet this essay's message is deeply ambivalent. On the one hand, Rome is a danger, a place where "you find every sort of horror." He calls it "the damnation of the half-educated," and warns readers that sending young architects there will leave

Figure 1.1 "The Lesson of Rome," Le Corbusier, *Vers une architecture*, 2nd edn (Paris: G. Crès, 1928 [1923]), 119. © Fondation Le Corbusier/ADAGP Copyright Agency, 2021.

them "crippled [mutilated] for life." But it also presents a test of an architect's worth. As Frederick Etchells's venerable translation has it, "the lesson of Rome is for wise men, who can resist and can verify."[1]

The Rome of Le Corbusier's Italy is a paradox. He insisted that architects must liberate themselves from the most pervasive form of influence it exercised in his own day: the academic myth of this ancient capital as a well-spring of the classical tradition, enthroned as the permanent capital of art. And yet, those architects who go there with discerning "eyes that can see" can also extract from the city's open-air classrooms of monuments and ruins valid forms of inspiration, which can, in turn, imbue their own work with authentic greatness. Such a lesson is hardly new to the modern age.[2] This discernment, insists Corbu, is what separated the architects of Michelangelo's circle from their lesser counterparts. The singular but Janus-faced "lesson of Rome" is a perilous promise. It is architecture's perennial proving ground.

In a cunningly oblique strategy, "la leçon de Rome" was also at the very center of Le Corbusier's frontal assault on his Beaux-arts foes. He equated the city's sacred icons—the Pantheon, St. Peter's dome, and the Palazzo Farnese—with grain silos, turbines, and automotive brake assemblies, all fodder for the architect's critique and appropriation. He neither ceded academicism its center of gravity by ignoring Rome outright, nor attacked it as a burden to be consigned to an inert, pre-modernist past. Rather than dismissing or demonizing the ancient city, he used new rhetoric, new associations, and doctored images to embed it in a new worldview that neutralized its long-standing symbolic charge before harnessing its energies to serve his own agenda.

These observations only begin to unpack the implications of Le Corbusier's Italian experiences and exhortations.[3] But his location of Rome at the heart of this modernist manifesto confronts us with a reality that sits at the heart of this book, too, and provides a clear starting point for the chapters that follow these introductory lines. It begins from a seemingly unwavering authority asserted by Rome that architects and scholars continue to wrangle nearly a century later. Rome had, indeed, only become Italy's capital mere decades before Le Corbusier first went there; and just fifty years before *Vers une architecture* was sent to press. Its claim on the title *caput mundi* was, though, millennia in the making, and its monuments long embodied the imperial, religious, and legislative power that flowed from the banks of the Tiber to the north and south of the peninsula. For some, that authority has been, or remains, natural and unassailable; for others, something dangerous and demanding correction. We see this tension presented vividly during the eighteenth century in Piranesi's carefully constructed cases for Rome and its architectural traditions as a welcome weight or a burden to throw off, presented in his fictional dialogue between Didascalo and Protopiro, and in his own debates with such contemporaries as Pierre-Jean Mariette.[4]

Perhaps we have begun with a burdensome assumption of our own. For all its prominence, Rome is not, of course, the encapsulation of Italy. But its status for architecture up to the period of Le Corbusier's text can be taken as a specific, *a fortiori* case of many issues and themes that emerge in considerations of the cities and landscapes of Italy across his century, including those one might wish to challenge. The observations

Le Corbusier made of the modern Italian capital pertain equally to the presence of Milan, Venice, or Florence in the critical landscape of architecture's twentieth century. He wrote on Rome's "lesson" for architects when the cities, architecture, and architects of Italy's aggregate history were still widely assumed to have special authority over his field, and when operating definitions of "architecture" and "the architect" continued to rely on distinctions first operationalized in Tuscany. The twentieth century held fast—albeit on an ever-expanding set of premises—to a sense of primacy that had been cultivated for centuries. Aesthetes, archaeologists, antiquarians, and architects of the eighteenth and nineteenth centuries had already turned their attention beyond Rome, looking carefully at the accumulated histories of Venice, Naples, Siena, and Ravenna—each distinct, yet together intertwined, and for modern readers foregrounding the unified modern polity. For the architect, though, Rome's singular aura and prestige were, arguably, chief among these, and Le Corbusier, in his turn, leveraged them boldly, even as he chafed against their existing forms and boundaries.

His urge to redefine the influence of historical figures and works on modern architectural culture—models of departure rather than exemplars to ape—would be typical of many other movements, designers, authors, and organizations who across the century, in locations reaching all around the globe, examined the power that precedents and predecessors had long asserted over their respective enterprises. The lesson of Rome was hardly his alone to discover, or new to the modern movement. But his location of this lesson at the center of his own radical vision makes this problem distinctive and compelling. He asserts his own claim to authority by turning to a place whose stature was once, but is no longer, considered unquestionable: Italy.

*　*　*

Despite the century that has passed since *Vers une architecture* first entered circulation, Italy retains its vast reach over the world of architecture—even if, for some, on terms that have become entirely different from those activated by Le Corbusier. The peninsula's ancient, medieval, and early modern sites, along with its spectrum of urban complexities, modernities, and debates, have been drawn into centuries of thinking and experimentation that "established" and extended architecture in productive ways. As such, Italy has variously formed a setting, a context, and a geographical limit for considering and practicing architecture; its very name invokes an historical field, a body of knowledge, and a cultural diaspora. In its long-standing centrality to architectural culture—a matter of education, erudition, and endurance—it constitutes one of modern architecture's many institutions. It is maintained in the rehearsal of a historical trajectory reaching from the Renaissance to the modern age; in the close study of traditions bound inextricably to the architecture and writing of ancient Rome; in the acculturating processes of studying in satellite campuses in Florence, Venice, or Milan; and in following field-trip itineraries in Naples, Palermo, or Turin.[5] Italy is upheld within the disciplinary canon, but it also figures in moments of anti-canonical resistance; in the sense of importance bestowed upon those prominent figures and debates around which the currents of modern and contemporary architecture flow; and in the dams formed by radicals and critics that make the passage of ideas through time uneasy. But what becomes of this system as historical knowledge and the imperatives behind its production change, as they surely must, and as they always have done?

At the core of this relationship between architecture and Italy is a sense, given voice across the last century, that architecture everywhere owed fifteenth-century Tuscany a foundational debt for fostering a concept, *disegno*, against which architecture was long tested.[6] Florentine architects had themselves long regarded Rome as a live lesson in their art, the ancient measure for all new ideas. Theirs was one of the many circles that could reach this city by road or sea, inscribing paths that became entrenched as the international *longue durée* of academicism's veneration of Rome and its antiquity brought this authority into the center of a modern architecture wary of history and precedent—something to extend, or to overcome—even as others looked towards new ideas and seemingly new authorities in Vienna, Paris, or Chicago. The shadow cast by beaux-arts academicism and the travel and mimetic practices that sustained it was just one of many phenomena drawing architects back to Italy again and again during the twentieth century. The dominance of Milan and Florence as bastions of Italian modernism sit alongside the Venice School's critical histories, postwar and postmodern investment in baroque space, Renaissance proportion, mannerist ambiguity, and manifold modes of historiographical referentiality as various kinds of "centers," each with a different locus of authority, or way of asserting it. The lesson of Rome—a singular lesson from a singular place—came to form part of a constellation of sites of architecture and debate. And this on top of designs by dozens of architects from Milan to Marsala with varying forms of magnetic appeal who shaped the trajectories and importance, on its own terms, of Italian modernism and postmodernism. Italy's footprints can consequently be found across histories of twentieth-century architectural culture, just as many parts of the world have found it important to "return" to Italy (modern and otherwise) for instruction, or to draw alternate pathways from these moments of architecture's "original sin"—as Manfredo Tafuri once put it.[7] These and other irreconcilable and yet interrelated "lessons" inflect and intensify Le Corbusier's own conflicted message of Italy's (and history's) complex place in modern architectural culture as both problematic foil and powerful inspiration. All collectively reinforce one condition: to understand twentieth-century architecture, one must (somehow) know Italy.

*　*　*

The chapters that follow have accepted an invitation to look at the imprints left by Italian architecture—however construed, from chapter to chapter—in the architectural culture of the long twentieth century. That Italy itself is a construction of nineteenth-century nationalism does little to counteract the clear sense that its cities and countryside have long formed a series of interrelated centers in which the production of buildings, treatises, manifestoes, events, and debates have proven important for architects and students of architecture beyond their most immediate constituencies. The confluence of this deep history and (yes) influence, which had been explored in modern terms by penetrating essays by Georg Simmel on Florence, Venice, and Rome, followed a twentieth-century path shaped by architecture's institutions in Italy and abroad; tourism, mobility, and migration; economic fluctuations and political imperatives; as well as the work of publishing houses, museums, archives, intellectuals, and architects.[8]

And yet, to assert (or indeed study) its pervasive impact on contemporary architecture inevitably invokes a contentious privilege. The enduring prominence of figures, works, and debates we can now claim for Italy in both the historiography of architecture and the contemporary artistic imagination demands reflection in the age of "global" architectural history. What are the corrective moves needed to read its architecture into those geographical, economic, racial, or cultural situations seemingly irreconcilable with narratives established over centuries of scholarly attention and architectural emulation? We recognize, naturally, the importance of pushing past the layer of abstractions and operative myths on which this authority rests to enter more deeply into the complexity of Italy's architecture when we study it on its own terms, as history. How can we, though, account both for the specificity of the social, cultural, and political settings in which buildings were realized, ideas committed to paper, images entered circulation, and for the abstractions and "lessons" derived from them? Does the study of Italian architecture—in curricula, and through institutions—reinforce an idea of architecture and the historical heft of a specific range of values that cannot be sustained either in professional education or historical research in the present moment? Does pursuit by twenty-first-century scholars and students of a deeper, broader Italy enrich the historical and critical references of contemporary architecture, or foster a rift between scholarship and its uptake? Does the "discovery" of a wider world of architecture—itself redefined on terms divorced from the regime of *disegno*—in which Italy is in no way involved, present a basic and unassailable challenge to the very measures we have used to call architecture "architecture" for centuries? Can we construct a history of architecture without an idea of architecture bound to traditions of representation or the anchor of antiquity? Or originating with entirely different ideas? How, all that is to ask, can we continue to study the history and reverberations of Italian architecture, locating the peninsula and all it contains on a more open disciplinary map?

The broadening of horizons Le Corbusier witnessed and furthered encompasses an even wider world of places, spaces, and structures, and an expanding range of questions, to grapple with the evolving meaning of "architecture." The obverse of this welcome development is that dealing with "Italian" topics in architecture now demands a more accountable disciplinary self-awareness. The aura Le Corbusier strategically undercut and cannily reclaimed has hardly dissipated, even as it relies on definitions that must be continually renegotiated in an age where national boundaries and cultural identity cannot be assumed to be coequal. How can we spread a broader net for our work while still approaching Italy—as students studying abroad, as scholars of the classical tradition, as historians of modern architecture—with new eyes, new questions, and new attitudes?

In this book we locate these questions in the long history of testing architectural history's tools, tasks, and premises by encountering architecture's edges and finding where those once rigid fences have a little give. Our old habits of casting eyes towards Rome, Venice, Paestum, Turin, or Siena, and of absorbing those treatises and debates that gave architecture shape in the early modern world, may remain compelling even as these sources cease to be as monumental as they appeared to earlier generations—or as that monumentality can itself be historicized and thus put in its place. Attending to Italy as we have will hardly presage the demolition of the edifice. As some readers might expect, a book accounting for Italy's imprints on the architecture of the twentieth century will recall the myriad ways that Italian architects and architecture *have* shaped that century, and hence the discipline's contemporary, historical, and critical landscape. This is no catalogue, however, and as much as it celebrates specific moments, works, and figures, it returns always and consistently to the problem we have set for it: reconciling the persistence with which architectural culture has turned to Italy as a wellspring and touchstone with the challenges posed and addressed by contemporary historiography.

How can we audit our admiration for the Italian example in the face of the changed critical fortunes of those very institutions (academic and avant-garde alike) whose legitimacy has been interwoven with its veneration? As we ponder the importance Italy has long held for architecture, we ask how else we can, or should, historicize its architectural culture. Is it possible to do so in ways that are consistent with a contemporary scholarly ethos—one that resists the rule of centers, that seeks to globalize, decolonize, and challenge inherited narratives we now find troubling, or limiting? We note, as an example of this effort in the twentieth-century Italian case, the important body of scholarship produced in recent decades on the architectural and urban impact of Italian imperialism in Libya and the Horn of Africa.[9]

This volume presents a series of paths into this problem offered by scholars who, each in different ways, navigate these waters by conducting critical interrogations of Italy's position in the architectural culture and ideology of the past century. In bringing their work together, under this question, we have sought to consider where, how, and why the disciplinary edifice of twentieth-century architecture—its canon of built, visual, textual, and conceptual works—relied on Italian foundations, and to identify where and how those foundations have already become insecure or might properly be made so. As a result, the linkages to Italy in the chapters that follow are sometimes overt and sometimes subtle. Our ambition is to offer more incisive perspectives on how this structure has shaped or distorted architecture's vision of itself, thereby turning to the question of how we might, today, understand architectural history's creative, theoretical, social, and historiographic horizons. Not just to declare the age of history's centers over, but to negotiate how they have led us here, and how those figures, sites and ideas that were their substance might now figure in architectural history. To put it simply, and to adapt an old phrase to our current problem, we ask what Italian architecture, as a modern institution, has meant up to now.[10]

Within this, our aim has been to reconsider a series of institutions on which "Italian architecture" is, in turn, constructed: the regime of *disegno* and its Florentine origins; the figure of the architect (as artist) and his (nearly always "his") masterworks; Rome; Venice; the canon of theory; the classical tradition; craft . . . the list is endless to the degree that we can draw all manner of architecture's founding premises and enduring techniques into play, as well as so many of the seemingly novel concerns addressed by architecture in the last few decades. But common to them all is a form of centrality to architecture itself, in which these dimensions of the history and status of Italian architecture can be found.

*   *   *

As we have worked through the process of transforming an open-ended exploration of these themes into resolved pieces of writing, we have encouraged our contributors to think through Italy as a "problem" bound to architectural history's geography and the privileged place Italy (and a particular constellation of Italian cities) have long occupied therein. From chapter to chapter, readers will encounter our questions intersecting with those brought to the project by each author; this, we believe, is one of the strengths of this collection. To the extent that what follows is resolved, it operates as a series of well-defined incursions into a topic that can sustain much more reflection and examination. When we first met together, with many of the authors whose work follows, we found value in the idea that we were collectively *worrying* at the question of Italy's authority, whether it was cast as absolute, tentative, challenged, or troubling. In many cases, individual contributions to this volume have used the questions at its center to consider aspects of larger projects where these issues may have remained latent. We hope that as readers ponder the work we have gathered into this book, that they will be drawn, too, towards those larger projects into which each chapter offers a glimpse.

Within the book's overarching conversation, a series of closely connected explorations frame its organizing structure. One study that stands apart is "The Architect as Intellectual" by Jean-Louis Cohen, a revised extract from his indispensable 1984 study of the entangled threads of influence between French intellectuals and architects and Italian architectural discourse in the twentieth century.[11] This argument, presented for the first time in English, unravels the historic conditions that shaped the distinctive character of Italian architecture culture. Cohen's illumination of the political, institutional, and cultural context in which Italian architects were nurtured and conducted their careers provides a crucial explanatory framework for the constellation of individual figures, centers of study and thought, and forms of practice whose creative and conceptual intensity exercised wider influence, in France as well as further afield. Close to four decades since its original publication, Cohen's analysis offers an incisive introduction to an idea that pervades the volume: if many facets of Italian architectural influence might be considered "natural" or "earned" due to the quality of individuals or projects as architects and architecture, these same figures and their works remain inextricable from contingent, constructed conditions.

Beyond this, then, and informed by its premises, contributors to this book have returned with fresh questions to key figures in the history of modern Italian architecture: Caspar Pearson revisits the question of origins in his writing on Leon Battista Alberti; Maristella Casciato draws out the women in Gio Ponti's ambit; and Diane Ghirardo restates the matter of tradition in the work of Aldo Rossi. They have located Italy and Italian cities as sites of formation within and beyond Italy itself: Giorgia Aquilar explores the lessons of Venice through the eyes of Peter Smithson and Arata Isozaki; Daniel Barber returns to Limone sul Garda to test its place in the history of climatic design;

Rosa Sessa follows Robert Venturi south to Campania to query his complex and contradictory relationship with Italy; and Dijia Chen reads Rossi in and through Chinese translation.

Our collaborators have explored the path of themes from Rome, Florence, and Padua to the world beyond: Raúl Martínez Martínez follows the path of an operationalized idea of aesthetics from Berenson's Villa I Tatti to Eisenman's Cambridge; Frank Bauer locates room for error in Alberti's typesetting and in the digital lessons drawn from his *quattrocento* ideas; Francesca Torello retraces the journeys of Henry Hornbostel across Italy and how they remained with him in Pittsburgh; and Lionel Devlieger takes pause to locate his encounters with Florence and the Florentine Aristotelians in his own formation. Authors have explored with new questions themes in which Italy has figured prominently in the architecture of the twentieth century: Ute Poerschke recalls the stakes of Italian thinkers in the evolution of functionalism; Federica Vannucchi teases apart the relationship of corporeality and diplomacy; Chris French the intimacies of territory and material for Vittorio Gregotti; and Silvia Micheli and Lorenzo Ciccarelli the institutional spaces between soft diplomacy and the cultivation of postmodern taste. The agency of Italian institutions in defining Italy's own authority is further explored by Ignacio Galan in his critical treatment of furnishing; by Daniela Ortiz dos Santos of the Italian architects, designers, and agencies implicated in the idea of an *architettura latinoamericana*; and by Philip Goad in his location of Italy in the world of Robin Boyd.

They together offer a sustained reflection on what Italy has been for architecture, suggesting new problems for us to pursue, new questions to ask of old materials, and new reservations to share with our students and colleagues. Amidst changing horizons and perspectives, the challenge remains: can a deeper, more critical consideration of the architectural legacies of Italy advance contemporary agendas as thoughtfully, incisively, and strategically as Le Corbusier's did?

Notes

1. Le Corbusier, *Towards a New Architecture*, trans. Frederick Etchells (New York: Dover, 1986), 173. In the original: "Il y a toutes les horreurs . . . La leçon de Rome est pour les sages, pour qui savent et peuvent apprécier, ceux qui peuvent resister, qui peuvent contrôler. Rome est la perdition de ceux qui ne savent pas beaucoup. Mettre dans Rome des étudiants architectes, c'est les meurtrir pour la vie." *Vers une architecture*, 2nd edn, rev. and ex. (Paris: Crès, 1928), 139–40.

2. On the way Le Corbusier's vision of Rome's instructive value parallels that of the early modern era, see Denise Costanzo, "Horrors and Heroes, Renaissance and Recent: Rome as Architecture School," in *Visualizing the Past in Italian Renaissance Art: Essays in Honor of Brian A. Curran*, ed. Douglas N. Dow and Jennifer Cochran Anderson (Leiden: Brill, 2021), 9–39.

3. On Le Corbusier's relationship with Italy, see *L'Italia di Le Corbusier*, ed. Marida Talamona (Milan: Electa, 2012).

4. All of which are contained in Giovanni Battista Piranesi, *Observations on the Letter of Monsieur Mariette: With Opinions on Architecture, and a Preface to a New Treatise on the*

Introduction and Progress of the Fine Arts in Europe in Ancient Times, trans. Caroline Beamish and David Britt (Los Angeles: Getty Publications, 2002).

5. Consider, for example, Kai Kappel and Erik Wegerhoff (eds), *Blikwendungen: Architektenreise nach Italien in Moderne und Gegenwart*, Römische Studien der Bibliotheca Hertziana 45 (Munich: Hirmer, 2019). Taking up the theme of travel, as it does, the opening question of its introduction is akin that which we pursue into different, if overlapping realms: "warum bloß italien?"—why just Italy?

6. See, for instance, Reyner Banhan, "A Black Box: The Secret Profession of Architecture," *New Statesman & Society* 3, no. 122 (1990): 22 5.

7. Manfredo Tafuri, *Ricerca del rinascimento. Principi, città, architetti* (Turin: Einaudi, 1992), xix; citing from the English edn, *Interpreting the Renaissance: Princes, Cities, Architects*, trans. Daniel Sherer (Cambridge, MA: MIT Press, 2006), xxvii. The question of exchange is explored in many ways, including in Lorenzo Cicciarelli and Clare Melhuish (eds), *Post-war Architecture between Italy and the UK* (London: UCL Press, 2021).

8. As a collection, in English, see Georg Simmel, *The Art of the City: Rome, Florence, Venice*, trans. Will Stone (London: Pushkin Press, 2019), the sketches originally published in *Die Zeit* in 1898; *Der Tag* in 1906; and *Der Kunstwart* in 1907, respectively.

9. For scholarship in this area published in English, see especially the work of Mia Fuller, Brian MacLaren, and David Rifkind.

10. Manfredo Tafuri, preface to *Teorie e storia dell'architettura* (1968), 2nd edn (Rome: Laterza, 1970).

11. Jean-Louis Cohen, *La coupure entre architects et intellectuels, ou les enseignements de l'italophilie* (Paris: Ecole d'architecture Paris-Villemin, 1984).

CHAPTER 2
THE ARCHITECT AS INTELLECTUAL
Jean-Louis Cohen

In 1984, I published a book-length scholarly paper entitled somewhat pompously *The Gap between Architects and Intellectuals, or Learning from Italophilia*, which sold out immediately and has been reissued thirty years later in an updated format.[1] This investigation of the differences between the French and Italian architecture scenes was born out of my research in both countries, but also from the experience I had acquired in teaching and as a contributor to Italian journals such as *Casabella*. My main point was that, in contrast to their French colleagues, whose anti-intellectualism had been nurtured by the École des Beaux-arts, Italian architects entertained for decades a dense web of relationships with culture beyond the boundaries of their discipline. Having noted this difference, I focused on the emergence of a discourse on urban form and a more refined architectural history in Italy and traced the impact Italian writings had on French scholars and architects.[2]

This chapter condenses the analysis I then offered of the condition of Italian architects from 1920 to 1980, beginning with the issue of continuity. In the postwar period, the theme of continuity was so salient that it was affixed to the title of the journal *Casabella* in 1953, when Ernesto N. Rogers relaunched its publication. It was certainly no accident that this expression of solidarity with the experience acquired under fascism would be invoked at the very heart of an early phase in the construction of a republican Italy. The importance of Italy's prewar architectural culture weighed significantly on both theoretical debate and the production of works of architecture.

An architecture of continuity

The continuity Rogers sought to maintain was intended, as he put it, as a "dynamic extension rather than a passive recopying."[3] This suggestion might appear astonishing against a naive image of Italian architecture during the fascist period. But if one wants to investigate the precise relations between architecture and culture in postwar Italy and to delineate the profile of the architect-intellectual, a figure whose contours emerged at this time, it is crucial to start by reconstructing the cultural and architectural endeavors which Rogers wished to continue, and thus one needs to return to fascist Italy. The first ambiguity that must be addressed concerns the relation between architecture and politics under fascism. However simplistic it may seem, one cannot simply dismiss the idea of a brutal and direct subordination of architectural debate to fluctuations in fascist cultural politics. The regime's interventions in the field of architecture, especially with regard to public buildings and urban projects, must be considered with all their implications.

In 1925, only ten days elapsed between the publication of Giovanni Gentile's "Manifesto of Fascist Intellectuals" and the response inspired by Benedetto Croce. Taken together, these established the bonds between Italian intellectuals and fascism.[4] Architecture soon became a significant concern for a regime that solidified its power the following year and would fully exploit new means of communication, such as radio and film.[5] In addition to creating a material infrastructure for taylorized mass leisure activities, the regime carried out a policy of brutal interventions in older city centers. Under the pretext of hygienic concerns and the need to clear space around historical monuments, the "regenerative" pickaxe was extolled by the press, practically attaining mythical status, especially once this tool became synonymous with urban renewal attacking dense central neighborhoods where working classes hostile to fascism were living. This policy of evisceration recast the face of larger cities such as Rome, Milan, or Bologna, as well as smaller cities such as Brescia.[6] It was taken to its conclusion after the Liberation, with the opening of the via della Conciliazone in Rome from Saint Peter's to the Tiber, completed in 1950.

But state intervention and the personal decisions of the Duce were not limited to public buildings, or to policies concentrating on urban centers and agricultural regions subjected to *bonifiche* strategies.[7] The regime saw fit to intervene in debates over architectural doctrine, just as it did in other domains of culture. In the early 1920s, fascism was at least partially rooted in various elements of Italian literature and culture, from Filippo Tommaso Marinetti to Gabriele d'Annunzio and Ardengo Soffici for the older generation, to Curzio Malaparte for the younger one.[8] But these ties to historical futurism or Malaparte's rancorous anti-intellectualism no longer sufficed for a power that became skilled at absorbing movements in culture and ideology, as Palmiro Togliatti clearly noted in his 1935 *Lectures on Fascism*.[9]

Modern architecture to the rescue

The rupture in the field of architecture that occurred in the pivotal years of the late 1920s did not go unnoticed: this was evident both in the creation of new movements, such as the Gruppo 7 in Milan in 1926, which later opened the way to the Movimento italiano per l'architettura razionale (MIAR); the Group of 6 in Turin, formed in 1928; as well as through spectacular events: the first exhibition of rationalist architecture that same year, and the second in 1931, both held in Rome. New journals appeared as well—both *La Casa bella* and *Domus* were founded in Milan in 1928. Faced with different incarnations of a movement that could easily conform to the established political order, the regime undertook various attempts at direct control, such as the creation of the Raggruppamento architetti moderni italiani (RAMI), meant to counter the MIAR.

The fascist critic Pietro Maria Bardi, who hosted an early exhibition of the rationalists in his Roman gallery, addressed his *Rapporto sull'architettura* of 1931 to Mussolini, giving formal notice to the Duce that he faced a choice between two alternatives: generally endorsing the ideals of the rationalist avant-garde, thus breaking with the architects and intellectuals of preceding generations, or else breaking with the younger generation and compromising the image of modernity the regime so intensely desired. The Duce received the message, and knew well enough to send out the manifesto of the organizers of the second national exhibition of rational architecture via the official telegraph agency, as Sigfried Giedion recounted at the time (see Figure 2.1).[10] He also knew to endorse the

Figure 2.1 Sigfried Giedion, "Situation of Contemporary Architecture in Italy," *Cahiers d'art* 6, no. 9-10 (1931), Cahiers d'art, Paris.

outcome of the competition for the new railway station in Florence, which awarded the prize to the modern project by Giuseppe Michelucci, with the Gruppo Toscano of Nello Baroni, Pier Niccolò Berardi, Italo Gamberini, Sarre Guarnieri, and Leonardo Lusanna, and was opposed by a segment of public opinion and by the railway administration. In 1934, he received the prizewinners, along with Luigi Piccinato's team working on the center of the new town of Sabaudia.

These signals to the younger generations absorbed their proposals for radical architectural forms into the regime's anti-capitalist proclamations. The Casa del Fascio in Como, that remarkable architectural manifesto built by Giuseppe Terragni between 1932 and 1936, can be read as a dialogue between the Duce, who sought to make a "glass house" out of fascism, and the architect, who specified that the "transposed meaning of the phrase points to and defines the organic qualities, the clarity, and the honesty of the construction."[11] The regime's decisions after the late 1930s took a different direction with the second competition for the Palazzo del Littorio and another for the 1942 Universal Exposition. During that same period, the rapprochement between fascism and Nazism, the war in Ethiopia, and the social ideals of young rationalist architects led several of them to adopt anti-fascist positions. Many participated in the Resistance, even at the cost of their lives.[12]

Regional diversity and architectural culture

In order to grasp the geographical features of fascist Italy's architectural culture, it is necessary to consider the distinct features of the three urban areas in which it was deployed—Turin, Milan, and Rome. The influence of this polycentrism on the beginnings of modern architecture is undoubtedly key to understanding the intensity with which its tenets were developed. In Turin, the most advanced Italian industrial firm supported a building that would assume the role of symbol, the Fiat factory of Lingotto, built between 1916 and 1926 by Giacomo Mattè-Trucco, while the research of Alberto Sartoris or Giuseppe Pagano was coming to fruition and would be on public display at the 1928 exhibition at the Parco Valentino.[13]

Milan was the birthplace of the Novecento movement, where the buildings of Giovanni Muzio and Giuseppe De Finetti were designed to echo the paintings of Giorgio de Chirico or Mario Sironi.[14] The city was the site of an encounter between two major underpinnings of the new culture. The exhibitions of the Milan Triennali were regular occasions for the public display of new ideas and forms of rational architecture, and a high-quality and consistent architectural press played a significant role in forming a generation of architects fully capable of functioning as both intellectuals and designers.[15] At the outset, *Domus* was directed by Gio Ponti, who was never overly concerned with doctrinal purity. As for *La Casa bella*, it changed its name to *Casabella* when Giuseppe Pagano took over as director in 1933 and set it on a new course to pursue the goals of the first rationalist generation.[16]

Figure 2.2 Irenio Diotallevi, Franco Marescotti, and Giuseppe Pagano, "La civiltà e la casa: note introduttive al progetto di quartiere di città orizzontale, studiato dall'ing. Diotallevi, Marescotti e dall'arch. Pagano," *Costruzioni casabella* 12, no. 148 (April 1948): 2–5. Collection Jean-Louis Cohen.

Casabella thus concentrated on building as well as thinking, with the help and subsequent instigation of Eduardo Persico who, like Pagano, had come from Turin. The review included non-architects, such as art historians Giulio Carlo Argan and Lionello Venturi, as well as the painter and future writer Carlo Levi.[17] Alongside the cultural density of *Casabella*, which provided a lucid perspective on the essential issues appearing on the Italian, European, and American scenes until it ceased publication in 1943, Milan witnessed between 1933 and 1936 the initial publication of *Quadrante*, an "engaged" publication led by Bardi and Massimo Bontempelli, which sought to combine a sincere commitment to the corporatism of Bottai with a strict allegiance to Le Corbusier and CIAM.[18] Commissions for apartment buildings of respectable size obtained by Terragni, Pietro Lingeri, Piero Bottoni, Lodovico di Belgiojoso and Muzio were additional signs of the new architecture's inroads into the urban culture of Milan.

The special role of private commissions is also undeniable, in light of Adriano Olivetti's initiatives for housing and factories built in Ivrea by Figini and Pollini, or the plan for the Val d'Aosta, in which BBPR (Gianluigi Banfi, Belgiojoso, Ernesto Peressutti and Rogers), Gino Figini, Luigi Pollini and Bottoni proposed a theatrical deployment of large architectural elements spread out on the broad and empty landscape.[19] Milan ultimately became the locus for more extreme urban propositions. In the late 1930s, the rationalists expressed their discovery of the shortage of working-class housing, a reaction delayed because of the intense demand for private commissions. This new area of interest led to the *Milano verde* project by Franco Albini, Ignazio Gardella, Pagano, and others, as well as for a neighborhood in the "horizontal city" by Irenio Diotallevi and Franco Marescotti, once again with Pagano (see Figure 2.2).[20]

The situation in Rome was quite different. This city lacked the sort of modernist bourgeoisie found in northern Italy. On the other hand, Rome was closer to the regime's centers of decision-making. The debates surrounding tradition and modernity, issues raised by Giuseppe Giovannoni and Marcello Piacentini, and questions of professional education emerged there. The aforementioned competition for the Palazzo del Littorio was held in the capital, as were preparations for the Universal Exposition of 1942, intended to burnish the regime's international reputation. Mario Ridolfi, Adalberto Libera, and Luigi Moretti further refined the language of modern Italian architecture, while Luigi Piccinato attended to its dissemination in the field of urbanism. A second generation, including Giuseppe Samonà, Ludovico Quaroni, and Saverio Muratori, also demonstrated its ambitions. In contrast to the rational construction and rigorous orthogonality of their contemporaries in Milan or Como, the Roman architects sought a balance between freer explorations of form and increasing curiosity regarding traditional rural vernaculars. While Pagano curated an exhibition on rural architecture for the Milan Triennale of 1936, partly based on his own photographs, and drew a doctrinal lesson from it regarding rationality, Ridolfi and Samonà used the same tradition to advance deliberate design strategies.[21]

Neorealism and organic architecture

This interest in the actual materiality of traditional architecture is all the more noteworthy in that it prefigured the general turn of Italian culture towards the realities of a nation that combined miserable conditions in the countryside with impoverished populations transplanted in cities. One can see this slow march towards neorealism, whose essential manifestoes were Elio Vittorini's book *Conversazione in Sicilia* and Lucchino Visconti's film *Ossessione* of 1941 and 1942, respectively, as a proof of the continuity between the struggles of the 1930s and those of the postwar republic, and as a testament to the capacity of Italian architects to shape the features of a broad culture in the same way as other intellectuals.

In the immediate postwar period, the contrasts between Milan and Rome persisted, but the capital played an increasingly significant role in public debate and as a source of architectural commissions. It was in Rome that Bruno Zevi proclaimed organic architecture as a new program for Italy, one he unpacked upon his return from the United States in 1945. He created a new journal, *Metron*, as well as a new organization, the Associazione per l'architettura organica (APAO). The APAO went so far as presenting a list of its own priorities during the municipal elections of Rome in 1946. Its goals were both vast and vague, as was evident in Zevi's report to the first meeting of the association, in December 1947.[22]

The new vectors of action were different in Milan, where the Movimento studi d'architettura (MSA) was established in 1945 and undertook the preparation of the VIII Triennale of 1948, which allowed for the migration of rationalist urban ideas from the drafting table to the city. The experimental neighborhood QT8, built under the leadership of Bottoni at the city's periphery, was the first to bear witness.[23] In addition, the enlightened national figure of Olivetti, who had already demonstrated his interest in architecture before 1940, re-emerged with the publication of the monthly *Comunità*, which brought together architects and other intellectuals who shared his interest in social and regional unity.[24] In 1949, Olivetti became director of the journal *Urbanistica*, which promoted the multi-disciplinary qualities latent in the work of the urban planner.

The Tiburtino episode and Quaroni's action

Experimental construction projects began to emerge from the encounter between new forms of public intervention in housing and the preoccupations of architects. The most important of these was no doubt the Tiburtino neighborhood outside Rome, built between 1950 and 1953 under the guidance of Quaroni and Ridolfi (see Figure 2.3). Their team included very young architects such as Carlo Aymonino and Carlo Melograni, alongside seasoned professionals like Federico Gorio or Mario Fiorentino. Like the Martella neighborhood built in Matera by Quaroni, Tiburtino integrated regionalist tendencies already manifest before 1940 in Rome or Naples. An image of rural life was communicated by the open brickwork of the drying spaces on the upper floors, window and masonry details, and especially how buildings were laid out along the length of the street. These features combined with the neighborhood's structural rationality, considered as a fully equipped and autonomous unit.[25] But the area's compact plan, along with the rejection of northern rationalists' orthogonal grids, was not enough to draw together a neighborhood intended to be a unified community, which would be occupied by refugees from areas that had been ceded to Yugoslavia.[26] The elapsed time since the first neorealist experiments in film or literature made these nods to rural tradition even more irrelevant; their primary purpose seemed to be providing a refuge for a group of architects seeking to exorcise the curse of modern construction techniques, as Manfredo Tafuri has observed.[27]

Figure 2.3 Ludovico Quaroni and Mario Ridolfi, with Carlo Aymonino, Mario Fiorentino, Carlo Melograni, et al., Tiburtino housing estate, Rome, 1950. Collection Jean-Louis Cohen.

Perhaps the most interesting feature of the Tiburtino experiment lies elsewhere: the recourse to a form of teamwork so fused that it became very difficult to identify the specific contributions of each architect. Quaroni provided an opportunity to resist the limits imposed by the traditional view of the architectural profession. Like Rogers or Samonà, he helped give birth to a new type of professional in his own image, one equally active in the field of culture as in design. Representing the second generation of modern Italian architecture in the same way as Rogers and Samonà, he maintained elements of continuity between debates prior to 1940 with the period of fulfillment and mastery of certain institutional domains that emerged after the war.

Quaroni did not return to teaching in Rome until 1963, but he developed his didactic agenda in Florence after 1955. Starting in the 1940s, a series of clashes between Quaroni and Zevi took place within the APAO in Rome regarding which attitude to adopt vis-à-vis the INA-Casa.[28] Quaroni participated forthrightly, as was evident in the case of Tiburtino. He not only confronted the realities of development, but also reflected on the relationship between architecture and the whole of urban culture – a subject on which he expanded in his lectures. Revisiting the Tiburtino experiment in 1957, he declared that "it was not the result of a unified culture, of a living tradition: it was the product of a state of mind."[29] Without the opportunity to listen to a living tradition, Quaroni contributed to the consolidation of Italian architectural culture and marked the successive stages of his evolution through his theoretical writing (*La torre di Babele*), his historical books (*Immagine di Roma*), and his didactic works (*Otto lezioni di architettura*).[30]

Rogers and the revision of the modern movement

Quaroni's persistence in identifying the limits of the architectural project can be compared to the energy with which Rogers attempted to recombine the pieces of Italian architectural doctrine within the cultural context of Milan, and his search for continuity with the vibrant rationalism of the 1930s, as indicated previously. *Domus* pursued its path under the direction of Ponti, who replaced Rogers in 1948. As for Rogers, he had re-established his ties to *Casabella* under Pagano and in 1952 resumed publication of the journal, with Giancarlo De Carlo, Vittorio Gregotti, and Marco Zanuso as editors. Rogers broadened the journal's scope to eliminate the ambiguities and false parallels between organic architecture and rationalism entertained by Zevi, who started publishing *L'architettura, cronache e storia* in 1955, as a replacement for *Metron*.

Rogers attempted to anchor his position on a critical revision of the heritage of the modern movement, whose two leading figures were, for him, Walter Gropius and Le Corbusier. Subsequent developments involving Rogers's three initial collaborators illustrated the highs and lows of the journal. De Carlo soon distanced himself from Rogers's approach. He resigned in 1957, reproaching Rogers for his excessive attachment to the language of modern architecture and his reticence towards social content. Gregotti adhered to the line for ten years and involved representatives of his generation such as

Guido Canella, Aldo Rossi, and Gae Aulenti. He later demonstrated his own abilities as a journal editor, with a memorable set of issues of *Edilizia moderna* between 1963 and 1966.[31]

The crisis of 1957 raised a broader set of issues: the polemics with De Carlo and others, addressed in Rogers's editorial "Orthodoxy of Heterodoxy," questioned the basic guidelines of the journal and organizations such as the MSA on a more fundamental level.[32] On the one hand, the CIAM meetings had come to an end, and on the other, new historicist directions such as "neoliberty" were posing new questions about the legitimacy of modern forms. In 1959 a heated polemic arose between Rogers and Reyner Banham that was emblematic of these confrontations. Banham had deplored the "retreat of the Italians from the modern movement" in the pages of the *Architectural Review*, which was widely read in Italy at the time.[33] The lesson in pragmatism that Rogers administered to Banham was not just in writing.[34] With the Torre Velasca, built in 1959 in the center of Milan by Belgiojoso, Peressutti, and Rogers himself, the revisionist impulse assumed a spectacular dimension. Instead of an aerodynamic skyscraper, like the Pirelli tower that Ponti completed in 1960, BBPR combined a tower's verticality with a blocky palazzo above the skyline of the existing city, recalling Milan's old apartment buildings by virtue of its openings and the shape of its roof. The architects' complete mastery of the structure's design and details at every scale, inspired by August Perret, absolved Rogers of any suspicion of neglecting modern technique (see Figure 2.4).[35]

The revisions that *Casabella continuità* undertook at the time were not simply a matter of taste. They were part of a methodical search for the historical sources and projects of modern architecture that dotted the journal's pages, so expertly laid out by Aulenti. Issues dealt with Frank Lloyd Wright, Adolf Loos (edited by Rossi), Henry Van de Velde (edited by Rogers), and Peter Behrens (edited by Gregotti), and with the architecture of expressionism. The question of urban form emerged as well, through initiatives such as a dossier on Berlin by Aymonino and Rossi.

Samonà's new urban dimension

Ernesto Rogers's deliberate efforts to mobilize a younger generation around a very public institution, in this case a journal, found its counterpart in Giuseppe Samonà's efforts from 1945 to 1971 as head of a similarly influential institution: the Istituto universitario di architettura di Venezia (IUAV). Before 1940, Samonà primarily worked on public buildings, as well as on the working-class neighborhood of Gaeta, where he combined typological elements from Le Corbusier's "immeubles-villas" with a vernacular vocabulary. Samonà was appointed dean of the IUAV in 1945 and his initiatives soon established an indispensable intellectual counterweight to the implacable control exerted by conservative architects on the faculties of Rome, Turin, and Milan. He invited the most dynamic representatives of Roman and Milanese movements to teach in Venice, which became a strategic arena where professional issues were subordinate to cultural debate.[36]

Figure 2.4 Ludovico Belgiojoso, Enrico Peressutti, and Ernesto Nathan Rogers, Torre Velasca, Milan, 1957. Mondadori Portfolio/Electa/Sergio Anelli.

Samonà's recruits for the institute's faculty privileged those excluded from other Italian universities for reasons of cultural or political incompatibility. In his own didactic and public roles, he engaged on a rather different front than the positions of *Casabella continuità*. He sought to maintain equal distance from both the positivism of "scientific" methods of urban design and planning, and the historicism of a culture solely oriented towards the past. This led him to advocate a determined program of urban analysis dealing with existing cities alongside the teaching of design studios. This would be the case for an investigation of Venice.[37] The search for a "new urban dimension" was at the heart of the book that Samonà published in 1959 on *L'urbanistica e l'avvenire della città* (Urbanism and the Future of the City).[38]

Samonà's positions foreshadowed the two guiding ideas that structured the Italian debate on the city between 1960 and 1980. He pinpointed issues pertaining to urban centers and their form, and thus paved the way for further research by several members of the Venice faculty, such as Aymonino and Rossi. He also championed the idea of inter-city planning, which became a consideration for the reforms of regional urbanism that came into play after 1971. Along with Quaroni and Rogers, albeit on a rather different playing field, Samonà's efforts shaped a new generation of architects who were active both on the level of design and on the level of culture. Through the writings and drawings it produced, this generation, which finished its training in the mid-1950s, framed an entirely new phenomenon that swept through Italy—and France, for that matter—in the late 1960s: the massification of the university in general, and of architectural schools in particular. And yet, despite their considerable symbolic and cultural impact, the shocks of the worker and student movements of 1968 and 1969 did not entirely overturn a pedagogical system whose conflicted transformation had started in Venice, Rome, Florence, and Turin.

An abundant printed production

One reason why the relations between Italian intellectuals and architects are so unusual is primarily because the architects themselves, following in the footsteps of the pioneers of rationalist architecture during the fascist period, were entirely capable of expressing and clarifying their intellectual points of reference and their approach to design. Importantly, changes in practice and the associated formal or conceptual ripples were generally accompanied by discursive justifications, some of them solidly argued and occasionally powerful enough to affect the national consciousness.

This intellectual quality of Italian debates was not the product of chance, but of necessity. After beaux-arts academies were shut down during the 1920s, architecture schools were incorporated into universities.[39] They recruited professors based on their cultural production (in the form of books or articles) as much as their architectural work. At the same time, obtaining commissions from INA-Casa or one of its counterparts—local authorities or enlightened industrialists—required wrapping professional expertise in a certain cultural aura. Developing a discourse about architecture was a pathway to notoriety, and thus to professional success (see Figure 2.5).

Another consideration should be added, one bound to Italy's historical and geographical structure. In a country so recently unified, that retained particularly vivid regional particularities, every major city supported its own distinct cultural life—at times provincial, and frequently intense and contradictory. Architectural themes often gained local cultural prominence, as seen in the press or through decentralized publications. At the same time, regional loyalties promoted solidarity among architects, constructed around journals and periodic exhibitions, which invited younger generations to publicly articulate their positions. Towards the late 1960s, the growing number of architects and teachers, along with increasing difficulty in obtaining commissions, inflating number of books, reviews, and discourse, indicated a displacement of energies that found little outlet in production, and hence turned towards intellectual speculation.[40]

Figure 2.5 Giuseppe Samonà, Luigi Piccinato, et al., INA-Casa housing estate, San Giuliano, Mestre, 1951-6. Collection Jean-Louis Cohen.

Architects and political life

This milieu of Italian architects was characterized by another feature adding to the proliferation of discourse: a sort of race towards differentiation. This latter quality seemed to motivate the main producers of architectural debate, with each participant in arguments seeking its own journal or collection of examples. This was due to their inability to control architecture schools, which had grown immensely. Like other Italian intellectuals, architects are stakeholders in the country's political life. Since the resistance and through the years of historic compromise, relations between architects and leftist parties have generally been productive.[41]

In addition to friendship and everyday sociability (De Carlo and Elio Vittorini lived in the same apartment building above the Naviglio canal in Milan), years of struggle alongside the workers' movement, from the collapse of the Popular Front in 1948 to the beginnings of the center-left in 1963, also contributed to this sense of common cause. In a country where political life was saturated with references to theoretical or philosophical debates, as occurred, for example, after the discovery of Gramsci's *Prison Notebooks*, politics was integral to the architect's *Weltanschauung*. Political life stimulated intellectuals in many ways, if only because party organizations provided opportunities for fruitful encounters between disciplines. Similarly, groups of intellectuals in the 1960s subverted the terms of political debate during the Cold War and dominance of Christian Democracy.

The renewal of architectural theory in the years before 1968 was consistent with new currents in Italian literature—the Gruppo 63, founded in Palermo, or the critical Marxism of Mario Tronti—that coalesced at the same time around journals such as *Il verri* and the *Quaderni rossi*. Gregotti's presence in Milanese discussions, as related by Umberto Eco, played a decisive role in the development of his positive doctrine and his criticisms attacking "illiterate architects."[42] Moreover, new questions in Marxism and the workers' movement were fundamental to the evolution of the Institute at Venice.

It was also thanks to universities, the audience they created, and the obligations they placed on professors—especially the requirement to publish for recruitment and promotion—that allowed debates about ideas to avoid remaining ephemeral and instead be condensed and crystallized as books. This sedimentation of ideas through education reached its ultimate limit with the transformation of the university into a facility opened to expanded masses of students after 1968. Some of the previous period's most prominent authors could not withstand the shock and refused to engage in a fundamentally altered teaching profession. Such was the case for Leonardo Benevolo and Bruno Zevi, who both left the university in the late 1970s. The issues that came out of the universities, such as discussions on the creation of new specialized departments, led to new currents within faculties of architecture. They also permeated design practice and had palpable effects on design culture by reshaping its perspectives.

Notes

1. Jean-Louis Cohen, *La coupure entre architectes et intellectuels, ou les enseignements de l'Italophilie* (Paris: École d'architecture Paris-Villemin, 1984; rev. edn, Brussels: Mardaga, 2015).

2. The corresponding chapter has been translated as Jean-Louis Cohen, "The Italophiles at Work," in *Architecture Theory since 1968*, ed. K. Michael Hays (Cambridge, MA: MIT Press, 1998), 506–21.

3. Ernesto N. Rogers, "Continuità," *Casabella continuità* 199 (December 1953–January 1954): 3.

4. Alberto Asor Rosa, "La cultura," in *Storia d'Italia*, vol. 4, part 2 (Turin: Einaudi, 1975), 1465.

5. See how the latter—film—gave an account of the former—radio—in Ettore Scola's *A Special Day*, released in 1977.

6. Leonardo di Mauro and Maria Teresa Perone, "Gli interventi nei centri storici: le direttive di Mussolini e le responsabilità della cultura," in *Il razionalismo e l'architettura in Italia durante il fascismo*, ed. Silvia Danesi and Luciano Patetta (Venice: La Biennale di Venezia, 1976), 38–42; Antonio Cederna, *Mussolini urbanista* (Bari: Laterza, 1979); Paolo Nicoloso, *Mussolini architetto. Propaganda e paesaggio urbano nell'Italia fascista* (Turin: Einaudi, 2011).

7. Riccardo Mariani, *Fascismo e città nuove* (Milan: Feltrinelli, 1976); Alberto Mioni, *Ricerche e saggi sulle città e il territorio e sulle politiche urbane in Italia tra le due guerre* (Milan: Franco Angeli, 1980). See also *Sabaudia città nuova fascista* (London: Architectural Association, 1982).

8. Asor Rosa, "La cultura," 1395.

9. Palmiro Togliatti, *Lectures on Fascism* (1973) (New York: International Publishers, 1976).

10. Sigfried Giedion, "Situation de l'architecture contemporaine en Italie," *Cahiers d'Art* 6, no. 9–10 (1931): 440–9.

11. Giuseppe Terragni, "La costruzione della casa del Fascio di Como," *Quadrante* 35–36 (October 1936): 5–27.

12. Asor Rosa, "La cultura," 1585–7.

13. On this building, see Carlo Olmo (ed.), *Il Lingotto, 1915–1939: l'architettura, l'immagine, il lavoro* (Turin: Umberto Allemandi, 1994).

14. Giorgio Gambirasio and Bruno Minardi, *Giovanni Muzio, opere e scritti* (Milan: Franco Angeli, 1982); Giovanni Cislaghi, Mara De Benedetti, and Piergiorgio Marabelli, *Giuseppe De Finetti progetti 1920–1951* (Milan: Clup, 1981).

15. Anty Pansera, *Storia e cronaca della Triennale* (Milan: Longanesi, 1978).

16. Giuseppe Pagano-Pogatschnig, "Programma 1933," *La Casa bella* 60 (December 1932): 9–10. See the anthology edited by Cesare De Seta: *Giuseppe Pagano, Architettura e città durante il fascismo* (Bari: Laterza, 1976).

17. See the commemorative issue prepared by then-director Tomás Maldonado: *Casabella cinquant'anni 1928–1978*, *Casabella* 440–4 (October–November 1978), and Chiara Baglione, *Casabella 1928–2008* (Milan: Electa, 2008).

18. Marida Talamona (ed.), *L'Italia di Le Corbusier* (Milan: Electa, 2012).

19. Carlo Olmo (ed.), *Costruire la città dell'uomo: Adriano Olivetti e l'urbanistica* (Milan: Edizioni di Comunità, 2001).

20. "Proposta di piano regolatore per la zona Sempione-Fiera a Milano," *Casabella Costruzioni* 132 (December 1938): 2–24; and "Quartiere della città orizzontale," *Costruzioni Casabella* 148 (April 1940): 14–16.

21. Giuseppe Pagano and Guarniero Daniel, *Architettura rurale italiana* (Milan: Hoepli, 1936). On Pagano's photographs, see Cesare De Seta, *Giuseppe Pagano fotografo* (Milan: Electa, 1979). See also Mario Ridolfi's 1940 design for a farm in Sant'Elia Fiumerapido, or those of Giuseppe Samonà for a working-class neighborhood in Gaeta, of the same year. On these design proposals and their context, see Michelangelo Sabatino, *Pride in Modesty: Modernist Architecture and the Vernacular Tradition in Italy* (Toronto: University of Toronto Press, 2010).

22. Bruno Zevi, "L'architettura organica di fronte ai suoi critici," *Metron* 23–24 (1947); and *Zevi su Bruno Zevi* (Rome: Magma, 1977), 58–64. English edn, *Bruno Zevi on Modern Architecture* (New York: Rizzoli, 1983).

23. Piero Bottoni, "Quarant'anni di battaglie per l'architettura," *Constrospazio* 4 (October 1973): 64–8. On QT8, see *Le case nella Triennale. Dal parco al QT8*, ed. Graziella Leyla Ciagà and Graziella Tonon (Milan: Electa, 2005).

24. Manfredo Tafuri, "Aufklärung I. Adriano Olivetti e la communitas dell'intelletto," in *Architettura italiana 1944–1981*, vol. 7: *Storia dell'arte Italiana* (Turin: Einaudi, 1982), 455–61; and Olmo, *Costruire la città dell'uomo*.

25. On Tiburtino, see the self-critical article by Ludovico Quaroni, "Il paese dei barocchi," *Casabella continuità* 215 (April–May 1957): 24–7.

26. The impact of the neighborhood on the inhabitants of Rome's suburban *Borgate* was depicted by Pier Paolo Pasolini in *Una vita violenta* (1959) (Milan: Garzanti, 1975), 173.

27. Manfredo Tafuri, *Ludovico Quaroni e lo sviluppo dell'architettura moderna in Italia* (Milan: Edizioni di Comunità, 1964), 90–100.

28. Tafuri, *Quaroni*, 90.

29. Quaroni, "Il paese dei barochi," 27.

30. Ludovico Quaroni, *La Torre di Babele* (Padua: Marsilio, 1967); *Immagine di Roma* (Bari: Laterza, 1969); *Progettare un edificio. Otto lezioni di architettura* (Milan: Mazzotta, 1977).

31. Gregotti explored themes in *Edilizia moderna* Gregotti that would later form the bulk of his discourse: *La forma del territorio, Edilizia moderna* 87–88 (1966).

32. Ernesto N. Rogers, with Eugenio Gentili, "Ortodossia dell'eterodossia," *Casabella continuità* 216 (September 1957): 2–4.

33. Reyner Banham, "Neoliberty: The Italian Retreat from Modern Architecture," *Architectural Review* 746 (March 1959): 231–5.

34. Ernesto N. Rogers, "L'evoluzione dell'architettura, risposta al custode dei frigidaires," *Casabella continuità* 228 (June 1959): 2–4.

35. "La Torre Velasca a Milano," *Casabella continuità* 232 (October 1959): 9–17; Leonardo Fiori and Massimo Prizzon, *BBPR, La Torre Velasca* (Milan: Abitare Segesta, 1982).

36. See the homage to Samonà published by his friends and disciples: Carlo Aymonino, Giorgio Ciucci, Francesco Dal Co, Manfredo Tafuri, et al., *Giuseppe Samonà: 1923–1975; cinquant'anni di architettura* (Rome: Officina, 1975).

37. Giuseppe Samonà, "Necessità di un studio di Venezia per la pianificazione urbanistica delle sue esigenze modern," in *L'unità architettura urbanistica* (Milan: Franco Angeli, 1975), 240–9.

38. Giuseppe Samonà, *L'urbanistica e l'avvenire della città* (Bari: Laterza, 1959), 304.

39. On the creation of the school network's main poles, see Loredana Compagnin and Maria Luisa Mazzola, "La nascita delle scuole superiori di architettura in Italia," in *Il razionalismo e l'architettura in Italia durante il fascismo*, 194–5.

40. The summaries of the main periodicals are to be found in Cina Conforto, Gabriele De Giorgi, Alessandra Muntoni, and Marcello Pazzaglini, *Il dibattito architettonico in Italia, 1945–1975* (Rome: Bulzoni, 1977).

41. See the stimulating reflections of Marco Biraghi in *L'architetto come intellettuale* (Turin: Einaudi, 2019).

42. Vittorio Gregotti, "L'architetto analfabeta," *Quindici* 6 (1967): 3–4. See also Umberto Eco's foreword to Vittorio Gregotti, *Le territoire de l'architecture* (1966) (Paris: L'Équerre, 1982), 7–10.

CHAPTER 3
ITALIAN AFTERTHOUGHTS: TRANSCODING *VENICENESS* FROM WITHOUT
Giorgia Aquilar

"Not so in Italy," wrote Peter Smithson of the "sense of being settled" through human construction, comparing the *Bel Paese* to his native England. Whereas in his homeland, place-making happens through the "ever-changing perfection of nature," the Italian peninsula is continuously "made and re-made" by the multiple authorship of "repeated additions and adjustments."[1] This reflection came to form part of Alison and Peter Smithson's pamphlet *Italian Thoughts*, self-published in 1993 as a compilation of arguments and design experiments developed over a number of years.[2] Therein, the British duo explores a territory they encountered "both as a fact and as an ideal," projecting Italy's traces from selected pasts towards potential futures.[3] Against this background, the Smithsons' *Thoughts* offers a premise for considering Italianness as a hypothetical space designed from without.

The Smithsons' account of their travels to Italy begins with the exhibitions *Wedding in the City* at the 1968 Milan Triennale and *Sticks and Stones* at the 1976 Venice Biennale and ends with the presentation of their work in Rome in 1991.[4] Their Italian reflections include a series of contributions, written by Peter alone, that had already appeared in the annual reports of the International Laboratory for Architecture and Urban Design (ILA&UD), founded by Giancarlo De Carlo in 1974. In the Smithsons' notes, Urbino, Siena, San Marino, and Venice—where the workshops organized by De Carlo took place—but also Florence, Rome, and Milan become vehicles for transcoding traits of Italianness to Cambridge, Bath, Stockholm, Athens, Paris, New York, Los Angeles, and other cities on both sides of the Atlantic.

Through an interplay between singularities and relations, the Smithsons' *Thoughts* presents a peculiar expression of Italianness focused on one famously distinctive city, participating in what John Dixon Hunt has defined as "Venicity (or Veniceness, from the Italian *Venezianità*)."[5] Throughout the English architects' Italian journeys from the 1960s to the turn of the millennium, Venice operates as an example of how existing conditions are continuously remade, "not as a single establishing act but as many reciprocal acts by many people."[6] In both its concrete substance and discursive conception, La Serenissima offers itself in its oxymoronic essence—exceptional and paradigmatic—as a place for the observation of broader discourses and critical issues for the built environment. The Smithsons looked at Venetian architecture as a "not-book-learned thing" and treated the "printed work" as an artifact, which "as a 'wrapped gift,' remain[s] to be discovered . . . and interpreted again and again by later generations."[7]

The Smithsons' *Thoughts* reveal one vision of Italianness, a late-twentieth-century concept also developed in the discursive space of North American architecture journals during these same years.[8] As the 1976 Venice Biennale (notably entitled *Europa-America*, and featuring the Smithsons' work) was taking place, another event established a significant axis: *Oppositions* 5, known as the "Italian issue." It connected the Istituto universitario di architettura di Venezia (IUAV) to the Institute of Architecture and Urban Studies (IAUS), founded by Peter Eisenman in 1967, where the journal was initiated in 1973. The link between the IUAV and the IAUS built a bridge from Venice to New York, and to other possible "Venices" reinvented further afield. Specific journal issues that owed a debt to Italy, and especially Venice, reveal conceptual imageries that unfold as instruments for rereading the built and the unbuilt and, potentially, as design tools.[9] *Oppositions*, later followed by the east coast periodicals *Assemblage* and *ANY*, and preceded by a backstory that links the birth of the IAUS journal to Italy via *Casabella*, together constitute the core of this discussion. Their Italy, as presented here, calls into play the definition of theory invoked by *Assemblage*'s founding editor K. Michael Hays, borrowing Fredric Jameson's notion of transcoding as "the invention of a set of terms, the strategic choice of a particular code or language, such that the same terminology can be used to analyze and articulate two quite distinct types of objects or 'texts,' or two very different levels of structural reality."[10] Such was the Smithsons' Italy, and their Venice in particular.

In their prologue to *Italian Thoughts*, the Smithsons investigated the influences of Italian Renaissance architects on the production of urban artifacts and theories of the twentieth century. The text, titled "Three Generations," entrusted Brunelleschi, Alberti, and Francesco di Giorgio with "the invention and the spread into ordinary use of a language whose intentions were wholly new," allowing the Smithsons to self-identify with "*[a]nother* third generation" with a corresponding drive.[11] They offer a potent analogue for the re-enactment of a comparable logic through a triad of media: made-out-of-Italy theoretical and design propositions emerging from the readings of such "territories made and re-made"; a meta-city that stands out both as paradigm and singularity; and a set of counter-narratives imprinted in the space of the page of architecture periodicals.[12] A sequence of thoughts is drawn into the tentative architectonics of strategic afterthoughts.

Prelude: entering from the backyard

"Arrival through the Back-Yard" is the title of Peter Smithson's proposal for Venice at the end of the millennium.[13] In it, a double backyard intervenes to situate the discussion between the guiding pretext of the Smithsons' thoughts and the discursive, paper space. The twofold dimension of doors and gateways as both entries and exits appears in the Smithsons' reflections as an Italian peculiarity. In his 1976 lecture "Doors in Italy," Peter Smithson addresses "real doors," that is, "cupboard doors."[14] In 1982, he casts the city of Genoa as the backdrop for discussing the "doors of the mind."[15] In their final ILA&UD project he presents Venice as a design laboratory that overturns the relationship between front and back through a reflection on the entry points into the city, and this by means of a specific scheme. After proposing an access to the city from Fondamenta Nove, which would thus become a threshold, he tables an alternative in "A Water-Biennale Park for the North End of the Darsena of S. Elena" (see Figure 3.1). Entering Venice from this backyard, a sequence of spaces and demountable artifacts would be made "available," connecting the hidden and the exposed. Extrapolating from Peter Smithson's other schemes for elsewhere in the lagoon city, this might entail including "all those things which are necessary but unpleasant," and accommodating "on the inside the sense of nature entering-in."[16] The available, the unpleasant, and the ingressive natures enabled by the gesture of door-opening, as shaping both forms and perceptions, emerge as elements for subverting the relationship between use and wear. The idea of a backyard—more than just a back door—suggests a reinterpretation of the yard as opposed or complementary to the garden, evoking a "changing, noisy" reservoir of "abandoned places, places for changing, spontaneous activities." Looking at Venice's "[g]ondola repair yard[s]" as prototypes for "shapes worn by that work," the garden's alter ego becomes at once a celebration of use and uselessness.[17]

Analogous backyard entries into this narrative appear in the paper spaces of certain American periodicals, and through another Venetian backyard—one in the city's vicinity, known as "Little Venice." Anticipating the birth of *Oppositions*, a double issue of *Casabella*

Figure 3.1 A Water-Biennale Park in the North of S. Elena from the *ILA&UD Annual Report* 1 (1997). Alison and Peter Smithson Archive, Frances Loeb Library, Harvard University.

was dedicated to the IAUS in 1971 (see Figure 3.2). Entitled "The City as an Artifact," it was assembled by Peter Eisenman, Pietro Sartogo, and Alessandro Mendini. "Marking the beginning of an enduring . . . transatlantic collaboration," the issue features William Ellis's article "The Natural Town and the Spaceless Milieu," an initial outcome of the partially unpublished study *New Urban Settlements: Analytical Phase*, developed within

Figure 3.2 Cover of *Casabella* 359‑60 (1971), special issue by the Institute for Architecture and Urban Studies. Mondadori/Electa/Marco Covi.

the Research and Development Program at the Institute since 1969.[18] Then a fellow at the IAUS, Ellis proposed a comparison that shifts the Smithsons' temporal reference. Discussing the development of new towns in England, Ellis envisioned a parallel between the case of Hook New Town and the medieval settlement of Chioggia, located at the southern edge of the Venetian lagoon. Chioggia was recognized as "the prerequisite for Hook," and Hook as a paradigm for "the designed, interpretive, artifice of a medieval city, in which there was a sense of point of contact." He presents both loci as cities in a garden because they share a close proximity of housing and nature, achieved through a compact density with open land on its outskirts, resulting in "a place that would accept change … but would be able to maintain its sovereignty by keeping its center protected from the ongoing traffic of automobiles."[19] For them, the "natural" is "the spatial street, exemplified by the Italian hill town," able to exceed "the artifice of the anti-artifice position."[20] This anticipates a possible rereading of non-natural natures, or the other side of nature and (simultaneously) the dark side of architecture, for which the built can be both the fencing in of the yard and, as a subversion, its doorway.

I. Janus-responses—doublings

The "first god of all doorways" is Janus, embodiment of Peter Smithson's Italophilic inclinations. In his 1987 "Janus—Thoughts for Siena," he presents twofold-ness as an inherent aspect of Italianness: "Janus is unique in that he was an essentially Italic god or, more precisely, Roman."[21] He presents Janus-thinking as a way "to observe both the exterior and the interior of the house, and the entrance and exit of public buildings," and also offers examples that describe a Janus-building. Together with a warehouse, a watermill, and a bastion, he names the palaces of three cities—those "with views high over the Mediterranean on one side and with steep dense streets on the other," like Genoa and Algiers, or "a palace, one side towards the wide water, the other towards the narrow street; Venice."[22] This inherent duality as a powerful expression of distinct, dominant external conditions becomes a trans-scalar medium to reread the relationships between fronts and backs, ups and downs, insides and outsides, from the single building to the whole city—where, as in the case of Venice, "every part" carries "the same message."[23] Italian thoughts are thus "Janus-thoughts" that become design strategies, or "Janus-responses."

The double-sided responses that Venice induces leads to the journal *Oppositions* through Peter Eisenman's acknowledgement of Venetian frontality during his Grand Tour with Colin Rowe:

> We then went to Venice. In retrospect, in Venice, interesting differences between Rowe and Tafuri became clear. Tafuri thought that Sansovino was important, while Rowe infinitely preferred Scamozzi. We saw two Palladian churches, San Giorgio and Redentore, and the layering and compression that occurred on the facades, their frontality. Now I was beginning to see things.[24]

If Eisenman's account of Venice interprets its frontality in formal terms, the shift from matter to metaphor may occur through Tafuri's idea of "doubling" as expressed in "L'architecture dans le boudoir," first published in *Oppositions* in 1974:

> At the origin of a critical act, there always lies a process of destroying, of dissolving, of disintegrating a given structure. Without such a disintegration of the object under analysis, no further rewriting of the object is possible. And it is self-evident that no criticism exists that does not retrace the process that has given birth to the work and that does not redistribute the elements of the work into a different order, if for no other purpose than to construct typological methods. But here criticism begins what might be called its "doubling" of the object under analysis.[25]

Transcoding Tafuri's doubling in this narrative, it is thus through "a process of destroying, of dissolving, of disintegrating" the "given structure" of Venice that the object-city starts duplicating itself. Janus thus becomes more than a physical double-sidedness: a strategic figure-device to reread what, in 1979, another Tafurian contribution to *Oppositions* defined as "the 'signifying traces' of events," a montage technique of transfiguration and recomposition from which any alleged beginning can become a multiplication of beginnings.[26]

II. Shells—whirlpools

The ideas of Venetian doublings and of the city of lagoons as a source for multiple beginnings meet and overlap in the second dyad of this narrative. For Peter Smithson, multiple others occupy and insufflate new lives into the "old hard shells" of the city:

> Venice is a collection of miraculously-still-lived-in shells, a domain of elegant crustaceans; many still living, shell and original occupier intact, many colonized by others: it is the surviving hard parts of the past kept alive new lives and uses, nothing on earth so much as some whiskery shell-formation.[27]

Looking at the Magazzini del Sale on the Fondamenta delle Zattere far beyond their original use as salt-warehouses, Smithson rereads "the public domain as the shell-formation." Traversed by different "degrees of accessibility," the "hard parts of the past" become the places in which "disuse" and "disbelief" make it possible to build up collective, "invisible territorialities."[28]

This idea for Venice returns through the book *Anywise*, a project emerging around the paper space of *ANY* magazine, within the milieu of the Anyone Corporation, founded in 1990 by Cynthia Davidson.[29] Anticipated by a conference held in Seoul in 1995, presented in preliminary form at the 1996 Venice Biennale, and then expanded to become the inaugural exhibition of the NTT Inter-Communication Center gallery in Tokyo, the project features an arbitrary Venice that emerges as the "point of reference" for a "fictional construct" designed by Arata Isozaki with Akira Asada.[30] *Kaihi/Haishi: The Mirage City, Another Utopia* responded to a request from the municipal government of Zhuhai City to transform the southern part of Hang-Qin Island, in the South China Sea, into a center for international exchange that would create an extension of the Special Economic Zone (see Figures 3.3, 3.4, and Plate 1). Isozaki designed an artificial island, set in the Hang-Qin Bay, "to be fabricated without any historicity."[31] Approximately the same size as Venice, Haishi seems to share with its Italian counterpart a vocation as "a whirlpool . . . of new encounters," among diverse authors and between the "West wind and the East wind."[32] In a coincidence of solitude and exteriority resembling that of the city of lagoons, Haishi is connected to the mainland by two bridges, like the island depicted on the frontispiece to the 1518 second edition of Thomas More's *Utopia*. At Mirage City, arbitrariness and randomness are pursued by means of a sequence of overlays, simulating "the state of tourbillion in constant flux."[33] Starting with a portion of the figure-ground composition of Piranesi's *Campo Marzio*, the design features a computer-generated pattern based on a diagram of church locations in Venice, whose "[a]ttributes of being a 'church' were stripped away."[34] This layout of appropriated traces of Italianness in turn permits the superimposition of other participants' "signatures," including the infestations of undesirable activities perpetrated by Diller + Scofidio, along with the contributions of

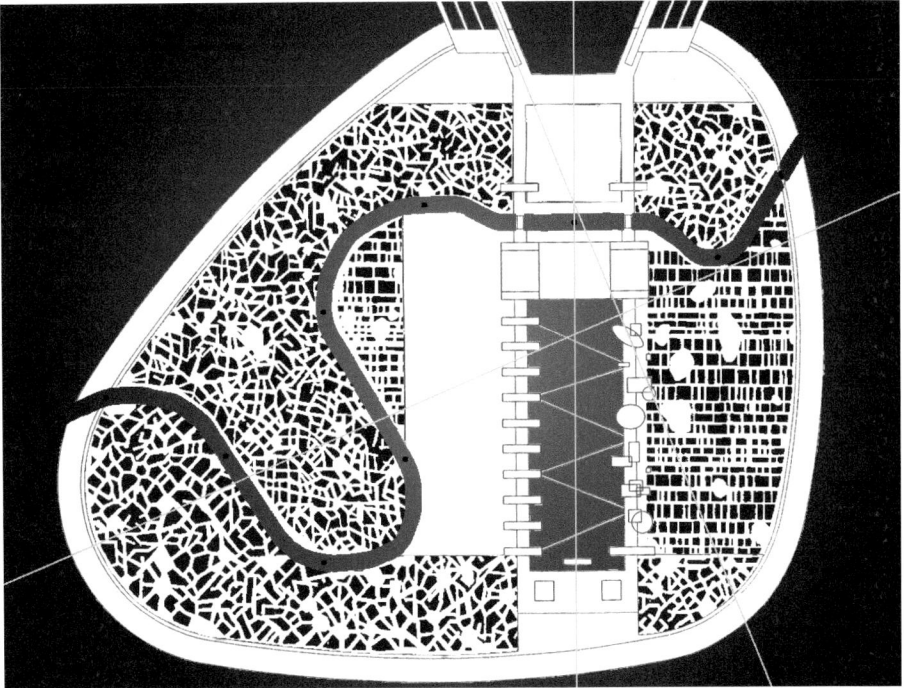

Figure 3.3 Arata Isozaki and Akira Asada, Haishi/Mirage City project, 1997. © Arata Isozaki, courtesy of Arata Isozaki & Associates.

Figure 3.4 Installation view of the exhibition *ISOZAKI Arata: SOLARIS*. Photo: KIOKU Keizo.

approximately fifty architects. Through a continuous process of negotiation between neighboring sites, "[a]rchitecture that has been designed for another location" would "create an entirely uncoordinated situation," destabilizing authorship and rejecting the imposition of any fixed image.[35]

III. Stages—armatures

This "Venetian" sense of multi-authorship and the coexistence of negotiation and deliberate lack of coordination configures another way of staging Italianness from the outside. Invoking Wittkower, Peter Smithson further describes the twofold-ness of Venice as "a piece of theater . . . the stone is big on its face, but thin, with its joints on the sides."[36] Built of such duplicitous matter, the city unfolds a continuous *mis-en-scène* of transient events, presenting opportunities for the new, "stage-architecture for the Court Masque."[37] These new spaces "made real for one day only perhaps, but still real," act as "intermediaries between actual and formal space . . . released from the cartouches and lozenge panels into which such objects are historically frozen."[38] The absence of historicity envisioned by Isozaki and Asada and the release from the paralyzing historicity of Smithson's "setting of a masque" share the design potential of an endless "re-arrangeability for different acts" and different spatiotemporal scenes: "The buildings along the Grand Canal are mostly façade . . . the city as a setting side-by-side of façade flats is consciously scenographic. It would seem therefore that the approach by water must, in the same scenographic way, seem to be all nature . . . to make a theatrical contrast between setting and city."[39]

This dimension of the city as a device for designing theatrical contrasts and transitory stages leads to the realm of *Assemblage*. Venice appears in the journal's 1998 issue, when the image of the Rialto Bridge is juxtaposed with the Turquoise Bridge under The Broadway in San Diego by Jon Jerde. Ann Bergren describes Jerde's borrowing of a form of Italianness and Veniceness as the architectural "armatures" of a shopping center and a theme-park as an "architecture of pleasure." In the space of the page, Venice flanks Jerde's 1985 Horton Plaza shopping center in San Diego to recount the process through which—twenty years after he traveled to Italy as a college student—he appropriated the model of the Italian hill town as "the greatest example of communality."[40] Bringing to California the idea of an "eclectic group of buildings with no single author, but built, as it were, by popular tradition," Jerde designs the Horton Plaza's "quest for communality" and pleasure. The specifically Venetian elements of this Californian project are crucial to his objective of designing "a 'mimetic double,' a competing twin."[41]

In Jerde's unbuilt project for Festival City on Mud Island near Memphis, these Italian borrowings become a bold framework for architectural reinvention (see Figure 3.5).

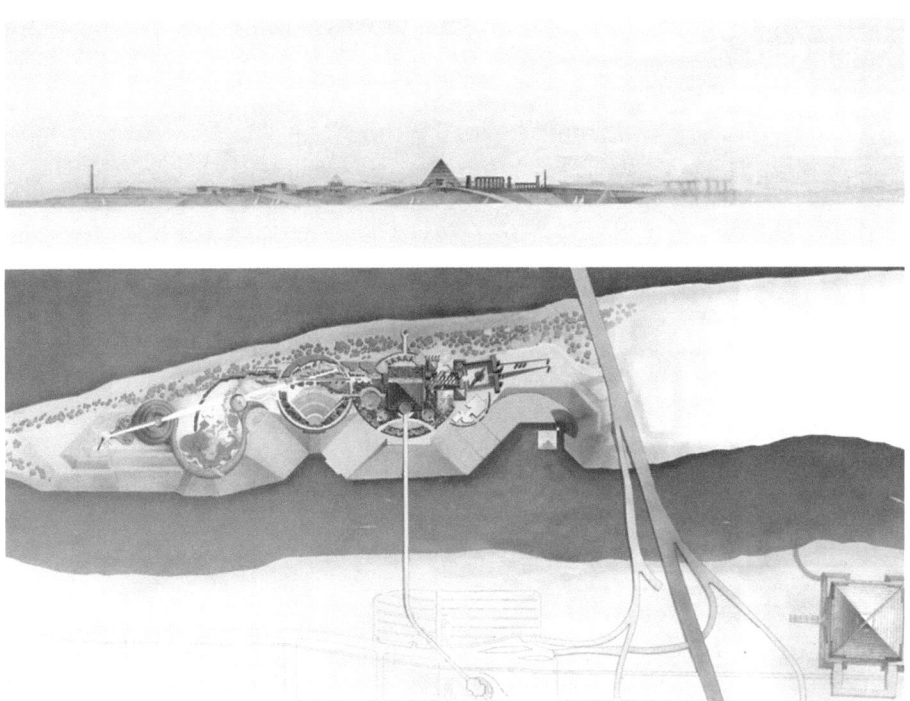

Figure 3.5 Jon Jerde's unbuilt design for Mud Island/Festival City near Memphis, 1998. Courtesy: JERDE.

Bergren's Freudian reading of Jerde's repetition compulsion at Mud Island takes it beyond the mere reiteration of the past. Although its namesake, the ancient Egyptian city of Memphis, is Jerde's most explicit reference, he also uses "various allomorphs of Italian urbanism ... in a kind of extended, honorific pun."[42] The muddy environment of the island in the Mississippi River resembles another Venice recounted by *Assemblage* one decade earlier. In 1987, the journal featured Peggy Deamer's account of Adrian Stokes's description of the facades of Venice "darkened by lichen."[43] Mud and lichens perpetrate a reading of Venice as a place shaped by murky non-human inhabitants, resembling those injections of natures and other "things on the outside" advocated by Peter Smithson and entailing "an empooling of the space-between," that is a shift "from the building as object to its action on the special shaping of the territory."[44]

Coda: imprints as anticipations, or "Hints of Attachments to Come"

"[H]ow does one return from a Venice that does not exist?" wonders Tafuri.[45] As a tentative conclusion, from the non-existent Venices floating within architecture periodicals through projects across diverse geographic realms—English new towns, the South China Sea, the western territories of North America—La Serenissima emerges as a relational matrix through which spaces and their imaginaries are re-examined in the rear-view mirror of second thoughts and reconsiderations. Returning to Jameson's idea of transcoding:

> New theoretical discourse is produced by the setting into active equivalence of two preexisting codes, which thereby, in a kind of molecular ion exchange, become a new one. What must be understood is that the new code (or metacode) can in no way be considered a synthesis between the previous pair ... It is rather a question of linking two sets of terms in such a way that each can express and indeed *interpret* the other.[46]

By its very nature resisting identification with a specific land (Italy or elsewhere), Venice stands out as a duplicitous metacode, paradigm, and outlier, a form of both belonging and enigmatic alienation. Archetype of the eternal and the ephemeral, with its sheltered yet precarious occupation of adjustable foundations, it resurfaces from its watery context as more than a space of deception and disguise. "Dressed for the seasons," Venice appears in the Smithson's *Italian Thoughts* as an "example of collective design," a paradigm of the "idea of triggering the design activities of others," and "open to the giving of others."[47] The rhythm of seasons seems to reverse the idea of possession and use: "... this happens in animal migrations; yet the various species seem to survive in their seasonally possessed shared habit. / Do we human animals feel it fresh / When at last we re-possess? / It would seem so. / Venice in winter is marvelous."[48]

The city's twofold-ness thus turns into an ode to uselessness: able to "suggest other uses," but having "permission to be otherwise useless."[49] Between new uses and non-uses, "the anticipated and un-anticipated are eagerly awaited," and a multispecies city seems to appear where "all inventions are an invention into nature; it is through them that we preserve our animal nature as the animals who wish to change things."[50] As an "Italian oddity," and perhaps a premonition for architecture, "[t]he texture, the graphics, the old city gave equal weight to men, to animals, to trees, to buildings," making the city itself a site for our "contract with nature."[51] If Italian Renaissance architecture has proven to be "rich in hooks and scaffoldings," perhaps between the strata of what already exists "there is room for illusion, and for activity."[52] And between illusion and activity, a city of non-alternate oppositions, of coexisting polarities stands out: a city of *Aufhebung*. Entering it from the backyard, a turning of Janus' head, changing its inhabitants into the crustacean's shell, and rendering it a transitory setting of stage-architecture—these are all acts of transcoding, anticipatory imprints or "hints of attachments to come."[53]

Notes

1. "A public space without trees is unimaginable in England. It is the ever-changing perfection of nature that 'settles' an English built-place. Not so in Italy. In Italy the sense of being settled—both as a fact and as an ideal—is consequent of man-devised additions and adjustments ... sometimes of a quality which seems beyond human capacity ..." Peter Smithson, "To Establish a Territory," *ILA&UD Annual Report* (Siena, 1986), 60.

2. Alison Smithson and Peter Smithson, *Italian Thoughts* (Stockholm: self-published, 1993), translated into German as *Italienische Gedanken: Beobachtungen Und Reflexionen Zur Architektur* (Basel: Birkhäuser, 2000).

3. Smithson, "To Establish a Territory," 60.

4. Further key dates include 1977, when Peter Smithson joined the ILA&UD Lab, working on projects in and for Urbino for five years; his first visit to the fortress of Sassocorvaro and the buildings by Francesco di Giorgio Martini in 1978; his ILA&UD design activities in Siena from 1982 until 1990; and finally, 1981 with the Smithsons' publication of the paperback edition of *The Heroic Period of Modern Architecture*, which was then disseminated by Alison Smithson through an Italian lecture tour.

5. John Dixon Hunt, *The Venetian City Garden: Place, Typology, and Perception* (Basel: Birkhäuser, 2009), 7.

6. Peter Smithson, "Risking More to the Future; Some Further Thoughts on Connection; Concerning Narrative and Change of Organizational Base," *ILA&UD Annual Report* (Urbino, 1977), 163.

7. Peter Smithson, "The Size of the Stones: S. Giorgio Maggiore and Il Redentore (13:6:97 and 12:9:97)," *Peter Smithson at ILA&UD*, ed. E.C. Occhialini (Milan, 2016), 147. Smithson and Smithson, *Italian Thoughts*, 14–15.

8. In the ILA&UD yearbooks, the most explicit theory on Italianness by Peter Smithson is the notion of *Conglomerate Ordering*, published in the same issue right after Manfredo Tafuri's *Humanism, Technology and Rhetoric in Renaissance Venice* (first delivered at Harvard that year). Peter Smithson, "Conglomerate Ordering," *ILA&UD Annual Report* (Siena, 1986), 54–9; in the same source, Manfredo Tafuri, "Humanism, Technology and Rhetoric in Renaissance Venice," 50–3.

9. Joan Ockman, "Venice and New York," *Casabella* 619–20 (1995): 57–71. Consider, too, *Perspecta* 9–10 (1965), edited by Robert Stern, which explored the contours of the so-called White/Gray divide; it was inspired by Ernesto Nathan Rogers's issue of *Casabella continuità* 281 (1963) on "Architettura USA." As Luciano Semerani wrote in *Phalaris*: "[Ideas] come and go across and over the Atlantic from Europe to America and from America to Europe, flocks of migratory ideas, perhaps always the same ideas, but each time they return from a journey they have changed because they are not eternal ideas, or perhaps they are traces, routes, points of departure and arrival that are always identical, but the journey and the time of the journey, by themselves, change us; in outward appearance at least." Luciano Semerani, "America–Europa," *Phalaris* 13 (1991): cover; translation by author.

10. Fredric Jameson, *The Political Unconscious* (Ithaca, NY: Cornell University Press, 1981), 40.

11. Peter Smithson, "Three Generations," *ILA&UD Annual Report* (Urbino, 1980), 88. The essay was later included in *Italian Thoughts*. Smithson, "Three Generations," 89–90. He goes on: "The founding generation of the Modern Movement were all born in the 1880s—Walter Gropius (1883), Mies van de Rohe (1886), Le Corbusier (1887)—and their style flowered in the 1920s. The parallel of that flowering with the early Renaissance seems irresistible: Pazzi Chapel 1429—the fourteen twenties. Villa Savoye 1929—the nineteen twenties. The generation who grew up with this style were born in the 1900s—Jean Prouvé (1901), Charles Eames (1907)—are the second generation. The work in parallel: Palazzo Rucellai 1446—the fourteen forties. Santa Monica House 1948—the nineteen forties. My own generation, the third generation, grew up to being working architects in an astonished daze with the originality, the daring, and the technical virtuosity of Jean Prouvé and the Eames. Our work, now under construction in the nineteen eighties, is, in this continuing parallel, to be seen in generation-time with Francesco di Giorgio's fort at Mondavio from the fourteen eighties (1482)."

12. Smithson, "To Establish a Territory," 60.

13. Peter Smithson, "Arrival through the Back-Yard," *ILA&UD Annual Report* (Venice, 1999), 136–7.

14. Peter Smithson, "In Praise of Cupboard Doors," *ILA&UD Annual Report* (Urbino, 1979), 40–53.

15. Peter Smithson, "To Open a Few Small Doors (Genova, 1982)," *Peter Smithson at ILA&UD*, 34–42.

16. Peter Smithson, "A Water-Biennale Park in the North of S. Elena," *ILA&UD Annual Report* (Venice, 1997), 162–3; "Outside the Arsenale," *ILA&UD Annual Report* (Venice, 1998), 170; and "Inside Outside: Outside Inside," *ILA&UD Annual Report* (Venice, 2000), 82.

17. Peter Smithson, "The Yard (Venice, 1997)," *Peter Smithson at ILA&UD*, 135–6.

18. See Beatriz Colomina and Craig Buckley (eds), *Clip, Stamp, Fold: The Radical Architecture of Little Magazines, 196X to 197X* (Barcelona: Actar, 2010), 127. William Ellis, "La città 'naturale' e i contesti a-spaziali"/"The Natural Town and the Spaceless Milieu," *Casabella* 359–60 (1971): 62–70. See also William Ellis, *New Urban Settlements: Analytical Phase* (New York: IAUS, 1970).

19. Suzanne Frank, *IAUS, the Institute for Architecture and Urban Studies: An Insider's Memoir* (Bloomington, IN: AuthorHouse, 2010), 89–91, 195.

20. William Ellis, cited in Frank, *IAUS, the Institute for Architecture and Urban Studies*, 231.

21. Peter Smithson, "Janus-Thoughts for Siena," *ILA&UD Annual Report* (Siena, 1987), 87.

22. Smithson, "Janus-Thoughts for Siena," 87, 89.

23. Peter Smithson, "Small Steps, Big Steps (18:4:99)," *Peter Smithson at ILA&UD*, 149.

24. "Interview with Peter Eisenman: The Last Grand Tourist: Travels with Colin Rowe," *Perspecta* 41 (2008), 133.

25. Manfredo Tafuri, "L'architecture dans le boudoir: The Language of Criticism and the Criticism of Language," *Opposition* 3 (1974); republished in *The Sphere and the Labyrinth: Avant-Gardes and Architecture from Piranesi to the 1970s* (Cambridge, MA: MIT Press, 1987), 272.

26. See Manfredo Tafuri, "The Historical 'Project,'" *Oppositions* 18 (1979); orig. 1977, and republished as "Introduction: The Historical 'Project,'" in *The Sphere and the Labyrinth*, 2. Tafuri, "The Historical 'Project,'" 3.

27. Peter Smithson, "Making Another Connection (part one, January 1977, edited April 1997)," *Peter Smithson at ILA&UD*, 132–3.

28. Smithson, "Making Another Connection," 132–3.

29. Cynthia Davidson (ed.), *Anywise* (Cambridge, MA: MIT Press, 1996).

30. Arata Isozaki (ed.), *kaishi/haishi: The Mirage City—Another Utopia* (Tokyo: NTT Publishing, 1997), 14. See also Akira Asada and Arata Isozaki, "Haishi Jimua," in *Anywise*, ed. Davidson, 24–31.

31. Isozaki, *kaishi/haishi*, 7. The Chinese term Haishi means both *city on the sea* and *mirage*.

32. Isozaki, *kaishi/haishi*, 9.

33. Isozaki, *kaishi/haishi*, 9.

34. Isozaki, *kaishi/haishi*, 13.

35. Isozaki, *kaishi/haishi*, 10. While Isozaki's proposal remained on paper, the Venetian theme he initiated seems to find an uncanny echo in the negotiations started in 2005 by the local government with the Las Vegas Sands Corporation—owner of the Venetian Resort Hotel Casino—to develop Hang-Qin Island through the company's design for the Venetian Hengqin International Convention and Resort Project, obliterating the "natural becoming" envisioned at Mirage City through the premise of welcoming *anyone* to the project.

36. Peter Smithson, "The Size of the Stones: S. Giorgio Maggiore and Il Redentore (13:6:97 and 12:9:97)," *Peter Smithson at ILA&UD*, 147.

37. Peter Smithson, "The Masque and the Exhibition: Stages toward the Real," *ILA&UD Annual Report* (Urbino, 1981), 62.

38. Smithson, "The Masque and the Exhibition," 62, 64.

39. Peter Smithson, "Venezia Scenographica," *ILA&UD Annual Report* (Venice, 2000), 72. Also citing from Smithson, "The Masque and the Exhibition," 67.

40. Jerde quoted in Ann Bergren, "Jon Jerde and the Architecture of Pleasure," *Assemblage* 37 (1998), 10.

41. Bergren, "Jon Jerde and the Architecture of Pleasure," 10.

42. Bergren, "Jon Jerde and the Architecture of Pleasure," 20.

43. Adrian Stokes quoted in Peggy Deamer, "Adrian Stokes and Critical Vision," *Assemblage* 2 (1987), 121.

44. Smithson, "Inside Outside: Outside Inside," 82; and "Empooling," *ILA&UD Annual Report* (San Marino, 1996), 42. He continues: "Where there is a sandy beach with rocks standing-up from it, as the tide recedes small pools are left at certain places where the rocks cluster. Similarly, the formation of buildings can curry [sic] with it an empooling of the

space-between and as with the rock-pools what is within the space-between seems extraordinarily vivid."

45. Tafuri, *The Sphere and the Labyrinth*, 41.

46. Fredric Jameson, *Postmodernism, or, the Cultural Logic of Late Capitalism* (Durham, NC: Duke University Press, 1991), 394–5.

47. Peter Smithson, "Making Another Connection, part three, January 1977, edited April 1997," *Peter Smithson at ILA&UD*, 134. Invoking, too, Manfrado Tafuri, "L'éphémère est éternel. Aldo Rossi a Venezia," *Domus* 602 (1980): 7–11; and John Hejduk, *Adjusting Foundations* (New York: Monacelli, 1995).

48. Peter Smithson, "To Work at the Gates," *ILA&UD Annual Report* (Siena, 1983), 69.

49. Peter Smithson, "Last Year in Urbino (17/19:5:82)," *Peter Smithson at ILA&UD*, 43; and "The Size of the Stones: S. Giorgio Maggiore and Il Redentore (13:6:97 and 12:9:97)," *Peter Smithson at ILA&UD*, 148.

50. Peter Smithson, "To GDC on Siena, for 1983 (18:11:82)," *Peter Smithson at ILA&UD*, 44; and "To Open a Few Small Doors," 35.

51. Smithson, "To Open a Few Small Doors," 41.

52. Peter Smithson, "Some further Layers: Work and Insights," *ILA&UD Annual Report* (Urbino, 1978), 78.

53. Smithson, "Some further Layers," 79.

CHAPTER 4
ITALY AS A METHODOLOGICAL TESTING GROUND FOR ARCHITECTURAL HISTORY
Raúl Martínez Martínez

The later decades of the nineteenth century witnessed developments both institutional and intellectual in the study of art in German-speaking nations. Art history found a secure footing in the university on the basis of a "scientific" approach to aesthetics. Such theoretical frameworks as aesthetic formalism, the psychology of form, and the aesthetic conception of space not only spurred on the study of this field; they also established a foundation on which the history of art could develop, everywhere, across the twentieth century. Few figures spanning this period of invention and institutionalization are as prominent as the Swiss art historian Heinrich Wölfflin. In a period of experimentation and reflection, Wölfflin found security in the art and architecture of Italy which, as an anchor for the history of art entire, offered a rich testing ground where novel methods of analysis could be leveraged to explore Italy's architectural heritage. In this, too, Wölfflin legitimized practices that would remain important for the study of architectural history (within and beyond the history of art) in the decades that followed his own highly influential contributions to the field.

Already in 1886, his doctoral dissertation "Prolegomena zu einer Psychologie der Architektur" (Prolegomena to a Psychology of Architecture) was, as Mark Jarzombek has observed, "one the earliest attempts to draw art and architecture into the emergent debates about psychology."[1] Wölfflin's study considered the psychological aspects of architectural apprehension by reading such buildings as the Villa Farnesina by Baldassare Peruzzi, the Tempietto of San Pietro in Montorio by Donato Bramante (both in Rome), the church of Santa Maria delle Grazie in Arezzo and the Palazzo Strozzi in Florence (both by Benedetto da Maiano). For Wölfflin, architectural style contained the character of the nation in which it developed. He could thus contrast the attitudes of northern and southern Europe and express his preference for the character of the peoples of the south. These differences were exemplified in the proportions of the Gothic; the Italian Gothic tended towards wide proportions and quiet existence, whereas its northern counterpart leaned towards vertical proportions and restlessness. The physical responses provoked by the perception of architectural forms produced in such countries as Italy and Greece were, for Wölfflin, more aligned with human organization and organic life through their tendency towards regularity and balance.

His study *Renaissance und Barock* (1888) is consumed with the Italian case, observing the forces informing stylistic change, its consequences for architectural composition, and its critical fortunes.[2] While Wölfflin's specific concern with psychology waned over the 1890s, his experimentation with method continued unabated.[3] This led him, ultimately, to a more formalistic approach based on a comparative method of visual appreciation, exemplified in his 1915 book *Kunstgeschichtliche Grundbegriffe* (Principles of Art History).[4] Together, these works explore a history of architecture that privileges the Italian past, in particular, among its materials. For Wölfflin, his contemporaries, and their disciples, Italy offered a consistent datum for evaluating new methods in "the search for universal laws governing artistic formation and stylistic evolution, the attempt to establish an expository *Kunstwissenschaft*."[5] Over subsequent decades, this project addressed very different problems in many distinct ways in the universities and museums of central Europe. The ideas and models these scholars developed, even in their disparity, formed an institutional common ground and, at times, an unconscious set of rules for architectural discourse with the history of art. Throughout, Italy continued to operate as a testing ground for novel approaches to the study of architecture. Methods developed thus assumed a life of their own, informing the study of architecture in other times and places, even as they continued to explore the history of art and architecture in Italy itself.

The acuteness of physical sensation

Consider the intellectual and artistic circle around Bernard Berenson and Villa I Tatti, outside Florence, which played a vital role in the diffusion of aesthetic theories developed in German-speaking Europe into the Anglophone world, with Italian Renaissance art as its primary vehicle. In 1893, Berenson wrote "A Word for Renaissance Churches," wherein he differentiated Italy's ecclesiastical architecture from that of northern Europe. Italian churches, he argued, "even in the darkest periods of medievalism," did not evoke the "vague emotions" and "sense of mystery" characteristic of northern churches.[6] Since Roman antiquity, he wrote, architects in Italy had aimed to reach a "perfect effect of space," an ideal that was ultimately expressed in the Renaissance with the domed central-plan church. The Renaissance architect, he believed, took an "effect of space and proportion" as the "principal aim of his art."[7] The first example of this Italian ideal of space was the Pazzi Chapel in Florence, and its "best realization" the church of Santa Maria della Consolazione at Todi.[8] Berenson held that the essence of Italian churches required a specific method for their full appreciation, discarding functional and structural interpretations. The empirical-psychological method he described follows that which is condensed in Wölfflin's dissertation, a work that contained, as Berenson later acknowledged, his "entire philosophy of art."[9] Berenson assumed the "point of view of the aesthetic spectator," whose analyses were based on the "acuteness of physical sensation."[10] He wrote perceptual descriptions of sensory experiences. When entering the church at Todi, for instance, "you feel as if you had cut loose from gravitation, and as if you took flight not only from the material universe, but also from all that is your conscious self."[11]

The stance in "A Word for Renaissance Churches" was expanded by Berenson's pupil Geoffrey Scott in *The Architecture of Humanism*, first published in 1914 and conceived as a study of Italian Renaissance architecture. Scott wrote that it was in Italy where

"Renaissance architecture was native ... yet, if we wish to watch architectural energy where it is most concentrated, most vigorous, and most original it is to Italy that we must turn."[12] While the book's first edition was well received and reviewed, its second edition (1924) saw a broader diffusion of Scott's ideas, to the point where it "almost could be taken for a book of the 1920s instead of something left over from before the war."[13] Reyner Banham attributes its popularity, in part, to Scott's broad interpretation of "humanism"—which Scott used "indiscriminately to refer either to the world of humane learning, or to the projection of human sentiments into the forms of architecture."[14] Scott's book has long been regarded as a study of the architecture of the long Italian Renaissance, even if, as John Macarthur has observed, his examples are "almost exclusively drawn from the Italian baroque."[15] However classified, the examples themselves are less significant than Scott's absorption and presentation therein of German empathy theory and its idea of space, which in turn enjoyed a wider diffusion within the field of modern architecture. *The Architecture of Humanism* provided an approach to architecture in which aesthetic experience revolved around an empathetic idea of form and space—Wölfflinian advances tested, once more, against an Italian measure. However, its open-ended nature invited an array of interpretations over the course of the twentieth century, and it became fundamental for classicists and modernists alike.

Vincent Scully and the empathetic response

Cast forward to the 1930s and 1940s, in which a diaspora of art historians carried models of art historical scholarship developed in central Europe into the rest of Europe, the United States, and elsewhere with a new level of visibility. Architectural historians educated around this time were exposed to their ideas both directly and indirectly, sometimes at the hands of first- or second-generation émigré scholars, sometimes in the implicit assumptions behind their exhibitions and popular histories. This wartime generation included such teachers as Vincent Scully, Bruno Zevi, and Colin Rowe, who themselves, in turn, promoted new readings of the history of Italian architecture in the second half of the twentieth century and cultivated what Anthony Vidler has described as the "flowering of history teaching."[16]

Vincent Scully's first article, for instance, considered the "live issue" of method. In "Architecture as a Science" (1948), he rejected the scientific interpretation of architecture since, as he argued, architecture could not be conceived as a systematic process governed by absolute and universal laws. The problem of architecture's relationship to science was at that time due to a misinterpretation of Louis Sullivan's aphorism "form follows function," through which modernist functionalism assumed in some quarters the character of a technological and functional determinism. As Scully stated, "today the vast body of architectural thought equates science and architecture more rigorously than at any time in the past." He argued that it was "impossible to deal with architecture in the abstract or in terms of formulas" because "architecture is not formula but form." It must be "seen and experienced."[17] He illustrated this position through the work of Leon Battista Alberti and Andrea Palladio. The architects shared similar theories—"ornament should express structure" and "the whole building should express the function it serves"— but the results differed in each case. Alberti's forms depicted "the confidence of fifteenth century experiment," whereas Palladio's displayed "the uncertainties of sixteenth century mannerism."[18] It was the architectural forms themselves, rather than the theory on which they drew, that revealed something of the authors or their time. This stance against the reductionism of scientific abstraction led Scully to develop an understanding of architecture through the visual analysis of its forms, under the maxim that all dogma "blinds men's eyes to that which they do not wish to see and thereby, so far as architecture is concerned, cuts them off from the roots of experience and knowledge."[19]

Scully put this approach into practice in an article in the first issue of *Perspecta* derived from research he had undertaken while a Fulbright Fellow at the American Academy in Rome: "Michelangelo's Fortification Drawings" (1952). He therein argued that the drawings made for Florence between 1527 and 1529 did not "seem yet to have attracted the attention they deserve" nor to have had the "effect upon architects and historians which they merit."[20] Scully's method consisted of analyzing Michelangelo's drawings by empathetically experiencing the design process through visual sensitivity to form. Privileging the artistic experience over historical facts, Scully sought to "work out Scott's concept of empathy in relation to his own sense of how one experiences art and writes about that experience."[21] This sense of empathy remained pivotal to Scully's work "as the basis of all perception." He acknowledged, "I talk about empathy a lot. It was very important to me … it came to me mainly from Louis Sullivan, and of course from Geoffrey Scott."[22]

Scully's explanations focused on wall planes, rhythm, and the angles of intersections, but they also embraced the third dimension, and hence space. He suggested that the energy of the "sensuously felt diagonal to destroy boundaries" and to "create reflex" made Michelangelo's fortification drawings "live and grow as spatial forms."[23] Michelangelo's use of the dynamic diagonal confounded those interpretations that characterized the architecture of the fifteenth and sixteenth centuries as based on a "system of rectangular and curvilinear rhythms" that pursued an "effect of static completeness," "spatial definition," and "rhythmical symmetry."[24] Scully believed that one of the historian's primary tasks was to continuously pose new questions of interpretations of the past. Architecture's history was "full of incomplete experiences" waiting to be "brought back into human focus" and to have "new effects."[25] His attitude reflected that of a generation of scholars looking forward by offering new readings of the (Italian) past. The history of architecture and its teaching thus emerged as a platform of great power that could nourish the architect's invention; it was a source full of lessons that, reinterpreted with contemporary eyes, could be applied in the present (see Figure 4.1).

Figure 4.1 Vincent Scully, "Michelangelo's Fortification Drawings: A Study in the Reflex Diagonal," in *Perspecta: The Yale Architectural Journal* (1952). Reprinted with the permission of *Perspecta*, Yale School of Architecture.

Bruno Zevi and the spatial experience

In Italy, Bruno Zevi advocated for a new critical method for the analysis of architecture that shared Scully's modernist sensibility. He believed the history of art had failed because it had considered architecture to be a "purely plastic phenomena," emphasizing solid exterior forms over the spatial conditions that were architecture's essence. In *Saper vedere l'archittetura* (1948, *Architecture as Space*), Zevi argued that the history of architecture had to become "primarily the history of spatial conceptions," its judgment based "fundamentally" on the "internal space of buildings."[26] To the eight most common bases of architectural interpretation (political, philosophical-religious, scientific, economic-social, materialist, technical, physio-psychological, and formalist), Zevi proposed a ninth lens: the "spatial interpretation," which did not "exclude but rather supports the first eight and shows their usefulness in architectural criticism when they are centered in space."[27] His chapter "Space Through the Ages" thus reviews the main conceptions of internal space in western culture. Zevi begins by analyzing the Greek temple as a deliberate de-emphasis of interior volume, with the Parthenon conceived as a sculptural monument and not an architectural work. The Greek temples of the south of

Italy and Sicily were, however, already spatial. As he argued, the "peristyle became broader and more spacious," a sign that "even at that time the Italic peoples were inclined to feel spatially" and to "give greater importance to space."[28]

Italy's prominence in Zevi's spatial history of architecture is hardly surprising. Besides being a Roman for whom much of this history was his own, he followed Berenson's argument that Italians possessed an innate sensibility towards space. This relationship may have been implicit in 1948, but Zevi later made his methodological alignment with Berenson and Scott clear. In 1978, Zevi established the series *Universale di Architettura*, a collection of essays presenting architectural ideas to a wider audience. Among its first volumes was a reprint of the 1939 Italian translation of *The Architecture of Humanism* by Elena Craveri Croce, daughter of philosopher Benedetto Croce. On the back cover, Zevi rhetorically asked, "Is it possible to understand painting without knowing Bernard Berenson? Similarly, you cannot understand architecture without reading Scott." This reasoning extended the methodological implications of *The Architecture of Humanism* to all architectural periods, through which "to understand and judge contemporary events."[29]

Zevi extended his spatial criticism into his teaching, where he saw an opportunity to intervene in the formation of new architects. In his course on Michelangelo taught at the Istituto universitario di architettura di Venezia in the late 1950s and early 1960s, conceived in preparation for the *quattrocentenario* of Michelangelo's death in 1964, Zevi's students developed a series of spatial models, assisted by the painter Mario Deluigi, with the intention of producing "three-dimensional translations of specific architectural thoughts."[30] This visual form of architectural criticism transformed the words of history into the "very language of the architects," a "three-dimensional reality,"[31] and offered a way of understanding Michelangelo with a modern sensitivity. As Zevi put it, their study of Michelangelo's spatiality provided an "effective instrument for evaluating the most current and pregnant themes of today's architecture."[32] Zevi proposed a novel pedagogy that showed how any past building seen with "modern eyes" and read with a "contemporary spirit" could become a "modern" building. He sought to reduce the gulf between architectural studios and history teaching by achieving a "complete coherence, almost a fusion between history courses and design courses."[33]

His views were shared by the architect Luigi Moretti, who similarly held that interior space is the "richest symbol of the entire architectural reality."[34] In an article published in 1952, Moretti focused on the spatial sequencing of internal volumes in works from ancient Rome to the baroque to offer a new account of their compositional structure. He visualized space three-dimensionally with evocative plaster models; the negative void suddenly became the protagonist, embodying spatial form. Moretti traced these ideas in his journal *Spazio*, addressing the concerns of modern architecture through an engagement with figures and works from across Italy's cultural history. His analyses of Italian painting, sculpture, and architecture spanned from the Romanesque to the baroque and emphasized artists like Michelangelo, Palladio, Caravaggio, and Borromini. While *Spazio* only lasted for seven issues, from 1950 to 1953, and reached a small audience, Zevi's influence was broader and spanned both hemispheres (see Figure 4.2 and Figure 4.3).

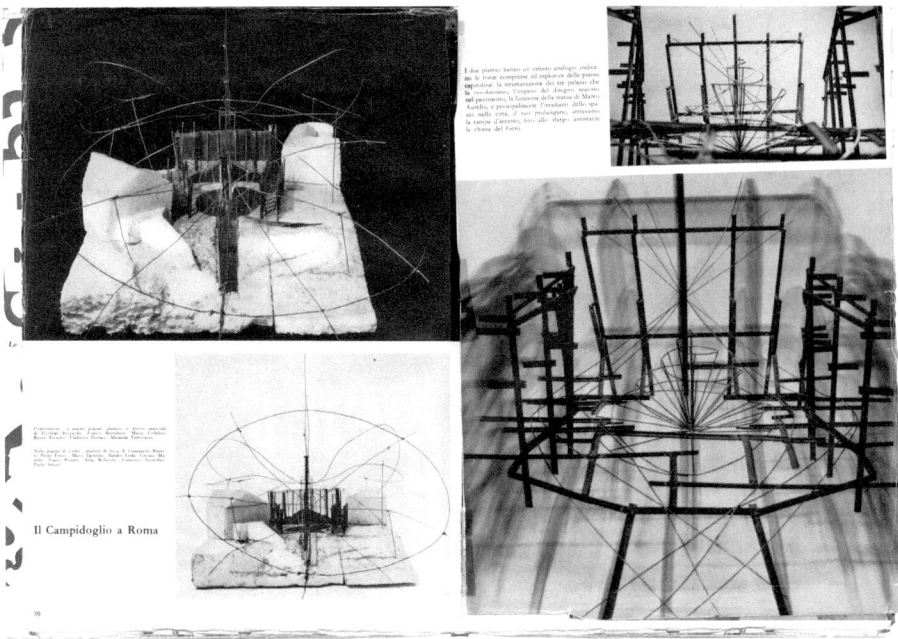

Figure 4.2 Student models, "Michelangiolo architetto," special issue of *L'architettura, cronache e storia* (1964). Fondazione Bruno Zevi, Rome.

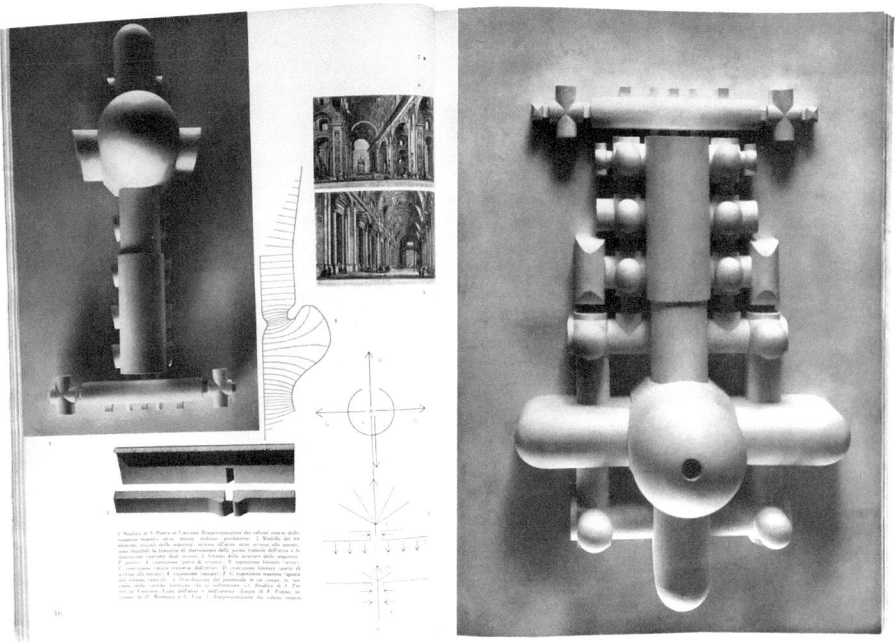

Figure 4.3 Luigi Moretti (models), "Strutture e sequenze di spazi," in *Spazio* 7 (December 1952-April 1953). Archivio Centrale dello Stato, Rome.

Zevi was particularly influential among the Spanish-speaking milieu on both sides of the Atlantic. Translations of his books, first published largely in Argentina, ensured the rapid diffusion of his ideas. During the 1950s and 1960s, Italian architects, critics, and historians offered crucial entry to discourse on modern architecture for their Spanish counterparts, but also new interpretations of the Italian past. For Rafael Moneo, the "Italy of the early sixties was a real model to follow, both from a cultural and political point of view."[35] In 1963, as a fellow of the Spanish Academy in Rome, Moneo had direct contact with Zevi and others at the Istituto nazionale di architettura, which ran programs to introduce foreign scholars from several academies to contemporary Italian architects, critics, planners, and engineers. Exposure to Zevi's ideas led Moneo to assimilate these "new" spatial theories within his own thinking and adopt an "ambition to make history the foundation of architectural knowledge." This moment, as he observed, was one in which "the study of the history of architecture itself was experiencing moments of indisputable interest." An historically self-aware architecture "became a methodological alternative to the purist rigorism of the modern movement."[36] This Roman cultural effervescence awakened widespread interest, not only of the past, but also of the present architectural scene in Italy. Figures like Carlo Scarpa, Ernesto Nathan Rogers, Gio Ponti, Zevi, Moretti, and Argan were joined by a new generation of scholars, including Vittorio Gregotti, Aldo Rossi, Paolo Portoghesi, and Manfredo Tafuri, who, in turn, reinvigorated Italian architectural discourse in the 1970s and 1980s through their multiform attention to history—both extending themes advanced by the likes of Zevi and Moretti and pushing back against them.

Colin Rowe and the abstract approach

In different ways, both Zevi and Scully extended Scott's postulate: while the scientific method was "intellectually and practically useful," the aesthetic method, which "humanizes the world," formed the very "foundation of architecture."[37] Scott's aesthetic criticism was, however, forcefully rejected by Rudolf Wittkower in *Architectural Principles in the Age of Humanism*, published in 1949. As Kenneth Clark later observed, the "first result of Professor Wittkower's studies" was to "dispose, once and for all, of the hedonist, or purely aesthetic, theory of Renaissance architecture."[38] Wittkower focused on the theory and practice of the period, again (like Scully) turning to Alberti and Palladio, but with a scientific method (in the tradition of *Kunstwissenschaft*) favoring a close reading of treatises and architectural forms in which the symbolic value of the Renaissance was manifest. His discourse avoided subjective judgments of taste and stylistic connotations and supported formal analyses on Pythagorean mathematics, Euclidean geometry, and harmonic proportion. His *Principles* opened a new paradigm for understanding Renaissance architecture after World War II by showing that Renaissance forms were the result of an intellectual framework rooted in Pythagoreo-Platonic philosophy. Wittkower's analyses of Renaissance architecture were eye-opening for the generation of architects educated under a dogmatic modernism. As Peter

Smithson declared in 1952, "Dr. Wittkower is regarded by the younger architects as the only art historian working in England capable of describing and analyzing buildings in spatial and plastic terms and not in terms of derivation and dates."[39] In 1955, Banham, too, conveyed the significance of his influence:

> The general impact of Professor Wittkower's book on a whole generation of post-war architectural students is one of the phenomena of our time. Its exposition of a body of architectural theory in which objective laws governing the Cosmos (as Alberti and Palladio understood them) suddenly offered a way out of the doldrum of routine-functionalist abdications, and neo-Palladianism became the order of the day. The effect of *Architectural Principles* has made it by far the most important contribution—for evil as well as for good—by any historian to English Architecture since *Pioneers of the Modern Movement*, and it precipitated a nice disputation on the proper uses of history.[40]

Architectural Principles was, as Wittkower acknowledged in 1971, a result of a "long period of gestation." Preparatory research began before the war with early studies on Alberti and Palladio that were published in the *Journal of the Warburg and Courtauld Institutes* "during the war" and were "extended" and "broadened in scope" for the book.[41]

Wittkower's studies on the architecture of Italy's fifteenth and sixteenth centuries, and on Palladio in particular, influenced his pupil Colin Rowe, whose 1947 master's thesis was a speculation on a hypothetical treatise by Inigo Jones based on Palladio's *Quatro libri dell'architettura* of 1570. Entitled "The Theoretical Drawings of Inigo Jones," Rowe's thesis was (as Anthony Vidler has observed) an "extraordinary synthesis of historical interpretation derived from Wittkower and formal analysis derived from Wölfflin."[42] This anchored Rowe's canonical article "The Mathematics of the Ideal Villa," also from 1947 and published in *Architectural Review*. Rowe established a relationship between Palladio's Villa Foscari, near Venice, and Le Corbusier's Villa Stein at Garches along the lines of the distinction in Wren's *Parentalia* between "natural" beauty—derived from geometry—and "customary" beauty—developed from use. Rowe's treatment of these two villas, their form and geometry, revolved around architecture's "natural" beauty through an analysis focused on the abstract realm of mathematics, geometrical analysis, and architectural proportion. By this means he conveyed the similarities and differences of their plans, elevations, and structural systems to reveal the diverse theoretical positions that guided the two architects—"symbolically and in the sphere of 'customary' beauty"—and to place their work within their own time.[43] Rowe made no direct reference to Wittkower in the article, but his influence is clear (as Vidler has argued) from Rowe's "analysis of the plans and their geometrical properties" to his "choice of illustrations"[44] (see Figure 4.4).

In 1973, Rowe wrote an addendum to this article for a broader audience, in which he pondered the method behind his critical speculation. He defined this criticism as "Wölfflinian in origin," since it began with "approximate configurations" and developed to "identify differences." It was unable to address "questions of iconography and content," relied on overly "symmetrical comparisons," and fostered a deep dependence on "close

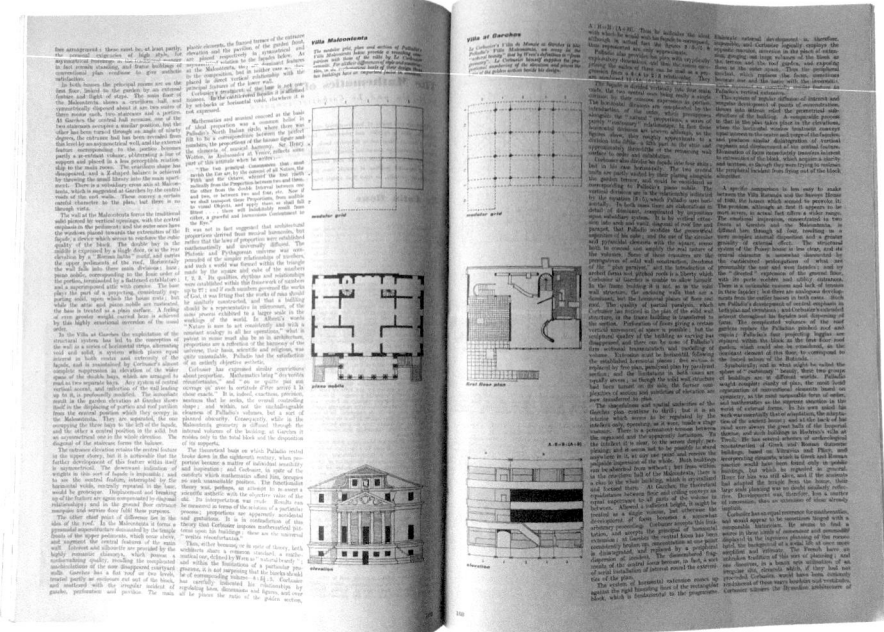

Figure 4.4 Colin Rowe, "The Mathematics of the Ideal Villa: Palladio and Le Corbusier Compared," in *Architectural Review* 101 (March 1947).

analysis"—yet Rowe acknowledged the value of this "Wölfflinian style of critical exercise."[45] Its value lay in its accessibility since it favored strictly visual appreciation over academic scholarship. This reflected Rowe's ambiguous relationship to two opposing attitudes: the "gentleman amateur," characteristic of English thought and exemplified in Berenson; and the "'professional' art history," represented by the Warburg Institute and witnessed by Rowe through Wittkower.[46]

Rowe's next article in *Architectural Review* was "Mannerism and Modern Architecture" (1950), in which he found commonalities between the architecture of sixteenth-century mannerism and that of the modern movement. Advancing a sense of mannerism bound to manifest periods of "acute spiritual and political crisis," Rowe compared the main facades of the so-called Casa di Palladio in Vicenza and Federigo Zuccheri's casino in Florence to Le Corbusier's Villa Schwob in La Chaux-de-Fonds; the interior spaces of Michelangelo's Capella Sforza in Rome to Mies van der Rohe's project of 1923 for the Brick Country House; Jacopo Barozzi da Vignola's and Bartolomeo Ammanati's schemes for the Villa Giulia in Rome to Mies's 1935 project for the Hubbe House at Magdeburg; and Michelangelo's apses in Saint Peter's in Rome to Le Corbusier's Cité de Refuge in Paris.[47] They together reveal a "Mannerist device," the "discord between elements of different scale placed in immediate juxtaposition."[48] The Wölfflinian method permitted Rowe to reveal a mannerist attitude in modern architecture before and after the 1920s. Robert Maxwell has observed that Rowe not only popularized the image of mannerism fostered by such figures as Nikolaus Pevsner and Anthony Blunt, but persuaded an architect like James Stirling to "become a modern Mannerist." Not only a "system for the periodization of art history," mannerism became a "system in the production of art."[49]

Rowe described himself as "thoroughly *Italianizatto*."[50] The attraction he felt towards Italy throughout his career was fostered by many of his students and followers, including Peter Eisenman, who, as Maxwell has noted, "fell under his spell and was induced to study Giuseppe Terragni closely and to become interested in Italian Mannerism."[51] In his first meetings with Rowe in Cambridge, Eisenman was "taught how to read" a "series of fantastic plans from the Renaissance" and to "see that specific plans showed certain ideas," but his "most important lecture in architecture" occurred in the summer of 1961, when he was taught how to "see as an architect."[52] During a trip with Rowe to Europe, Eisenman visited a Palladian villa (Villa Pisani in Montagnana) for the first time and Rowe demanded, "tell me something about what you are looking at that you cannot see!" Thus, for Eisenman, the "idea of the 'presence of the unseen'," became a central tenet in his career as an architect, theorist, and professor.[53]

For Rowe, no book on architecture from the second half of the twentieth century was comparable to those by Scott and Wittkower.[54] These two works represented the intellectual stances of connoisseurship and science: Anglo-American experiential subjectivity and German intellectual objectivity. This frame must be expanded to fully understand the impact that these competing methods of interpreting architecture had in breaking old paradigms and further propelling artistic and scientific understanding. Italy, with its rich history and extensive heritage, was not only the critical laboratory in which these new frames of thought were tested, but it was instrumental to their legitimization and their widespread acceptance in architectural discourse. Though built on an Italian foundation, with the limitations that this implies, these methods are not unchanging instruments of analysis rooted in a specific country or culture—they are open-ended, as their readers have shown, and evolve and adapt to an ever-changing world. The scope of these methods far transcends their original application. They both maintain the past's relevance to architecture and guide architectural history toward future landscapes built on shifting cultures. Furthermore, methods of architectural analysis cannot be understood separately from the tools or tasks of the historian; these intangible lines of influence, running through generations, provoke an unending chain of growth within that field.

Notes

1. Mark Jarzombek, *The Psychologizing of Modernity: Art, Architecture, and History* (Cambridge: Cambridge University Press, 2000), 38. Heinrich Wölfflin, "Prolegomena zu einer Psychologie der Architektur" (diss., Ludwig Maximilian University of Munich, 1886).

2. Heinrich Wölfflin, *Renaissance und Barock: Eine Untersuchung über Wesen und Entstehung des Barockstils in Italien* (Munich: Theodor Ackerman, 1888). English edn, 1964.

3. Harry Francis Mallgrave and Eleftherios Ikonomou (eds), *Empathy, Form, and Space: Problems in German Aesthetics, 1873–1893* (Santa Monica, CA: Getty Center for the History of Art and the Humanities, 1994), 51.

4. Heinrich Wölfflin, *Kunstgeschichteliche Grundbegriffe: Das Problem der Stil-entwickelung in der neueren Kunst* (Munich: F. Bruckmann, 1915). First English edn, 1932.

5. Mallgrave and Ikonomou, *Empathy, Form, and Space*, 40.

6. Bernard Berenson, *The Study and Criticism of Italian Art: Second Series* (London: George Bell and Sons, 1902), 66. Orig. in "A Word for Renaissance Churches," *Free Review* (November 1893): 178–89.

7. Berenson, *Study and Criticism of Italian Art*, 66.

8. Berenson, *Study and Criticism of Italian Art*, 70.

9. Bernard Berenson, *Sunset and Twilight* (New York: Harcourt, 1963), 22.

10. Berenson, *Study and Criticism of Italian Art*, v.

11. Berenson, *Study and Criticism of Italian Art*, 69.

12. Geoffrey Scott, *The Architecture of Humanism: A Study in the History of Taste* (London: Constable and Company Ltd., 1924), 10–11.

13. David Watkin, foreword to *The Architecture of Humanism: A Study in the History of Taste* (London: Architectural Press, 1980), xxiv.

14. Reyner Banham, *Theory and Design in the First Machine Age* (1960) (Cambridge, MA: MIT Press, 1980), 67.

15. John Macarthur, "Geoffrey Scott, the Baroque, and the Picturesque," in *The Baroque in Architectural Culture, 1880–1980*, ed. Andrew Leach, John Macarthur, and Maarten Delbeke (Farnharm: Ashgate, 2015), 61.

16. Anthony Vidler, "Troubles in Theory Part III. The Great Divide: Technology vs Tradition," *Architectural Review* 232 (August 2012), 98

17. Vincent Scully, "Architecture as a Science: Is the Scientific Method Applicable to Architectural Design?" *Yale Scientific Magazine* 22 (May 1948), 5.

18. Scully, "Architecture as a Science," 6, 18.

19. Scully, "Architecture as a Science," 20, 22.

20. Vincent Scully, "Michelangelo's Fortification Drawings: A Study in the Reflex Diagonal," *Perspecta* 1 (1952), 38.

21. Neil Levine, "Vincent Scully: A Biographical Sketch," in *Modern Architecture and Other Essays*, ed. Neil Levine (Princeton, NJ: Princeton University Press, 2003), 16.

22. Vincent Scully in Yehuda Safran and Daniel Sherer, "An Interview with Vincent Scully," *Potlatch* 4 (2016), 9.

23. Scully, "Michelangelo's Fortification Drawings," 43.

24. Scully, "Michelangelo's Fortification Drawings," 40.

25. Patricia Leighten and William B. Stargard, "Interview with Vincent Scully," *The Rutgers Art Review: The Journal of Graduate Research in Art History* 2 (January 1981), 98.

26. Bruno Zevi, *Architecture as Space: How to Look at Architecture* (New York: Horizon Press, 1957), 32. Orig. *Saper vedere l'architettura* (Turin: Einaudi, 1948).

27. Zevi, *Architecture as Space*, 223.

28. Zevi, *Architecture as Space*, 78.

29. Geoffrey Scott, *L'architettura dell'umanesimo*, trans. Elena Craveri Croce (Bari: Dedalo, 1978), back cover.

30. Bruno Zevi, "Visualizzare la critica dell'architettura," *L'architettura, cronache e storia* 103 (May 1964): 2. For a close reading of this project, see Tiffany Hunt, "Michelangelo in 1964: The Critical Model as Dialectical Image in Bruno Zevi's Renaissance Architecture," *Architectural Theory Review* 24, no. 2 (2020): 144–63.

31. Bruno Zevi, *Michelangiolo architetto* (Milan: Etas Kompas, 1964), 4.

32. Zevi, *Michelangiolo architetto*, 2.

33. Bruno Zevi, "History as a Method of Teaching Architecture," in *The History, Theory and Criticism of Architecture. Papers from the 1964 AIA-ACSA Teacher Seminar*, ed. Marcus Whiffen (Cambridge, MA: MIT Press, 1965), 14, 17.

34. Luigi Moretti, "Strutture e sequenze di spazi," *Spazio* 7 (1952–3), 10.

35. Rafael Moneo, *L'altra modernità. Considerazioni sul futuro dell'architettura* (Milan: Christian Marinotti Edizioni, 2012), 107.

36. Moneo, *L'altra modernità*, 109.

37. Scott, *Architecture of Humanism*, 218.

38. Kenneth Clark, "Humanism and Architecture," *Architectural Review* 107 (February 1951), 65.

39. Alison Smithson and Peter Smithson, "Correspondence: *Architectural Principles in the Age of Humanism*," *RIBA Journal* 59 (1952), 140.

40. Reyner Banham, "The New Brutalism," *Architectural Review* 118 (December 1955), 361.

41. Rudolf Wittkower, *Architectural Principles in the Age of Humanism* (London: W. W. Norton & Co., 1971), n.p. The articles were published in issues 4, 7, and 8 of the *Journal of the Warburg and Courtauld Institutes*: "Alberti's Approach to Antiquity in Antiquity" (1940–1), "Principles of Palladio's Architecture" (1944), and "Principles of Palladio's Architecture: II" (1945).

42. Anthony Vidler, *Histories of the Immediate Present: Inventing Architectural Modernism* (Cambridge, MA: MIT Press, 2008), 66.

43. Colin Rowe, "The Mathematics of the Ideal Villa: Palladio and Le Corbusier Compared," *Architectural Review* 101 (March 1947), 103.

44. Vidler, *Histories of the Immediate Present*, 81–2.

45. Colin Rowe, *The Mathematics of the Ideal Villa and Other Essays* (Cambridge, MA: MIT Press, 1978), 16.

46. Vidler, *Histories of the Immediate Present*, 63.

47. Rowe, *Mathematics of the Ideal Villa*, 43.

48. Rowe, *Mathematics of the Ideal Villa*, 50.

49. Robert Maxwell, "Mannerism and Modernism," in *Reckoning with Colin Rowe: Ten Architects Take Position*, ed. Emmanuel Petit (New York: Routledge, 2015), 27, 30.

50. Maxwell, "Mannerism and Modernism," 37.

51. Maxwell, "Mannerism and Modernism," 31.

52. Peter Eisenman, "Interview with Peter Eisenman: The Last Grand Tourist—Travels with Colin Rowe," *Perspecta* 41 (2008), 131, 133.

53. Peter Eisenman, "Bifurcating Rowe," in *Reckoning with Colin Rowe: Ten Architects Take Position*, ed. Emmanuel Petit (New York: Routledge, 2015), 57.

54. Alfonso Corona Martínez, "Respe(c)to a Colin Rowe," *Summa+* 47 (2001), 132.

CHAPTER 5
FUNCTIONALISM AND ITS ITALIAN ENTANGLEMENTS

Ute Poerschke

The topic of functionalism in modern architecture is not typically associated with Italy. Functionalism is primarily tied to developments in northern Europe and North America, while Italy is often associated with rationalism and, in the second half of the twentieth century, critiques of functionalist standpoints. A widely known example of the latter is the dispute at the 1959 meeting of the Congrès Internationaux d'Architecture Moderne (CIAM) about the functionality and historicity of the 1958 Torre Velasca in Milan by BBPR, in which Peter Smithson accused Ernesto Rogers of having abused "function" as "the handmaid of form."[1] Another example is Aldo Rossi's rejection of "funzionalismo ingenuo" (naive functionalism) in his 1966 *L'architettura della città*.[2] The prominence of these critiques of functionalism, however, has obscured just how deeply Italian thinkers have been involved with the idea's development from its outset in the Age of Enlightenment to contemporary architectural discourse.

The introduction of the term "function" in seventeenth- and eighteenth-century language has its roots mainly in France and Germany. In natural history, René Descartes used it in his writings on human physiology of 1632 and 1648. In mathematics, Gottfried Wilhelm Leibniz established it in 1673 and it became accepted through Leonhard Euler's *Introduction to Analysis of the Infinite* in 1748. In philosophy, Immanuel Kant utilized the term in his 1781 *Critique of Pure Reason* as part of an epistemic dichotomy between intuition/sensing and conceptualization/thinking, in which the former "rests on affections," the latter "on functions."[3] However, when it comes to architecture, it was Italian scholars who introduced the term in the eighteenth century, namely Francesco Algarotti, Francesco Milizia, and Andrea Memmo. The three authors referred in their writings to a scholar they much admired, the Venetian padre Carlo Lodoli, whom Emil Kaufmann in 1955 and Joseph Rykwert in 1976 called "the first advocate of functionalism" and "one of the founding fathers of all functionalism and rationalism" in architecture.[4] Aside from two small book outlines, Lodoli left no writing of his own, but his ideas lived on in the treatises of Algarotti, Miliza, and Memmo and, through them, in the twentieth-century architectural discourses of both functionalism and rationalism as distinct and yet closely related legacies (see Figure 5.1).

Lodoli's two key terms in the above-mentioned outlines were "retta funzione e rappresentazione" (proper function and representation), later often translated as "function and form." He described function and representation as "the only two final, scientific aims of civil architecture" and required that, in order to achieve good architecture, function and representation must "come together to be nothing but a single thing."[5] Lodoli critiqued his contemporaries' focus on architecture as imitation of historic

Figure 5.1 Portrait of Carlo Lodoli framed by the banderole "One must unite fabrication and reasoning / And function shall be representation." Portrait published in Andrea Memmo, *Elementi d'architettura lodoliana o sia l'arte del fabbricare con solidità scientifica e con eleganza non capricciosa* (Rome: Pagliarini 1786).

forms whose justification relied on accepted authorities. Reinterpreting one such authority, he reminded architects that their judgments should be built on "fabbrica" and "ragione." Vitruvius had stated that the "architect's expertise ... is born both of *practice* [*fabrica*] and of *reasoning* [*ratiocinatio*]. *Practice* is the constant, repeated exercise of the hands by which the work is brought to completion in whatever medium is required for the proposed design. *Reasoning*, however, is what can demonstrate and explain the proportions of completed works skillfully and systematically."[6]

Lodoli praised only a few masterpieces and architects, particularly the Pantheon and Palladio, and criticized most architectural works for not being true to their "medium" (Latin, *materia*). He developed the idea that each construction material must have its own forms. By proposing an architecture that is true to its materials, he aimed at a timeless aesthetic norm and, at the same time, rejected an authoritative historic standard that did not allow any progress in architecture. Lodoli did not reject history per se, but asked architects to approach it critically rather than adopting and repeating established habits without applying rational criteria.

The ways in which the three authors Algarotti, Milizia, and Memmo discussed their master's ideas give us a foretaste of the sort of appropriation and criticism that would recur in the twentieth century. In his popular *Saggio sopra l'architettura*, published in Italian, French, and German in 1756, Algarotti explained Lodoli's dictum of "funzione e rappresentazione" as follows: "Nothing, he insists, must be put in representation that is not also truly in function; and with this proper term one must call everything an abuse, the more it departs from this principle, which is the true foundation, the cornerstone, on which architectural art must be placed."[7]

But Algarotti was concerned that this rigorous dictum might go too far. Providing the example of stone lintels, he argued that stone had no flexible fibers when compared to wood and therefore, if "stone were put in representation as it is in function, the apertures in buildings could not turn out other than very narrow." This would lead to doors and windows "of a narrowness unpleasant to behold and inconvenient to use."[8] This reservation shows that the first architectural treatise to ever contain the word "function" already included a critique that has continued into the present: that a focus on functions and strict adherence to rational principles might ignore engagement with questions of beauty and lead to ugly buildings. Algarotti concluded that a stringent functionalism bans all ornament: "Wanting everything that is in representation to also truly be in function ... is wanting too much. Whatever can be the function of the foliage of the Corinthian capital, the volutes of the Ionic, the fluting of the columns, the animals and other similar things commonly chiseled into the frieze?"[9]

Milizia, a widely read author, claimed in at least five of his books that "whatever is in representation must be in function."[10] However, he only provided three examples to illustrate how he understood this phrase. All three referred to the column orders and their rational rules within the structure of a building. In his view, the only building that showed a column order with exemplary function and representation was the Pantheon with columns "*in vera funzione:* with the attempt to remove a single one, suddenly everything is ruined." By contrast, in the Colosseum and the Porta del Popolo, the columns had "poca funzione."[11] The examples show that Milizia was less interested in actual building materials and their resulting structural logic than in the relationship of building parts within a compositional whole. Through this interpretation—and different from Algarotti—Milizia was able to reconcile the "funzione e rappresentazione" dictum with neoclassicism and its emphasis on Greek and Roman building principles.

Memmo claimed to be the true interpreter of Lodoli's theses and defended his master's theory against Algarotti's critique, harshly calling the latter a "nuovo ridicolo" (new absurdity).[12] For Memmo, the function-representation dictum would help architects to practice "not eloquently with the authority of antiquity at hand, but with bare, demonstrative reason" and resist the habit of imitation, which he called "un morbo" (a plague).[13] The references to rigorous reasoning—Lodoli's followers were also called "rigoristi"—found in all these publications explain how architectural functionalism and rationalism can have the same roots and why Lodoli was called a father of both movements.

The ideas of Lodoli, Algarotti, Milizia, and Memmo were circulating in the western world early in the nineteenth century. In the United States, for instance, Milizia had gained popularity through Thomas Jefferson, who in 1824 commented that "searching, as he does, for the sources and prototypes of our ideas of beauty in that fine art, he appears to have elicited them with more correctness than any other author I have read," and proposed Milizia's writings as a textbook "for a course of lectures on the subject, which I shall hope to have introduced into our institution."[14] Milizia's *Memorie degli architetti antichi e moderni* of 1781 was published in English in 1826, but his phrase "onde quanto è in rappresentazione, deve essere sempre in funzione" was translated (without "function") into "whatever is represented must appear of service."[15] Another route was through the American sculptor Horatio Greenough (1805-52), who studied Memmo's and Milizia's publications while living in Italy. In his own writings, Greenough often referred to the idea of function in a work of art. He proclaimed, "Beauty as the promise of Function; Action as the presence of Function; Character as the record of Function."[16] Several authors have speculated (without direct evidence) about a possible path of the function-representation dictum from Lodoli, Algarotti, Milizia, and Memmo through Greenough and Ralph Waldo Emerson to Louis Sullivan's phrase "form follows function," as first used in his 1896 essay "The Tall Office Building Artistically Considered."[17]

Despite their dissemination in Europe and the United States, by the 1920s, Lodoli's ideas were being addressed not by architects, but by art historians. The first to do so was likely the Vienna School stalwart Julius von Schlosser in his seminal 1924 book *Die Kunstliteratur*, which provided a historical overview of art theories and was translated into Italian in 1935. Schlosser emphasized Lodoli's modernity and rationalism in linking his theories to the avant-garde: "Lodoli is interesting for us, because he anticipates certain modern concepts. His study is directed toward the rational substantiation of style, in the spirit of the rationalism of enlightenment of his time."[18] Schlosser also invoked the padre's dictum: "Lodoli insists that a building's vital 'function' must be clearly expressed in its 'representation,' and he firmly refuses the ornamental facades visible in Italy since antiquity, which are put in front of a diversely built and concealed structure."[19] Schlosser thereby provided bridges to modern rationalism and functionalism. Shortly after *Die Kunstliteratur* appeared, similar attempts at describing Lodoli as a pioneer of the modern movement were made by such Italian historians as Michele de Benedetti in 1930 and Nino Gallo in 1935.[20] Carlo Ragghianti published on Algarotti and "architecture in function" in *Casabella* in 1936.[21] Maria Louisa Gengaro, in an article of 1937, not only described Lodoli as a "precursor of modern razionalismo," but embedded his thoughts in a "definition of modernity" based on an "uninterrupted continuity of thought." She argued that Lodoli's eighteenth-century theory "is particularly up-to-date, not because it shows a system of rational architecture, but because it suggests a value of architecture per se."[22]

This merging of functionalist and rationalist thinking among historians during the 1920s and 1930s also appears in Italian architects' writings of that same period—albeit without explicit reference to Lodoli or his followers. Consider Gruppo 7, renamed later as Movimento italiano per l'architettura razionale (MIAR), which began publishing in December 1926 its four-part manifesto, in which they called for a "new spirit" in architecture that reflects a "desire for truth, logic, order, and Hellenic lucidity." They referred to Le Corbusier as "one of the most noteworthy initiators of a rational architecture," the Dutch development of "architectural forms composed of the most rigorous and constructive rationality, perfectly attuned to the country's climate and landscape," Russia's "technical aesthetic ... in a full and flourishing development," and German architects, who have developed, based on their experience "in the construction of purely industrial buildings . . . the essence of pure rationality." To distinguish themselves from these rationalist-functionalist movements, Gruppo 7 asked Italian architects to invoke Roman monumental proportionality and rhythm. To renew architecture, they aimed at an abstraction of classical formal principles, but insisted these should "respond only to the character of necessity" and "result from rigid adherence to logic, to rationality."[23] Neither Lodoli, his circle nor the term "function" appears, but they clearly indicated a correspondence between the rejection of historicism and an embrace of rationalism. Their attitude to history was similar to Le Corbusier's in his 1923 *Vers une architecture*, which rejected historicism while also praising what he called the "seed" of antiquity, "which is to say the sense of relationships, the mathematics thanks to which perfection becomes attainable."[24] This twofold approach to history could rarely be found among modern architects outside of France and Italy. Particularly in Germany, it was common to reject all references to history, as can be seen in the Bauhaus's exclusion of architectural history courses from its curriculum.

The ambiguous overlap between the concepts of the "functional" and the "rational" is also evident in an episode concerning Alberto Sartoris's 1932 book *Gli elementi dell'architettura funzionale*. Sartoris had originally intended to label the architecture presented in his book as "*architettura razionale*"— akin to Gruppo 7's attitude above. In place of a preface, Sartoris published a letter from Le Corbusier that was meant to explain why he changed "*razionale*" to "*funzionale*":

The title of your work is limited ... Aside from rational you can also say *functional*, but for me the word *architecture* has in itself something more magic than the rational or the functional, something that dominates, prevails, succeeds ... In a few words, what I want to say: our rationalist artistic circles negate, in fact only theoretically, the fundamental human function of beauty, that is the beneficial and stimulating effect that harmony has on us.[25]

In 1960, Reyner Banham would claim that this was a breakthrough for the term "functionalism," insisting that "there is little doubt that the first consequential use was in Alberto Sartoris's book" and that "[r]esponsibility for the term is laid on Le Corbusier's shoulders."[26] Both claims are an overstatement and show Banham pushing his own agenda of defining functionalism as a joint French-Italian enterprise. The episode certainly shows Le Corbusier's influence on Italian modernism, but Banham's translation of Le Corbusier's advice to Sartoris is misleading: "The title of your book is limited ... Instead of Rational say *Functional*."[27] As the longer passage above shows, Le Corbusier did not tell Sartoris how to title his book. Rather than preferring one of the two terms, Le

Figure 5.2 Alberto Sartoris, *Gli elementi dell'architettura funzionale* (Milan: Hoepli, 1932). Using a letter from Le Corbusier as the preface, Sartoris suggests the equivalence of "funzionale" and "razionale."

Corbusier considered the concepts of "architecture" and "harmony" more important. Not only did he find the title limited but regarded its emphasis on the "rational" and the "functional" as impairing the intuitive aspects of architectural practice.

What certainly had a greater impact on the popularity of "functionalism" as a term among architects was the famous CIAM congress "The Functional City" held on the ship *Patris II* and in Athens in the summer of 1933. While there were several proposals for the title of that event—ranging from "constructive city" (original title) to "organic city" (Ernst May) and "new city" (Walter Gropius)—the title "functional city" seemed to materialize during a CIAM meeting in Berlin from June 4 to 7, 1931. Le Corbusier's letter to Sartoris was written only three days later, on June 10, 1931, which may explain why Le Corbusier was referring so pointedly to the "functional." Based on this episode of finding an appropriate theme for the meeting, Banham might have been right that "[m]ost critics of the Thirties were perfectly happy to make this substitution of words."[28] On the other hand, it shows that architects often preferred terms aligned with their own national discourses. The term "constructive city," for example, was used when the congress was planned for Moscow. Gropius's proposal for the "new city" might have been intended to evoke the phrases *Neues Bauen* or *Neue Sachlichkeit*. Italy's modernists were active in CIAM, but there was no proposal for naming the congress "rational city." This may have been because no Italian delegates participated in the meeting in Berlin. With this in mind, Sartoris's decision to remove the term *razionale* from the title of his book on modern architecture might have had two reasons beyond the generally unsettled relationship between rationalism, functionalism, and modernism: offering an homage to Le Corbusier, and linking the book and congress titles to increase the visibility and marketability of his work.

While architects propagated functionalism in architecture and urban planning without recalling Lodoli directly, historians continued to establish the padre and his students as the founding fathers of architectural rationalism and functionalism. With Rudolf Wittkower and Emil Kaufmann, Lodoli and his circle arrived for a second time in Anglophone architectural discourse. Wittkower, who emigrated from Germany to England in the 1930s and later to the United States, claimed in a 1938 article that Lodoli's "influence seems to have been more vital than that of any other theorist of architecture of the 18th century" and explained that Giovanni Battista Piranesi's "rationalist approach to architecture" was "under the spell of Padre Lodoli."[29] Kaufmann, who emigrated from Austria to the United States in 1940, described in a 1944 article that "Lodoli was imbued with the concepts of rationalism," aiming at "an architecture independent of authorities, and one in which function spoke by itself."[30] In his *Architecture in the Age of Reason* of 1955, Kaufmann became more direct, calling Lodoli "the first advocate of functionalism" and stressing the dichotomy of function and form: "Quite suddenly, in the midst of the eighteenth century, a new theory arose in Italy which diametrically contradicted all earlier doctrines. These doctrines were entirely formalistic and supported the contemporary aesthetic pattern. The newly arisen doctrine, however, was strictly functionalistic."[31] Kaufmann's discussion of Lodoli's theories ended with this insight: "one should not think that all formal aspirations were gone forever and the rule of a Lodolian functionalism about to start. The perennial competition between form and function went on."[32] It is important to note that in Lodoli we do not see any hint of a hierarchy between function and form, as is most prominently visible in Sullivan's dictum. Lodoli instead demanded that function and representation must "come together to be nothing but a single thing," which corresponds better to Frank Lloyd Wright's view that "form and function are one."[33] Kaufmann's understanding of "function" to mean "practicality" and "materiality," and his interpretation of Lodoli as favoring function over form, is misled by the discourse of his own time.[34] At the same time, Kaufmann's writings fed this same discourse by providing arguments for the historicity of functionalism and early hints of skepticism towards functionalism, as when he stated regarding Algarotti that "[f]unctionalism appeared to him morbid; formalism, however, right."[35]

In the decades following Wittkower and Kaufmann, Lodoli and his circle gained more and more popularity in the United States as theorists of modernity, rationalism, and functionalism.[36] In 1964, Edgar Kaufmann, Jr. was the first author to present and translate what survived of Lodoli's original writings—the two short manuscripts mentioned above. This Kaufmann called Lodoli "the first man to draft a constitution for architecture suited to the modern world," and, like the elder Kaufmann above, he translated Lodoli's phrase "funzione e rappresentazione" as "function and form," which deviates from the original meaning to favor a post-Sullivan terminology.[37] It took another decade to reconsider this translation. In his 1976 essay "Lodoli on Function and Representation" and, more prominently, in his 1980 book *The First Moderns*, Joseph Rykwert described Lodoli as "one of the founding fathers of all functionalism and rationalism" before discussing Lodoli's terminology in the scientific context of its time.[38] Rykwert concluded that, for Lodoli, "*function* was the mechanical working of the forces within the structure translated into graphic terms."[39] He proposed that Lodoli borrowed the term function from mathematics, and specifically from Bernoulli's definition of a mathematical function.

Late in the twentieth century, both historians and architects started to shift from thinking of form and function as competitors toward a more nuanced understanding of their interdependencies. Here, particularly, Rossi stands out. Making his case against naive functionalism (introduced above), he clarified that this "does not entail the rejection of the concept of function in its proper sense, however, that is, as an algebra of values that can be known as functions of one another, nor does it deny that between functions and form one may seek to establish more complex ties than the linear ones of cause and effect."[40]

Rossi discussed the confusion of cause and effect as a problem within architectural functionalism, which he understood as a movement that "pervades the entire course of architectural thinking since Vitruvius."[41] By misunderstanding the relationship of cause and effect, functionalism tried to determine architecture from forces outside of architecture rather than from intrinsically architectural questions.[42] Rossi overcame the apparent architect-historian divide by discussing Lodoli and his circle directly. As early as 1956, he referred to Lodoli's "*stretto funzionalismo*," although he was more interested in discussing Milizia, whom he embedded in his discussions on neoclassical and rationalist architecture and, more generally, on reclaiming architects' "*coscienza storica*" (historical consciousness), which twentieth-century modernism (especially functionalist modernism) had supposedly abandoned (see Figure 5.3).[43]

Figure 5.3 Aldo Rossi, *L'architettura della città* (Padua: Marsilio, 1966). While disapproving of "funzionalismo ingenuo," Rossi also clarifies that this "does not entail the rejection of the concept of function in its proper sense."

With Rossi, we see how "rationalism" and "functionalism" acquired new meanings and deeper differentiations. However, not everybody put Lodoli on the side of functionalism. Instead, theorists enjoyed the resonance of Lodoli's multilayered ideas with those of postmodern discourse, opening new ways of thinking about not only his "*funzione e rappresentazione*," but also of the relationships of function and form in general, in which subordination of one under the other was left open. Alberto Pérez-Gómez, who vehemently critiqued modernism and its grounding in a scientific worldview, argued that "Lodoli's understanding of architecture and history appears to be more profound than even that of most nineteenth- and twentieth-century theoreticians." For the *Rigoristi*, "the relations between form and matter had to be metaphoric and imaginative, not merely rational. This is far indeed from nineteenth-century structural determinism or the reductionistic obsessions of functionalism. Function, for the *Rigoristi*, retained the ambiguous dual connotation of abstract mathematics (number) and visible representation (quality). It could therefore be a symbol of human order."[44]

The shift in interpretation from "form" to "representation," which started with Rykwert, also opened connections to semiotic discourse about architecture as a sign and signifier of meaning. The beginning and end of Marco Frascari's brilliant 1985 essay, "Function and Representation in Architecture," provides an idea of this shift:

> As a semiotic device architecture operates between two spheres of production of signs. In Vitruvian literature those have been named *ratiocinatio* and *fabbrica* [sic], or in Renaissance terminology *theorica* and *practica*. The spheres can be characterized as the general and the individual, the abstract and the concrete ... An architectural semiotician should be someone able to merge in an architectural production, the two spheres in which architecture as a semiotic device operates. An architecture which unifies the *theorica* with the *practica*. An architecture in which the function is merged with the representation.[45]

Pérez-Gómez and Frascari set the record straight, asserting that the eighteenth-century Italian treatises do not support a simplified deterministic interpretation of "form follows function." Widening our understanding of functionalist theory, they exemplified how the discourse on functionalism could progress toward becoming a part of postmodernism.

Since then, a steady flow of new interpretations has continued to the present day. Refocusing on Lodoli, publications have investigated such specific issues as Lodoli's application of mathematics, physics, and philosophy to architecture (Diana Bitz); or his understanding of function as performance between parts and whole (this author); and, most extensively, Lodoli's Socratic approach to teaching and his practice as an educator (Marc Neveu).[46] From the overview provided in this chapter, it is evident that Italian theories of the eighteenth century have become, in various ways, a benchmark in the debates on functionalism, rationalism, postmodernism, and beyond—both explicitly and implicitly in the foundations of a modernist discourse. The appropriations of these theories are quite diverse, even contradictory. They have served to critique the eighteenth-century *Quarrel of the Ancients and the Moderns*; in support of eighteenth-century neoclassicism; in nineteenth-century debates on organic architecture; as a historical trace to ground rationalism and functionalism throughout the twentieth century; in the semiotic discourse of postmodernism; and in today's diverse discourse. In all cases they were utilized as a method to rethink well-trodden paths in architecture. Here lies their abiding value.

Notes

1. In Oscar Newman, *New Frontiers in Architecture: CIAM '59 in Otterlo* (New York: Universe Books, 1961), 96.

2. Aldo Rossi, *The Architecture of the City*, trans. Diane Ghirardo and Joan Ockman (Cambridge, MA: MIT Press, 1982), 46–8.

3. René Descartes, *Traité de l'homme* (1632) and *Descriptio corporis humani omniumque ejus functionum* (1648); Gottfried Wilhelm Leibniz, *Methodus tangentium inversa, seu de functionibus* (1673); Immanuel Kant, *Critique of Pure Reason*, ed. and trans. Paul Guyer and Allan Wood (Cambridge: Cambridge University Press, 1998), 205.

4. Emil Kaufmann, *Architecture in the Age of Reason: Baroque and Post-Baroque in England, Italy, France* (Cambridge, MA: Harvard University Press, 1955), 95. Joseph Rykwert, "Lodoli on Function and Representation," *Architectural Review* 160 (1976): 21–6, esp. 21.

5. Lodoli's outlines were first published in Andrea Memmo, *Elementi d'architettura lodoliana ossia l'arte del fabbricare con solidità scientifica e con eleganza non capricciosa*, vol. 2 (Milan: Zara, 1834), 51–62, esp. 59.

6. Vitruvius, *Ten Books on Architecture*, trans. Ingrid D. Rowland (Cambridge: Cambridge University Press, 1999), 21.

7. Francesco Algarotti, "Saggio sopra l'architettura," in *Opere del Conte Algarotti*, vol. 2 (Livorno: Coltellini, 1764), 62–3.

8. Algarotti, "Saggio sopra l'architettura," 73.

9. Francesco Algarotti, "Lettere sopra l'architettura," in *Opere del Conte Algarotti*, vol. 6 (Livorno: Coltellini, 1764), 169–278, esp. 209.

10. Francesco Milizia, *Vite de' più celebri architetti d'ogni nazione e d'ogni tempo* (Rome: Monaldini, 1768), 14; *Memorie degli architetti antichi e moderni* (Parma: Stamparia Reale, 1781), xv; *Principj di architettura* civile (1781, here Bassano: Remondini, 1785), 31; *Dell'arte di vedere nelle belle arti del disegno secondo i principi di Sulzer e Mengs* (1781, here Genoa: Caffarelli, 1786), 95; *Dizionario delle belle arti del disegno*, vol. 2 (Bassano: Remondini, 1797), 90; Ute Poerschke, *Architectural Theory of Modernism: Relating Functions and Forms* (New York: Routledge, 2016), 48–51.

11. Francesco Milizia, *Dell'arte di vedere*, 103–5; Francesco Milizia, *Roma delle belle arti del Disegno* (Bassano: Remondini, 1787), 160.

12. Memmo, *Elementi d'architettura lodoliana*, 20: "Ecco un nuovo ridicolo che il signor conte procura di dare al suo amico."

13. Memmo, *Elementi d'architettura lodoliana*, 128 and 110.

14. William O'Neal, "Francesco Milizia, 1725–1798," *Journal of the Society of Architectural Historians* 13, no. 3 (1954): 12–15, esp. 12.

15. Francesco Milizia, *The Lives of Celebrated Architects, Ancient and Modern*, trans. Eliza Cresy (London: Taylor, 1826), xix.

16. Horatio Greenough, "Relative and Independent Beauty," in *A Memorial of Horatio Greenough, consisting of a Memoir, Selections from His Writings, and Tributes to His Genius*, ed. Henry Tuckerman (New York: Putnam, 1853), 131–45, esp. 132.

17. Edgar Kaufmann, "Memmo's Lodoli," *Art Bulletin* 46 (1964): 159–75; Rykwert, "Lodoli on Function and Representation"; Louis Sullivan, "The Tall Office Building Artistically Considered," *Lippincott's Magazine* 57 (1896): 403–9.

18. Julius Schlosser, *Die Kunstliteratur: Ein Handbuch zur Quellenkunde der neueren Kunstgeschichte* (Vienna: Schroll, 1924); *La letteratura artistica. Manuale delle fonti della storia dell'arte moderna*, trans. Filippo Rossi (Florence: Schroll, 1956), 666.

19. Schlosser, *La letteratura artistica*, 666.

20. Michele de Benedetti calls Lodoli "[u]n precursore dell'architettura funzionale nel settecento," Nino Gallo "un scrittore razionalista del '700." Emil Kaufmann, "At an Eighteenth Century Crossroads: Algarotti vs. Lodoli," *Journal of the American Society of Architectural Historians* 4, no. 2 (1944): 23–9, esp. 25. Kaufmann, "Memmo's Lodoli," 159. Edgar Kaufmann listed several more publications on Lodoli in the 1930s.

21. Carlo L. Ragghianti, "F. Algarotti e l'architettura in funzione," *Casabella* 9, no. 105 (1936): 4–6.

22. Maria Louisa Gengaro, "Il valore dell architettura nelle teoria settecentesca del Padre Carlo Lodoli," *L'arte* 8, no. 4 (1937): 313–17.

23. The manifesto was published in the journal *La rassegna italiana*, 1926-7. "Architecture. Architecture II: The Foreigners. Il Gruppo 7," intro. and trans. Ellen R. Shapiro, *Oppositions* 6 (Fall 1976): 85–102.

24. Le Corbusier, *Toward an Architecture* (1923), trans. John Goodman (Los Angeles: Getty Publications, 2007), 201. Le Corbusier referred here to ancient Greece. Similarly, he praised the Byzantine church of S. Maria in Cosmedin for its "signal splendor of mathematics, the unbeatable power of proportion, the sovereign eloquence of relationships" (201).

25. Alberto Sartoris, *Gli elementi dell'architettura funzionale* (Milan: Hoepli, 1932), 1–2.

26. Reyner Banham, *Theory and Design in the First Machine Age* (London: Architectural Press, 1960), 320.

27. Banham, *Theory and Design*, 320.

28. Banham, *Theory and Design*, 320.

29. Rudolf Wittkower, "Piranesi's 'Parere su L'Architettura'," *Journal of the Warburg Institute* 2, no. 2 (Oct. 1938): 147-58, esp. 150. Later, Wittkower called Lodoli a "prophet of rationalism": Rudolf Wittkower, *Art and Architecture in Italy 1600 to 1750* (Baltimore, MD: Penguin Books, 1958), 243.

30. Kaufmann, "At an Eighteenth Century Crossroads," 26 and 29.

31. Kaufmann, *Architecture in the Age of Reason*, 89.

32. Kaufmann, *Architecture in the Age of Reason*, 141.

33. In Memmo, *Elementi d'architettura lodoliana*, 59; Frank Lloyd Wright, *The Natural House* (New York: Bramhall House, 1954), 20, 45; Frank Lloyd Wright, *The Future of Architecture* (New York: Mentor, 1963), 246, 319, 348.

34. Kaufmann, *Architecture in the Age of Reason*, 89.

35. Kaufmann, *Architecture in the Age of Reason*, 98.

36. Additional important publications not discussed here include Gianfranco Torcellan, *Una figura della Venezia settecentesca: Andrea Memmo; Ricerche sulla crisi dell' aristocrazia veneziana* (Venice: Istituto per la collaborazione culturale, 1963); Ennio Concina, "Per padre Carlo Lodoli. Giovambattista Lodoli ingegnere militare," *Arte Veneta* 30 (1976): 240; Georg German, *Einführung in die Geschichte der Architekturtheorie* (Darmstadt: Wiss. Buchgesell, 1980).

37. Kaufmann, "Memmo's Lodoli," 172.

38. Rykwert, "Lodoli on Function and Representation," 21.

39. Rykwert, "Lodoli on Function and Representation," 25.

40. Rossi, *The Architecture of the City*, 46.

41. Aldo Rossi, "Architettura per i musei" (1968), in *Scritti scelti sull'architettura e la città 1956-1972* (Milan: Clup, 1975), 323–39, esp. 325. The English translation in Aldo Rossi, *Selected Writings and Projects* (Dublin: Gandon Editions, 1983), 14–25, does not include this sentence. A similar phrase can be found in "Introduzione a Boullèe," in *Scritti scelti sull'architettura e al città 1956-1972*, 346–64, esp. 346 and 353.

42. This interpretation of Rossi's understanding of functionalism is from Angelika Schnell, *Aldo Rossis Konstruktion des Wirklichen. Eine Architekturtheorie mit Widersprüchen* (Basel: Birkhäuser, 2019), 224 and 233.

43. Aldo Rossi, "Il concetto di traditoze nella architettura neoclassica milanese" (1956), in *Scritti scelti sull'architettura e alcittà 1956-1972* (Milan: Clup, 1975), 1–24. In "Emil Kaufmann e l'Architettura del'Illuminismo" (1958), in *Scritti scelti sull'architettura e al città 1956-1972* (Milan: Clup, 1975), 62–71, he referred to "Milizia e rigoristi italiani."

44. Alberto Pérez-Gómez, *Architecture and the Crisis of Modern Science* (Cambridge, MA: MIT Press, 1983), 6–8, 253–6.

45. Marco Frascari, "Function and Representation in Architecture," *Design Methods and Theories: Journal of DMG* 19, no. 1 (1985): 200–16, esp. 200 and 211–12. In addition, see Marco Frascari, "*Sortes Architetii* in the Eighteenth-Century Veneto" (Ph.D. diss., University of Pennsylvania, 1981), Marco Frascari, "The *Particolareggiamento* in the Narration of Architecture," *Journal of Architectural Education* 43, no. 1 (1989): 3–11.

46. Diana Hibbard Bitz, *Architettura Lodoliana: Topical Mathematics as Architecture* (Ph.D. diss., Emory University, 1992); Poerschke, *Architectural Theory of Modernism*; Marc Neveu, "Architectural Lessons of Carlo Lodoli. Indole of Material and of Self" (Ph.D. diss., McGill University, 2005), and "The *Indole* of Education: The Apologues of Carlo Lodoli," *Getty Research Journal* 1 (2009): 27–38.

CHAPTER 6
THE ITALIAN RENAISSANCE AS REBIRTH AND RETURN
Caspar Pearson

Against all odds, the Italian Renaissance is still with us. Whether one conceives of it as a wellspring of inexhaustible vitality, or as an unkillable, undead creature, its longevity is not in doubt. Time and again, modern and contemporary architectural practitioners and writers have returned to the Renaissance, often positing it as a privileged point of origin or rupture, or as a moment of exceptional cultural decline or flourish. For Manfredo Tafuri, for example, the Renaissance activities of Brunelleschi and Alberti constituted the "epicenter" and "true origin" of modernity (a notion with which Jakob Burckhardt might well have agreed), while more recently Françoise Choay has persuasively located the birth of the modern discourse of urbanism within the fifteenth-century architectural treatise of Leon Battista Alberti.[1] We need not look far to find others placing similar emphasis on the Renaissance, even if they interpret it in very different ways. We might consider the centrality of the period in the thinking of Colin Rowe, the sustained interest in mannerism expressed by Robert Venturi and Denise Scott Brown, Richard Rogers's many appeals to the ideas of humanism and the Renaissance, or the New Urbanists' admiration for the city of Pienza.[2] Just a few years ago, Rem Koolhaas opened the *Monditalia* exhibition at the Biennale di Venezia (an exhibition in which he sought to explore the relevance of Italy in a thoroughly globalized world) with what he termed a "Renaissance façade," and included an installation in which he reflected on his experience of what he described as "revisiting—or visiting for the first time" the Italian Renaissance at Michelangelo's Laurentian Library vestibule.[3]

In all of this, we might sense a nagging and persistent "will to return," or at least a special fondness for a privileged cultural reference point, one that is shared among professionals educated within systems that frequently accorded the Italian Renaissance an especially high status. For some scholars and architects, in fact, the Renaissance could perhaps be considered a sort of figurative home for the discipline of architecture, albeit an exclusive one, and one that is accompanied by many of the ambivalences and complications associated with homes of all kinds. In this view, it is the moment in which the modern notion of the architect was formed and a locus to which one can always return for solace or new inspiration. Such a conception of the Renaissance is of course a thoroughly modern one. And yet, the connection between architecture and the ideas of home, return, and rebirth arguably has its roots in the fifteenth century itself, where it was already alive in some of the pivotal texts that initiated the historiographical reception of the era's major building projects. To explore this idea further, we might consider two of the most frequently cited examples from the period: Alberti's letter to Brunelleschi celebrating the cupola of Florence Cathedral and Pius II's account of the origins of Pienza.

The making of the cupola of Florence Cathedral

Battista Alberti, who is better known to us, on account of an ostentatious act of self-naming, as Leon Battista Alberti, was born in Genoa in 1404. As is well known, the Alberti had formerly been one of Florence's most prominent families; bankers unmatched in wealth and also, for a brief period after 1378, in political power. By the end of the 1380s, however, their fortunes turned, and a series of measures eventually resulted in the 1401 exile from Florence of all adult males of the clan. It was not until 1428 that these provisions were finally annulled, allowing the Alberti to return. Battista, who, after his family left Genoa, had undergone a rigorous humanist training in Padua, attained a degree in civil and canon law from the University of Bologna, and subsequently began a career in the papal chancellery in Rome, visited Florence shortly afterwards. From 1434 he took up residence in the city for an extended period, following in the train of his employer, Pope Eugenius IV.[4]

The return to Florence was highly significant for Alberti, and there is no document that attests to this more than the letter, dated July 17, 1436, that he appended to a manuscript of his treatise on painting and sent to Filippo Brunelleschi. The letter was no doubt occasioned by the fact that the cupola of Florence Cathedral, whose construction Brunelleschi had supervised, was at the time just weeks away from completion, an event that must have caused considerable excitement in the city (see Figure 6.1).[5]

Figure 6.1 The Cathedral of Santa Maria del Fiore, Florence. Photograph by the author.

In his epistle, Alberti praises a number of Florentine artists, and singles out Brunelleschi in particular for his engineering achievement in building a dome of such size and doing so without the support of wooden centering. In a much-quoted passage, he says:

> What man, however hard of heart or jealous, would not praise Pippo [Filippo Brunelleschi] the architect when he sees here such an enormous construction towering above the skies, vast enough to cover the entire Tuscan population with its shadow, and done without the aid of beams or elaborate wooden supports? Surely a feat of engineering, if I am not mistaken, that people did not believe possible these days and was probably equally unknown among the ancients.[6]

The notion of having outdone the ancients is particularly significant coming from a humanist like Alberti, but there is more to the letter than simple wonder at a great building achievement. Alberti is keen to connect this tectonic undertaking, albeit in a rather opaque and elliptical manner, with his own overcoming of adversity and restoration to his ancestral home.[7] Thus, he begins the letter by saying that he had formerly believed what he heard many say, that nature had grown old and no longer produced great geniuses any more than giants:

> But after I came back here to this most beautiful of cities from the long exile in which we Albertis have grown old, I recognized in many, but above all in you, Filippo, and in our great friend the sculptor Donatello and in the others, Nencio, Luca and Masaccio, a genius for every laudable enterprise in no way inferior to any of the ancients who gained fame in these arts. I then realized that the ability to achieve the highest distinction in any meritorious activity lies in our own industry and diligence no less than the favors of Nature and of the times.[8]

The works of the Florentine artists, Alberti claims, had brought about an extraordinary change in him. They had caused him to abandon his prior belief that nature had fallen into terminal decline and that the whole of culture had degenerated with it. Instead, he now saw that his own age could match, and in outstanding works such as the cupola even surpass, the achievements of antiquity.[9]

This idea about history as a whole was clearly linked, for Alberti, to his understanding of his own personal and familial history, to which he refers in the same passage. It is only his return to Florence, he implies, that made his revelation possible, a return that brought an end to a "long exile" and that allowed him finally to enjoy a much longed-for home. That sense of recuperation, and of a homeland (*patria*) recovered, seems to have been instantiated for him in the great cupola. Towering over the city, it acted not only as an outstanding instance of human ingenuity but also perhaps as an exemplary center-point or anchor of meaning. Exiles such as the Alberti continued to inhabit a Florence-centered world, even during their banishment, but they were confined to its margins. Now, however, Alberti stood at its center, and what he found there was truly remarkable.

Nonetheless, it must be recognized that Alberti's "return" to his long-lost home was really a semi-fictional event. Born in 1404, he had not grown up in Florence or visited the city before his adulthood. It was thus a new and previously unknown city that he became acquainted with in the 1430s, though the return of the *family* was real enough. Undoubtedly, Alberti was aware of the long tradition, especially prevalent in Tuscany, in which exile was mined for its poetic potential, and while we can understand him, on the one hand, as expressing genuine feelings of joy, we can also see him, on the other hand, as consciously going about the forging of an authorial identity, utilizing the distancing effects of exile and playing upon the melancholia and euphoria associated with estrangement and familiarity. In fact, the fragility of his return and of the home that he found in Florence would quickly become apparent, as Alberti would take an ever more critical stance towards many aspects of Florentine culture. In his writings, he would return time and again to his lingering feelings of marginalization. The recuperation of a home that is associated, in the letter to Brunelleschi, with a great architectural feat, can thus be seen from the outset to belong as much to myth as it did to history.

The making of Pienza

Turning to Pienza, the same issues of exile, estrangement, and the search for a home also loom large. Enea Silvio Piccolomini, who later became Pope Pius II, was also born into the context of exile. Indeed, his family, who were formerly wealthy international bankers, had been pushed out of Siena as part of the general expulsion of the nobility from the city in 1385, just two years before the first of the Alberti were exiled from Florence. In this case, however, the Piccolomini were not compelled to go so far. The future pope's grandfather retired to property that he owned in Corsignano, a small hill town in the Val d'Orcia, south of Siena. Like the Alberti, the Piccolimini had formerly controlled a large international banking business, but this had already collapsed a generation before Enea Silvio was born in 1405. Though his father received an education befitting a nobleman, he was not able to live as one, and he eventually turned to farming in Corsignano. It was thus in this village, which at the time was populated almost entirely by agricultural workers, that the young Enea Silvio, named after one of the most famous wandering exiles in all of literature, Aeneas, spent his childhood.[10] He finally left in 1423 to pursue his education in Siena, and afterwards he did not, for a long time, look back. Indeed, he seems not to have set foot again in Corsignano until, on route to Mantua in 1459, as the newly elected Pope Pius II, he visited the town in the company of a great retinue of courtiers and retainers. In his memoires, which contain detailed, third-person accounts of his life, he explains that he had great hopes for the occasion, but he also says that those hopes were immediately dashed. In a passage that reads almost as though it could have been written for him by a psychoanalyst, the pope describes how:

> Returning there [to Corsignano] at this time he hoped to have some pleasure in talking with those with whom he had grown up and to feel delight in seeing again

his native soil; but he was disappointed, for most of those of his own generation had died and those who were left kept to their houses, bowed down with old age and illness, or, if they showed themselves, were so changed as to be hardly recognizable, for they were feeble and crippled and like harbingers of death. At every step the pope met with proofs of his own age and could not fail to realize that he was an old man who would soon drop, since he found that those whom he had left as children had sons and were already well along in years.[11]

It was at that moment, rocked by unexpected feelings of estrangement and determined to make a home matching his expectations, that Pius resolved to start building in Corsignano, initiating a project that would ultimately lead to him granting the town the status of a city and renaming it Pienza.[12] The largest of the new buildings, exceeding even the size of the cathedral, would be the pope's own residence, the Palazzo Piccolomini, designed by Bernardo Rossellino in the most up-to-date Renaissance idiom, with facades covered in shallow rustication and divided into bays by tiers of antique-style orders, much in the manner of the Palazzo Rucellai in Florence, a building often attributed to Alberti (see Figures 6.2 and 6.3).[13] At the rear, a large hanging garden gives on to sweeping

Figure 6.2 Palazzo Piccolomini (right), Pienza, designed by Bernardo Rossellino. AKG Images/ Erich Lessing.

Figure 6.3 Palazzo Rucellai, Florence, attributed to Leon Battista Alberti. Photo 1890. AKG Images.

views of the Val d'Orcia, and these are so breathtaking that it is easy to miss a small detail on the east perimeter wall (see Figure 6.4 and Plate 5). Here, what appears to be the doorway of a medieval building has been preserved, and there is good reason to believe that this is in fact the entrance to Pius's childhood home, or at the very least that it has been mocked up to seem so.

The Papal Bull of July 14, 1463, which makes provision for new building works, refers to the palace as standing "in fundo paterno, destructa domo" (on our ancestral estate, the [old] house now being destroyed).[14] Similarly, Flavio Biondo, a prominent humanist writer who travelled in Pius II's retinue, described the palace, in his *Italia illustrata*, as "palatium tuo natali cubiculo superaedificatum," that is to say, "the *palazzo* built over the bedroom where you were born."[15]

Undoubtedly, this tells us a great deal about Pienza and its origins in Pius II's own search for a home. As with Alberti, there is a sense that home might be actualized through architecture, via the making of new and magnificent buildings in an antique-modern style, and as with Alberti, the home that is sought is essentially a fictional one. That is not to say that Pius did not really grow up in Corsignano—undoubtedly, he did—but to acknowledge that the actual Corsignano fell so short of his imaginative requirements

Figure 6.4 Doorway in the east wall of the garden of the Palazzo Piccolomini, Pienza. Photograph by the author.

that it could only be, in a very strange sense, retrieved by the making of something entirely new and different. In the relic-like preservation and display of the fragments of his ancestral house, Pius manifested very effectively the temporal anxiety and uncertainty pervading his project, juxtaposing conspicuous signs of contingency, change, and the forces of history, with an Albertian mode of building that perhaps sought, albeit in a partial and equivocal manner, to stand outside of time by appealing to generative rules that could be naturalized as universally valid.[16] In this way, he set up a confrontation that seems to speak to the kinds of temporal dualities that Alexander Nagel and Christopher Wood have associated with a Renaissance fascination with anachronism.[17]

The making of the Renaissance

Perhaps the longing for a home—albeit a fictionalized and unrecoverable one—that we encounter within these emblematic architectural projects has stayed with the Italian Renaissance. Perhaps it was even crucial to its formation. It is notable that in the case of both Alberti and Pius II, the preoccupation with home is linked inextricably to a concern with life—or, to be more precise, with *new* life. Pius II was motivated by the apprehension of his impending death to renovate the place where he once was young and thereby in some sense to evade the workings of time, while Alberti speaks of his family having "grown old" in their exile, implying that their return might bring about a kind of rejuvenation. It is striking, in this regard, that the very word *re-naissance* of course denotes a re-birth. Indeed, the Renaissance is unusual as a term for a historical period in that it makes a direct reference, via birth, to life. One of the first great formulators of the Italian Renaissance as an idea about history, the historian Jules Michelet, certainly saw it that way, and it is worth noting that architecture played a crucial role in his thinking. Indeed, Brunelleschi and the cupola, he argued, had really brought the Renaissance into being. Arriving at the culmination of an extraordinary passage, in which he moves fluidly back and forth between architectural metaphor and the analysis of architecture itself, Michelet says of the cupola:

> Behold then, the cornerstone of the Renaissance is set in place, the permanent objection to the crippled art of the Middle Ages, the first attempt, but a triumphant one, at a serious construction that supports itself, based on calculation and the authority of reason.
>
> The reconciliation of art and reason, that is the Renaissance, the marriage of beauty and truth.[18]

The cupola was, for Michelet, emblematic of the ethos and achievements of the entire Renaissance. There is something rather Albertian in this faith in the ability of a building—this building in particular—to encapsulate such epoch-making significance.[19] Indeed, Michelet's own motivations might well have been just as personal as those of Alberti and Pius II.

That, at any rate, was certainly the view of Lucien Febvre, the historian of the Annales School, whose essay of 1950, "Comment Jules Michelet inventa la Renaissance?" (How Jules Michelet Invented the Renaissance) is an extraordinary, lyrical paean to the birth of an idea. Pointing out that Michelet embraced the Renaissance during a period of euphoria when he found a new love, following a long depression caused by the death of his first wife, Febvre writes:

> [F]ollowing a death surrounded with sentiment, new life flowered again in his heart, *una vita nuova. Mors et vita*—in Michelet-the-mystic the two terms were indissolubly linked and necessarily bound up with one another. Life arose out of death and death opened the gateway to new life. Birth, death, renaissance—it is a trio that was familiar to the historian. Just as the alliteration "*ne, re-ne*" (born, reborn) was familiar to him too.[20]

In this inspired condition, Michelet, Febvre suggests, stumbled across the word Renaissance: "he stopped and smiled at the word which smiled back at him and set it apart for a higher destiny."[21]

What is so striking about this essay is the sense of a chain of desire and inspiration stretching from figures such as Alberti and Pius II, up to Michelet and on to Febvre—fanning out from history and embracing also architecture, with which it was always anyway linked from the start. In fact, Febvre's broader purpose in his essay is to show how the Renaissance, which he considers a tyrannical concept, came to imbed itself so firmly in our historical thinking, since, as he puts it:

> We like to talk about the machines which we create and which enslave us. But machines are not made only of steel. Any intellectual category we may forge in the workshops of the mind is able to impose itself with the same force and the same tyranny—and holds even more stubbornly to its existence than the machines made in our factories. History is a strongbox that is too well guarded, too firmly locked and belted. Once something has been put in it for safe keeping it never gets back out.[22]

The Renaissance, we might think, is not only fully present in the "strongbox" of modern architectural history but has sometimes even been treated as the "cubiculum natale" upon which modern architecture was "superaedificatum": the birthplace over which it was built and a site that continues to exert a definite pull.

And yet, it may be that that desire is finally reaching its limit and starting to dissipate. Perhaps with the acceleration and huge expansion of horizons inherent in contemporary life, we are unable, like Alberti, Pius II, or even Michelet, to grant new buildings such extraordinary epoch-making powers. Perhaps, in the age of globalization—when the Italian Renaissance seems suddenly a much more regional, local, or even parochial phenomenon than before—in the age of megacities, "bigness," and anti-humanism, the Renaissance simply cannot maintain the same kind of purchase on our thinking as it once did. After all its multiple births, it may at last be growing old. If so, that might itself allow us to see in ways that we have not done before—and thus to make it new once more.

Notes

1. Manfredo Tafuri, *Theories and History of Architecture*, trans. Giorgio Verrecchia (London: Granada, 1980), 14, 30; Françoise Choay, *The Rule and The Model: On the Theory of Architecture and Urbanism*, trans. Denise Bratton (Cambridge, MA: MIT Press, 1997), 3–6.

2. Rowe engaged closely with the Renaissance throughout his career. Perhaps his most celebrated essays linking the Renaissance and modern periods are "The Mathematics of the Ideal Villa: Palladio and Le Corbusier Compared," *Architectural Review* 101 (March 1947): 101–4; and "Mannerism and Modern Architecture," *Architectural Review* 107 (May 1950): 289–99. Likewise, Mannerism remained a sustained interest of Venturi and Scott Brown, first articulated in Robert Venturi's *Complexity and Contradiction in Architecture* (New York: Museum of Modern Art, 1966). On the relationship between Rowe's thought and that of Venturi and Scott Brown, see Denise Costanzo, "Text, Lies and Architecture: Colin Rowe, Robert Venturi and Mannerism," *Journal of Architecture* 18, no. 4 (2013): 455–73. Rogers has

long highlighted the importance of the Renaissance for his own thinking. Visitors to the Royal Academy's major retrospective of the architect in 2013 were greeted by a video in which Rogers emphasized the centrality of humanism, Italy, and the Renaissance to his work. Pienza featured regularly in discussions of New Urbanism, and not least in the naming of the Pienza Seaside Institute for Building and Land Stewardship, founded in 2002 by Robert Davis, Raymond Grindoz, and Leon Krier.

3. See Rem Koolhaas, *Fundamentals Catalogue* (Venice: Marsilio, 2014), 404.

4. For Alberti's biography, see Girolamo Mancini, *Vita di Leon Battista Alberti*, 2nd edn (Florence: Carnesecchi, 1911); and Anthony Grafton, *Leon Battista Alberti: Master Builder of the Italian Renaissance* (New York: Hill and Wang, 2000). For Alberti's career at the papal Curia, see Brigide Schwarz, "Die karriere Leon Battista Albertis in der päpstlichen Kanzlei," *Quellen und Forschungen aus italienischen Archiven und Bibliotheken* 93 (2013): 49–103.

5. The letter is appended to one of three surviving manuscripts of the vernacular version of the *De pictura*, none of which are autograph. Long regarded as a self-translation from the original Latin, the vernacular version is now considered to have precedence. On this, see Lucia Bertolini, "Sulla precedenza della redazione volgare del *De pictura* di Leon Battista Alberti," in *Studi per Umberto Carpi. Un saluto da allievi e colleghi pisani*, ed. Marco Santagata and Alfredo Stussi (Pisa: ETS, 2000), 181–210; and Rocco Sinisgalli's introduction to Leon Battista Alberti, *Il Nuovo* De pictura *di Leon Battista Alberti = The New* De pictura *of Leon Battista Alberti*, ed. and trans. R. Sinisgalli (Rome: Kappa, 2006), 25–45. On Alberti's broader motivations and practices in writing and disseminating the vernacular version of his treatise, see Bertolini's introduction in Leon Battista Alberti, *De pictura (redazione volgare)*, ed. Lucia Bertolini (Florence: Polistampa, 2011), 37–58; and by the same author, "Come 'pubblicava' l'Alberti: ipotesi preliminari," in *Storia della lingua e filologia: per Alfredo Stussi nel suo sessantacinquesimo compleanno*, ed. Michelangelo Zaccarello and Lorenzo Tomasin (Florence: Fondazione Franceschini, 2004), 219–40; and "Nouvelles perspectives sur le *De pictura* et sa réception," in *Alberti: humaniste, architecte*, ed. Françoise Choay and Michel Paoli (Paris: École nationale supérieure des Beaux-arts, 2006), 33–45.

6. Leon Battista Alberti, *On Painting and On Sculpture: The Latin Texts of* De pictura *and* De statua, ed. and trans. Cecil Grayson (London: Phaidon, 1972), 33. For the original language, see Alberti, *De pictura (redazione volgare)*, 204: "Chi mai sì duro o sì invido non lodasse Pippo architetto vedendo qui struttura sì grande, erta sopra e cieli, ampla da coprire con sua ombra tutti e popoli toscani, fatta sanza alcuno aiuto di travamenti o di copia di legname? Quale artificio, certo, se io ben iudico, come a questi tempi era incredibile potersi, così forse a presso gli antichi fu non saputo né conosciuto."

7. On this topic, see Caspar Pearson, "The Return of the Giants: Reflections on Technical Mastery and Moral Jeopardy in Leon Battista Alberti's Letter to Filippo Brunelleschi," *Journal of the Warburg and Courtauld Institutes* 83 (2019): 113–41.

8. Alberti, *On Painting and On Sculpture*, 33; and *De pictura (redazione volgare)*, 203–4: "Ma poi che io dal lungo esilio in quale siamo noi Alberti invechiati, qui fui in questa nostra sopra l'altre ornatissima patria ridutto, compresi in molti, ma prima in te, Filippo, e in quel nostro amicissimo Donato scultore e in quelli altri, Nencio e Luca e Masaccio, essere a ogni lodata cosa ingegno da non postporli a qual si sia stato antiquo e famoso in queste arti. Per tanto m'avidi in nostra industria e diligenzia, non meno che in benificio della natura e de' tempi, stare il potere acquistarsi ogni laude di qual si sia virtù."

9. On history as progress rather than decline in Alberti's letter, see Christine Smith, *Architecture in the Culture of Early Humanism: Ethics, Aesthetics and Eloquence 1400-1480* (Oxford: Oxford University Press, 1992), 19–53.

10. For accounts of Pius's early life, see, among others, Gioacchino Paparelli, *Enea Silvio Piccolomini: L'umanesimo sul soglio di Pietro* (Ravenna: Longo Editore, 1978), 18–29; R. J. Mitchell, *The Laurels and the Tiara: Pope Pius II 1458-1464* (London: Harvill Press, 1962), 27–34; Charles-Édouard Naville, *Enea Silvio Piccolomini: l'uomo, l'umanista, il pontefice (1405-1464)* (Bologna: Analisi, 1984), 53–57; and Arthur White, *Plague and Pleasure: The Renaissance World of Pius II* (Washington, DC: Catholic University of America Press, 2014), 48–53. Both Pius's early life and the condition of Corsignano at the time that he was born are considered in Charles Mack, *Pienza: The Creation of a Renaissance City* (Ithaca, NY: Cornell University Press, 1987), 26–7.

11. Pope Pius II, *Secret Memoires of a Renaissance Pope: The Commentaries of Aeneas Sylvius Piccolomini*, trans. Florence A. Gragg (London: Folio Society, 1988), 96; Enea Silvio Piccolomini, *Commentarii rerum memorabilium*, ed. Luigi Totaro, 2 vols (Milan: Adelphi, 1984), 1: 312 (Bk. 2, Ch. 20): "Quo tunc rediens speravit voluptatem aliquam sumere, eos allocuturus quibuscum adoleverat et aspectum natalis soli cum gaudio revisere. Sed contra evenit, quando maior pars aequalium vita excesserat et qui adhuc spirabant, gravati senio morbisque, domi detinebantur et si qui sese exhibebant, mutatis vultibus vix agnosci poterant, exhausti viribus, deformes et quasi mortis nuncii. Offendebat Pontifex ubique suae senectutis inditia: non poterat se non senem et cito casurum recognoscere, cum iam aetate graves filios inveniret eorum quos pueros reliquerat."

12. For an account of the entire project in English, see Mack, *Pienza*.

13. Tradition holds that Alberti was the architect of the Palazzo Rucellai, though no document contemporary with the building of the palace attests to his involvement. Recent major works on Alberti's architecture have accepted his authorship. See Robert Tavernor, *On Alberti and the Art of Building* (New Haven, CT: Yale University Press, 1998), 94–5; and Massimo Bulgarelli, *Leon Battista Alberti 1404-1472: Architettura e Storia* (Milan: Electa, 2008), 47–51. For a statement of the contrary view, see Charles Mack, The Rucellai Palace: Some New Proposals," *Art Bulletin* 56 (1974): 517–29.

14. For the Latin text of the Bull, see Mack, *Pienza*, 205-6, n. 87. Mack (62–3) connects the doorway with the text in the Papal Bull and suggests that "the pope evidently wished to preserve a portion of his humble birthplace as a reminder of his origins and a contrast to the sumptuous palace he had erected in its stead. It was a nostalgic statement of both humility and pride."

15. Flavio Biondo, *Italia illustrata*, trans. Jeffrey A. White (Cambridge, MA: Harvard University Press, 2016), 388–9 (Appendix, Additiones correctionesque, 3.23); and Mack, *Pienza*, 167, 169.

16. On Albertian architecture and the desire to stand against or outside of time, see Choay, *The Rule and the Model*, 134; and Marvin Trachtenberg, *Building-in-Time: From Giotto to Alberti and Modern Oblivion* (New Haven, CT: Yale University Press, 2010), 357–83.

17. Alexander Nagel and Christopher Wood, *Anachronic Renaissance* (New York: Zone Books, 2010).

18. Jules Michelet, *Histoire de France au seizième siècle*, vol. 7: *Renaissance* (Paris: Chamerot, 1861), 97: "Voilà donc la forte pierre de la Renaissance fondée, la permanente objection à l'art boiteux du moyen âge, premier essai, mais triumphant, d'une construction sérieuse qui s'appuie sur elle-même, sur le calcul et l'autorité de la raison. L'art et la raison réconciliés, voilà la Renaissance, le marriage du beau et du vrai."

19. There is no indication that Michelet was familiar with Alberti's letter, though he may have picked up on echoes of it in Vasari's life of Brunelleschi, which takes up Albertian themes such as the rhetoric of outdoing, and which Michelet clearly studied closely.

20. Lucien Febvre, *A New Kind of History: From the Writings of Febvre*, ed. Peter Burke, trans. Keith Folca (London: Routledge and Kegan Paul, 1973), 262: ". . . voilà qu'après une mort

sentimentale une vie nouvelle, *una vita nuova*, refleurissait dans son cœur. *Mors et Vita:* chez le mystique Michelet, les deux termes étaient liés, indissolublement, par un lien nécessaire—la vie sortant de la mort, la mort ouvrant la porte à de nouvelles vies. Naissance, mort, Renaissance: triade familière à l'historien. Comme lui était familière l'allitération 'né, re-né', qu'il emploie si souvent." All quotations in the original language are from the reproduction of the text in *Le Genre humain* 27, no. 1 (1993): 77–87.

21. Febvre, *A New Kind of History*, 263: ". . . il s'arrêtait, il souriait à ce mot qui lui souriait, il le retenait pour de plus hauts destins."

22. Febvre, *A New Kind of History*, 258: "Nous parlons volontiers de la machine que nous créons et qui nous asservit. Il n'est pas de machine que d'acier. La catégorie intellectuelle que nous forgeons dans nos ateliers cérébraux s'impose à nous avec la même force, la même tyrannie— et d'ailleurs vit d'une vie autrement tenace que la mécanique fabriquée dans nos usines. Histoire, coffre-fort trop bien gardé, trop bien verrouillé. De ce qu'il a une fois mis à l'abri, rien ne sort."

CHAPTER 7
FROM RENAISSANCE PRECISION TO COMPUTATIONAL UNCERTAINTY
Frank Bauer

Inventing a notation

Emerging technologies are prone to errors. Late-fifteenth-century readers of Leon Battista Aberti's first printed edition of *De re aedificatoria* of 1485 were presumably unsurprised to encounter errata in this early typeset. But why do blind spots populate some of its passages, and what is the peculiar two-headed letter conjoining a capital "L" to an inverted "C" (see Figure 7.1)? These appear less like errors than deliberate, if mysterious, formatting decisions. The hybrid figure appears at the end of a section on building ornamentation, where Alberti arranges the traditional Vitruvian columnar systems ("classical orders"), painstakingly describing their constitutive elements. Instead of using many words to delineate molding contours, however, the author simply invokes their resemblance to a few letters: an L, C, or S, variously manipulated through their inversion, superimposition, and attachment. When he construes profile cuts, such as astragals or ovoli, Alberti therefore directs readers to that which follows (*sic*, or "thus"): the model of his writing, which appears as a void on the printed page.[1]

Alberti mistrusted imagery. Using instead what Mario Carpo famously christened "alphabetic code," he sought to communicate the language of architecture.[2] His dismay for the flaws and deviations to be found in manually copied images and text reflected his opposition to the traditions of scriptoria and libraries, just as it somehow anticipated the media revolution born in Johannes Gutenberg's workshops across the Alps.[3] Notes Veronica Biermann: "His recognizing, describing, determining and denominating of individual profiles and moldings corresponds with a mode of representation, which incorporates its handwritten mode of publication and replication."[4] Dario Donetti has drawn analogies in Alberti's work between bodies of language and of ornament, both constituted from letters and profiles.[5] Both are also abstractions, requiring interpretation. A scholar above all else, Alberti preferred what was written and seemingly more ambiguous over what was drawn and seemingly more precise. Drawings could be distorted, and to him were "in many cases inopportune, *i.e.* not necessary, of no use, or even inappropriate," as Francesco Furlan has observed.[6] Alberti's demand to his copyists not to tamper with his work, nor even to replace written-out numbers with numerals, is in this respect revealing, as is his stated intention to "make a brief digression, for the sake of clarity."[7] He finds clarity, too, in a literally lexical dissection of forms into typographic models.

As Biermann has noted, it is curious that Alberti's first typesetter denied him the courtesy of printing his experiment, beyond using movable letters to set a translation for "channel" by inverting the C and hanging it from the L´s bottom bar.[8] Here, new

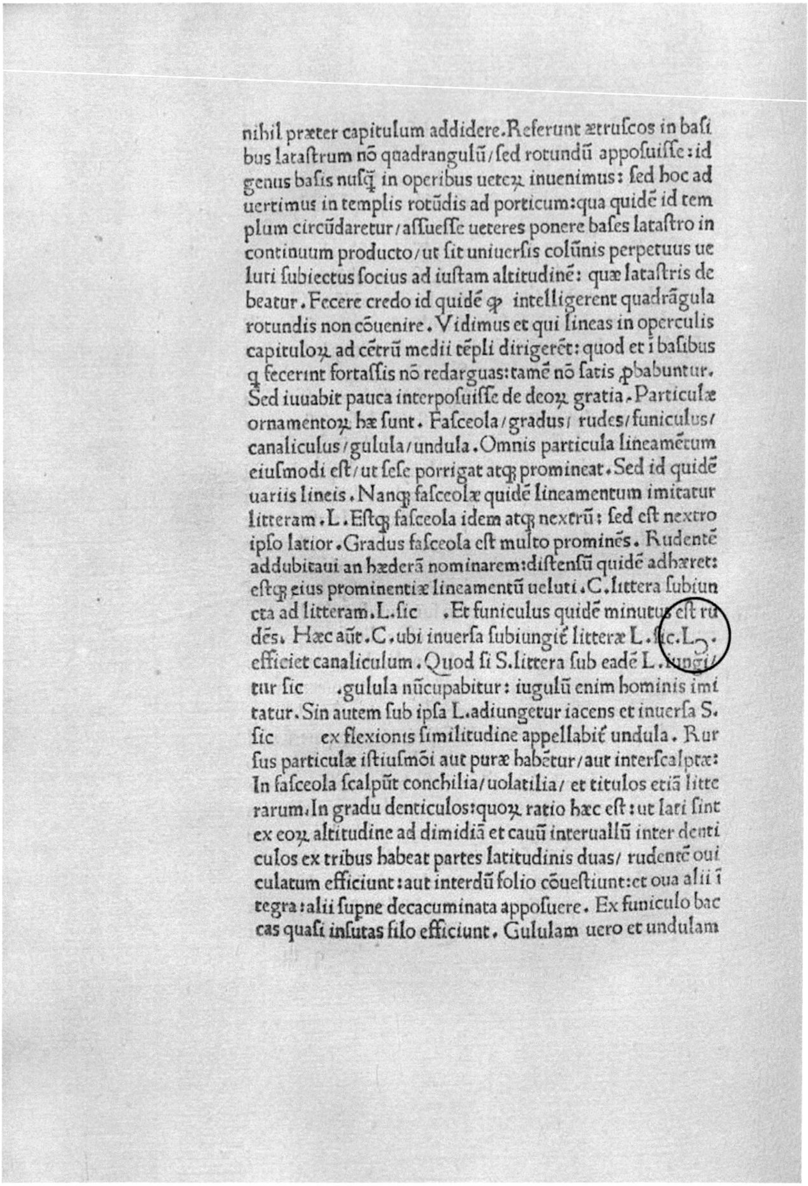

nihil præter capitulum addidere. Referunt ætruſcos in baſi
bus lataſtrum nō quadrangulū/ſed rotundū appoſuiſſe : id
genus baſis nuſ̃ in operibus ueteꝛ inuenimus : ſed hoc ad
uertimus in templis rotūdis ad porticum : qua quidē id tem
plum circūdaretur/aſſueſſe ueteres ponere baſes lataſtro in
continuum producto/ut ſit uniuerſis colūnis perpetuus ue
luti ſubiectus ſocius ad iuſtam altitudinē : quæ lataſtris de
beatur. Fecere credo id quidē ꝗ intelligerent quadrāgula
rotundis non cōuenire. Vidimus et qui lineas in operculis
capituloꝛ ad cētrū medii tēpli dirigerēt : quod et i baſibus
ꝗ fecerint fortaſſis nō redarguas : tamē nō ſatis ꝓbabuntur.
Sed iuuabit pauca interpoſuiſſe de deoꝛ gratia. Particulæ
ornamentoꝛ hæ ſunt. Faſceola/gradus/ rudes/funiculus/
canaliculus/gulula/undula. Omnis particula lineamētum
eiuſmodi eſt/ut ſeſe porrigat atꝗ promineat. Sed id quidē
uariis lineis. Nanꝗ faſceolæ quidē lineamentum imitatur
litteram. L. Eſtꝗ faſceola idem atꝗ nextrū : ſed eſt nextro
ipſo latior. Gradus faſceola eſt multo prominēs. Rudentē
addubitaui an hæderā nominarem : diſtenſū quidē adhæret :
eſtꝗ eius prominentiæ lineamentū ueluti. C. littera ſubiun
cta ad litteram. L. ſic   . Et funiculus quidē minutuꝭ eſt ru
dēs. Hæc aūt. C. ubi inuerſa ſubiungiē litteræ L. ꝭc. L.⸲.
efficiet canaliculum. Quod ſi S. littera ſub eadē L. ꝭungiꝰ
tur ſic   . gulula nūcupabitur : iugulū enim hominis imi
tatur. Sin autem ſub ipſa L. adiungetur iacens et inuerſa S.
ſic   ex flexionis ſimilitudine appellabiē undula. Rur
ſus particulæ iſtiuſmōi aut puræ habētur/aut interſcalptæ :
In faſceola ſcalpūt conchilia/uolatilia/ et titulos etiā litte
rarum. In gradu denticulos : quoꝛ ratio hæc eſt : ut lati ſint
ex coꝛ altitudine ad dimidiā et cauū interuallū inter denti
culos ex tribus habeat partes latitudinis duas/ rudentē oui
culatum efficiunt : aut interdū folio cōueſtiunt : et oua alii ī
tegra : alii ſupne decacuminata appoſuere. Ex funiculo hac
cas quaſi inſutas filo efficiunt. Gululam uero et undulam

Figure 7.1 Leon Battista Alberti, *De re aedificatoria*, first typeset edition (Florence: Nicolaus Laurentii, Alamanus, 1485), vol. Universitätsbibliothek Freiburg i.Br., 120b.

technology lags behind the old, since a manuscript from that same year better accommodates his "model" (see Figure 7.2). Although most later-printed editions left blank spots or added alternative representations of these instructions, Cosimo Bartoli, who first translated Alberti's book into Tuscan, printed his textual models along with discrete figures.[9] While his edition met a sixteenth-century demand for illustrated architectural treatises, it also suggests a conscious decision to be as precise as possible.

Some 500 years later, emerging technologies appear prone to similar demands for precision, while tensions persist around representation and exactitude. Against such insistent precision, Alberti's errata might suggest a productive vagueness.[10] Then as now, modeling is a trans-medial catalyst for communicating ideas which operate between precision and uncertainty. Attempting to re-embed the "digital turn" within the discipline's putative humanist legitimization reinvigorates long-standing questions about architecture's professionalization, technological appropriation, and concurrent forms of authorship.

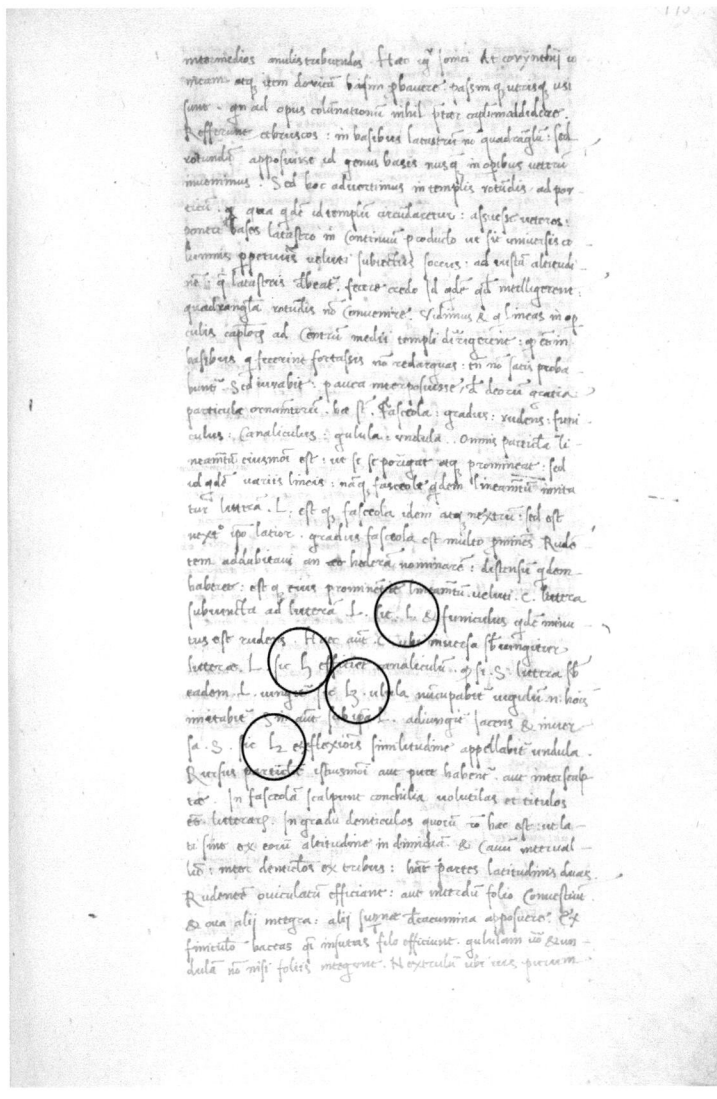

Figure 7.2 Leon Battista Alberti, *De Re Aedificatoria*, manuscript, Codex Ms1, ca. 1485. Hanna Holborn Gray Special Collections Research Center, University of Chicago Library, 173a.

Inventing a profession

Counterintuitively, establishing Alberti's present-day relevance requires establishing him as an author of his own time. Amidst the social stratification, urbanization, and emancipation of early modern Italian city-states, new realities in politics and building drove an improvement in architects' standing. To fully understand their role within the building, cultural, and social enterprises now conjoined under the concept of "Renaissance architecture," one must remember that, since Vitruvius, architecture had been considered an *arte mechanica*, a physical practice of craft and skill. Regarding it instead as an *arte liberale*, Alberti established architecture as an intellectual endeavor—relying not least on the concept of *disegno*. As Stephen Parcell explains, "not only the builder is absent from *disegno* in Book 1, the physical building is also absent … Although he presents many building principles, there are no particularities of site, material, or program, to make them tangible."[11]

Alberti's *disegno* anticipates much that would be reworked by Giorgio Vasari in the following century. Following Wolfgang Kemp's analysis of this term's complex development in sixteenth-century Florence, Heinz Hirdina has shown how the manifold definitions of *disegno* operate between mental and formal principles, communication between artist and client, or the process by which the arts are elevated over craft.[12] As an early modern identity, the "architect" mirrored this term's practical and epiphanic notions, along with its etymology: *disegnare* means to scheme or find, as well as to draw. The drawing could become an immaculate act of creativity, a moment of inception. It was revolutionary to think that *disegno* established the architect with an artistic and intellectual capacity to anticipate or imagine buildings, unlike the medieval master mason whose authority lay in productive, dirty hands from dust-filled workshops and muddy construction sites.

This is where Alberti's notion of *lineamenta* comes in—giving "an appropriate place, exact numbers, a proper scale and a graceful order for whole buildings and for each of their constituent parts."[13] Susanne Lang has revealed how this Albertian term, which Branko Mitrović has more recently translated as "shape" in a purely geometrical sense, located where "the essential features of a building, especially the proportions, were laid down."[14] This not only differentiates proportional systems from those information-driven models of today, but also suggests their independence from his typographic models—complementary abstractions.

Alberti describes architectural design as an imaginative process whose essence exists beyond the physical: "nor do lineaments have anything to do with material."[15] The result is what Carpo has framed "the Albertian paradigm—the definition of architecture as an allographic art, and of building as the notationally identical copy of a singular, authorial act of design," from which the architect should maintain distance.[16] Consequently, lineaments enter in the first of Alberti's books while materials and construction appear later—and only after his repeated claim that architects should first finish an iterative and rigorous process of planning and drawing the building in all consistency, so "that were you to add, change, or take away anything, it would be to the detriment of the whole."[17] This threshold between designing and building has remained codified in architecture, centuries later and worldwide.

But how did earlier generations of readers understand this claim? Consider Philibert de l'Orme, author of the first French architectural treatise (*Premiere Tome de l'architecture*, 1567). Christopher Hight has recently described him as "embedded into the material logics of the drawing as a 'manner of working.'"[18] De l'Orme deals with the architect, as a figure, by means of another contemporary printing innovation: the woodcut. He created two allegories, figures presenting opposing architectural dispositions, that encapsulate a whole set of Renaissance revolutions (see Figure 7.3). A prudish, isolated scholastic contrasts with an inspiring humanist teaching a student; a barren wasteland versus a flourishing Edenic landscape; a disabled figure without eyes to behold, ears to understand, or hands to shape against one endowed with manifold abilities. In a likely self-portrait, de l'Orme presents an architect with many hands, winged feet, and an extra eye to supervise multiple building sites. This "good architect," master of tools, material, and men, can translate a design into drawings, and direct their realization as building projects, like the Renaissance palace and cathedral in the foreground. Returning to Alberti: "Should you propose to supervise and execute the work, you will hardly be able to avoid having the sole responsibility for all the errors and mistakes committed by others, whether through inexperience or neglect. Such projects require zealous, circumspect and strict clerks of works, to supervise the necessary work with diligence, application, and their constant presence."[19]

Figure 7.3 Philibert de l'Orme, "The Bad Architect, the Good Architect," woodcut illustrations, 1567. Source: Philibert de l'Orme, *Le Premier Tome de L'Architecture*, Bibliothèque nationale de France (Paris: F. Morel, 1568), 281r, 283r.

These sources suggest how the Renaissance project as a projection of *disegno* into reality also implied new modes of communication and interpretation. The relation of master builder and craftsman was not discarded but translated into drawings and other mediating forms and figures. Such mediating devices as plans and models produced a dialogic space that might now be considered productive rather than problematic. Renaissance notation systems as embodied in orthographic and perspectival drawings are commonly regarded by authors of recent digital technologies as maintaining a representational gap that has now been overcome. While we need greater media literacy to challenge this view, is it really the task of drawing and notation to communicate the architect's intentions with ever greater precision, accuracy, and efficiency? Or to enable more ambivalent, collaborative, and diachronic approaches to production?[20] To what extent, that is, do contemporary technologies realize or reverse the precedent set by Alberti?

Inventing a reversal?

De re aedificatoria has been read as a justification for architecture's self-conception as an autonomous, authoritative, and intellectual creative practice, in which is legislated the fundamental divide between design and construction. In recent years, Alberti's treatise and its relevance have been rediscovered repeatedly. Andrew Witt used Albertian methods to develop a machine epistemology aimed at a new paradigm of digital instrumentation, and Mitrović located the foundations of contemporary three-dimensional modeling environments in his work.[21] These extend observations by Robin Evans, who associated architecture's disciplinary project with a confluence of Renaissance construction and a turn from orthogonal to perspectival projection:

> Alberti's construction is a set of conventions *without* any necessary relation to reality. Using it, we can go fishing for real objects to catch within its net. We can also use the net to make imaginary objects that exist only in the picture … Alberti's perspective has the power to make reality in its image precisely because it is not reality.[22]

Alberti's invocation of moldings with letters may be powerful for this same reason: not because they represent reality, but because they abstract it and thus require interpretation. Carpo takes an alternative stance when he "recounts the rise and fall of the paradigm of identicality and shows that digital and pre-mechanical variability have many points in common."[23] He reads the "digital turn" as an "Albertian paradigm" in reverse, reinstating master builders who exert direct control over computational production. This anchoring of emerging technologies both in and against the Italian Renaissance is widespread. For instance, Anthony Hauck and others identified similarities between Building Information Modeling (BIM) and Alberti's advocacy of operative models to simulate and manage design parameters (like costs, engineering, and construction sequence): "As BIM environments and their analytical elaborations and generative design successors gain computational capabilities and information access through resources available through cloud connectivity, the architectural profession has an opportunity to assert a role explicitly ceded by Alberti and implicitly occupied by Brunelleschi: that of the master builder."[24]

The model as an epistemic device has long occupied a productive position within architectural history. Werner Oechslin has shown how its definition as an *idea materialis* between abstraction and physicality, linking ideation and reality, has challenged and advanced architecture over centuries.[25] BIM provides a computational sequel to construction's industrial rationalization, as a tool to design, realize, and monitor a building from conception to demolition.[26] Breaking with many representational customs and traditions, notably the venerable plan, elevation, and section drawings, BIM's three-dimensional representations have been described as a building's "digital twin." This kinship is not limited to a notation of form, but includes semantic, functional, relational, and processual information using Industry Foundation Class (IFC)-coded building elements. Such expansive notions of the model generate a dynamic yet precise representation of the building and its many boundary conditions, fostering feedback-driven processes which integrate project delivery and post-occupation scenarios while offering unprecedented degrees of coordination across specializations and trades.[27]

Looking at BIM from outside the discipline, one might follow Horst Bredekamp's description of models as both guide and shackle, at once a liberating catalyst and self-formative agent. He emphasizes the visual agency that animates all sorts of images (meaning "every form of conscious shaping"), from altarpieces to X-ray scans.[28] Presenting the scale model as the paradigm of an "image act," he uses the wooden model of the dome of Florence Cathedral by Filippo Brunelleschi to make his case.[29] During the planning process from 1420 to 1436, the architect was not restricted to using the famous model preserved in the Museo dell'Opera del Duomo (roughly 1:50). He also had four bricklayers construct a far more massive (estimated 1:8 to 1:12) model to test his vaulting proposal, as the building commission had requested of him.[30] This large-scale model served as what would today be called a proof of method: that the ribbed dome could be erected as a self-supporting two-shell structure using wooden chains, herringbone brick bond, and two load-bearing systems, and abandoning costly wooden centering.[31]

Brunelleschi thus provides an early example of a new and more diverse culture of models that expanded medieval practices. As Alberti indicates, they served to verify a design, relate it to the site, develop variations, and evaluate construction methods, but always remained abstractions:

> [T]he presentation of models that have been colored and lewdly dressed with the allurement of painting is the mark of no architect intent on conveying the facts; rather it is that of a conceited one, striving to attract and seduce the eye of the beholder, and to divert his attention from a proper examination of the parts to be considered, toward the admiration of himself.[32]

It is tempting to hear Alberti, albeit indirectly, referring to the typographic experiments described at the outset. Regardless, such models accomplished more than was originally intended of them, developing into active agents of their own construction.[33] For his part, Brunelleschi's model tested his design from an architect's perspective, less to augment his internal workflow while he was developing solutions than to verify it externally. In this way, his models anticipated BIM: "Renaissance architects used models as an extended medium for planning—open for further elaboration, open for experiments in scale," while for clients the model offered "an opportunity to seize control over a building prior to completion."[34]

Modeling practices thereby participated in larger struggles for power and authority over building, extending what Antoine Bousquet calls a "dual process of rationalization of vision and mathematization of space" in perspectival construction.[35] Following Oechslin, one may see this dualism of theory and practice (or design and making) in Alberti's use of *modulus* and *exemplar* (scale or module, and example or prototype).[36] This is also evident when Alberti outlines the iterative logic of working between design, drawing, and model.[37] But is this not a moment when representational guides become shackles, to invoke Bredekamp, when the model pivots from an exploratory tool for an architect to a tool used by authorities to control what is built? This question recurs whenever models (be they made of bricks or bytes) gain renewed importance in the production of architecture. For Marco Frascari, "in an age in which unconsidered consumerist interests have exploited architecture, when a hasty abuse of public and private edifices has reached institutional intensity, and when buildings are the target of technologies of absurd variations, it is imperative to re-evaluate the graphical procedures involved in the conceiving of buildings."[38]

Frascari assumed a skeptical stance towards stock phrases like "virtual to actual," "file to factory," and "mass customization," which seek to "bridge the gap" and abolish projective distances in building representation, seen as a problematic legacy of architecture's Renaissance traditions. He contemplates how the latest revolutions in architectural media prevent imagination, highlighting issues of authorship and ownership, software ontologies and uncertainty. Will architects overcome embedded notions of creative and productive control, and develop a more collaborative and ambiguous vision of their profession? Would overcoming the skepticism to which he gives voice require somehow measuring the wiggle room offered by modeling and its manifold mediations from idea to materialization? Should we continue considering the "digital turn" as a reversal of an Albertian paradigm dividing architects from production (increasing their status while decreasing control), or instead conceive of computational technologies as just another chapter in the grand narrative of optimization and standardization? Perhaps there is a third possibility, where digital virtualization technologies do not offer a return to an imagined prelapsarian condition, but a much more final realization of Alberti's paradigm than he could have imagined when he construed *lineamenta* to consist exclusively of geometrical properties—constraining architectural agency to an initiating act of design, yet also anchoring a contemporary drive to an idea of precision and control bound to Renaissance Italy.[39]

On reinventing a discipline from without

If the Albertian media revolution introduced the architect as a design generalist, the latest one has produced increasingly isolated roles as "BIM Manager" and "BIM Designer." Yet instead of fostering disciplinary silos, the "digital turn" may open design discourse to all those other domains that deal with modeling multi-variable and dynamic systems. Modeling complexity as an epistemic technique could effectively bridge research cultures, given that different digital models often use similar (typically quantitative) means to justify and substantiate their legitimacy.[40] Bernd Mahr has argued for a transdisciplinary approach to modeling based not on contents, but practices:

> While their model-ness [*Modellsein*] is slowly recognized, models detach themselves from the conditions of their emergence and turn into empirical objects. This is when they stop being bound to either situation or subject of their construction and become independent. They turn into ontological beings and often acquire a status which withdraws them from any call for justification.[41]

One generation earlier, Horst Rittel described similar logics in his "model of design as argumentation,"[42] a decision-making process that introduces informed, tentative, and balancing logics to resolve complexity, and whose productivity rests in questions and uncertainties rather than clear answers. Most architects would probably recognize this model, placing their work's interrogative and speculative dimensions among its more fascinating qualities. This reflects the productive antagonism of precision and uncertainty in design practice, where a second-year student's clumsy cardboard model can outperform a classmate's shiny ArchiCAD simulation: one nurtures, the other suppresses the epistemic power of openness. Reinhard Wendler posits this as a contrast between vagueness and exactitude: "open" models would seem to invite more creativity than seemingly exhaustive ones. This antagonism between a curiously productive "precision of uncertainty" versus an impeding, sometimes misleading "uncertainty of precision" means that "the more complete the model is considered to be, the more it blurs with its reference object."[43]

This epistemological condition applies to design *and* research, both cultures that use modeling as a form of construction, so to speak. What emerges from reading Mahr, Rittel, and Wendler is that ambiguity can enrich how we construe models of realities, as well as realities of modeling, both past and future. Given this, scholarly efforts to anchor the digital model in (or before) Alberti and Brunelleschi's "Renaissance" should be challenged, if one embraces the history of architectural making as a productive enterprise—not despite but rather because of projective distance. While decentering the idea of the master builder, these studies distance Albertian notation from a controlling mode of communication whose apotheosis emerged through industrialization, computer-aided manufacturing chains, and intelligent building elements. If each of these reservations introduces its own distinct bottlenecks, cultivating historical narratives to connect a specific past to our present, is it not time to interrogate the complexity of trans-temporal architectural mediacy instead of pursuing some elusive dream of immediacy for design and production? Telling the history of architectural practice as one of figments, failures, and formations through modeling might allow us to consider, say, IFC-coded building elements as a return to the discursive blank spots of Alberti's typeset some 500 or so years later.

This new moment of virtualization risks otherwise becoming yet another "redundant precision iceberg," as Francesca Hughes has beautifully framed it.[44] Today, architectural culture produces an "uncertainty of precision" that may eventually become constitutive, if not detrimental, to building. Although Beetz and others have tackled many crucial questions of standardization, planning policy, and accessibility concerning BIM, little attention is devoted to its intrinsic logic.[45] Correcting this deficit would potentially entail trading a productive openness and abstraction for an increased definitiveness and precision—as Daniel Cardoso Llach has put it, "we build our conceptions of design out of the technological discourses and apparatuses with which, and within which, we design."[46] We encounter related issues when Nat Oppenheimer advocates bespoke, problem-specific solutions using emerging technologies that operate "beyond the more standard uses and preferred rhetoric of BIM."[47] They are also manifest when Phil Bernstein states how an "ability to integrate meta-design into design is critical to the future of the practice of architecture and design itself."[48] Architects should either design by thoroughly deploying all emerging technologies to manage their work's physical realization, or else simply contribute an abstracted image of their vision of the work—anything from a napkin sketch to a shiny rendering—with everything that follows being a process of negotiation in which an architect plays, if anything, just one role among many others.

That said, there exist alternative realities of digital practice in which models support both designing *and* making, yet they are used beyond efficiency and optimization to advance epistemological or aesthetic qualities. The emerging field of computational art production may be a catalyst for such urgent questions. It includes the work of artists who produce sculpture approaching the scale of buildings, which involve various professionals for planning and production through bespoke digital workflows ranging from three-dimensional sketches to manufacturing data sets. This work aligns with a growing interest in art's productive and procedural dimensions, exposing the material basis of the digital and exploring collaborative forms of practice.[49]

This growing awareness of the relevance of computational production in art has made it a testing ground for alternative digital workflows.[50] Notorious projects like *B of the Bang,* a public art project in Manchester by Heatherwick Studios from 2005, made such ramifications prominently visible. The project received widespread attention until its demolition only four years after its production, as it employed contemporary methods of 3D simulation and manufacturing to develop the fabrication sequence.[51] Experimental use of 3D wax prints permitted only the structure's core and framework to be designed and tested, which produced an "epistemological surplus" throughout its chains of mediation and realization. Just as Alberti developed bespoke typographic models to bypass a notational bottleneck—that is, the drawing copyist—this project's construction required new forms of notation to extend shortcomings of conventional representation: most contributions by production agents (CNC machinery, craftsmen, and engineers) could otherwise simply not be adequately shared (see Figure 7.4 and Plate 2).

Radically changing forms of practice (whether for the Renaissance architect or the BIM operator) introduce entirely new means of approaching models, as is evidenced by the work of companies like designtoproduction or Carlson Baker. Custom workflows are collaborations between craft specialists, material scientists, and structural engineers developed to address surprising and unconventional boundary conditions. Herwig

Figure 7.4 Engineer Michael Jay works on the *B of the Bang* sculpture at the AK Heavy Engineering Factory in Sheffield, northern England, May 25, 2004. Reuters Pictures. Photograph by Ian Hogson.

Bretis, lead engineer at ArtEngineering, has described how this can take projects into new territory, as with their column production for the Roots by Olafur Eliasson, whose bent, twisted forms and continuously changing diameters were realized with custom timber templates in a pressure chamber workflow.[52] If comparisons to Brunelleschi seem far-fetched, one can invoke Oppenheimer by comparing all workflows in their use of emerging technologies beyond notions of tradition and control. Such new tools support problem-specific, non-standard solutions which can provide a catalyst for architects confronting issues of visual agency and authorship.

In 1485, when Alberti's notational experiment for architecture met movable typesetting, it produced gaps. A second techno-epistemic revolution established the architect's modern role as both designer and communicator of solutions. A third innovation in the wake of emerging technologies sought to establish a Renaissance foundation for the contemporary drive towards precision, which perhaps fulfilled epiphanic notions of *disegno* beyond any anticipated by the "Albertian paradigm." Connecting these revolutions in bespoke forms of architectural modeling, production, and practice invites a transdisciplinary approach to contemporary digital modeling practice that sees spaces of ambiguity in communication and visualization as productive rather than problematic. More than five centuries ago, a goldsmith carving turnip models and a humanist polymath invented a new profession by embracing both the possibilities and uncertainties of new technologies.[53] This truly collaborative, innovative, and creative spirit is something a twenty-first-century architectural profession may well learn from its Italian Renaissance birthplace.

Notes

The author acknowledges the support of the "Matters of Activity. Image Space Material" Cluster of Excellence funded by the Deutsche Forschungsgemeinschaft (DFG, German Research Foundation) under Germany's Excellence Strategy – EXC 2025 – 390648296.

1. Nathalie Bredella, "Modell," in *Werkzeuge Des Entwerfens*, ed. Barbara Wittmann (Zurich: Diaphanes, 2018), 107–9.

2. Mario Carpo, *The Alphabet and the Algorithm* (Cambridge, MA: MIT Press, 2011), 44–8.

3. Veronica Biermann, "Der Architekturtraktat. Leon Battista Alberti: *De re aedificatoria*, 1452," in *Das Buch Als Entwurf*, ed. Dietrich Erben (Munich: Fink, 2019), 32–3.

4. Biermann, "Der Architekturtraktat," 51; unless otherwise noted, all translations are by the author.

5. Dario Donetti, "Crafting Perfection: Leon Battista Alberti, Language and the Art of Building," in *Perfection: The Essence of Art and Architecture in Early Modern Europe*, ed. Elisabeth Oy-Marra and Lorenzo Pericolo (Turnhout: Brepols, 2019), 75–7.

6. Mario Carpo and Francesco Furlan, "Introduction: The Reproducibility and Transmission of Technico-Scientific Illustrations in the Work of Alberti and in His Sources," in *Leon Battista Alberti's "Delineation of the City of Rome" ("Descriptio Vrbis Romæ")*, ed. Mario Carpo and Francesco Furlan (Tempe, AZ: ACMRS, 2007), 20.

7. Leon Battista Alberti, *On the Art of Building in Ten Books*, trans. Joseph Rykwert, Neil Leach, and Robert Tavernor (Cambridge, MA: MIT Press, 1988), 204; see also 200–1, 211; and Mario Carpo, *Architecture in the Age of Printing: Orality, Writing, Typography, and Printed Images in History of Architectural Theory*, trans. Sarah Benson (Cambridge, MA: MIT Press, 2001), 119–21, 124.

8. Biermann, "Der Architekturtraktat," 32–57.

9. Leon Battista Alberti, *L'architettvra*, trans. Cosimo Bartoli (Venice: F. Franceschi, 1565), 166b.

10. Compare Frank Bauer, "On the Visual Agency of Manufacturing Models," *Bitacora* 46 (2021): 130–9.

11. Stephen Parcell, *Four Historical Definitions of Architecture* (Montreal and Ithaca, NY: McGill-Queen's University Press, 2012), 143–4.

12. Wolfgang Kemp, "Disegno. Beiträge Zur Geschichte des Begriffs Zwischen 1547 und 1607," *Marburger Jahrbuch Für Kunstwissenschaft* 19 (1974): 219–40; Heinz Hirdina, "Design," in *Ästhetische Grundbegriffe*, ed. Karlheinz Barck et al. (Stuttgart and Weimar: Metzler, 2001), 42.

13. Alberti, *On the Art of Building*, 7.

14. Susanne Lang, "De Lineamentis: L. B. Alberti's Use of a Technical Term," *Journal of the Warburg and Courtauld Institutes* 28 (1965), 335; Branko Mitrović, *Serene Greed of the Eye: Leon Battista Alberti and the Philosophical Foundations of Renaissance Architectural Theory* (Berlin: Deutscher Kunstverlag, 2005), 49.

15. Alberti, *On the Art of Building*, 7.

16. Carpo, *The Alphabet and the Algorithm*, 117.

17. Alberti, *On the Art of Building,* 37.

18. Christopher Hight, "Manners of Working: Fabricating Representation in Digital Based Design," in *The SAGE Handbook of Architectural Theory*, ed. Greig C. Crysler, Stephen Cairns, and Hilde Heynen (London: SAGE, 2012), 427. He builds on Robin Evans, *The Projective Cast: Architecture and Its Three Geometries* (Cambridge, MA: MIT Press, 1995), 179–240.

19. Alberti, *On the Art of Building*, 318.

20. Ludger Hovestadt, Urs Hirschberg, and Oliver Fritz, "Introduction," in *Atlas of Digital Architecture*, ed. Ludger Hovestadt, Urs Hirschberg, and Oliver Fritz (Basel: Birkhäuser, 2020), 34–7.

21. Andrew Witt, "A Machine Epistemology in Architecture. Encapsulated Knowledge and the Instrumentation of Design," *Candide* 3, no. 12 (2010): 37–88; Branko Mitrović, "Leon Battista Alberti, Mental Rotation, and the Origins of Three-Dimensional Computer Modeling," *Journal of the Society of Architectural Historians* 74, no. 3 (2015): 312–22.

22. Evans, *The Projective Cast*, 140; see also 136–42, 107–19.

23. Carpo, *The Alphabet and the Algorithm*, x; see also 77–9.

24. Anthony Hauck, Michael Bergin, and Phil Bernstein, "The Triumph of the Turnip," in *Fabricate 2017*, ed. Achim Menges, et al. (London: UCL Press, 2017), 19; see also 16–21.

25. Werner Oechslin, "Architekturmodell—'Idea Materialis'," in *Die Medien und die Architektur*, ed. Wolfgang Sonne (Berlin: Deutscher Kunstverlag, 2011), 131–56.

26. Jakob Beetz et al., "Building Information Modeling (BIM)," in *Atlas of Digital Architecture*, 509; see also 507–29.

27. Richard Garber, "No More Stopping," *Architectural Design* 86, no. 1 (2016): 120–7.

28. Horst Bredekamp, *Image Acts: A Systematic Approach to Visual Agency* (Berlin: De Gruyter, 2018), 16; see also 242–8.

29. Horst Bredekamp, "Das Modell als Fetisch und Fessel," in *Bild und Bildlichkeit*, ed. Otfried Höffe (Halle (Saale): Leopoldina, 2012), 61–70. Bredekamp offers the concept of an "image act" as a counterpart to the "speech act."

30. Andreas Lepik, "Das Architekturmodell der frühen Renaissance—Die Erfindung eines Mediums," in *Architekturmodelle der Renaissance. Die Hamonie des Bauens von Alberti bis Michelangelo*, ed. Bernd Evers (Munich: Prestel, 1995), 63–4.

31. Frank D. Prager and Gustina Scaglia, *Brunelleschi: Studies of His Technology and Inventions* (Cambridge, MA: MIT Press, 1970), 23–44, 47–61; Udo Peil, "Die Große Kuppel von Florenz—Statik und Intuition im 15. Jahrhundert," *Bautechnik* 84, no. 1 (2007): 47–59.

32. Alberti, *On the Art of Building*, 34.

33. Bredekamp, "Das Modell als Fetisch und Fessel," 67–8.

34. Lepik, "Das Architekturmodell der frühen Renaissance," 19; see also Andreas Lepik, *Architekturmodell in Italien 1335–1550* (Worms: Werner, 1994), 166–79; Matthew Mindrup, *The Architectural Model: Histories of the Miniature and the Prototype, the Exemplar and the Muse* (Cambridge, MA: MIT Press, 2019), 92–102.

35. Antoine Bousquet, *The Eye of War: Military Perception from the Telescope to the Drone* (Minneapolis: University of Minnesota Press, 2018), 23; see also 21–40.

36. Werner Oechslin, "Das Architekturmodell zwischen Theorie und Praxis" in *Architekturmodelle der Renaissance. Die Hamonie des Bauens von Alberti bis Michelangelo*, ed. Bernd Evers (Munich: Prestel, 1995), 43–6.

37. Alberti, *On the Art of Building*, 317; Carpo, *The Alphabet and the Algorithm*, 20–1. Garber sees Alberti partially contradicting his own paradigm through such operative use of models, paralleling its purported reversal in BIM practices. Richard Garber, "Alberti's Paradigm," *Architectural Design* 79, no. 2 (2009): 88–93, esp. 92.

38. Marco Frascari, "Introduction: Models and Drawings—the Invisible Nature of Architecture," in *From Models to Drawings: Imagination and Representation in Architecture*, ed. Marco Frascari, Jonathan Hale, and Bradley Starkey (London: Routledge, 2007), 1; see also 2–8.

39. Mitrović, *Serene Greed*, 49–50.

40. Friedrich Balke, Bernhard Siegert, and Joseph Vogl, "Editorial," in *Modelle und Modellierung*, ed. Friedrich Balke, Bernhard Siegert, and Joseph Vogl (Munich: Wilhelm Fink Verlag, 2014), 5–8.

41. Bernd Mahr, "Modelle und ihre Befragbarkeit. Grundlagen einer allgemeinen Modelltheorie," *Erwägen Wissen Ethik* 16, no. 3 (2015), 332.

42. Horst Rittel, "The Reasoning of Designers," working paper A-88-4 (Stuttgart: IGP, 1988).

43. Reinhard Wendler, "Zu einer Unschärferelation der Modelle. Präzision und Produktivität mehrdeutiger Modelle in der Gestaltung," in *Haare Hören—Strukturen Wissen—Räume Agieren. Berichte aus dem interdisziplinären Labor "Bild Wissen Gestaltung*," ed. Horst Bredekamp and Wolfgang Schäffner (Bielefeld: transcript, 2015), 138–39.

44. Francesca Hughes, *The Architecture of Error: Matter, Measure, and the Misadventures of Precision* (Cambridge, MA: MIT Press, 2014), 5.

45. Beetz, et al., "Building Information Modeling (BIM)," 523–5.

46. Daniel Cardoso Llach, "Builders of the Vision. Technology and the Imagination of Design" (Ph.D. diss, Massachusetts Institute of Technology, 2012), 164. See also Daniel Cardoso Llach, *Builders of the Vision: Software and the Imagination of Design* (London: Routledge, 2015).

47. Nat Oppenheimer, "An Enthusiastic Sceptic," *Architectural Design* 79, no. 2 (2009): 105.

48. Phil Bernstein, "Intention to Artefact," in *Digital Workflows in Architecture*, ed. Scott Marble (Basel: Birkhäuser, 2012), 70; see also 64–71.

49. Michael Petry, *The Art of Not Making: The New Artist/Artisan Relationship* (London: Thames & Hudson, 2012), 6–11.

50. Greg Lynn, "Everybody's An Architect These Days," in *Out of Hand: Materializing the Postdigital*, ed. Ronald T. Labaco (London: Black Dog, 2013), 14–19.

51. Bob Sheil and Ron Packman, "Making a Bang," *Architectural Design* 75, no. 4 (2005): 70–7.

52. Herwig Bretis, "ArtEngineering—Ingenieurleistungen für die Kunst," *DETAIL Structure* 2 (2016): 8–9.

53. Lepik, "Das Architekturmodell der frühen Renaissance," 84–5.

CHAPTER 8

THE HUMAN BODY AS A SPACE OF DIPLOMACY: *STUDI SULLE PROPORZIONI* AT THE IX MILAN TRIENNALE IN 1951

Federica Vannucchi

Presented at the IX Milan Triennale in 1951, the exhibition *Studi sulle proporzioni* (Studies on Proportion) revived an architecture centered on human proportions. The exhibition was designed by architect Francesco Gnecchi-Ruscone and curated by Carla Marzoli, the owner of the antiquarian bookshop La Bibliofila, a well-known meeting place for Italian and European intellectuals alike in Milan.[1] *Studi sulle proporzioni* collected manuscripts, works of art, photographic reproductions, and objects that demonstrated how proportional systems had shaped architecture from antiquity to modernity. It asserted the contemporaneity of the topic by systematically arranging the exhibited materials on a black thin tubular structure designed strictly following Le Corbusier's Modulor. This system of proportional measurements was outlined by the Swiss architect in a book dedicated to the topic published only one year before the Triennale (see Figure 8.1 and Plate 6).[2] A few months after the opening of the exhibition, Marzoli also organized an international conference entitled *De divina proportione: Il primo convegno internazionale sulle proporzioni nelle arti* (On Divine Proportion: The First International Conference on Proportion in Arts, September 27 to 29, 1951), in which an exceptional coterie of North American and European speakers would participate. James Ackerman, Max Bill, Gillo Dorfles, Matila Ghyka, Sigfried Giedion, Le Corbusier, Pier Luigi Nervi, Ernesto N. Rogers, Alfred Roth, Giuseppe Samonà, Andreas Speiser, Eva Tea, Rudolf Wittkower, and Bruno Zevi, among others, discussed systems of proportions in architecture and art as well as in mathematics, engineering, physics, biology, music, and sociology.[3] In the conference, proportional systems were understood as sets of organizing principles that were intended to enable a "harmoniously" integrated form of design knowledge that extended beyond disciplinary divisions. But, most importantly, its participants agreed on what seemed, in the aftermath of World War II, to be a necessary and universal quest for the "humanization" of modern architecture through the application of human proportions to its construction.

As the conference discussed the use of proportions in contemporary architectural practice, however, the human body presented at the exhibition was not simply a model for buildings design but also—and most importantly—a carefully crafted vessel for diplomatic exchange. Its assumed universality was confined to specific geographic boundaries and ideological claims with clear ties to the international tensions that were escalating into the Cold War. Marzoli's exhibition and conference took form against this backdrop, in the office of the Triennale's president Ivan Matteo Lombardo, who had served as Italy's Minister of Industry and Trade until 1950 and was its Minister of Foreign

Figure 8.1 Carla Marzoli with Francesco Gnecchi-Ruscone, view of *Studi sulle proporzioni*, IX Milan Triennale, Milan, 1951. Courtesy of the Archivio Fotografico, La Triennale di Milano, Milan.

Trade in 1951. Lombardo's exchanges with Marzoli hardly concealed the political utility of the Milan Triennale and, in particular, the *Studi sulle proporzioni*. In keeping with the politics of Italy's center-right, Lombardo turned the Milan Triennale into a diplomatic enclave for the European Recovery Program, which Lombardo had himself negotiated with the United States.[4] *Studi sulle proporzioni* demonstrates how the Milan Triennale was able to present a new architecture paradigm—the "humanization" of modern architecture by proportional systems—to a national and international audience, and, at the same time, how the latter served a specific geopolitical end in the diplomatic negotiation of the Atlantic Alliance, the precursor to NATO.

Prelude: the meeting between Marzoli and Lombardo

Dedicated to *Merce e Standard* (Products and Standards), the IX Milan Triennale was the second exhibition to be presented to the public since the end of World War II. As organization of this event started in early 1948, the Triennale was subjected to a plethora of media attacks because of lingering controversies surrounding the previous exhibition.[5] The VIII Milan Triennale, entitled *L'abitazione* (Habitation, 1947), did not simply display its exhibits at the Palazzo dell'Arte, the show's traditional venue. Its curator, rationalist architect and communist activist Piero Bottoni, constructed a low-income housing complex in Milan named the "Quartiere Triennale 8" (QT 8, for short). Labeled derogatively the "communist Triennale" by members of center-right political parties, this show became a battleground for the electoral campaign of 1948.[6] After the Christian Democrats' pivotal victory over their left-wing rivals, a center-right alliance—the so-called *centrismo*—was established that would dominate the Italian parliament without interruption until 1962. At the same time, the Italian Communist Party left parliament in a concession to the government, so that Italy could benefit from the European Recovery Program.

It was during *centrismo*'s reign that the Milan Triennale was restructured. In 1949, the parliament approved a new statute for the Milanese institution, one that reorganized the institution into two distinct wings: the Administrative Council, its explicitly political organ, and a newly defined architectural division. The latter was subdivided into two committees whose departments stressed the importance of research over physical realization. Although the plan fell through, the intent was to use the Milan Triennale as a national research center for the development of urbanism, architecture, and industrial design. Of the two committees, the Study Center was supposed to examine the current state of architecture as well as define the exhibition's theme and overall articulation, while the Executive Committee was to carry out the program. The members of the Administrative Council were to be appointed by the President of the Republic based on the suggestions offered by various actors that included government ministers, Milan's city hall, architectural leagues, and artist and artisan unions. The Administrative Council reflected a plurality of the various political parties then sitting in parliament, while also restoring political control to the Triennale.

As the Triennale was undergoing its political restructuring, Marzoli held a series of meetings with Lombardo and the administration of the Palazzo dell'Arte. In early September 1950, the Executive Committee had contacted several publishing houses, asking them to curate an exhibition under the rather generic theme of the evolution of the Italian art book during the twentieth century. Marzoli accepted the appointment and proposed a program that went well beyond the initial ambition. Already well known in Milanese architectural circles for her antiquarian bookshop and for editing several books for the publishing houses La Chimera and La Bibliofila, Gillo Dorfles recalled that:

> Carla Marzoli was an extremely interesting figure: at that time, she had an antiquarian bookshop in via Manzoni and she was on very friendly terms with all of us, that is, with the BBPR, with Albini, with Zanuso, and we—this group of architects and sympathizers—met her very often. She had no particular academic qualifications but she was a very intelligent and moderately well-connected woman, so she was able to gather people from the academic world and at the same time from the *haute* society. I remember seeing at her book shop Le Corbusier, Roth, Bill and all these intellectuals who often came to Milan at the time.[7]

Her correspondence with the Triennale organizers and various participants in the conference—in particular with Le Corbusier and Wittkower—together with her conversations with the Museum of Modern Art in New York and UNESCO (the former regarding a proposed second conference on proportions to be held in New York, which was never realized) were evidence of Marzoli's exceptional ability to establish a network of key players. Often the only woman operating in a world of men, Marzoli rose to a vital role in the post-World War II discussion of proportional systems in architecture, thanks to her determination, foresight, mediating skills, and proficiency in speaking English and French as well as Italian.[8]

In Marzoli's correspondence with Lombardo at the end of February of 1951, she discussed the program of her exhibition, scheduled to open in May of the same year. Marzoli asked Lombardo to meet a few days later to define the exhibition program and form. Between Marzoli's initial involvement and her letter to Lombardo, the exhibition went through several changes of program and title. In her February letter, Marzoli proposed the title *Exhibition on the Studies of Proportion through Ancient and Modern Treatises* or, more simply, *Harmony*. A few days later, *Harmony* became "divine."[9] The two interlocutors agreed on the provisional title *Divine Harmony*. Although inspired by Pacioli's treatise entitled *De divina proportione* (1509), "divine" did not qualify "proportion," as it would later in the international conference *De Divina Proportione* at the Palazzo dell'Arte. In place of "proportion," it was the concept of "harmony" that was characterized as "divine." Interestingly, while "proportion" belonged to a specifically architectural design language, "harmony" could speak to both an architecture audience as well as to a wider public. It was towards the latter that Marzoli's description of the exhibition was directed. In the catalog entry for what would finally come to be named *Studi sulle proporzioni*, she explained that "this exhibition aims to bring together cultures of different and distant times and countries according to that universal harmony that, without minimally limiting them, informs and supports every invention and every creation of man, whether artistic or scientific or technical."[10] In its plural declination, "cultures" here referred to ideas and customs of those societies which Marzoli wished to see unified through their shared artistic, scientific, and technical discoveries. "Harmony" referred to the relationship among these cultures. In other words, through her use of the term "harmony," Marzoli turned an architectural precept into an argument about cultural politics.

To the architectural scholars invited to participate in the conference *On De divina proportione*, "harmony" referred to the Albertian *concinnitas* as defined in *De re aedificatoria* (1485) and interpreted in Wittkower's *Architectural Principles in the Age of Humanism* (1949).[11] Alberti had famously defined *concinnitas* as "a harmony of all the parts ... fitted together with such proportion and connection that nothing could be added, diminished, or altered but for the worse."[12] Wittkower followed suit, noting that "according to Alberti's well-known mathematical definition, based on Vitruvius, beauty consists in a rational integration of the proportions of all the parts of a building in such a way that every part has its absolutely fixed size and shape and nothing could be added or taken away without destroying the harmony of the whole."[13] The British art historian used the terms harmony and proportion interchangeably as both a mathematical equation of proportionality between parts and the whole (i.e. harmonic ratio) and an aesthetic category qualifying the application of such proportionality in design.[14] But the two terms did not refer simply to architecture. Wittkower added that the fascination of the architects of the fifteenth and sixteenth centuries with harmony and proportions was to be found in the Vitruvian figure described by the ancient Roman author in the Third Book of his *De architectura* (first century BCE). There, Vitruvius spoke of a human body inscribed in a circle and a square which to the Renaissance architects suggested a metaphysical relationship between the macrocosm—in its various forms of nature, the universe, and God—and the microcosm—the perfection of the human body.[15] To express this fascination, Wittkower collected a selection of Vitruvian figures in his publication, while, of all available Renaissance architects, he cited Pacioli's *De divina proportione* to explain the cosmological parallelism. It was thus not at all surprising that the exhibition reserved a central space for Pacioli's manuscript and the portrait of him attributed to Jacopo de' Barbari, while the conference was named *De divina proportione*.

Whereas Wittkower's influential publication offered a framework for the exhibition, in the *De Divina Proportione* conference it was Sigfried Giedion who defined the terms of the debate since, for personal reasons, Wittkower could not attend the entirety of the event. In his talk on "The Whole and the Part in Contemporary Architecture," Giedion explained his understanding of harmony, which came to define a general intention of the event. For the Swiss historian, "harmony" qualified, once again, Alberti's relationship between the whole and the parts, but, unlike the Renaissance architect, this relationship identified an epistemological shift. In his talk, Giedion stated:

> The renewed interest in proportions as a relationship between the whole and the parts is a symbol of a movement of revolt, of a movement of revolt against specialism, and above all the sign of a process of humanization … of a deep aspiration of our age, of a long-term path that cannot be stopped …
>
> Thus, we have entered a period in which in the sciences, hitherto absolutely specialized and closed in on themselves, have returned to thinking about the problems of form resumes (perhaps in the terms in which they are spoken of today, perhaps also for the needs of nuclear power, for example, but this need is felt in all fields of investigation).[16]

As much discussed in the arts as in the sciences, proportional systems were for Giedion viable principles enabling the definition of a universal form of knowledge, one that encompassed the specialization of modern disciplinary fields. Interestingly, this universalism was advocated while another was undergoing erosion because of the geopolitical reconfiguration of international powers after World War II.[17] Simply put, Giedion promoted a totalizing system of knowledge just when this idea showed its greatest fragility. In light of this, Marzoli's understanding of "harmony" seemed closer to Giedion's than initially expected. In her explanation for the catalog, "harmony" did not refer to the unity of different disciplines, as in Giedion's case, but rather to a general state of being in accord among what was defined as the "cultures" of different societies. And yet, the will to advance a totalizing apparatus was common to both.

In Marzoli's description, harmony was produced by "cultures of different and distant times and countries" which coexisted, by means of their texts, in the exhibition space. While her explanation was rather unexpected within the context of an architectural audience, it was perfectly in tune with the initial directives of the Triennale Executive Committee. Her quest directly reflected the general intention expressed by the Triennale organizers. As the organ entrusted with staging the Triennale every three years, the Executive Committee had presented an early version of the program to the Administrative Council in January of 1950. The program stated:

> As the only periodic international exhibition of modern decorative and industrial arts and modern architecture, the Milan Triennale is in a position to offer artists, architects and manufacturers from all over the world a meeting point and a way to place the problem on that larger plane that goes beyond the borders of any nation and that alone can determine a result that is universally valid.

It then added that "today, alongside a revision of artistic positions and the recognition of the unity of cultural and social problems, new ways of understanding formal and technical problems arise, and the inseparable link between architecture and other disciplines is reaffirmed."[18] The Executive Committee implicitly referred to the Milan Triennale as the first and only established, recurring architecture exhibition recognized by the Bureau International des Expositions (1928 to the present), the international organization that regulates international fairs.[19] Given this unique status, the Triennale organizers envisioned the Palazzo dell'Arte as an international catalyst for discussing architecture's universal values. The organizers shied away from more detailed indications, and the generality of the Executive Committee's programmatic lines reflected the heterogeneity of its members and the incompatibility of their positions. Chosen by an Administrative Council that was equally diverse, the members of the Executive Committee included architects Franco Albini and Piero Bottoni, Luciano Baldessari and Gio Ponti, graphic and industrial designer Marcello Nizzoli, educator Elio Palazzo, and painter Adriano di Spilimbergo. The diversity of views was apparent in the different programs formulated by each member. The interest in the *pezzo unico* (unique object) of Ponti could not possibly coincide with Bottoni's industrial object for the everyday. In the absence of a clear direction, Ponti played the leading role. Labeled by Ernesto N. Rogers "le leader de la bourgeoisie,"[20] Ponti was asked by Lombardo to head the Executive Committee. Although Ponti declined this role, the Executive Committee chose to follow his program, according to which the Triennale should promote "in fatto di cultura e di progresso, valori universali" (universal values in terms of culture and progress) by proposing new models of habitation.[21]

In 1951, the quest for universal harmony among different cultures in the aftermath of World War II did not come as a surprise. And yet, seen in light of Marzoli and Lombardo's meeting, a harmony among cultures acquired a rather specific meaning. While Lombardo was negotiating a place for Italy within the Atlantic Alliance, *Studi sulle proporzioni* aspired to promote a parallel state of consensus, accord, and unity—in other words, of harmony—among people. This hoped-for state of accord was mediated by the display of an idealized human body described for centuries in architectural treatises. Architectural history and disciplinarity—from the Vitruvian figure to Le Corbusier's Modulor—was put to the service of diplomatic affairs.[22] Presented in the early 1950s as a modern statement, this idealized body begged the question of whose "cultures of different and distant times and countries" were mentioned by Marzoli in the catalog and represented in the exhibition. That the idealized body presented by a female curator was gendered male as well as ethnically specific only highlights the many questions it raises. In other words, if a unity was wished for, who were the members of this unity? And, by the same token, who was excluded?

The exhibition

By walking into *Studi sulle proporzioni*, one might find some answers. Located on the second floor of the Palazzo dell'Arte, *Studi sulle proporzioni* consisted of an elongated rectangular room furnished with thin tubular profiles painted black. Gnecchi-Ruscone designed the tubular structures following the sequence 16, 36, 52, 88, 140, and 228, inspired by Le Corbusier's Modulor (see Figure 8.2). These minimal, precisely designed frames supported manuscripts, works of art, photographic reproductions, and objects. The manuscripts displayed were often rare first editions, loans that required endless negotiations with libraries and institutions around Europe. The curator divided them in two sections: "Studies on Proportion from Antiquity to the Seventeenth Century" and "Studies on Proportion During Modernity." The material was displayed in thirty-two separate vitrines, arranged following both a chronological and thematic succession. Works of art included paintings such as the fourteenth-century *Ideal City* from the Palazzo Ducale of Urbino and Bruno Munari's *Concave-Convex* of 1947. The exhibition included thirty photographs, mostly enlarged reproductions of images taken from the manuscripts. These represented buildings and projects whose designs followed a proportional system and included a view of the Great Pyramid of Giza, diagrams of the Parthenon, a plan of an ideal Greek theatre, and proportional diagrams of the Milan Cathedral, as well as the more recent enlarged reproduction of "Diagram 1. Point: Cool tension towards the center" from Wassily Kandinsky's book *Point and Line to Plane* (1926) and BBPR's *Monument to the Victims of the Concentration Camps* (1946). Importantly, these reproductions also included four scaled-up studies of the "ideal" human body. These were what the catalog described as "proportions of the male body" generically attributed to Leonardo's manuscripts; Albrecht Dürer's sketches of both a male and female body from his *Four Books on Human Proportion*; "the axial diagram of figure in motion" from Abraham Bosse's *Manière universelle de Monsieur Desargues pour pratiquer la perspective* (1648); and, of course, Le Corbusier's Modulor.[23]

Central to the exhibition was an extraordinary collection of medieval, early modern, and modern manuscripts that narrated a history of proportional systems from antiquity to the present. The itinerary started in ancient Greece, with texts by Pythagoras,

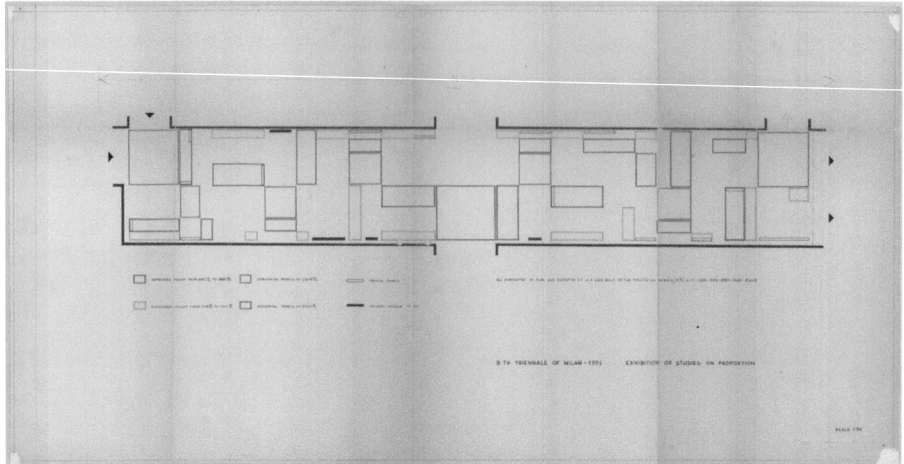

Figure 8.2 Francesco Gnecchi-Ruscone, Project for *Studi sulle proporzioni*, 1951. Courtesy of Archivio Francesco Gnecchi-Ruscone, CASVA, Milan.

Herodotus, Euclid, Aristotle, and Plato. The selection spoke of the intersection between architectural knowledge and the study of human proportions, and more generally, of proportional systems as means for decoding the laws of the natural world. The array of manuscripts continued into ancient Roman literature through Vitruvius' celebrated *De architectura*. It entered the Middle Ages with Villard de Honnecourt's *Sketchbook* and arrived at the Renaissance with Leon Battista Alberti, Filarete, Francesco di Giorgio Martini, Piero della Francesca, Leonardo da Vinci, Albrecht Dürer, Sebastiano Serlio, Andrea Palladio, Vignola, Vincenzo Scamozzi, Pietro di Giacomo Cataneo, and Girolamo Maggi. Luca Pacioli's *De divina proportione* was central to the exhibition as one of the most persuasive attempts of the Renaissance to relate the mathematical precision of proportions to the arts. Following Pacioli, it was mathematics—with the exactitude of its numbers—that revealed the divine law of creation.[24] This law was to find its application, Wittkower argued while citing Pacioli, in "the proportions of man . . . 'because from the human body derive all measures and their denominations and in it is to be found all and every ratio and proportion by which God reveals the innermost secret of nature.'"[25]

The exhibition continued with Viollet-le-Duc, then shifted from architects to trace the scientific revolution with Johannes Kepler, René Descartes, and Galileo Galilei, and entered what the exhibition defined as modernity with Albert Einstein and Enrico Fermi. From the discovery of the perpetual motion of celestial bodies to the equivalence of energy and mass, and finally the release of energy through atomic fission, the exhibition drew attention to the translation of natural phenomena into mathematical formulae and demonstrated the harmonic relationships between macrocosm and microcosm. The collection also encompassed the more contemporary and speculative work of Max Bill's *Fifteen Variations on One Theme* (1938), Matila Ghyka's *The Geometry of Art and Life* (1946), and Leonardo Sinisgalli on *Furor mathematicus* (1950). Finally, it featured the latest architectural scholarship on proportion that had inspired the exhibition: Le Corbusier's *Modulor*, along with Rudolf Wittkower's *Architectural Principles in the Age of Humanism* and James Ackerman's article "'Ars sine Scientia nihil est': Gothic Theory of Architecture at the Cathedral of Milan."[26]

The exhibition narrative sent visitors on a journey through an evolution of knowledge during the last 2,500 years. Although the exhibition focused on the question of proportions, the manuscripts shown were considered among the most important texts demonstrating the development of human thought. And yet, they described the evolution of knowledge of a specific part of the world: western (primarily European) thinking. The prototypical man advertised by *Studi sulle proporzioni* transcended national borders and temporal periodization but only, needless to say, within the limits of the Atlantic Alliance. Italy was strategically—and no less artificially—positioned within the Alliance's geography as its cultural epicenter, representing a lineage that dated back to the Roman Empire and the Renaissance. For Minister Lombardo and the center-right government, on the other hand, the inclusion of the Italian peninsula in the Atlantic Alliance followed the political strategy of *centrismo* as a means to negotiate a place for the country in the global chessboard of the Cold War. This was clear in a letter to the undersecretary of the Presidency Council, the Christian Democrat Giulio Andreotti, where Lombardo described the preparatory stages of the Triennale and the diplomatic relationships he had established. Switzerland, Spain, and West Germany had already agreed to participate. But the acceptance for which Lombardo expressed the most pride was the one he received from the United States, which had required "un lavoro estremamente delicato" (an extremely delicate negotiation).[27] Lombardo was used to the United States as an interlocutor. As part of the De Gasperi administration, he had conducted an extensive diplomatic exchange with American officials prior his Triennale appointment.

In February 1948, Italy and the United States negotiated the terms and conditions of the Treaty of Friendship, Commerce and Navigation in Rome. Lombardo was the politician chosen to lead the Italian delegation, while the treaty effectively anticipated the terms and conditions of the recovery plan announced by Secretary of State George Marshall in the same year. This occasion granted Lombardo a privileged position in the exchange between the two countries. A few months later, the American Ambassador to Italy, James Clement Dunn, wrote to George Marshall about Lombardo's anti-communist campaign within his party, the Socialist Party. While forcing the center-left coalition of De Gasperi to exclude the Communist Party from the government, Marshall identified Lombardo as the political leader most capable of directing Italy away from Soviet influence.[28]

Architecture exhibitions were used as a means of propaganda at the time of these negotiations between Italy and the United States over the European Recovery Program.[29] Both Dunn and Lombardo were present at the inauguration of the pavilion dedicated to the European Recovery Program at another event, the Fiera Campionaria in Milan in 1949, as well as at the exhibition *The City of the European Recovery Program* in Rome at the end of 1950 (see Figure 8.3). Although these exhibitions were intended to showcase the first urban projects sponsored by the Recovery Program, the new buildings were

Figure 8.3 Opening of the exhibition *La città dell'ERP*, November 22, 1950. Courtesy of Archivio Istituto Luce, Rome.

often lost in the background, overshadowed by other items. In the Rome exhibition, for instance, public attention was captured by a television set enclosed in an armillary sphere—interestingly, alluding once again to a cosmological relationship—surrounded by full-scale portraits of Italians commenting on the benefits of the Recovery Program. As pointed out in footage from the Luce Institute, *The City of the European Recovery Program* presented scaled-up portraits of a chef, a schoolteacher, a nurse, a postman, and so forth, that is, of common people captured in their daily lives.[30] The message was simple: the Recovery Program was explained to Italians by the faces of their compatriots who directly benefited as a result of the aid.

Studi sulle proporzioni adopted a similar strategy: it still displayed the human body. But in Marzoli's exhibition, the human body was not simply the inhabitant of architecture but rather the measurement system for the production of architectural knowledge and constructions. Following the exhibited treatises, architecture was the result of the measurement, calculation, and systematization of the human body. This process of systematization was clear in the framing system on which the figures of *Studi sulle proporzioni* lay. Uncannily, the thin black tubular structure running for the entire length of the elongated room recalled a tracing in black ink of a perspectival drawing (see Figure 8.4). It offered the visitor a sense of having entered Brunelleschi's discovery literally transposed into a three-dimensional space. Perspective was indeed central to the

Figure 8.4 Carla Marzoli with Francesco Gnecchi-Ruscone, view of *Studi sulle proporzioni*, IX Milan Triennale, Milan, 1951. Courtesy of the Archivio Fotografico, La Triennale di Milano, Milan.

exhibition. But what was provided in Marzoli's exhibition went beyond the intention of Renaissance architects.

In Pacioli's *De divina proportione*, perspective provided the mathematical formulation—the "mathematical vocabulary," Pacioli would argue—of space that has finally made architecture "disciplined." In other words, it was the mathematical rigor of perspective that allowed architecture to become a discipline, that is, a field of knowledge. Equally, in Marzoli's exhibition, the perspective "drawn" by the tubular structure also measured and controlled the space of the room along with the depictions of human figures in the room—from the Renaissance reinterpretations of the Vitruvian Man to Le Corbusier's Modulor. And yet, the thin black structure not only framed and measured the bodies drawn from the architectural treatises, but also measured the people moving through such space, namely, the exhibition visitors. From the photographs of the exhibition one can imagine a field of bodies—both drawn on the surfaces and moving through the exhibition—populating the three-dimensional perspective. It was this field of bodies framed by the perspectival structure that crafted the Milan Triennale as a diplomatic enclave. It did so to the extent that architecture served as a means of claiming the universality of a system holding people together.[31] The rigid, tense, and highly delicate "framework" ultimately turned the multiple pretexts for holding these people together—a universalizing aesthetic and political system—into matter. This frame was, without a doubt, a western construct. As the exhibition expressed its hope for this western universality, differences fell out of the picture. Without these differences, desired exchanges—including the diplomatic agreements of the Marshal Plan—seemed far more attainable.

Notes

1. Designed by Renzo Mongiardino, the bookshop was famous for its public talks by intellectuals such as Jean Starobinski, Jean-Paul Sartre, and Simon de Beauvoir. See "La Bibliofila de Carla Marzoli," *L'Illustré* 45 (November 7, 1946).

2. Le Corbusier, *Le Modulor: Essai sur une mesure harmonique à l'échelle humaine, applicable universellement à l'architecture et à la mécanique* (Boulogne: Éditions de l'Architecture d'aujourd'hui, 1950). After the IX Milan Triennale in 1951, Le Corbusier published his *Le Modulor II. 1955 (la parole est aux usagers), suite de "Le modulor" "1948"* (Boulogne: Éditions de l'Architecture d'aujourd'hui, 1955). For the conception and evolution of Le Corbusier's Modulor, see Jean-Louis Cohen, "Le Corbusier's Modulor and the Debate on Proportion in France," *Architectural Histories* 2, no. 1 (2014): 1–14, DOI: http://dx.doi.org/10.5334/ah.by.

3. For the conference proceedings, see Fulvio Irace and Anna Chiara Cimoli (eds), *La divina proporzione. Triennale 1951* (Milan: Electa, 2007).

4. See Agostino Giovagnoli, *L'Italia nel nuovo ordine mondiale: politica ed economia dal 1945 al 1947* (Milan: Vita e pensiero, 2000); and Kaeten Mistry, *The United States, Italy and the Origins of Cold War: Waging Political Warfare 1945–1950* (Cambridge: Cambridge University Press, 2014).

5. On negative reviews of the 8th Milan Trinnale, see Raffaele Calzini, "Quartiere modello a Milano," *Corriere della sera* (April 13, 1947): 3; "Ultimo atto alla 'Triennale,'" *Corriere della sera* (August 14, 1947): 2; Raffaele Calzini, "L'Ottava Triennale si è aperta. Molti problemi e poche soluzioni," *Corriere della sera* (June 1, 1947): 3; Leonardo Sinisgalli, "Bilancio dell'Ottava Triennale," *Comunità* (November 15, 1947): 5.

6. Ernesto N. Rogers, "Esperienza dell'Vlll Triennale," *Domus* 221 (July 1947): 2.

7. "Carla Marzoli è stata una figura estremamente interessante: a quell'epoca aveva una libreria antiquaria in via Manzoni ed era molto amica di tutti noi, cioè dei BBPR, di Albini, di Zanuso, e noi—questo gruppo di architetti e di simpatizzanti—la vedevamo molto spesso. Non aveva particolari titoli accademici ma era una donna molto intelligente e moderatamente ben introdotta, per cui riusciva a raccogliere persone del mondo accademico e insieme anche della haute cittadina. Mi ricordo di aver visto da lei Le Corbusier, Roth, Bill e tutti questi intellettuali che allora venivano spesso a Milano." Gillo Dorfles, "Gillo Dorfles," in *La divina proporzione. Triennale 1951*, ed. Fulvio Irace and Anna Chiara Cimoli (Milan: Electa, 2007), 140.

8. Proof of Marzoli's position in the international scene is, for instance, the request to contribute to the exhibition *The Modern Movement in Italy: Architecture and Design* (1954) at the

Museum of Modern Art in New and its catalog by G. E. Kidder Smith, *Italy Builds—Its Modern Architecture and Native Inheritance* (New York: Reinhold Publishing Corporation, 1955). For the exchange of Marzoli and Smith, see Anna Chiara Cimoli, "Il Primo Convegno Internazionale sulle Proporzioni nelle Arti: una storia interrotta," in *La divina proporzione. Triennale 1951*, ed. Fulvio Irace and Anna Chiara Cimoli (Milan: Electa, 2007), 202–37.

9. Carla Marzoli, Letter to Ivan Matteo Lombardo, dated February 23, 1951, and Giuseppe Gorgerino, Letter to Carla Marzoli, dated February 27, 1951, TRN_09_DT, Box 113—Mostra Studi sulle proporzioni, Archivio Storico La Triennale di Milano, Milan.

10. "Questa mostra si propone di avvicinare culture di età e paesi diversi e lontani in funzione di quell'armonia universale che, pur senza minimanete limitarle, informa e regge ogni invenzione e ogni creazione dell'uomo, sia artistica che scientifica o tecnica." Carla Marzoli, "Studi sulle proporzioni," *Nona Triennale di Milano* (Milan: SAME, 1951), 114.

11. See Alina A. Payne, "Rudolf Wittkower and Architectural Principles in the Age of Modernism," *Journal of the Society of Architectural Historians* 53, no. 3 (September 1994): 322–42; and more recently, Francesco Benelli, "Rudolf Wittkower versus Le Corbusier: A Matter of Proportion," *Architectural Histories* 3, no. 1 (2015): 1–11, DOI: http://doi.org/10.5334/ah.ck.

12. Leon Battista Alberti, *On the Art of Building in Ten Books*, trans. Joseph Rykwert, Neil Leach, and Robert Tavernor (Cambridge, MA: MIT Press, 1988), 156.

13. Rudolf Wittkower, *Architectural Principles in the Age of Humanism* (1949) (London: Academy Edition, 1988), 18.

14. For "proportion as ratios" and "proportion as architectural beauty," see Matthew A. Cohen, "Introduction: Two Kinds of Proportion," *Architectural Histories* 2, no. 1 (2014): 1–25, DOI: http://dx.doi.org/10.5334/ah.bv.

15. See Spyros Papapetros, "Architecture, Cosmology, and the Real World," *Perspecta* 42 (2010): 108–25.

16. "La rinascita dell'interesse per le proporzioni come rapporto tra il tutto e le parti è simbolo di un movimento di rivolta, di un movimento di rivolta contro lo specialismo, e soprattutto il segno di un processo di umanizzazione … di una profonda aspirazione della nostra epoca, di un percorso a lungo termine che non può essere arrestato …

"Così, siamo entrati in un periodo in cui nelle scienze, fino ad ora assolutamente specializzate e chiuse in se stesse, si torna a pensare ai problemi della forma (forse nei termini in cui se ne è parlato oggi, forse anche per le necessità della fisica nucleare, ad esempio, ma quest'esigenza si avverte in tutti i campi di indagine)." Sigfied Giedion, "Il tutto e la parte nell'architettura contemporanea," in *La divina proporzione. Triennale 1951*, ed. Fulvio Irace and Anna Chiara Cimoli (Milan: Electa, 2007), 74.

17. As noted already in Papapetros, "Architecture, Cosmology, and the Real World."

18. "La Triennale di Milano, per essere l'unica Esposizione internazionale periodica delle arti decorative e industriali moderne e dell'architettura moderna, è nella posizione di offrire agli artisti, agli architetti, alla produzione di tutto il mondo un punto di incontro ed il modo di porre il problema su quel piano più vasto che supera i confini di ogni Nazione e che solo può determinare una risultante che sia valida universalmente." And also: "Nel presente periodo accanto ad una revisione delle posizioni artistiche, ed al riconoscimento della unità dei problemi culturali e sociali, sorgono nuovi modi di intendere i problemi formali e tecnici, e si riafferma il nesso inscindibile fra l'architettura e le altre discipline." Executive Committee, Allegato B. al verbale e della seduta del Cons. Di Amm. Dei giorni 9/10 gennaio 1950, TRN_9_DT, Box 13—Consiglio di Amministrazione, Archivio Storico La Triennale di Milano, Milan.

19. See Bureau International des Expositions, https://www.bie-paris.org/site/en/.

20. Ernesto N. Rogers, *Architettura, misura e grandezza dell'uomo: Scritti 1930–1969*, vol 1, ed. Serena Maffioletti (Padua: Il Poligrafo, 2010), 42.

21. Gio Ponti, Program Summary dated November 25, 1949, TRN_9_DT, Box 162—Programma Nona Triennale, Archivio Storico La Triennale di Milano, Milan.

22. On the "ideal body" in architecture, see, among others, George Dodds and Robert Tavernor (eds), *Body and Building: Essays on the Changing Relation of Body and Architecture* (Cambridge, MA: MIT Press, 2005); and Fabiola López-Durán, *Eugenics in the Garden: Transatlantic Architecture and the Crafting of Modernity* (Austin: University of Texas Press, 2019).

23. Abraham Bosse's complete title is *Manière universelle de Monsieur Desargues pour pratiquer la perspective par petit-pied, comme le géométral, ensemble les places et proportions des fortes & faibles touches, teintes ou couleurs.* Carla Marzoli, "Studi sulle proporzioni," *Nona Triennale di Milano* (Milan: SAME, 1951), 116–17.

24. Pacioli claimed that architecture could be disciplined through the application of "a mathematical vocabulary," which, he believed, allowed perspective to be calculated. As he explained, "Questo vocabolario matematico, excelso Duca, fia greco derivato da μαθηματικός, che in nostra lengua sona quanto a dire disciplinabile; e al proposito nostro per scienze e discipline matematici se intendano aritmetica, geometria, astrologia, musica, prospettiva, architettura e cosmografia e qualunc'altra da queste dependente." Luca Pacioli, *De divina proportione* (1497), in *Scritti rinascimentali di architettura*, ed. Arnaldo Bruschi (Milan: Edizioni il Polifilo, 1978), 67.

25. Wittkower, *Architectural Principles in the Age of Humanism*, 25.

26. Le Corbusier, *Le Modulor*; Wittkower, *Architectural Principles in the Age of Humanism*; James Ackerman "'Ars sine Scientia nihil est': Gothic Theory of Architecture at the Cathedral of Milan," *Art Bulletin* 31, no. 2 (June 1949): 84–111.

27. Ivan Matteo Lombardo, Letter to Giulio Andreotti, dated September 23, 1950, TRN_9_DT, Box 172, Folder 03—Andreotti S.E. Dr. Giulio / Roma, Archivio Storico La Triennale di Milano, Milan. See also "Ivan M. Lombardo Oral History Interviews" at the National Archives and Records Administration, https://www.trumanlibrary.gov/library/oral-histories/lombardo.

28. Giovagnoli, *L'Italia nel nuovo ordine mondiale*, 147–53.

29. See, for instance, Raffaele Bedarida, "Operation Renaissance: Italian Art at MoMA, 1940–1949," *Oxford Art Journal* 35, no. 2 (2012): 147–69.

30. La Settimana INCOM / 00518, "Alla presenza dell'ambasciatore Dunn e di autorità italiane e statunitensi, si apre a Roma la mostra 'Città dell'ERP' con opere e progetti frutto dei contributi del piano Marshall," November 22, 1950, Archivio Istituto Luce, Rome.

31. As Joseph Nye states in *Soft Power*, a country is most likely to establish lasting international relationships when it promotes values that can be understood as universal. Joseph Nye, *Soft Power: The Means to Success in World Politics* (New York: Public Affairs, 2004).

CHAPTER 9
MODELS AND METHODS OF ARCHITECTURE AND CLIMATE

Daniel A. Barber

The received traditions of modern architecture have drawn on strong connections to Italy: its natural splendor, its refined urbanism, its cultural sophistication. Many of the tropes and narratives that center Italy as the locus of architectural tradition also center a premise of architecture as an art of form-giving, be that decorative and linguistic or spatial and affective. Other lineages of this heritage are similarly robust. This chapter is concerned with yet another: the influence of Italy on a substantive, though heretofore under-recognized, thread of modern architecture focused on designing a relationship to climate. It tells the story of a pair of architects—the Olgyay brothers—working in the mid-twentieth century, for whom the relationship between architecture and climate was foundational.

As an aspect of modern architectural research and practice, climate encompasses both regional weather patterns and thermal conditions (exterior and interior).[1] The story of the Olgyays is instructive in that it provides evidence of an ambitious attempt to focus architectural knowledge on climate's dynamics—an attempt that emerged, as will become clear, in relationship to an Italian sojourn—while also allowing for a wider reconsideration of the progressive contours of modern architectural ideas. It presents a shift in context that allows for a rich understanding of the broader stakes of climatic interventions in architecture.

I

The brothers Victor and Aladar Olgyay are best known for their development of a climate-focused design method from the 1930s to the 1960s—one that, indeed, serves as the basis for computational climate performance methods in use today.[2] Victor's experience in Italy early in his career was formative. He went to Rome in 1935, soon after completing his degree at the Royal Hungarian Technology University in Budapest, having been awarded a prize to study at the Scuola Superiore di Architettura at the age of twenty-five.

Interest in modern architecture preoccupied discussions in Budapest and Hungary while the Olgyays were in school. The Technology University was mired in controversy in the late 1920s as modern techniques were proposed and rejected. By the mid-1930s, many advocates for the new architecture had left to join their young compatriot Marcel Breuer, who joined the Weimar Bauhaus in 1921 (he would be instrumental in bringing the Olgyays to the United States in the 1940s). Though the situation at the university was contested—a complex of influences involving both modernists and the then-illegal Communist Party—the Hungarian CIAM group was active in the early 1930s, mounting three exhibitions, including one whose title translates as "For the New Buildings" in early 1932, of which we can assume the Olgyays, then studying in Budapest, were aware. Modernism was seen in many quarters as the design strategy of the future, a premise clearly impressed upon the young twins.

Victor Olgyay's year in Rome was an opportunity to search for aesthetic and social trajectories amidst this contested milieu, and to devise an architecture appropriate to the emergent *esprit nouveau*; a term used here pointedly given Le Corbusier's evident influence. Rome was, for Olgyay, and somewhat contrary to its deeply layered historical richness and the internal tussles of the faculty at the Valle Giulia, a blank slate on which he could project his ambitions.

Following Victor's return from Rome and over the next decade, the Olgyays completed more than forty commissions in Hungary. Arriving in the United States in 1945, following a brief spell in Indiana at Notre Dame, the twins soon made their way to the Massachusetts Institute of Technology to work on the Solar Energy Fund projects being supported there right after the war. They were preceded, though, by a volume that served as a sort of thick calling card: *The Work of Architects Olgyay + Olgyay*, published in 1944.[3] Targeting an American audience, it nonetheless appeared in both Hungarian and English, with a cover by Gyorgy Kepes, a preface by Breuer, and an introduction by the New York architectural critic Peter Blake. It described their trajectory over the previous decade— that is, after Victor Olgyay's return from Italy. The first project it presents is "Apartment House, Roma 1936" (See Figure 9.1).

It would take another move, to Princeton in 1952, and the establishment there of a climate-method-focused project at the Princeton Architectural Laboratory, and then the publication of *Solar Control and Shading Devices* in 1957, before design commissions started to materialize in the US. These were mostly houses around Princeton, as well as a few solar or climate design-focused experimental buildings. Most of their work was as specialists, providing tools and techniques to assess a building's climatic opportunities. Building on their connections to Breuer (then at Harvard), they consulted for Josep Lluis Sert, Walter Gropius, and others. They established themselves as experts in the functional process of understanding how and where to place *brise soleil* and other shading mechanisms to mitigate solar radiation, and later developed a more comprehensive climate-modeling method involving a range of design, material, and site-based factors, with multiple phases and extensive research required. Indeed, having experienced a period of relative prominence in the Hungarian architecture scene, a decade "in the wilderness" saw them relegated to a more junior professional status, which explains, in part, a sort of retreat to the laboratory. For the ten years or so following their arrival in the US, the Olgyays were consumed with research in the solar and climatic capacities of architecture, seen as the legacy of interwar modern design techniques, and serving as the crucible from which their mature work and publications would materialize.

Barely noted in architectural-historical narratives until recently, climate was nonetheless a prominent concern for a range of well-known projects in the mid-century

Figure 9.1 "Apartment House, Roma, 1936," in *The Work of Architects Olgyay + Olgyay*, 1944. Courtesy Victor Olgyay.

period. Consider the work of the Ukranian architect Piotr Kowalski, a former MIT student of the Olgyays, who assisted Breuer in designing the UNESCO Headquarters in Paris, completed in 1958. His sun shading diagrams were essential to the orientation of the Y-shaped building and to the placement of the (somewhat ineffective) heat-absorbing glass elements protruding from this iconic facade.

The Olgyays were innovative in their specific realm of expertise; but they are also significant as an important case in the broader emergence of architects as researchers and of environmental research as a substantive trajectory for the design professional. This was evidenced not only at MIT and Princeton, in the Olgyays' own orbit, but also in such settings as the new Department of Architectural Science at the University of Sydney, established in this same period largely through the figure of Henry (Jack) Cowan, and the University of California Berkeley, after founding the new College of Environmental Design in 1959.[4] Practice, climate, and research were all aspects of the epochal shift to a modern disposition and design idiom, and help to understand how the events that shaped the Olgyays' work also opens up a more substantive analysis of new narratives and their integration into architecture's history.

II

The Roman apartment block with which the Olgyays' 1944 book opens was drawn during Victor's time in Italy. Among the familiar modernist tropes it exhibits is an interior flexibility: part of the living room can be turned into a study, the chairs can become a bench, the bedroom is separated by a collapsible screen. The interior views presented in the book frame the project in the stream of then-recent ideas around new ways of living and the role of the designer as both accommodating and engendering the new habits and practices imagined as part of the modernist *esprit nouveau*.

Also of interest is the pictorial framing of the elevation from a window across the street, invoking the building's presence in the city; and the slightly awkward "view from above" drawing that accompanies it. It takes a second to get one's visual bearings, suggesting that the project is part of a larger intervention in ways of thinking about and representing urban form and urban development being played out largely in the city's suburbs and periphery. "The rows of buildings," the Olgyays write, "were constructed East and West … a type of back-to-back house with four symmetrical flats on each floor."[5] Use of the phrase "were constructed" for this unbuilt project is likely an artifact of mistranslation (there are a number of such errors in tense and verb agreement throughout the book). Their mention of East and West, however, is highly significant, an early indication of their attention to solar orientation as being instrumental to integrating a building into both its urban and climatic contexts.

These concerns took on increasing importance in their work. Their first major built project, the so-called "House Reversed" in Budapest, designed right after Victor's return to Hungary from Italy, was completed in 1939. They turned the building towards the garden rather than to the city, facing the more prominent facade away from the street,

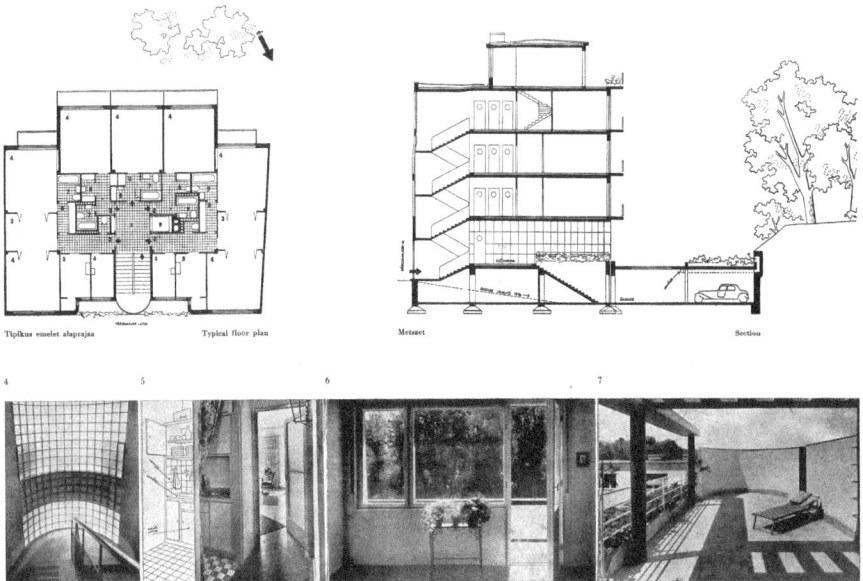

The most essential characteristic about this house is its preferring not to face the street. Not because this particular street in Buda would be distasteful. On the contrary, it is attractive. No architect would have dared twenty of thirty years ago to build a house in which the inhabitants would have no view of the street. The street is the living artery of the town. Why should we hate it ? But the street represents noise, dust and distraction ; why — we ask today — should the house be overwhelmed by it, with our leisure disturbed, and even our breathing poisoned by infected air ? When the architects of this house glanced through the other buildings in the street, which forgot the trees, bushes, the green splendour of the fresh grass behind their thick walls, they obviously thought, that men are slaves of queer customs : those also, the owners of luxury apartments the windows of which face not the sun with its healthy air, but the dusty street. So the two designers planned a reversed house backing the street, facing completely the garden.

We have advanced a long way from the „fashionable-front" architecture ; no one believes any longer the ceremonial attitudes of facades. Here, however, not only the front of the building was turned round, but the whole constructive rhythm of the architectural organism was reversed. Every room faces the hill and the big trees of the garden. Only the staircase incorporated into a glass cylinder, and the windows of the accessory units face the street. This elevation is closed, while the opposite side opens freely and sensitively to the garden with a pulsating lively rhythm born from the architecture itself. Here we see the creative power of architecture which is able to create something of a new expressive and practical nature without weighing considerations and huge fantasies, yielding without restraint and scruple to the right of inner rhythm. The building is erected on two levels, the street being lower — here the ground floor correspodents to the basement of the garden side — which is cleverly used as a garage. The tenant opens the garage with his key and after parking his car can, without leaving the building, reach the lift which takes him to his flat. Rational as this arrangement is, just as great attention and consideration were paid by the architects to all the details of the house, with the aim of perfecting the use of the flats for the inhabitants. By the use of balconies and large windows along the whole length of the building, every flat can enjoy the garden air. On the top floor is a roof terrace with semi-covered verandah, garden and shower.

The two architects did not follow the principle which ignores everything but the eloquence of extravagant palaces. They thought only of the eighteen families moving into the building and trying to make their lives healthier and brighter. And just because they scorned rhetoric, they justified themselves.

arch. Giancarlo Palanti. Milano, 1942 "DOMUS"

Kerti homlokzat
The garden front

16

Figure 9.2 Olgyay + Olgyay, "House Reversed," Budapest, 1939. Courtesy Victor Olgyay.

113

and towards the sun-exposed south—an intervention that defies modern architecture's general focus on the city. This unorthodox approach suggested that orientation was of primary concern—climatic context trumped urbanistic considerations—thus the sun-facing facade was both more climatically and formally active (see Figure 9.2).

The garden facade had a massive shading frame as part of an extruded, boxed balcony to mitigate the entrance of the sun into the interior. This was not done with the sort of careful scientific attention to the details of the local climate the Olgyays would later employ, because these precise calculation tools were not yet available. The 1939 project instead benefited from a more impressionistic sun-path analysis, which clarified the extent of the extrusion, the character of the secondary shades, and the general orientation to the garden. The sort of gestural climatic moves made in "House Reversed" were inadequate for impacting the thermal interior, relatively ineffective and not quite realizing their climatic ambition. Perhaps they did not quite justify the turn away from the city. "House Reversed" illustrated, to the Olgyays, the need for greater technical and methodological precision in articulating an effective and convincing climatic modernism.

Reviewing the project in 1942, Giancarlo Palanti emphasized the open-ness of "House Reversed" to the parkland behind, writing that, "Every room faces the hill and the big trees in the garden." Yet his interest was drawn to new architectural parameters: "[H]ere we see," Palanti continued, "the creative power of architecture which is able to create something of a new expressive and practical nature without . . . huge fantasies . . . yielding without restraint the inner rhythms."[6] The brothers themselves celebrated the shading effectiveness of the balcony, though they lamented the lack of specificity in understanding how the extruded elements performed.

A commission for the Stühmer Chocolate Factory outside Budapest, in 1941, saw a turn from this more impressionistic approach to a focused climatic engagement—in modeling, experimenting, and calculating to determine a facade system appropriate to the needs of the interior. The architect Donald Watson, a prominent solar designer in the 1970s, would later describe the building as "Corbu with numbers . . . [an] architectural design with the tools of the formative science of building climatology."[7] Indeed, we could credit the thermal complications of chocolate production—where it could be warm, where the goods needed to be protected from sunlight—as essential to refining the aspirations for a climate focused design method (see Figure 9.3).

At the Stühmer Factory it becomes clear that the tools and techniques of the new architecture were often, in the interwar period, articulated according to their capacity to manage climatic conditions. One is left to consider how these narratives were so effectively suppressed over the last century. Put somewhat differently, the celebration of steel, concrete, and glass as the primary building materials of modernism is also a frustration of methods and traditions that had adapted a building to its regional weather conditions: thick masonry and limited fenestration, for example, in much of northern Europe; complex facade shading, natural ventilation, and volumetric considerations, for another, in Brazil. The purported universality of modernism was elaborated through new materials with dramatically different thermal properties. Before air conditioning

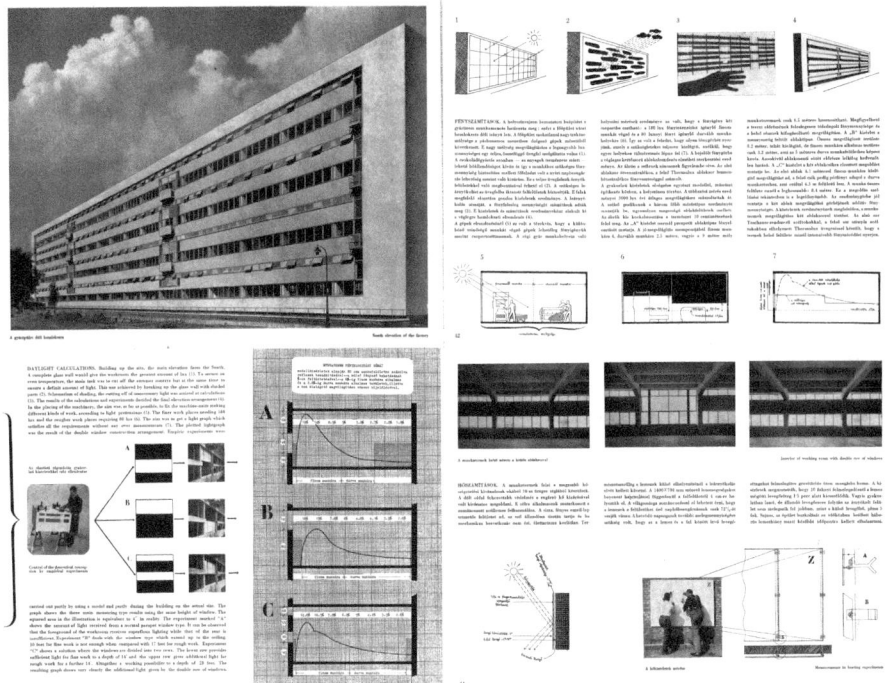

Figure 9.3 Olgyay + Olgyay, Stühmer Chocolate Factory outside Budapest, Hungary, 1941. Courtesy Victor Olgyay.

allowed for a universal approach, architects were concerned with how to adjust their methods to allow the facade to manage interior climate.

Glass was essential to modernism's cultural promise, but architects had to overcome its remarkably poor insulative qualities. Le Corbusier's statement, in Buenos Aires in 1930, that "architecture is about sunlight on floors" indicates, if a bit too poetically, how the basic question of solar incidence played a role in such well-known designs as the Villa Savoye, a project with which the Olgyays were of course familiar.[8] This capacity for climatic adaptability was essential to what one could call the globalization of the international style. Architects in Europe, Brazil, India, parts of West Africa, and across the Middle East, not to mention the United States, saw that the technological and social innovations of modernism not only allowed for open-ness in facade and plan, and the exhilaration of new spatial experience, but also led to a need to orient and selectively screen the facade according to the details of site-specific solar incidence and climatic patterns, with direct results on the daylight and thermal conditions of the interior. To pursue its self-appointed global mandate, modern architecture became a flexible mechanism of regional adaptation, a device for climatic engagement. That is, at least, until air conditioning systems filled these open spaces with mechanically cooled or heated air, finally fulfilling modernism's universal premise premise yet obviating the need for a climatic design-methodological approach.

In the late 1930s, the Olgyays were beginning to articulate and emphasize a climatic trajectory of modernist thought and experimentation with which they would be consumed, in building and writing, until the mid-1960s. The complexities of the chocolate factory, as suggested in their climatic-analytic diagrams and other drawings, among these other moments and events, were instrumental to the more elaborate method they developed to connect a building to its climate and site. Their research on a method for climatic analysis and adaptation captured in *Solar Control and Shading Devices* and *Design with Climate* (1963) led to the refined articulation of the concept of the comfort zone—a regulated condition for the thermal interior—and the charts and techniques to help architects understand this concept and design for it.

III

There are profound discursive obstacles to embracing the repositioning of architectural history and discourse according to its relevance to climatic debates, or to environmental considerations, or even relative to the broader construct of design research. As a general concept and perceived legacy of modernist experimentation, formalism is perhaps the most potent of these obstacles. A history of architectural modernism with a focus on the production of novel form has largely dominated the field's narratives since the 1960s. This preoccupation was rendered explicit in Peter Eisenman's 1963 doctoral thesis, "The Formal Basis of Modern Architecture," completed the same year as the publication of Victor Olgyay's best known book, *Design with Climate*. Eisenman's premise was that the iterative manipulation of platonic solids held a capacity to resolve the purported paradox of form and function. He claimed that this "autonomous" mode for architectural exploration was the essential influence of the modern movement. Modern architecture's "basis," as Eisenman's title has it, was "formal," with other concerns of the building following behind.[9]

This mode of formalist influence, as well as a discursive mechanism to elide socio-political context, was derived at least in part in Eisenman's well-known case from a close reading of Giuseppe Terragni's Casa del Fascio in Como.[10] In his reading, modern architecture's historical significance rests in the formal design tools that it engendered. This stance has shaped much of how architecture has been taught and debated for the last half-century. The formalist project involved a turn away from the social and political effects of architectural ideas and practices, towards an emphasis on its disciplinary "autonomy"—a premise that, with several substantive exceptions, continues to drive purportedly novel practices and pedagogies in the present.[11]

Behind this well-rehearsed facade of formalist experimentation, the history of architecture's relationship with climate is robust: it offers tantalizing context for many familiar projects and ideas, and opens out to new ways of thinking about architectural engagement with technology, environment, and society. Particularly in light of the escalating climate emergency, it also allows for a new sense of architecture's cultural resonance. How do we assign excellence to a given design project, according to what terms and parameters; according to what hoped-for consequences of the design intervention in the broader social realm? The computational production of novel form is still seen by many historians, critics, and practitioners as the metric of value. Innovation in architecture tends to involve the production of heretofore unimagined spatial experiences, generated through computational means. Concern over how those spaces and structures relate to the environmental conditions of the building has recently, again, become a topic of discussion.

There is of course, and increasingly, excellent work occurring in architecture focused not only on technical questions in search of energy efficiency, but also on histories of environmental culture and the relationship of patterns in the natural world to principles of design practice: on the elaboration of environmental cultures. Though, again until quite recently, such questions tended to not appear as central to the value of a building. Think, for example, of the Pritzker Prize, or high-profile building competitions, or global events such as the Venice Biennale. Climate might be seen as a technical concern, but it is less frequently seen as a cultural issue. While a comprehensive analysis of how architecture is valued—arguments about what, in fact, constitutes a substantive distinction in the context of differential evolution—exceeds the scope of this chapter, the historically conditioned terms of the formalist framework nonetheless become apparent. New narratives can begin to suggest alternative legacies and emphasize new criteria for assessing architectural ideas and practices, resonant with contemporary challenges.

One of the effects of inserting climate into architecture's histories is that it opens them towards a new set of events, and a new set of criteria, for understanding how that history has developed in relation to the present. Isabelle Stengers recently observed, "What is proper to every event is that it brings the future that will inherit from it into communication with a past narrated differently."[12] This is a complex formulation that bears rereading. The history described here, and the broader prospect for an environmental history of architecture to which it relates, starts to reframe the terms by which we consider a given architectural phenomenon to be seen as an *historical event*—a building, a drawing, an idea that opens up a different causal chain, with novel relationships to the present. Describing such events allows one to narrate the past differently, drawing out threads that have been concealed or ignored, so as to communicate with, and pose trajectories for, an as yet undetermined future. This causal complication, of a past rearticulated according to its relevance to possible futures, is the framework for the effect of climate on the history of architecture—its narratives and its implications.

How does Stengers help us to adjust our approach to questions of foundation, of origins, of imprints and footprints? How do buildings, events, and individuals, their interests and interventions, resonate across time and space differently in consequence of contemporary concerns? And how can we perform this sort of broad rescripting of architectural histories and their weight as we collectively consider the dynamics of buildings and the forces that construct them in the context of carbon emissions, climate disruptions, of settler colonialism, and economic inequities spiraling out of control? We search for some *ground*, albeit a different ground, but a means to establish novel conditions for the production of architectural knowledge, a surface to imprint.

IV

Consider as an event, in Stengers' terms, an episode from Victor Olgyay's Italian sojourn. It could be framed as an origin story: the moment when he visited the lemon houses on the shores of Lago di Garda and had something of an epiphany. While an origin implies an essential imprint, breadcrumbs left on the trail, the threads of emergence are a bit more scattered. Olgyay is, after all, just one of a number of possible figures to support a shift in the narration of mid-century modernism around the importance of climatic methods to developments in architectural design and its social effects.

To return, then, to Italy, and to the substance of this event that draws to the fore the significance of a different past—an Italian imprint left on the climate design discourse. In a recent essay on his father's life, Victor Olgyay (the son of the Victor Olgyay being discussed) writes that beyond the training his father received in Rome, the most influential aspect of his time in Italy was a visit, in 1935, to Limone sul Garda—here almost a decade before Limone became the southernmost extent of the Nazi advance. As the younger Olgyay writes:

> Nestled in the Italian Alps is the village of Limone . . . The area is temperate, warmer than the surrounding areas. The Dolomites rise thousands of feet to the north of the village, and Lake Garda hugs the southeast edge. These geographic conditions create the distinctive climate that allows the cultivation of lemons in this area, but not a few miles away. The opportunity to grow lemons in the Alps gave rise to the distinctive architecture of the "lemon houses," terraced structures with movable roofs and walls . . . Facing southeast and warmed by the sun, these buildings, which protect and nourish the delicate citrus in the variable alpine weather, are designed in *direct response* to the character of their place.[13]

An event, this visit, leads the older Olgyay to a perspective on architecture that connected it to climate, less on scientific terms and more according to a sort of mythopoetics of balance and harmony, of the uniqueness and natural splendor of an Italian place (see Figure 9.4).

The contradiction here, or at least a complication, is that in the face of what now might seem to be a progressive ambition to use design and technology to correlate a building to its climate was, in fact, somewhat regressive, a conservative gesture in this mid-century moment of exploration. This would translate from the unique atmospheric conditions of Limone sul Garda to the climate-focused design methodology of the Olgyays' later work: how to coordinate a building precisely to its regionally specific climatic surround; and how to do so according to the framework of the "comfort zone." The comfort zone was at the epistemological center of the Olgyays' methods: an attempt

Figure 9.4 Victor Olgyay at Limone sul Garda, Italy, 1935. Courtesy Victor Olgyay.

to *regulate*; to normalize a space of consistency amidst the diurnal and seasonal vicissitudes of climate; to reshape the building process to produce a normative, predictable interior, appropriate to a culturally specific concept of comfort that was posed as universal. The Olgyays' analysis of modern architecture's climatic capacities had as its goal a sort of profound, eventually planetary, normalization of interior thermal experience. It was in this sense only partially preoccupied with the climatic parameters of a given site.

What the Olgyays could not have predicted was that their ambition to integrate climate knowledge into the design process—to use novel design techniques to produce a consistent interior space—developed parameters, metrics, and values that would be taken up by the air conditioning industry. ASHRAE regulations and HVAC industrial standards reinterpreted the comfort zone in the language of mechanical systems, ideally behind sealed, unshaded facades. In stark contrast to the Olgyays' method and purported sources of inspiration, mechanical air conditioning is completely inattentive to the climatic vicissitudes of the surroundings, or to the details of design, materials, and orientation. With air conditioning, architecture was no longer a designed system of climatic adaptability, but a mechanical system for interior thermal consistency—a universal force for fossil-fueled planetary consistency.

The ascendancy of mechanical systems had a significant impact on the framing of the experience of the interior as universal, and on the cultural construction of comfort. The building became a system of energy processing, of turning petroleum into conditioned air, keyed to an "optimized" and normalized interior environment. The lesson learned in Limone sul Garda—that a detailed understanding of a site's climate allows for attention to the kind of life, and the kind of architecture, appropriate to that site—was overwhelmed by this universal imperative for consistency; and by the flood of oil that architects, and others, are now desperate to stem.

This past can, returning to Stengers, be narrated differently: the Olgyays' methodological exploration contains additional resonance into the present, and near future. Some decades after their research, in the late 1990s, as concerns around environment and climate were returning to the field of architecture, the Olgyays' design method was rendered computational through the design and performance assessment software Eco-tect. The software platform, produced by the Australian architect Andrew Marsh, drew directly on the Olgyays' method as laid out in the 1963 *Design with Climate*; other architectural scientists and engineers continue to draw inspiration from their method. Computational knowledge, in the face of the climate emergency, has reopened the ambition to carefully adjust a building to its micro-climate.[14]

The Olgyays' ideas, innovations, and designs were generally well received in the 1960s and 1970s. While physical and meteorological principles were well integrated into their work, the field of climate architecture they pioneered was left fallow as engineering and architecture schools went through a decades-long lull in supporting such collaborations and shared climate knowledge—overwhelmed, as these discussions were by the end of the 1950s, not only by oil and the industrial supply chains of glass, concrete, steel, and HVAC, but also the formalist imperative.[15]

The Olgyays' method was developed at a time when issues of climate and comfort were seen as an expression of the clarity and brilliance of an architectural idea. This was a moment of excitement over applying scientific knowledge to architecture, long an ambition of modernism, and essential to its logic of innovation. The architectural manipulation of climate was seen as a means to improve the experience of a building's interior, to improve quality of life, and also to demonstrate the skill, creativity, and adeptness of the designer. Such issues were, however briefly and partially, an aspect of how architecture was valued.

An origin, an essential story, about the uniqueness of place, about a capacity to understand the values and vicissitudes of a specific village and its architecture, in the end masks the potential of this Italian imprint for a history of the near future. Instead, the insertion of the lemon house as event, as one among many in a complex process of knowledge production, opens towards the possibility of recursivity. Might our current anxiety about climate instability encourage an inversion of this imprint and its apparent origins, as the *progressive trajectory* of modernist realizations gives way to attention to the *cyclical patterns of climate*? This poses the possibility, if not the imperative, to explore some of these climatically engaged architectures as not only relevant to an expanded architectural history, but also as instrumental insertions in the vocabulary of architectural practice. A cyclical approach that looks to the past to open up possibilities for the future.

Notes

1. For a more general indication of this climate-focused narrative, see Daniel A. Barber, *Modern Architecture and Climate: Design before Air Conditioning* (Princeton, NJ: Princeton University Press, 2020).

2. The biographical details in this chapter come from the Olgyay collection at the Library of the Design School at Arizona State University; see also the essay written by his son, of the same name, Victor Olgyay, "A Rational Regionalism," in *Design with Climate: Bioclimatic Approach to Architectural Regionalism* (Princeton, NJ: Princeton University Press, 2015), xii–xv; one of four introductory essays to the reprint of this 1963 book.

3. Aladar Olgyay and Victor Olgyay, *The Work of Architects Olgyay + Olgyay* (New York: Reinhold, 1952). The 1944 edition was in Hungarian.

4. See, for example, Daniel Ryan, "Architects in White Coats," in *The Sydney School: Formative Moments in Architecture, Design, and Planning at the University of Sydney*, ed. Andrew Leach and Lee Stickells (Carleton, Victoria: Uro Publications, 2018); and Avigail Sachs, *Environmental Design: Architecture, Politics, and Science in Postwar America* (Charlottesville: University of Virginia Press, 2018).

5. Olgyay and Olgyay, *The Work of Architects Olgyay + Olgyay*, 11.

6. The Olgyays credit this statement to "arch. Giancarlo Palanti, Milano, 1942 'DOMUS'" in their book *The Work of Architects Olgyay + Olgyay*, 16, although *Domus* did not publish that year.

7. Donald Watson, "Who was the First Solar Architect?" in *Environmentally Friendly Cities: Proceedings of the PLEA 1988/Passive and Low Energy Architecture, Lisbon, Portugal, 1988*, ed. Eduardo Maldonado (London: Routledge, 2014), 216.

8. Le Corbusier, *Towards an Architecture*, trans. John Goodman (Los Angeles: Getty Publications, 2007), 172.

9. Peter Eisenman, *The Formal Basis of Modern Architecture: Dissertation, 1963, Facsimile* (Zurich: Lars Müller, 2006); see also a series of editorials in the journal *Oppositions* in the 1970s, including Mario Gandelsonas, "Neo-Functionalism," *Oppositions* 5 (1976), and Peter Eisenman, "Post-Functionalism," in *Oppositions* 6 (1977).

10. See Peter Eisenman, *Giuseppe Terragni: Transformations, Decompositions, Critiques* (New York: Monacelli, 2003).

11. For a concise explanation of the autonomy thesis, see K. Michael Hays, "Introduction," in *Architecture Theory since 1968* (Cambridge, MA: MIT Press, 1998): x–xv.

12. Isabelle Stengers, *In Catastrophic Times: Resisting the Coming Barbarism*, trans. Andrew Goffey (Lüneburg: Open Humanities Press, 2015), 39.

13. Victor Olgyay, "A Rational Regionalism," xii.

14. In 2008, Eco-tect was purchased by AutoCAD and is now a part of their broader CAD packages, an integrated element rather than a stand-alone platform, with potential implications for the dissolution of the specificities of climate knowledge.

15. See John Reynolds, "The Roots of Bioclimatic Design," in Victor Olgyay, *Design with Climate: Bioclimatic Approach to Architectural Regionalism* (Princeton, NJ: Princeton University Press, 2015), ix–xi; xi. Reynolds writes, "Ten years after Victor Olgyay's death, the widely used Wiley textbook *Mechanical and Electrical Equipment for Buildings, 6th Edition* featured Olgyay's map of the US' four climate regions, and his recommended plan volume and shape characteristics for buildings in those four regions."

CHAPTER 10

"SLOW DOWN YOUR KUNSTWOLLEN, YOUNG MAN" OR, WHAT A PRACTICE IN BUILDING DECONSTRUCTION LEARNED FROM TUSCAN ARISTOTELIANISM

Lionel Devlieger

I must warn the reader first: this is an embarrassingly self-centered chapter, in which I use the pronoun "I" far more often than I would have liked. And were it not for the constant insistence of the editors of this book, it would probably never have been written.

I

I studied architecture at Ghent University, in Belgium, in the early 1990s. This is a program in the polytechnic tradition, where the Department of Architecture and Urban Planning is part of the Faculty of Engineering Sciences. We shared many courses with the other engineering students. Our building, a typical neoclassical engineering school in the beaux-arts tradition, completed in 1890, stood in the shadow of the famous Ghent University Library by Henry van de Velde, the art nouveau designer and architect who morphed after World War I into a prophet of modernism. His "Tower of Books," the central feature of his library, meant to have the beauty of an industrial complex, was imagined like an automated silo for the storage of books. The building was entirely proportioned, down to its window profiles, according to the golden section.[1]

The taste for architecture instilled in us by our professors was a form of neo-modernism. Our own student designs generally mimicked Mies or Corbu in the best cases. Most of the time it was just questionably detailed minimalism. We had no idea of materiality; whenever possible, our buildings were to be clad in white plaster. It appeared to me and my fellow students that this was the best way to underscore the geometric appeal of our neatly stacked volumes under the sun. We very much disliked, I remember, brick facades, even if painted white. The texture of brick felt ugly because it all too bluntly underscored architecture's own materiality. I guess we thought of designers who inserted into their designs all too "material" features such as brick, or rusticated stone, like an author who would give his main character chronic bad breath as a reminder of this person's base mortality.

In fact, we were largely uninterested in materials. Only one material held our attention, thanks to the fact that its plasticity made it, in a way, immaterial: concrete. Ghent University, it is often forgotten, is an important sanctuary in the world-church of concrete. Gustave Magnel taught in the engineering school. He was a pioneer in the testing and calculation of pre-stressed concrete structures, who collaborated with Henry van de Velde in the late 1930s on the building of the Tower of Books, and who also built the first bridge in pre-stressed concrete girders in the US, the Walnut Lane Memorial Bridge in Philadelphia, in 1951.[2] The fact that concrete was all numbers, calculation, and hardly anything else made it even more noble.

The kind of architectural history that was conveyed to us was pretty consistent with this pedagogical program. Our history courses were good—they triggered our intellects— but they had that teleology inscribed in them: the trajectory of Western architectural history was presented as a gradual emancipation of the art of building from cruder earlier forms towards something that was more intellectual, more scientific, more abstract, less material, and less reliant on the primitive bent (as Loos would put it) towards ornamentation.

Highly valued but remote eras in that genealogy, such as the Italian Renaissance, were approached in a way that made these as palatable as possible for our modernist minds. We did not immediately get to read Erwin Panofsky's *Idea* or Rudolf Wittkower's *Architectural Principles in the Age of Humanism*, but it was clear that the perspective of these authors heavily influenced the light under which we were taught to approach the Italian Renaissance.[3]

I graduated from Ghent in 1996. Ten years later, I met Maarten Gielen and Tristan Boniver and we founded Rotor, an organization dedicated to finding uses for derelict building materials. I would have been utterly incapable of doing this in 1996. Not a single hair on my head would have thought it interesting, relevant, or challenging. What exactly happened in the intervening decade is what I shall explore here. It was a personal journey that took me to Italy and helped to undo much of the education I received at university.

Chronologically, things went like this. In my final master's year, I went to Rome on an Erasmus Scholarship for one semester. I started my master's thesis there on an abstract topic: the analogy between good buildings and nicely proportioned human bodies in the Italian Renaissance. It dwelled upon the great treatises of the 1400s, of course—Alberti, Francesco di Giorgio, and Filarete—but also on the way in which anatomy, the science of the thorough and detailed observation of the human body, gained traction in the habits of certain artists and came to be perceived as a legitimate source of architectural insight. My research led me to written sources that shed light on the way in which such figures as Leonardo or Michelangelo conceived of the human body: in terms of its shape and dimensions, of course, but also of its functioning and growth. Reading these sources, it gradually dawned on me that, for *Quattrocento* and *Cinquecento* inhabitants of the Italian peninsula, the origination process of art objects and baby humans held much in common.

After graduation, I completed a mandatory period of internships in design firms to qualify to practice architecture in Belgium. In 1999, I resumed my education thanks to a doctoral research scholarship at Ghent University that allowed me to continue the research initiated with my thesis. I picked up the research where I had left it, on the topic of the parallel between artistic and natural generation. I realized I needed to better delineate the specific period and geographic region for which I wanted to study prevalent conceptualizations of human biology. I decided to take a closer look at the context in which the doctrine of *disegno* originated: Florence and Tuscany under Duke (later Grand Duke) Cosimo de Medici (whose reign started in 1537), and for whom Giorgio Vasari worked most of his professional life.[4]

II

As a primary source for bodily conceptualizations, I used the writings of Benedetto Varchi (1502–65), a poet, scholar of literature and art, and historian who was befriended by Vasari and close to many other artists working for the regime. Varchi was an excellent orator hired to talk in public on significant occasions. He wrote the funeral oration for Michelangelo in 1564; he also delivered lectures, meant as a form of civic education, on a wide range of topics that caught general interest—on the question of love, that of which of the visual arts is noblest, and many others. His lectures, the manuscripts of which have been conserved, often took the form of commentaries on poetry, preferably of masters such as Dante or Petrarch, or equally famous authors.

One of his lectures is a commentary on Michelangelo's famous sonnet *Non ha l'ottimo artista*, in which the orator details both the physics and the physiology of artistic creation. It is echoed by another lecture, commenting on a passage of Dante's *Divina commedia* on embryology. Here Dante details how a human child is formed in his mother's womb.[5] Varchi's learned commentaries on Dante are particularly convincing because, as a well-read Aristotelian, he fully grasps the biology of Dante that is informed by Thomas of Aquinas, Averroës, and ultimately by Aristotle's own writings on the subject.

I was supposed to continue my career as a researcher in architectural history and theory by way of a postdoctoral project in the Netherlands, but for a variety of reasons I will not detail here, I cut it short. At the end of 2005, I traveled to Venice to learn how to make Italian terrazzo floors the traditional way. Back in Brussels, for a short while, between 2006 and 2008, I worked as a part-time, self-employed contractor building crushed marble floors. Like the architects of Duke Cosimo de Medici, I worked with local resources, such as the famed Rouge Royal marble found in the Belgian provinces of Hainaut and Namur—the remains of a 380-million-year-old coral reef.

In parallel, as mentioned, I co-founded Rotor, which was incorporated as a non-profit organization in 2006. We worked initially on the steady flow of recurrent waste materials constantly produced by the manufacturing industry in Belgium. We tested the relevance of these leftovers, available for free in gigantic amounts, for applications in design, architecture, or other fields. From a broad interest in industrial waste materials, our attention gradually narrowed towards those from the building industry, which constitutes a third of all waste flow in Europe. In Belgium, a tiny country of about 11 million inhabitants, building and demolition waste material presently amounts to 20 million tons yearly, and is rising.[6] If thrown on a heap, they would form a mound almost twice the height of the pyramid of Giza. In the best case, the inert bulk of these materials is reduced by crushers to a fine rubble that is used as backfill for roadbuilding.

We defined it as our task to help authorities divert the largest possible portion of that waste from this depressing fate through reuse: by carefully identifying those materials that are robust, functional, and valuable enough to live a second (and possibly third, fourth, and fifth) life in a new building. We quickly understood the best way of preserving the value of a tile, a door, a ceiling panel, a brick is not to wait until the crane of the demolisher comes by, but to do a careful and selective dismantling, on the building site, of those elements that come into consideration. We call this practice *deconstruction*. In 2014, we launched a spin-off cooperative company, Rotor DC, which has become a busy actor in the emerging circular economy in Brussels. Our workers undertake selective deconstruction operations in buildings slated for demolition or facing a significant refurbishment. This operation must take place before the demolition contractor begins their work. Usually the window of opportunity, timewise, is very short. Dismantled elements are then packaged and transported to our workshops in Brussels, where they are cleaned, prepared for reuse, and resold to local contractors, designers, or private homeowners.

In parallel, Rotor has also developed into a design and consultancy firm, realizing small- to middle-scale design projects that include reused building elements, or providing design advice to architects and clients willing to apply reuse on a bigger scale. We also have a steady flow of exhibition projects and installations that document and critically reflect upon our society's use of material resources. The first of these shows to create a genuine buzz was our installation for the Belgian Pavilion at the 2010 Venice architecture biennale. The exhibition, entitled *Usus/Usures*, looked at how human use alters contemporary building materials. It asked the question: when is a building element so worn it is deemed unfit for purpose?[7] I could digress on this for several paragraphs, but the point is to return to those mental clicks I underwent in Italy that made my contribution, as an architect, to the project of Rotor possible in the first place.

Staying in Italy during my Erasmus semester in Rome, and on several occasions during my doctoral study in Florence, helped. But more so was bathing intellectually in what I will call, for the lack of a better alternative, "Tuscan Aristotelianism," which helped me read what I saw in a different way. When you walk around in Florence with Panofsky's *Idea* in mind, you will constantly be on the lookout for works of art that will validate the Neoplatonic take on what art is, including architecture. Good art embodies, even if only as a feeble echo, the transcendent qualities of the eternal Ideas, contained in the divine mind, that shine over the world like undying lights—thus states the doctrine. As the human mind contains a few sparks of that light, it recognizes these features, and yearns for them. These qualities usually are thought to be geometric and numerical, a question of measurable proportion, or the dialectics of how parts relate to a whole. You will see beauty in a church by Brunelleschi, a facade by Alberti, a perfectly proportioned human body by Michelangelo sculpted from Carrara marble, a material which owes its nobility to the fact that its immaculate whiteness almost suggests immateriality, like the pervasive white plaster we venerated at Ghent.

The theory of *disegno*, when read from that perspective, posits that the sparks of divinity contained in the artist's mind allow artists to act as God when shaping their own works. That is why Michelangelo is said to be *divino* and why Federico Zuccari explains the term's etymology as meaning the "segno di dio in noi" (sign of God in us). For Panofsky, when Michelangelo used the term "concetto" in his poem, he actually meant "idea."[8] This celebration of the ideas of the artist, which resonated deeply in twentieth-century art and architecture and led to such phenomena as conceptual art, is also intrinsically disdainful of materiality, as (following Plotinus) matter, and especially unformed matter, is intrinsically vile, even evil.[9] It is to be noted, furthermore, that plants and animals, which, unlike humans, are not shaped in the image of God, receive hardly any attention. They just fall under the category of "living matter."

a. Things are either made by nature, art, or chance

Tuscan Aristotelianism takes a very different view of these matters. It first posits that, in the sublunary world, things are either made by nature, by art, or by chance. Things created by chance are intrinsically ignoble; they are unique, meaning impossible to repeat. They show no mastery. Between art and nature, there are similitudes, but nature's creations are decidedly nobler. All that is under the moon is subjected to cycles of generation and corruption. Nothing here is eternal, but what approaches eternity best are the living creations of nature, which have the capacity to reproduce themselves, and thus attain, if not immortality for the individual, the immortality of the species. When Aristotle speaks about the appearance of an animal, like that of an octopus, he uses the term *eidos*, translated in Latin and Tuscan as *forma*.[10] It is worth remembering that *eidos*, as a commentator like Varchi knew well, also has the meaning of species—that is, a form with self-reproductive capacities. With *eidos*, we are at the same time very remote from, and very close to, *idea*.

Also, "art" translates as *technê* in Greek, as Tuscan Aristotelians understood. The term exceeds what we understand as art today. It comprises all artificial things humans create, and in many cases translates better as technology. When Varchi provides examples of "artistic" creations, he talks about the making of a knife or the building of a house. There is also a scale of nobility in these creations; whatever helps for the conservation of the human species, and is hence of greater utility, is nobler. That is why for Tuscan Aristotelianism, the arts of architecture and medicine are to be ranked decidedly above, for instance, painting and sculpture.

b. A concept is not an idea

Concetto means two things in Tuscan: the mental representation of something to be made; and a fetus, or freshly formed baby. To put it differently, a *concetto* is the product of two types of conception: the first one in the female womb; the other one in the mind. Interestingly, Aristotelian Tuscans, like Leonardo da Vinci, thought of the brain as the indistinct mass surrounding three cavities in which the real action of the mind is taking place, through the motions and circulations of a series of spirits. It is here that sensory impressions mediated by these spirits arrive, memories are stored, and new images or instructions are recombined.[11]

c. Matter and form are the two sides of a coin

In Aristotelianism, all things existing stand on one of the ten grades of the great chain of being. Its extremities are pure matter (*prima materia*) on the lowest scale, and pure form, on the other, highest scale. Everything else, and certainly everything that can be known by the senses, is the conjunction (*composto*) of a principle of form and a principle of matter.

Form, rather than just a two- or three-dimensional shape, is best seen as the process that will shape matter and will draw the potential entity out of matter into its actuated state. I sometimes compare it with the little whirlwinds you see in comic strips around a character who undergoes a sudden transformation. In Aristotelian embryology it is the action of the hot vapor contained in the male seed that will shape, mold, coagulate, and infuse life into the material principle that is in the womb, as this stop-motion from Jacob Rueff (1554) shows (see Figures 10.1 and 10.2).

But the action of the formal principle can also be very simple. It can be the heat that transforms a piece of dough into bread, or a raw egg into a hard-boiled one. One important point is posited with great emphasis: it is impossible to distinguish form and matter in a *composto*. When you have a wooden ball, it is impossible to extract the roundness from the object and consider it separately. This principle is the *unità del composto*, the integrity of the compound. Matter and form are interdependent.

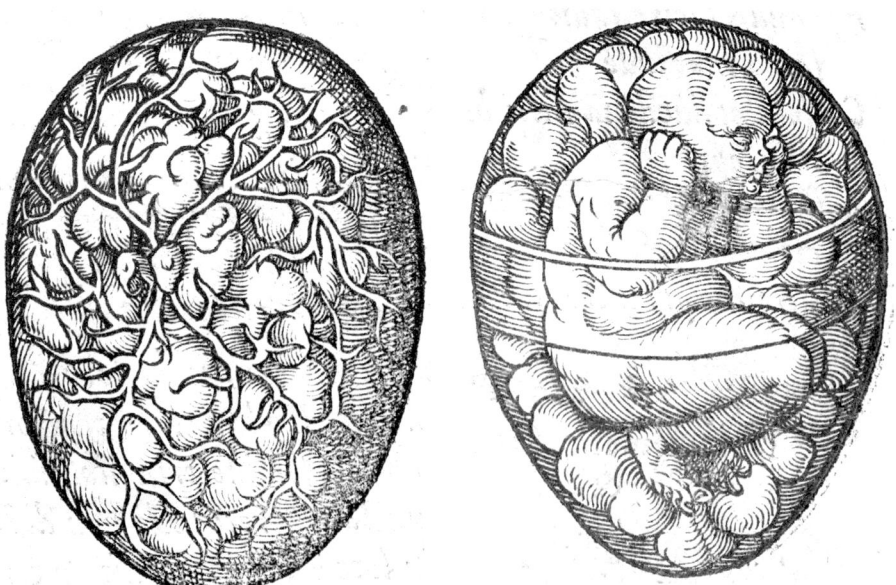

Figures 10.1 and 10.2 Jacob Rueff, The successive stages of the development of the human embryo inside the womb, from *De conceptu et generatione hominis* (Tiguri: Christoffel Froschouer, 1554). Courtesy the Wellcome Institute via Wikimedia Commons.

d. The patient has agency

From a political point of view, and to the contemporary mind, Aristotelian conceptions of animal biology and physics are plain infuriating. Consider the following statements by Benedetto Varchi: "primal matter desires form like the female desires the male, which is like the imperfect desires the perfect." Or even better:

> Quasi monsters is the name given to females and all those children that are not resembling their fathers; since, although woman belongs to the same species as men, as Aristotle says, she is nonetheless dissimilar from the generator, and every man desires to generate something resembling himself, and thus always a boy and never a girl.[12]

We can take this the bad way and dismiss Aristotelianism as the doctrine of aggressive patriarchy. I would fully understand. And yet, I think it is worth looking past this offensive, apparently absolute denigration of woman. Because, as Aristotle, Varchi, and all these patriarchs will have known, a woman has very clear agency, not least in transmitting, as a mother, parts of her own nature to her fetus. This means that, as absurd as a theory stemming from before the discovery of female (and male) reproductive cells might seem, the feminization of matter is not necessarily depriving it of importance or capacity to exert action. But it is a different, less transparent kind of agency, the cogs and wheels of which remain mostly hidden and mysterious. This also has consequences for artistic creation. If making "art" is drawing into actuality a potentiality that lies within the matter with which you work, the first thing to do is to listen to your material, instead of rushing to subject it to your mental representations, as the Neoplatonic doctrine would have us do. The job of the artist then becomes akin to the job of a wet nurse.

e. Anatomy and perfette proporzioni

One last thing I want to mention here is that Aristotelianism invites us to revisit the practice of anatomy. From a Neoplatonic perspective, if the human body is the image of God, a decent observation of its features, ruler in hand, makes sense. Cutting up dead bodies and observing their inner workings can be seen as a slightly overzealous desire to understand what lies behind the scenes of the beautiful skin-shapes, but it is less evident.

My contention is that for Renaissance artists bent towards Aristotelianism, *anatomia* and *perfette proporzioni* are code-words for the kind of careful observation an artisan is meant to engage in before he attempts to hatch anything useful. It is a form of reverent reverse-engineering. As becomes very clear from the *Trattato delle perfette proporzioni* of Vincenzo Danti (whom David Summers sees as Michelangelo's intellectual heir), who allegedly dissected about ninety human bodies and many more animals and plants, as a way to uncover the intrinsic intelligence of these assemblages.[13] The good anatomist is always on the lookout for how finely nature has crafted the members of plants and animals in order to contribute to their ultimate end, the conservation and the reproduction of these species. A perfectly proportioned animal member, we understand, is one that maximizes its *attezza*, that is, its "aptitude" to perform the desired task.

III

Being in Italy for longer stretches of time during my Ph.D., and simmering, so to speak, in these Aristotelian writings, gradually chipped away my old convictions. It blew my mind step by step and changed my outlook radically. It became possible to look at the situations I was encountering, when coming out of my research into the Brussels of the early twenty-first century, with a fresh pair of eyes. My short stint in the terrazzo business was probably therapeutic, but it was also the result of a fascination with the idea that you could let form—unexpected colored patterns—emerge by first preparing matter, or putting it in the right conditions, and then exerting upon it a simple action that would then reveal its full glory. To make a terrazzo floor, in fact, it is first necessary to pour a carefully measured mix of crushed marble aggregate, cement, and pigments. You then obtain a floor that initially appears no less dull than a concrete slab. But, once hardened, when you then patiently grind that floor with a heavy, wheel-mounted power-tool, decreasing the grain-size of your polishing stones at each step, you eventually draw your terrazzo floor from potentiality into actuation, as Aristotelians would put it. You hatch, so to speak, your shiny and bright floor (see Figure 10.3).

Rotor, at first sight, was a slightly different story, yet it was grounded in the same sort of considerations. At first, we focused on leftovers from industrial production. These are

Figure 10.3 Hand-made terrazzo floor with aggregate in Rouge Royal marble, Chaumont-Gistoux (Belgium), 2007. Photograph by Lionel Devlieger.

Figure 10.4 Cones of dripped PU from a Flemish boot factory, as displayed in *Deutschland im Herbst* by Rotor. Kraichtal (Germany), 2008. Photograph by Rotor.

objects that have an ambiguous status, if you look at them from the position that things are either made by chance, art, or nature. Issued from industrial production plants, these are clearly the result of *art* (technè), but they are the involuntary by-products of a process, so *chance* equally plays a role. A good example of this are the cones of polyurethane (PU) foam that caught our attention in 2008 while researching for *Deutschland im Herbst*.[14] These are stalactites of PU that dripped from the injection molds in a rubber boot factory during the chemical reaction between the two components of the synthetic resin (see Figure 10.4). Once one such pile on the floor grows high enough to interfere with the machines, it is thrown away as rubbish, amounting to entire containers of these cones. No two of these cones are similar, in shape or color. And yet, they all look quite alike, as if different individuals of the same species.

Later, when we became interested in salvaged building components for their secondary use-potential, this meant interrogating a material or element for its capacity to become a part again in a new whole. Elsewhere, I have compared this to the act of casting actors for a play. The designer then becomes a director—the French term *metteur en scène* is even more explicit.[15] In Rotor's design projects we often have the impression that we are "staging materials." We actively solicit dormant agencies which only need the right context to emerge again.

Figure 10.5 Dismantling by Rotor DC of ceramic floor tiles in the former Institut de Génie Civil (architect Joseph Moutschen), Liège (Belgium), 2014. Photograph © Olivier Beart.

This explains why, at Rotor, we have never been enthusiasts of upcycling and other forms of *détournement*: design situations in which you divert an element, material, from its originally intended use. A close reading of salvaged elements, such as suspended ceiling panels, ceramic floor tiles, or bricks, reveals how much intrinsic aptitude (*attezza*) these already have for performing exactly those tasks: that of a ceiling panel, tile, brick. From imposing mental form on passive matter, designing instead becomes a dialogue between the functional and aesthetic intentions in the mind of the designer, and the available resources, human and material.

IV

Now, you might argue, Aristotelianism is a tradition, derived from the writings of The Philosopher, which spread over the whole of Europe and beyond. What might make its Italian or Tuscan variant so interesting? To which I respond that its relationship with the notion of *time* is crucial.

The Italians of what we end up calling, following Vasari's hint, the Renaissance, were acutely aware of the passing of time. Many of the great architects of that era, like Brunelleschi, Alberti, da Sangallo, and Michelangelo, spent quite some time rifling through the rubble of collapsed Roman monuments for hints of grandeur, inhaling the dust of decay at every step. But the philosophy of the author of *On Generation and Corruption* seems to have prepared them for a more relaxed take on the all-pervading laws of entropy than we Moderns tend to possess. Pervaded by Platonic obsessions with eternal (geometric, mathematic, purely mental) forms as we are, we miss the fundamental wisdom that lies in this peripatetic truth: nothing, under the moon, is forever, except maybe, as we saw above, the forms of living species—the shape and nature of the almond tree, of the turtle, or of the octopus. The rest (all things made by chance and art) is doomed to decay. From that fundamental observation you have the impression that the Aristotelian Italians made the best of it by displaying in their architecture the art of slowing, as best they could, the (eventually inevitable) degrading action of time.

We Moderns from the twentieth and twenty-first centuries seem to have totally lost that capacity. We so yearn for the pristine, platonic shapes and immaculate surfaces to which industrial production has accustomed us, in our objects of daily use, our interior design, or architecture, that we engage in a Sisyphean war against wear and tear that we are bound to lose. That war is not waged with lenience and concessions, as in the days of wainscots, but with materials that promise eternal gloss, such as polished granite and brushed stainless steel. And there is the strategy of the outright denial, or the refusal to live in the presence of palpable signs of the passage of time: once a cupboard surface is chipped, a wall dented, a facade cladding weathered, we often prefer to toss it away, to demolish it and buy or build anew.[16] For decades, mechanized, fossil-fuel-powered heavy machines allowed us to haul all that trash to faraway backstage places, where it remained hidden from sight. But, as recent planetary developments show, ever more blatantly, the backstage tends to return to the forefront, and our little manicured, staged, artificial environments will not stand the assault for long.

Given all this, going back to environments that function in acceptance with the physical traces of time's passage can be, I believe, therapeutic. Being in the proximity of Rome, for instance, simultaneously reading the traces of the republic and the empire, and whatever great civilizations came before or after, provides a sense of the fragility of cultural production which, I believe, can be healthy, especially for designers and architects. It's even better if, while doing so, you can also dive into texts which celebrate the sublunary world, or the Critical Zones, as Bruno Latour would have it, with their natural process of generation and decay, collisions of matter and form, as the places where the real action is going on.[17]

Notes

1. Geert Bekaert, Ronny De Meyer, Edgar Barbaix, et al., *Hommage: Universiteitsbibliotheek Gent* (Ghent: Vlees en Beton, 2004).

2. It was reported, for instance, in "Elastic Concrete Pinch-Hits for Steel," *Popular Science* 160, no. 3 (March 1952): 146.

3. Erwin Panofsky, *Idea: A Concept in Art Theory*, trans. Joseph J. S. Peake (1924) (Columbia: University of South Carolina Press, 1968); Rudolf Wittkower, *Architectural Principles in the Age of Humanism* (London: Warburg Institute, 1949).

4. Lionel Devlieger, "Benedetto Varchi on the Birth of Artefacts: Architecture, Alchemy and Power in Late-Renaissance Florence" (Ph.D. diss., Ghent University, 2005).

5. Benedetto Varchi, *Due lezioni* (Florence: Lorenzo Torrentino, 1549); and *Lezzione sulla generazione del corpo*, lecture to the Fiorentina (Florence, December 1543, published 1560). See Devlieger, "Benedetto Varchi on the Birth of Artefacts," 80–94.

6. StatBel, "Waste Production," https://statbel.fgov.be/en/themes/environment/waste-and-pollution/ (figures up to 2018); and *OECD Environmental Performance Reviews: Belgium 2021*, https://www.oecd-ilibrary.org/, esp. "Waste, Materials, and the Circular Economy."

7. Rotor (Tristan Boniver, Lionel Devlieger, Maarten Gielen, et al.), *Usus/usures. Etat des lieux–How Things Stand*, exhibition catalog (Brussels: Éditions de la Communauté française Wallonie-Bruxelles, 2010).

8. Federico Zuccari, "L'idea de' pittori, scultori, ed architetti" (1607), II.16; discussed in Panofsky, *Idea*, 88; Devlieger, "Benedetto Varchi on the Birth of Artefacts," 80, 82–3.

9. Panofsky, *Idea*, 118.

10. Aristotle, *On the Generation of Animals*, trans. A. L. Peck (London: William Heinemann, 1943).

11. As depicted in his studies of the head, in (for instance) Martin Clayton and Ron Philo, *Leonardo da Vinci: Anatomist* (London: Royal Collection, 2012), 60–1.

12. Benedetto Varchi, "Della generazione de' mostri," in *Opere di Benedetto Varchi* (Trieste: Lloyd Austraico, 1859), 663.

13. Vincenzo Danti, *Trattato delle perfette proporzioni* (Florence, 1567), I: 244.

14. Tristan Boniver, Lionel Devlieger, Maarten Gielen, et al., *Deutschland im Herbst*, exhibition catalog (Kraichtal: Ursula Blickle Stiftung, 2008).

15. In the same vein, Aude-Line Dulière recently used the metaphor of the designer as a shepherd.

16. Note a twentieth-century counter-current to this pursuit of the ever-new in the phenomenology nurtured in Italy by Ernesto Nathan Rogers and Vittorio Gregotti. See, for

example, Ernesto Nathan Rogers, *Esperienza dell'architettura* (Turin: Einaudi, 1958); and the essay by Chris French later in this volume.

17. Bruno Latour and Peter Weibel (eds), *Critical Zones: The Science and Politics of Landing on Earth* (Cambridge, MA: MIT Press, 2020).

CHAPTER 11
ROBERT VENTURI AND NAPLES: THE COMPLEXITY OF THE SOUTH
Rosa Sessa

Love yourself a little too, and take every proper advantage of your stay in Italy.[1]

Letter from Vanna Venturi to Robert Venturi, January 5, 1955

In histories of recent architecture and architectural culture, the widely established idea that Italy is a rich depository of historical examples presents many questions, especially in relation to the revolution propelled by the modern movement. After World War I, many modern architects refused direct inspiration from the distant past, and thus drew less directly on Italy's architectural heritage in the design of new works. This conditional turn away from history shaped the geography of attention to Italian architecture over the middle decades of the twentieth century. While in previous centuries architects' interests were homogeneously distributed among the country's north, center, and south, modern architects were generally less inclined towards Italy's southernmost regions, and appear less informed, or simply uninterested, about their most recent architectural expressions.

This shift can be read as the result of the propagation of an image of southern Italy as a place defined by premodern and archeological heritage, traditional folklore, rural habits, and reactionary cultures. The image circulated in the late nineteenth century as a product of Italy's unification in 1861, itself a political project through which northern elites absorbed the former Kingdom of Naples and the Two Sicilies (the largest state in Italy before unification). The new state perceived these regions as culturally distinct from the peninsula's north and center, and intentionally alien from the rapid modernization transforming those areas of the country. The image of a bifurcated Italy symbolically divided by Rome became common among Italians, and also affected foreign perceptions. The so-called Southern Question was not only a matter of prejudice towards the *Mezzogiorno*: the mass internal migration away from the former Kingdom of Naples was the result of national politics favoring industrial development in certain areas, particularly around Milan, Turin, Genoa, and Rome.[2]

For centuries, though, southern Italy had featured prominently on the map of international travelers and intellectuals, gaining in importance after the discovery of Herculaneum and Pompeii in the mid-eighteenth century. This helped the city of Naples, especially, to become a vibrant center for foreign artists and intellectuals, attaining a cultural prominence that paralleled its new political role as capital of the Bourbon Kingdom. The ancient remains preserved by Vesuvius became a shared reference for western architects, the most powerful inspiration for that era's international Neoclassicism.[3] During that epoch, foreign interest in Naples and its region of Campania went beyond archeology. Since the sketches of the vernacular architecture of Capri by architect Karl Friedrich Schinkel, who first visited the island in 1803, and the enthusiastic descriptions of the area by Goethe in his *Italienische Reise* (*Italian Journey*) of 1816–17, European intellectuals, artists, and architects were preoccupied with the landscape and the architecture of coastal Campania.[4]

As Naples' stature within the new Kingdom of Italy diminished in the late nineteenth and early twentieth centuries, the South primarily attracted archeologists and anthropologists to its ancient sites, while new architecture in Italy's central and (especially) northern regions participated in the international discourse on modernism on its own terms. It is no coincidence that the most renowned Italian architects of the past century, such as Giuseppe Terragni, Pier Luigi Nervi, Ernesto Nathan Rogers, and the nation's two Pritzker Prize winners, Aldo Rossi and Renzo Piano, were all born in northern Italy, nor that their built projects were mostly located in the country's northern and central regions.

Against that larger tendency, some foreign architects continued to show interest in the South. Josef Hoffmann was the first modernist pioneer to credit the Mediterranean buildings of southern Italy as an inspiration for his architecture in 1897, describing the vernacular architecture of Capri as "a harmonious expression in absolute simplicity, free from artificial superstructures and tasteless decorations . . . a simple whole that responds to the needs of rationality and comfort of the individual."[5] A decade later, Hoffmann wrote of the gulf of Naples: "there, for the first time, it became clear to me what matters in architecture."[6] Fifty years later, a similarly warm acknowledgment of the architecture of the Amalfi Coast came from the American Louis Kahn, who, in 1959, described how in the winter of 1928–9, "I came to a little village, and this village was very unfamiliar. There was nothing there that I had seen before. But through this unfamiliarity – from this unfamiliar thing – I realized what architecture was."[7]

Before World War II, Campania was still, for some, a must-see destination on the itinerary of the traditional Grand Tour, which brought Le Corbusier to Pompeii in 1911.[8] Among those architects who decided to reside in the region for a longer period was the Austrian Bernard Rudofsky. Thirty years before his acclaimed exhibition *Architecture Without Architects* (Museum of Modern Art, 1964), he lived in Naples, Capri, and Procida, collaborating with the Italian architects and designers Gio Ponti and Luigi Cosenza. With the latter he designed some of the most refined examples of modern architecture in the region, such as the unbuilt project for a Villa in Positano (1937) on the Amalfi Coast, or Villa Oro in Naples (1937), a building celebrated in Italy as an intelligent and poetic encounter between Germanic rationalism and the Mediterranean *genius loci*. Despite its apparently enduring magnetism, Campania begins to lose the foreign architect's attention after World War II. Why might this be?

We might pose this question to Robert Venturi, the prominent American architect who devoted much of his formative years in the 1940s and 1950s to experiencing Italian cities and their historic architecture. The influence of Italy, and in particular of Rome, in his early biography is well known.[9] His first day spent in Rome, on August 8, 1948, was described by Venturi as an epiphany: in his words, the Eternal City was still able to reveal valuable architectural and urban lessons through spontaneous absorption of the city's context, color, scale, and natural monumentality.[10] In fact, challenging academic as well as personal expectations, for the twenty-three-year-old architect the city of Rome provided a place for new reflections on topics such as decoration in architecture, the dynamism of Baroque buildings and urban spaces, and the spatial character of the Italian piazza.

Venturi was in Rome as part of a longer summer journey through Europe, undertaken after completing his bachelor's degree in Architecture at Princeton University. In nine weeks, the American traveled through England, France, and Italy, deliberately dedicating half of that time to Italian explorations. Once there, Venturi followed a rather traditional travel itinerary, visiting Rome, Florence, and Venice, including excursions to Siena, Ravenna, and the buildings of Palladio in Vicenza. Following the classic Grand Tour trajectory, Naples was his southernmost destination. Venturi only spent two days in Naples, including a one-day visit to Pompeii.

At that time, Naples was not completely unknown to the young architect. On the contrary, two of his best friends at Princeton had lived there while serving in the American army during World War II. Both had passionately discussed that city. While Venturi's roommate, the historian Everett de Golyer ("Ev"), described Naples as "a filthy hole [with] compensatory beauties of artistic nature," his friend Bill, the literature scholar William Weaver, was a true enthusiast, to the point that he went back immediately after the end of the conflict in order to correct his wartime image of a "false Naples that only existed for soldiers: the city composed of brothels, bad bars, Army messes and hotels, and officer's clubs."[11] The life of the real city, finally free from the war, was later described by the young writer as "more fascinating, more inexhaustible than ever."[12] Weaver, who later became the most prominent English translator of twentieth-century Italian literature, would spend six weeks in 1947 as a guest of Neapolitan author Raffaele La Capria in the baroque Palazzo Donn'Anna.[13] He there found inspiration for his first book on the lifestyle of locals and foreigners in Naples, *A Tent in This World*.

Despite his friend's passion for the "tangible history" of Naples, when Venturi visited the place one year later, he was less impressed.[14] The young traveler described the bay of Naples as "very beautiful," adding, however, that the city "includes little of architectural interest."[15] Echoing his friend Ev, and much of the travel literature on that topic, Venturi reported that "the beauty of the city of Naples lies in its situation, the bay, the sky and the mountains, including Vesuvius, rather than the city itself. I found the city as dirty and sordid as its reputation holds."[16] The only building he mentioned in his letters is a modern one, the Postal Office by Giuseppe Vaccaro and Gino Franzi, completed in 1936, writing to his parents that it is "good (= bad) Mussolini modern architecture."[17]

Six years later, Venturi received a hard-won Rome Prize in Architecture from the American Academy in Rome. All three of Venturi's fellowship applications present Rome as the primary focus for his architectural and urban investigations. And yet, the records of his stay from 1954 to 1956 reveal that gradually, and surprisingly, Naples became its silent counterpart, a place where the young American would test his theories of the Roman baroque and mannerism. The city's proximity to Rome, and its distinctive seventeenth- and eighteenth-century architectural heritage, together turned Naples into Venturi's most favored destination for trips beyond Lazio.

Figure 11.1 Robert Venturi, the elliptical double-ramp staircase of the Certosa in Padula, 1955. The Architectural Archives, University of Pennsylvania, by the gift of Robert Venturi and Denise Scott Brown.

In 1955, during his long journey through southern Italy, Venturi followed a baroque itinerary suggested by the German art historian Richard Krautheimer, a renowned scholar then residing at the American Academy. He began in Sicily, where Venturi visited the Noto area, then continued up the peninsula through Calabria. In Campania, he stopped in the small village of Padula to visit its famous Certosa, the largest Carthusian charterhouse in Italy. There, he was impressed by one peculiar element at the monastery, an elliptical double-ramp staircase enclosed in an octangular tower, added to the existing structure in the late eighteenth century. Venturi described this dramatic construction as "a great staircase, very daring and dynamic structurally and spatially – the quintessence of Baroque"[18] (see Figure 11.1).

After returning to the Academy after a long visit home to Philadelphia, Venturi went back to Campania in January 1956 and looked at its architecture with new interest. Following a more extensive itinerary, the young American visited Pompeii and Herculaneum as well as the late baroque architecture of Luigi Vanvitelli around the city of Caserta. Most importantly, he seems to look at the city of Naples with fresh eyes, and far greater appreciation. He wrote:

> I consider my trip to Naples which I expected to be a three- to four-day one, and which lasted eight days – a success … In fact, it is to me one of the most beautiful examples of city I have seen – not because of the setting only, but architecturally – and this aspect of it is not generally appreciated.[19]

Plate 1 Installation view of the exhibition *ISOZAKI Arata: SOLARIS*. Photo: KIOKU Keizo.

Plate 2 Engineer Michael Jay works on the *B of the Bang* sculpture at the AK Heavy Engineering Factory in Sheffield, northern England, May 25, 2004. Reuters Pictures. Photograph by Ian Hogson.

Plate 3 Marking: Lioz limestone cladding, Centro Cultural de Belém, Lisbon. Photograph © Maria Mitsoula. Reproduced with permission.

Plate 4 College of Fine Arts, Carnegie Mellon University, Pittsburgh. Detail of mural in the Great Hall. Henry Hornbostel, architect; James Monroe Hewlett, muralist, 1914-15. Creative Commons CC0 Universal Public Domain Dedication.

Plate 5 Doorway in the east wall of the garden of the Palazzo Piccolomini, Pienza. Photograph by Caspar Pearson.

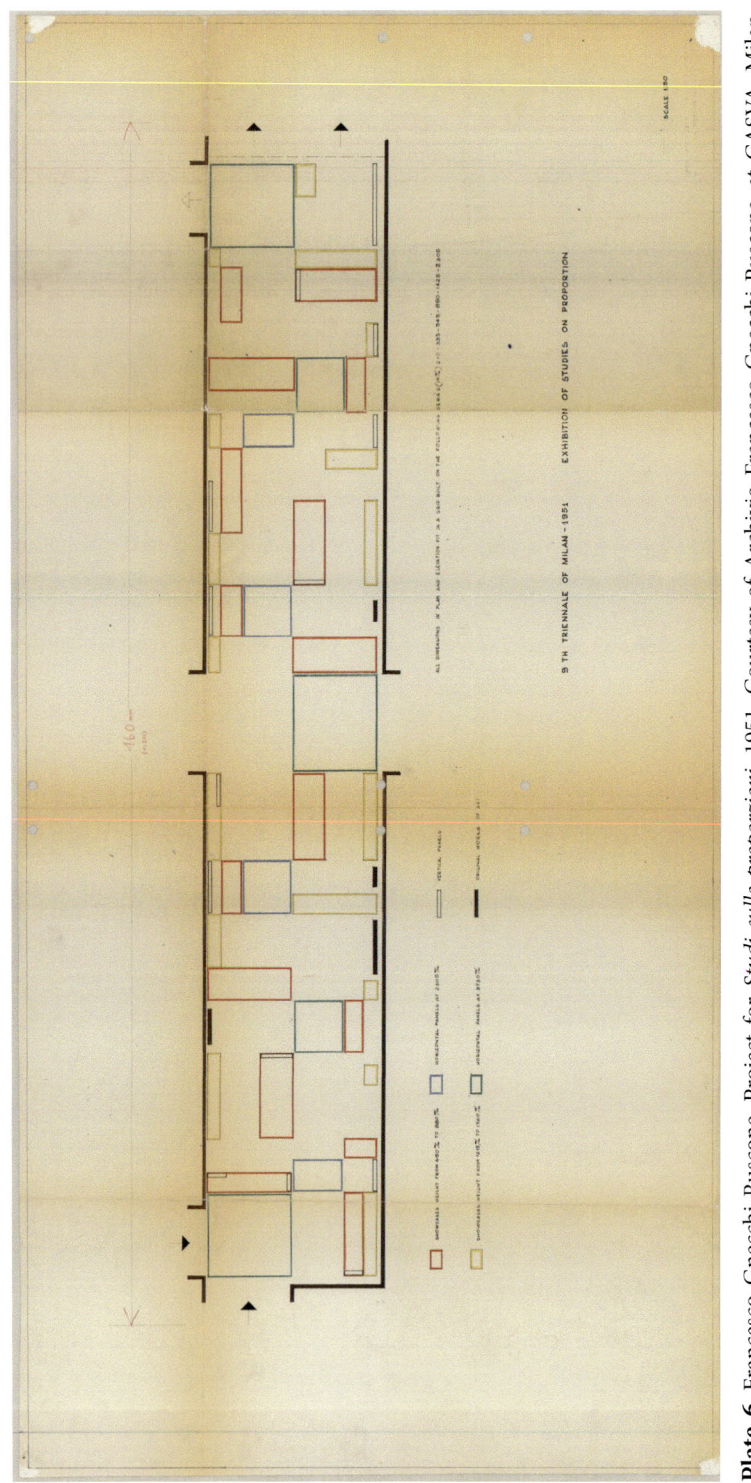

Plate 6 Francesco Gnecchi-Ruscone, Project for *Studi sulle proporzioni*, 1951. Courtesy of Archivio Francesco Gnecchi-Ruscone, at CASVA, Milan.

Plate 7 Robert Venturi, details of the baroque staircase and the facade of the Basilica of San Paolo Maggiore in Naples, framing the view of the lively facade of a residential building, 1955-6. The Architectural Archives, University of Pennsylvania, by the gift of Robert Venturi and Denise Scott Brown.

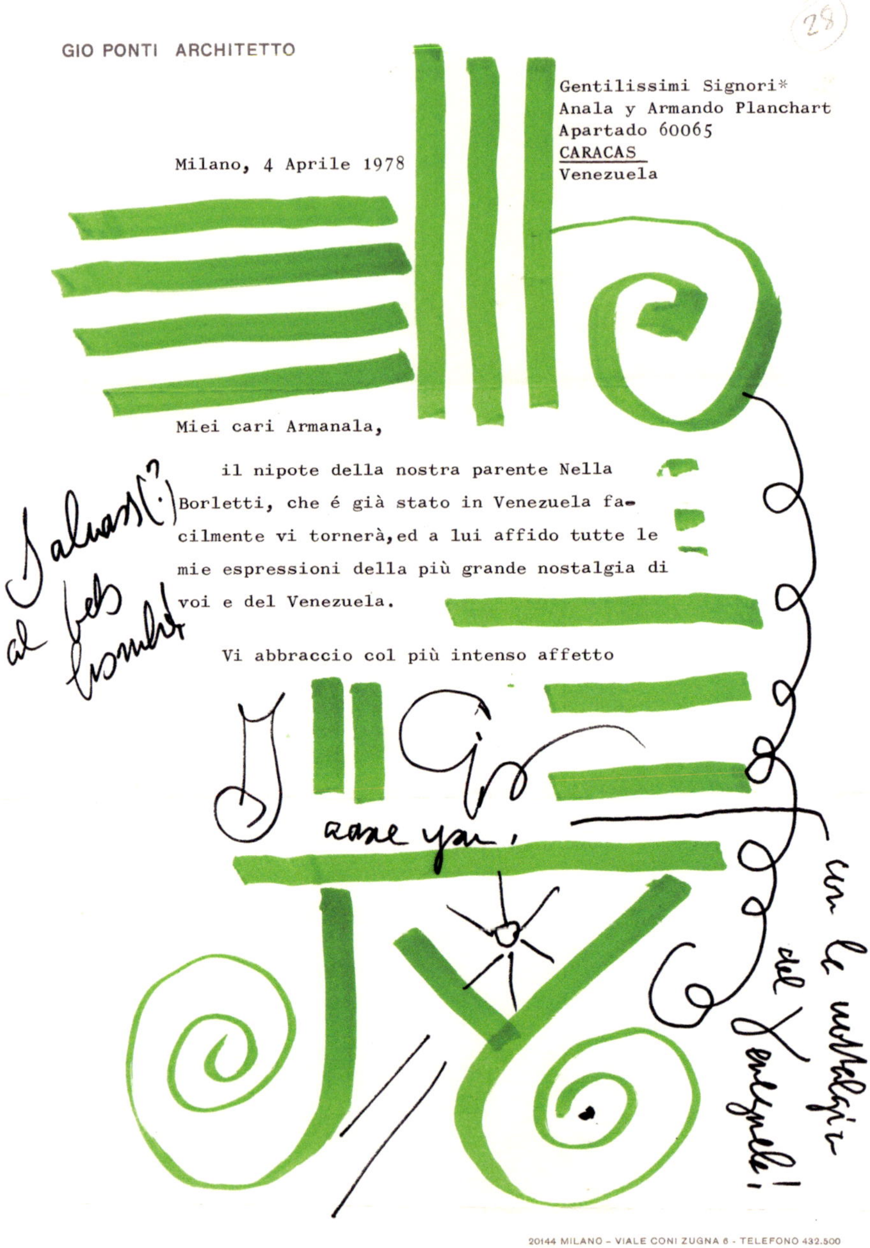

GIO PONTI ARCHITETTO

Gentilissimi Signori*
Anala y Armando Planchart
Apartado 60065
CARACAS
Venezuela

Milano, 4 Aprile 1978

Miei cari Armanala,

il nipote della nostra parente Nella Borletti, che é già stato in Venezuela facilmente vi tornerà, ed a lui affido tutte le mie espressioni della più grande nostalgia di voi e del Venezuela.

Vi abbraccio col più intenso affetto

20144 MILANO - VIALE CONI ZUGNA 6 - TELEFONO 432.500

Plate 8 Gio Ponti, letter to Anala and Armando Planchart, Milan, April 4, 1978. Courtesy of Archivio Gio Ponti Caracas: Correspondencia.

Plate 9 Aldo Rossi, San Cataldo Cemetery, Modena, 1971. Photograph courtesy Diego Terna.

Plate 10 Wang Shu, Amateur Architecture Studio, Youth Center, Haining, Zhejiang, China, 1990. Photograph courtesy Cole Roskam.

For the young architect this was a new start, even a second epiphany on the architecture of Italy. Venturi took beautiful pictures of the city, capturing the dramatic details of its baroque architecture, and the way it shaped the life of its inhabitants. His photographs emphasized the ever-surprising interactions between Neapolitan buildings and their users. The human body was always present, not to indicate architectural dimensions or scale but to convey a sense of liveliness and vibrancy to the scene. The staircases are often the protagonists in his photographs: Venturi is intrigued by Naples' distinctive open baroque staircases, which serves as a functional as well as a decorative element, and works as both an intricate facade and gathering point.

A month after the trip, Venturi wrote to his parents that he was still working on his impressions of Naples, reading books about the city in the Academy library. In a note he listed all the buildings he had visited, a comprehensive investigation of every neighborhood in the city, with a special predilection for the baroque buildings of Ferdinando Sanfelice (1675–1748), particularly Palazzo Sanfelice, Palazzo dello Spagnuolo, and Palazzo Serra di Cassano, which all feature famous open staircases (see Figures 11.2, 11.3, 11.4, and Plate 7).

In March 1956, Venturi visited Naples again to see Maria Callas perform at the San Carlo Theater in *Lucia di Lammermoor*, but also "to wander through 'my' parts of Naples."[20] A few months later, at the end of his stay at the Academy, the final journey of his fellowship was again dedicated to Naples and its bay, with short trips to the islands. He wrote of his fourth visit in two years:

> The trip back that evening through the Bay of Naples I will never forget. A lovely sunset, and surrounded by Capri, Ischia, Procida, the glorious city of Naples, Vesuvius with Portici at its foot, and Sorrento and its Peninsula, in a 360-degree arch. That evening in Naples I took a lovely *passeggiata*, and the next morning also revisited my favorite things, and said farewell.[21]

Despite the intense and knowledgeable relationship with Campania captured by Venturi's fellowship letters and photographs, very few traces of the region would appear in his subsequent works. Venturi cited the region's buildings only four times in his first major publication, *Complexity and Contradiction in Architecture* of 1966, a book that collected much of his early investigations on the architecture of Italy. Of the dozens of baroque works illustrated throughout, only two are Campanian: in "Contradiction Adapted," the facades of two Neapolitan villas—Villa Pignatelli in S. Giorgio a Cremano and Villa Palomba in Torre del Greco—are shown.[22] In the book's concluding chapter, "The Obligation Towards the Difficult Whole," Venturi selected a photograph of the historic center of Naples, in which a woman animates an intricate interplay of volumes and stairs, to represent the "plastic forms of indigenous Mediterranean architecture."[23]

It is the image of Piazza Plebiscito, however, that best reveals how Venturi used examples from Naples. In the chapter "The Inside and the Outside," a view of the space's colonnade and Pantheon-inspired central church parallels a plan of St. Peter's Piazza in the Vatican. For Venturi, both colonnades are designed to exclude "the city complex, in

Figure 11.2 Robert Venturi, the details of the baroque staircase and the facade of the Basilica of San Paolo Maggiore in Naples framing the view of the lively facade of a residential building, 1955-6. The Architectural Archives, University of Pennsylvania, by the gift of Robert Venturi and Denise Scott Brown.

Figure 11.3 Robert Venturi, the staircase of Palazzo Sanfelice in Naples and its inhabitants, 1955-6. The Architectural Archives, University of Pennsylvania, by the gift of Robert Venturi and Denise Scott Brown.

Figure 11.4 Robert Venturi, the main staircase of Palazzo Sanfelice in Naples, 1955–6. The Architectural Archives, University of Pennsylvania, by the gift of Robert Venturi and Denise Scott Brown.

order to achieve unity for their piazzas."[24] Here, Naples serves as a counterpoint to the dominant theme of Rome, reinforcing and sustaining Venturi's reflections on the architecture of the Eternal City. Yet the vibrant and distinctive complexity of the many layers of interpretation of Naples, so profoundly experienced and examined by Venturi during his many visits, remains left out of *Complexity and Contradiction*.

The limited presence of Naples in Venturi's theoretical writings of the 1960s is consistent with the general contours of postwar US discourse about Italy's modern architecture. One example is the complete absence of Neapolitan references in the early work of Ada Louise Huxtable, who otherwise played a key role in redefining the Italian architecture scene for a US audience. From 1950 to 1952, the young curator spent two years in Milan as a Fulbright grantee studying the professional activity of Pier Luigi Nervi, at that time little known outside Italy. Her first article on Nervi appeared in *Progressive Architecture* in 1953; he figured in her exhibition on Italian modernism, held at the Museum of Modern Art in New York the following year; and her first book *Pier Luigi Nervi* was published in 1960.[25] These three cultural products helped Huxtable situate herself as a prominent architectural critic and author, and shaped how Americans perceived Italian architecture and design during the postwar period.

The exhibition that Huxtable curated for MoMA, *The Modern Movement in Italy: Architecture and Design*, was organized as a traveling exhibition through the United States and Canada and was on display in New York from August 18 to September 6, 1954.[26] It was the museum's first monographic exhibition on Italian architecture, and it addressed the topic from a unique perspective for that period.[27] Until the mid-1950s, MoMA had given almost no indication that Italy had produced modernist architecture. The pivotal *Modern Architecture: International Exhibition* curated by Philip Johnson and Henry-Russell Hitchcock in 1932 included a single Italian building, the Electrical House of the 1930 Monza Exposition, designed by the young Milanese architects Luigi Figini and Gino Pollini. The exhibition directed by Huxtable was significant in establishing an alternative, modernist narrative for a country traditionally associated with its historical heritage. However, by selecting projects primarily located in Milan, Turin, and Rome, Huxtable presented a highly incomplete version of Italian contemporary architecture. Her exclusion of Naples is most conspicuous, given that both Nervi and the Olivetti Company (whose activities were well represented in the show) had built there.[28]

During this same period, the American architect and photographer George E. Kidder Smith took a more geographically inclusive approach to Italian architecture. Smith traveled around Italy from 1950 to 1951 on a fellowship from Brown University, taking pictures and notes on architecture throughout the country, from the vernacular to the latest projects.[29] This research was disseminated in two ways. In 1952, Smith delivered a lecture at the RIBA in London on "Contemporary Italian Architecture and the Italian Heritage," sharing reflections on his travels.[30] The most extensive result of his research was a book Smith considered his best: *Italy Builds: Its Modern Architecture and Native Inheritance*, published in 1955 both in English and in Italian. The author reflected on both "Italy's incomparable inheritance" and its attempts to adapt an architectural modernity of Germanic origins to the nation's distinctive needs and characteristics.[31]

With this double effort, Smith stressed the correlation, even continuity, between Italy's traditional architecture, its landscape, and new construction, presenting this as a lesson that might be profitably assimilated by foreign architects.

The first chapter, "The Inheritance: The Land and Its Architecture," presents the multifaceted geography of the country and the variety of traditional buildings associated with its different landscape and climatic conditions. In this comprehensive overview from the Alps to southern coastal towns, Campania appears through the pure volumes and sensuous curves of the vernacular architecture of the Amalfi Coast and the islands of the Bay of Naples, and local climate mitigation systems such as the porticoes of Pompeii and the inner open court of the Positano houses. The second chapter, "The Urban Setting," includes several southern examples, among them the topographically distinctive castle of Ischia, the famous *piazzetta* in Capri, and the monumental fountains of the Royal Palace of Caserta and Taormina.

The balanced presentation of the country's three main geographical areas is abandoned in the final chapter, "The Modern Architecture of Italy." Of fifty-one projects, only five are from the South: two social housing complexes in Naples (one by Cocchia, De Luca and Della Sala, the other by Cosenza and Coen), a low-cost housing project in Palermo, an apartment house in Taranto, and a Neapolitan coffee shop and bar designed by Della Sala, D'Ambrosio and Salvatori. The latter was praised for its "Mondrian-inspired façade," somehow suggesting the Neapolitan reception of a diversity of international references, well beyond the *Siedlungen* widely reinterpreted in the social housing projects built after the end of the war.[32]

In the book, the Neapolitan cafeteria is displayed next to a Milanese perfume shop; the large photographs of their fronts underline the similarities between their full-height windows, the glamorous fonts of their shop signs, and the interiors flooded with natural light. Those pages seem to allude to a higher level of taste and design sophistication for commercial spaces that—as Smith timidly suggests—has an equal chance to flourish in the whole country, from north to south.

In the early 1950s, Huxtable had excised the south from her exhibition on Italy's modern architecture, while Smith portrayed, however marginally, the South as part of the Italian conversation on modern architecture. Although his book is regionally even-handed when discussing geography and heritage, he demonstrates a selective, frequently negative view of southern Italy's contemporary architecture. He tried to explain the overrepresentation of northern and central architecture in his book compared to the South by claiming that the region's new architecture was of lesser quality, a symptom of the south's inferior industrial development. As he put it, "The contemporary architectural level of southern Italy, reflecting its wealth distribution and industrial output, has always been of lower order than that of the northern part of the country."[33] Significantly, in the section on "Museums and Exhibitions," he shows great interest in the pavilions and exhibits presented in Milanese shows and fairs (the Triennale is mentioned three times, the Milan Trade Fair four times), while never citing any pavilions from the Mostra d'Oltremare exhibition in Naples (from 1940), despite the many renowned architects and landscape designers (both local and not) involved in this event and its resumption after the war.[34]

It is the way Robert Venturi dealt with the architecture of Naples, however, that reveals the most ambivalent attitude towards the South of any American architect during the postwar period. While a Rome Prize fellow, Venturi traveled extensively through that part of the country, taking photographs and notes while deepening his knowledge through his studies at the library and conversations on baroque architecture with Krautheimer at the American Academy. Back in Philadelphia, however, his theory teaching at the University of Pennsylvania and the long process of writing *Complexity and Contradiction in Architecture* both demonstrate a drastic reduction of Naples' importance in his thinking. The book, a sharp but "gentle manifesto" that presents his theory through formal analysis of an eclectic collection of architectural examples, historic and modern, European and American, positions the architecture of Rome prominently across its pages.[35] Venturi has no fear of discussing even the city's most controversial buildings: the "orgy of inflections" of the new mannerism he saw in work by the idiosyncratic fascist architect Armando Brasini, for instance, stands out in the last two chapters.[36] Naples, however, while present, remains in the background, in a supporting role. Despite his brilliant interpretation of two baroque facades as a manifestation of two types of contradiction in architecture, there is no trace of the ardor present in his fellowship writings: his passionate discussions about the vernacular architecture of the bay, his strolls with Weaver and the designer Roberto Mango through the city, his intense analysis of the baroque open staircases.

The deliberate minimization of Naples in Venturi's work may intersect with his own complex and contradictory biography. Venturi was himself a son of southern Italy; his father, Robert, was born in Abruzzo, while his mother, Vanna, had Apulian origins.[37] Both his parents were determined to leave their past of misery and deprivation to successfully enter the life of the Philadelphian elite. To avoid the degrading clichés identified with Italian immigrants, especially southerners—commonly referred to disparagingly as *terrone, paesano,* or worse—they chose to forge a new identity. To free themselves from pejorative stereotypes after their marriage in 1924, Robert and Vanna renounced the most recognizable aspects of their identity that impeded their assimilation into mainstream American society: they moved to suburban neighborhoods not associated with Italian communities, only spoke English at home, left Catholicism to become Quakers, and even banned pasta from their family diet.[38] The only aspects of "Italianness" that survived this transition were those associated with high culture: opera, literature, fine arts, and architecture. Intimate connections with these more elite and intellectual aspects of Italy were ones that Mr. and Mrs. Venturi were very proud to possess.

Venturi never openly states any rationale for the changes in his relationship with Naples or southern Italy. As an only, devoted son, however, this might have been a means (conscious or otherwise) to defend his parents' choices to selectively reframe their ethnic identity. In addition to possible familial motivations, Venturi's limited deployment of southern themes may have been professionally strategic. Given the heritage evident in his name, he may have wondered whether his attention to southern themes might be received as obsolete and provincial, a sort of resurgence of nostalgia for the lost homeland. Perhaps the ambitious young architect believed that overly frequent references to

Neapolitan architecture might have a destabilizing effect on his emerging career in the America of the late 1950s and early 1960s, a concern consistent with the image of Italy's contemporary architectural relevance propagated by Huxtable and Smith. To avoid being identified with the Italy his parents left behind, and to align himself with the Italy he thought would serve his professional ambitions, the architecture of Naples to which he was drawn so deeply, in so many ways, during his stay at the American Academy, was suppressed in *Complexity and Contradiction*, published by MoMA and the Graham Foundation ten years after his return from Rome. The many complexities of his relationship with Naples and the South, though dear to Venturi's heart, would remain untold.

Notes

1. Letter from Vanna Venturi to Robert Venturi, January 5, 1955, Venturi Scott Brown Collection, 225.RV.43, Architectural Archives of the University of Pennsylvania, Philadelphia.

2. A large literature exists on this topic. The books published in English include Jane Schneider, *Italy's "Southern Question": Orientalism in One Nation* (London: Routledge, 1998); those affected regions are Abruzzo, Apulia, Basilicata, Calabria, Campania, Molise, and Sicily.

3. Maria Teresa Caracciolo, Luigi Gallo, and Massimo Osanna (eds), *Pompei e l'Europa, 1748–1943* (Milan: Electa, 2015); Fabio Mangone, *Immaginazione e presenza dell'antico. Pompei e l'architettura di età contemporanea* (Naples: ArtstudioPaparo, 2017).

4. Andrea Maglio, *L'Arcadia è una terra straniera. Gli architetti tedeschi e il mito dell'Italia nell'Ottocento* (Naples: Clean, 2009).

5. Josef Hoffmann, "Architektonisches von der Insel Capri," *Der Architekt* 3 (1897): 13; in Eduard F. Sekler, *Josef Hoffmann, 1870–1956* (Milan: Electa, 1991), 518.

6. Josef Hoffmann, "Meine Arbeit" (1911), in Eduard F. Sekler, *Josef Hoffmann, 1870–1956* (Milan: Electa, 1991), 486.

7. Louis Kahn, keynote address at the CIAM Otterlo congress (1959), in Alessandra Latour, *Louis I. Kahn. Writings, Lectures, Interviews* (New York: Rizzoli, 1991), 93.

8. Orfina Fatigato, *Napoli est réussi. Il ritorno in Occidente di Le Corbusier* (Rome: Officina Edizioni, 2013).

9. Rosa Sessa, *Robert Venturi e l'Italia. Educazione, viaggi e primi progetti, 1925–1966* (Macerata: Quodlibet, 2020); Denise Costanzo, "The Lessons of Rome: Architects at the American Academy, 1947–1966" (Ph.D. diss, Pennsylvania State University, 2009), and "I'll Try My Best to Make It Worth It: Robert Venturi's Road to Rome," *Journal of Architectural Education* 70, no. 2 (2016): 269–83; Martino Stierli, "In the Academy's Garden: Robert Venturi, the Grand Tour and the Revision of Modern Architecture," *AA Files* 56 (2007): 42–63.

10. Robert Venturi, Princeton, September 30, 1948, *Summer Activities: Report and Some Impressions*, Venturi Scott Brown Collection, 225.RV.34, Architectural Archives of the University of Pennsylvania, Philadelphia.

11. Letter from Everett de Golyer to Robert Venturi, August 12, 1945, Venturi Scott Brown Collection, 225.RV.4, Architectural Archives of the University of Pennsylvania, Philadelphia; William Weaver, *A Tent in This World* (Kingston, NY: McPherson & Company, 1999), 21.

12. Weaver, *A Tent*, 21.

13. "William Weaver, Influential Translator of Modern Italian Literature, Dies at 90," *New York Times*, https://www.nytimes.com/2013/11/17/arts/william-weaver-influential-translator-of-modern-italian-literature-dies-at-90.html.

14. Weaver, *A Tent*, 106.

15. Letter from Robert Venturi to his parents, August 22, 1948, Venturi Scott Brown Collection, 225.RV.25, Architectural Archives of the University of Pennsylvania, Philadelphia.

16. Venturi to his parents, August 22, 1948.

17. Venturi to his parents, August 22, 1948.

18. Letter from Robert Venturi to his parents, June 12, 1955, Venturi Scott Brown Collection, 225.RV.70, Architectural Archives of the University of Pennsylvania, Philadelphia.

19. Letter from Robert Venturi to his parents, January 16, 1956, Venturi Scott Brown Collection, 225.RV.77, Architectural Archives of the University of Pennsylvania, Philadelphia.

20. Letter from Robert Venturi to his parents, March 28, 1956, Venturi Scott Brown Collection, 225.RV.98, Architectural Archives of the University of Pennsylvania, Philadelphia.

21. Letter from Robert Venturi to Hamilton Smith (Marcel Breuer Architects), March 28, 1956, Venturi Scott Brown Collection, 225.RV.46, Architectural Archives of the University of Pennsylvania, Philadelphia.

22. Robert Venturi, *Complexity and Contradiction in Architecture* (1966), 2nd edn (New York: Museum of Modern Art, 1977), 45, figs 62–3.

23. Venturi, *Complexity and Contradiction*, 103, fig. 249.

24. Venturi, *Complexity and Contradiction*, 72, fig. 145.

25. Suzanne Stephens, "Ada Louise Huxtable," in *Women in American Architecture: A Historic and Contemporary Perspective*, ed. Susana Torre (New York: Whitney Library of Design, 1977), 141–3.

26. "The Modern Movement in Italy," MoMA, https://www.moma.org/interactives/exhibitions/2016/spelunker/exhibitions/2648/.

27. The first MoMA exhibitions fully dedicated to Italy had been *Italian Masters* in 1940, and *Twentieth Century Italian Art* in 1949. The following decade saw a rise in the interest of the institution in Italian design, and the organization of an exhibition presenting the products of the Olivetti company in 1952.

28. The main railway station of Naples, designed by Nervi together with an impressive team of architects (among them, Bruno Zevi, Luigi Piccinato, and Giuseppe Vaccaro), was under construction at the time (1954–60), as well as the Olivetti factory in Pozzuoli designed by Luigi Cosenza (1953–5).

29. Angelo Maggi, "Re-Interpreting Kidder Smith's *Italy Builds*: Crossovers Between Photography and Architecture," *Sophia Journal* 2 (2017): 1–9.

30. Maggi, "Re-Interpreting Kidder Smith's *Italy Builds*," 2.

31. George E. Kidder Smith, *Italy Builds: Its Modern Architecture and Native Inheritance/L'Italia costruisce. Sua architettura moderna e sua eredità indigena* (Milan: Edizioni di Comunità, 1955), 4.

32. Smith, *Italy Builds*, 215.

33. Smith, *Italy Builds*, 215.

34. The others include Marcello Canino, Michele Capobianco, Carlo Cocchia, Giulio De Luca, Stefania Filo Speziale, Luigi Piccinato, and Roberto Pane. Many pavilions were restored after the war under the supervision of Delia Maione and Elena Mendia.

35. "Nonstraightforward Architecture: A Gentle Manifesto" is the title of the first chapter.

36. Venturi, *Complexity and Contradiction*, 77, 90–3.

37. Vincenzo Di Florio, *Robert Venturi. Una esplorazione delle origini atessane* (Atessa: Grafiche Caporale, 2019).

38. "Without disowning his roots, [my father] still felt that one did everything one could to become typically American. His lifestyle showed this . . . He 'assimilated'." This quote by Venturi is taken from Linda Brandi Cateura, *Robert Venturi: Upbringing Among Quakers*, in Linda Brandi Cateura, *Growing Up Italian: How Being Brought Up as an Italian American Helped Shape the Characters, Lives, and Fortunes of Twenty-Four Celebrated Americans* (New York: William Morrow & Company, 1988), 198.

CHAPTER 12
GIO PONTI: A CLOUD OF AFFINITIES
Maristella Casciato

In November 1967, Gio Ponti published a small format book, a poetic-visual experiment that might be considered an example of concrete poetry. Entitled *Nuvole sono immagini* (Clouds are Images), it presented a short poem in fifty rhyming couplets in Italian and simultaneously translated in another five languages, accompanied by vaporous drawings. With each passing page, the clouds accumulate and drift apart like notes on a staff, and just before a downpour, there is a battle among them, until "clouds in a goblet" appear.[1] The publication, conceived as a gift for Christmas and the New Year, was entrusted to Vanni Scheiwiller (see Figure12.1).[2]

Fifty years go by. In the Milanese premises of the Whiters law firm, Lisa Licitra Ponti, then almost one hundred years old, agreed to exhibit a selection of her own delicate drawings, accompanied by a few words. Of these drawings, one that is especially striking for its immateriality is entitled "Una tazza d'aria"; it pictures a cerulean, ethereal cloud captured in a bowl.[3]

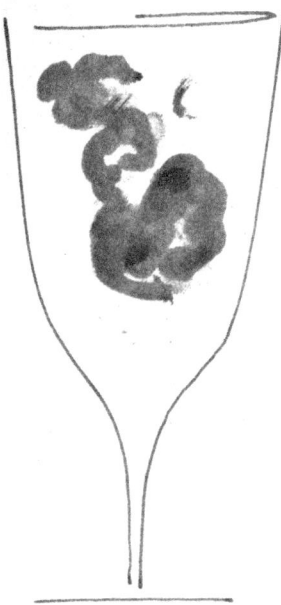

49   nuvole nel bicchiere

Figure 12.1 Gio Ponti, "Nuvole nel bicchiere," drawing published in Ponti's book of poems, entitled *Nuvole sono immagini* (Milan: All'Insegna del Pesce d'Oro, 1967), 49. Courtesy Gio Ponti Archives.

Many critics have written about the elective affinities that marked the lives of the world-renowned architect and his daughter Lisa, and this chapter will revisit certain aspects of that connection. But these correspondences of ideas, thoughts, and feelings were in the case of Gio Ponti substantially inflected by a universe profoundly indebted to the feminine: in his family, where his wife Giulia Vimercati Ponti and three daughters, Lisa, Giovanna, and Letizia, all figured prominently; in his encounters with Daria Guarnati, a still-young and immensely talented Lina Bo, the decorator Edina Altara, and the fashion journalist Irene Brin; in the ambit of his own *Domus*, where Lisa and Enrichetta Ritter worked side by side and where, from the mid-1960s, Marianne Lorenz managed the editorial staff; in his professional exchanges and friendship with Anala Planchart; and finally in the devoted affection of a multifaceted artist like Nanda Vigo. In their own ways, each of these women was "enchanted by clouds." They behaved like acrobats; they followed the unexpected; they achieved the unimaginable; they knew the lightness of being and followed "joy, strength, courage, and youth, imagination, goodness"—the values in life that were quintessential to the Pontian ethos.[4]

* * *

In the Milan apartment where Giovanna Ponti, Gio's second daughter, lived with her husband, the architect and designer Alberto Rosselli (first an assistant then, after 1951, partner in the firm of Fornaroli Ponti) and their son Paolo, an entire wall of the living room came to be occupied by the painting *La famiglia dell'architetto* (The Architect's Family) by Massimo Campigli (1934; see Figure 12.2). The portrait was bequeathed to Giovanna by her father, who died in 1979. Ponti had met the painter around 1930, and he became "a cornerstone of the architect's artistic life, someone he conversed with at length."[5] Campigli was among the most admired "heroes" of mural painting, alongside such figures as Sironi, Severini, and Carrà.[6]

Exhibited at that year's Venice Biennale, the portrait of the Ponti family captures through its "figurative abstraction" the subtle psychological ties between the four women flanking the architect.[7] To the left is Giulia Vimercati Ponti, "a gorgeous woman," whom the architect married in 1921, soon after he graduated from the Politecnico di Milano.[8] Giulia, a young daughter of Milan's wealthy, came from an old aristocratic family in Brianza; she was the hub of a wheel whose spokes connected all aspects of the architect's private and professional lives. She was wife, mother, household manager, counselor, collaborator, ambassador; she was by his side his entire life, and accompanied him on his most important trips. Giulia's sister Maria Vimercati had married Aldo (Romualdo) Borletti, heir of one of Milan's most influential industrial families, long active in the production of design objects. This connection opened the door to encounters that would have a significant impact on the architect's career.[9] Regarding her parents' relationship, Giovanna Ponti recalled:

> He fought with Mother all his life. They argued and made up, made up and argued. She was the only one able to defy Gio, to disrupt the order that Papà, having been born for this, wanted to see perfected, from clothes to the table settings . . . He

Figure 12.2 Gio Ponti, apartment of Ponti's family in Casa Laporte (via Brin, Milan), 1936. On the wall, Massimo Campigli, *La famiglia dell'architetto*, oil on canvas, 1934. Courtesy Gio Ponti Archives.

would prepare for the holidays down to the last detail, and she would purposefully move a fork, a chair: she hated static perfection as much as he loved it … she objected to work, and he lived to work.[10]

In Campigli's painting, Giulia holds Letizia (Tita), then two years old. Lisa, born in 1922, stands at center, next to Giovanna, born in 1924. The older daughters hold each other's hands affectionately, showing a lifelong connection that would grow stronger with the passing years. The figures of Giulia and Gio frame the moment of suspension portrayed by the artist: the former, in a pose like a Renaissance Madonna, extends her arm to rest her right hand on Letizia's leg; the latter, arm stiff, rests his left hand on Giovanna's shoulder.

Of the three daughters, Giovanna Ponti would have the least professional interaction with her father, perhaps (among other reasons) to protect her husband, Alberto; from the early 1950s, he shared his days, career, office, problems, and triumphs with Ponti. In contrast, Tita Ponti, the youngest, was involved in countless civic causes as an activist with Amnesty International and supporter of Milanese Radio Popolare. Because of her fluent Spanish, she was at her father's side for at least a decade starting in 1953, during his years of work in Latin America.

We thus arrive at Lisa, who described her interactions with Gio as follows:

I had the good fortune to be at the journal *Domus* with a father who said, "do as you like." It was great there. Things were published freely, you met people, and spent time together. It was a long and incredibly beautiful period. I was very fortunate because I met so many extraordinary people ... every month there were so many pages where we could experiment, commission artists, and produce them together. *Domus* was distributed all around the world, in the most discerning locations. It was a magnificent venue. Not only architects, but even many artists produced work specifically for the magazine.[11]

Lisa Licitra Ponti, an intellectual and a refined artist who expressed herself through words and drawings alike, was much more than a mere assistant at Ponti's side; she was a partner, the one able to connect her father's editorial activity to literature, art, and criticism. She joined her father at *Domus* in the late 1930s and returned with full authority in 1948, when Ponti regained control after a six-year interval at *Stile*, for which Lisa wrote short articles, commentary on the artists she considered the most promising against a backdrop of war and bombings.

Domus, founded in 1928, was subtitled "architecture and interiors of the modern city and country home." It immediately became one of the most effective and active instruments of Italian architecture in the early fascist period. Often contrasted, almost ideologically, with *Casabella*, then led by Giuseppe Pagano, Ponti's magazine distinguished itself with its graphic design as much as through its content.[12] The architect conceived of it as an informative periodical that could make its way into every Italian home while winking at female readers; the monthly's scope included architecture, interiors, domestic economy, and home decoration. Yet from the very first issue, with an editorial entitled "La casa all'italiana" (The Italian Home), Ponti set out to show a national and fascist path to achieving a modern way of living: "[This home] is not only a '*machine à habiter*,' but offers 'comfort' and something higher: it is 'suited to our ideas' and 'healthy for our lifestyle.'"[13]

After twelve years, Ponti left the management of his creation, and the following year, in 1941, was when he founded another journal, the aforementioned *Stile* (Style), which he also led.[14] He abandoned his first editor, Gianni Mazzocchi, for Aldo Garzanti, who had arrived in Milan from Forlì in 1939 and decided to focus on publishing.

Ponti's move from *Domus* to *Stile* had a significant impact on the way he thought about his role as chief editor. In the years before the war, he thought he had accomplished *Domus*' initial mission and was eager to reach a new public. He took a fresh look at all managerial issues and invited younger colleagues to create an editorial team, where women became more and more pivotal.

Stile—sometimes written as "*lo Stile* (article in lower case, noun capitalized, or "the Style") *in homes and interiors*," the subtitle varying over the years—was intended as an art monthly that could also speak to a readership beyond the art world. Born at the start of the war, it aimed to be the most beautiful and elegant Italian magazine, and succeeded in doing so—at least during its first three years.[15] Ponti changed his way of working, gathering a large editorial staff that included Carlo Pagani, Piero Gadda Conti, Gian Galeazzo Severi, and Carlo Enrico Rava, in addition to Lisa Ponti, to whom was entrusted each issue's final section, which became "the Style newsletter."[16] Its editorial position remained moderate; the goal was to proceed on the basis of accumulated experience, to spread a culture of modern living, to go further and "demonstrate the connections between the many things that are *expressions*, *ornaments*, or *tools* for our way of life."[17]

Yet Italy's fortunes changed in 1943 as its allegiances shifted; the magazine became less appealing as the war approached people's doorsteps. In the summer of that year, the bombing of Milan damaged the offices of both the publisher and the editors. This led to an "impoverished" *Stile*, not in terms of ideas but of resources. While producing *Stile*, Ponti wrote under twenty-four pseudonyms, and from 1945 to 1947 managed every issue. As soon as *Domus* was reborn from the ashes of war, Lisa Ponti was ready to resume her role in that journal. She wrote that "'Stile' is an island. A magazine that was born and then died a few years later. 'Domus' is a river."[18] In a letter to his friend Gigi Radice, Ponti affirmed that "my daughter is so much like myself at *Domus* that it is best to negotiate with her."[19]

These densely interwoven histories of publishing houses that shift from accounts of *Domus* to *Stile*, and back to *Domus*, include a third periodical beginning in 1939: *Aria d'Italia* (Italian Air) and its founder and editor, Daria Guarnati (see Figure 12.3). Who was Daria and what affinities connected her to Ponti? The young Daria Lapauze (better known as Guarnati, the name of her husband Giacomo Francesco, an art writer and ardent collector) was born in Paris in 1891. Her father was a conservator at the Petit Palais and director of two major journals on Renaissance art. In 1936, the newly widowed Daria Guarnati moved to Milan and brought Paris to the Lombard capital, where she formed numerous acquaintances among collectors and intellectuals, such as Piero Maria Bardi, already very close to Ponti. Lisa Ponti, a teenager at the time, remembered:

> . . . the endless squabbles between Daria and Gio, as intense and deep as the affinity they shared . . . If Paris was where art reviews like *Verve* and *Minotaure* were born, it was with Daria and Gio that *Aria d'Italia* was born, the most Italian of the Parisian journals and the most Parisian of the Italian journals and a point of connection—during years of isolation—between artists and writers: Italian/Parisian artists and writers, like de Pisis, Cocteau, Malaparte . . .[20]

Aria d'Italia had seven quarterly issues from 1939 to 1941. Each had a seasonal reference and a monographic quality, constructed around the idea of an Italian style and artistic culture. The images were always far more important than the text. The layout was sophisticated, with foldout pages; sometimes the drawings were at full scale; sometimes they played with the juxtaposition of larger and smaller images, so they could be studied comparatively. From the project's beginnings, Ponti supported Daria Guarnati with his intellectual proximity and his words of encouragement and comfort: "I believe that *Aria d'Italia* is a most noble undertaking, through which you honor Italy … I thus repeat my advice: clear your mind of everything except *Aria d'Italia*."[21] But the

Figure 12.3 Daria Guarnati (right) and Gio Ponti (left) meeting in front of the architect's country house in Civate, a small town in the province of Lecco, early 1950s. Courtesy Gio Ponti Archives.

architect was also among its most active partners, and even more, as we shall see. Ponti designed the cover of the first issue (winter 1939), in which Lisa Ponti published two items, a Christmas carol and a short story. Moreover, in the first issue of *Stile* (January 1941), he included a promotion of Guarnati's magazine, calling it "the most graphically beautiful and artistically important publication in Europe ... [one that anticipates] the twentieth century's 'second avant-gardes' like Pop Art or the verbal-visual intervention *ante litteram* ..."[22]

If, as already stated, *Aria d'Italia* is positioned both chronologically and culturally in a transition phase between two key moments in Ponti's editorial production, his return to editorial control over *Domus* in 1948 did not end his intellectual ties to Guarnati.[23] This is shown by the release of an eighth issue of *Aria d'Italia*, published in 1954 under the title "Espressione di Gio Ponti" (The Expression of Gio Ponti). The publication was a tribute to one of Daria's sources of intellectual inspiration, whose significance the volume presented as a rejection of artistic ideologies or fixed historiographic perspectives through a montage of text and images. As James Sachs Plaut wrote in the preface, these were demonstrations "of the special quality of Italian genius which through the centuries has so frequently yielded the *complete* artist." The author rejoiced at the opportunity to introduce "a provocative and noteworthy chapter in the art of our day ... and to welcome and introduce Gio Ponti to an ever-growing and appreciative audience."[24] In fact, the Institute of Contemporary Art (ICA) in Boston, of which Plaut was director, was organizing a show of Ponti's work that would travel to several cities across North America.

To conclude this chapter, it is worth underscoring that it was Guarnati who, in 1939, proposed to Bardi the production, however precocious, of a monographic work on Ponti. Bardi seemed favorably inclined towards the project but did not pursue it. She revisited the idea in 1957, in the wake of the work done for "Espressione di Gio Ponti," proposing to gather the material and ask him only for a one-page preface. It all remained on paper.

While the small exhibition at the ICA in Boston indicated Ponti's success, it remained unique until the architect's death in 1979; an international retrospective was not staged until 1986, this time in Japan, curated by Arata Isozaki.[25] A few years later, it was Lisa Licitra Ponti who undertook the daunting task of telling the story of Gio Ponti the architect and designer, which she had witnessed first-hand, by publishing the first book dedicated entirely to her father's work. Her volume covered, in objective and essential detail, the many chapters in a career that encompassed every spatial, formal, structural, material, and cultural aspect of design practice.[26]

*   *   *

In the second part of this study, I will focus briefly on a few other female figures who intersected with Ponti's professional world in ways that were somewhat less structured than those discussed so far. Yet they did not count any less; indeed, their collaboration demonstrates how much the architect sought and greatly appreciated these happy synergies with women.

I have previously written briefly about Lina Bo, who recalled Gio as "the last of the Humanists."[27] Lina Bo landed in Milan in 1940, the year Italy entered the war. In her words, "I escaped the ruins of antiquity reclaimed by the fascists. Rome was a closed-off city, fascism was there … but Milan, no."[28] She arrived in the Lombard capital with her Milanese colleague Carlo Pagani who, like her, had graduated in Rome. She was twenty-six years old when she entered Gio Ponti's office as an intern. He published their project for a "Seaside House in Sicily" in *Domus* (August 1940); the Mediterranean atmosphere pervading its living room design, as drawn by Lina Bo, has a De Chirico-esque quality. She and Pagani followed Ponti to the editorial staff at *Stile*. Of the two, Lina seemed particularly gifted at absorbing Ponti's suggestions, especially regarding the interiors, as her beautiful drawings demonstrate. During those same years, Lina Bo developed many other journalistic activities and, in collaboration with Pagani, edited five *Quaderni di Domus* (Domus Notebooks) that focused on research into handicraft and industrial design. In 1945 the war ended, and hope was reborn. Lina Bo rediscovered her nomadism and returned to Rome, where she met Bruno Zevi. Together, with the consent of the editor of *Domus* and in partnership with Pagani, they decided to establish the journal *A—Cultura della Vita* (A—Culture of Life), the first issue of which appeared on February 15, 1946.

This extraordinary experience demonstrates their cultural, ethical, and civic commitment to national reconstruction. *A* lasted only one year and produced nine issues. During that same year, Lina Bo married Pietro Maria Bardi, whom she certainly met through Ponti. That October, the couple embarked for Rio de Janeiro, a destination that became permanent: "I felt I was in an unimaginable land, where everything was possible. I felt so happy; in Rio there was no rubble."[29]

We now return to *Domus*, where the number of women working alongside Lisa Ponti multiplied over the decades. In 1952, Gio Ponti was primarily occupied with a project that synthesized three aspirations drawn from his way of understanding his contribution to architecture: professional practice, education, and editorial engagement. All this manifested itself in the renovation of an abandoned shed, formerly a garage, a long, narrow space measuring 15 m x by 45 m, where he located his office with adjoining areas for a small exhibition space, an educational center for students and artists, and the *Domus* headquarters.[30]

The magazine's editorial office occupied an area at the back of the shed, near the garden exit. The detailing of each interior space was carefully considered to create a pleasant and relaxing environment, even during the frenetic periods as each issue was completed. The editors, two at that time (Lisa Po and Enrichetta Ritter), shared a large worktable.

Enrichetta Ritter, born in Italy to a Waldensian family from Switzerland, was the same age as Lisa. She focused on design that was especially creative. She arrived at *Domus* in July 1951, when Ponti had decided to dedicate the second half of the year (issues 260 to 264–5) to the meticulous presentation of international pavilions and national exhibitions, with sections on industrial design objects and on ceramics, textiles, and plastics, the crafts presented at the IX Milan Triennale. Ritter was certainly entrusted with following this very important event, the first to leave behind the social issues of the immediate postwar era of reconstruction.

The following year Lisa Licitra Ponti and Enrichetta Ritter produced a volume entitled *Furniture and Interiors* for Domus Editions. Their partnership during the *Domus* years was very direct, productive, and enduring, lasting until the summer of 1961 (see Figure 12.4). After leaving the magazine, Ritter published *Italian Design: Furniture* (1968), a very thorough and well-documented book whose production was supported by Bruno Munari and Gillo Dorfles. It included works by Gio Ponti, Franco Albini, Ettore Sottsas, Joe Colombo, and Vico Magistretti, among others.

The Austro-Italian Marianne Lorenz joined the *Domus* editorial staff in April 1965. After a brief period working in his architecture office, Gio wanted her at the magazine alongside Lisa, with whom she developed a deep friendship. This was the golden age at *Domus*, by then a landmark for an increasingly global architecture, yet also a training ground for young critics and emerging photographers. Lorenz's rigor and professionalism, plus a sincere generosity, were in perfect harmony with the two Pontis.[31]

Among the authors who first worked at *Stile*, then *Domus*, there were also Edina Altara and Irene Brin. The former began contributing fashion illustrations to *Bellezza* (Beauty), a women's magazine also managed by Ponti, in 1942. Her extensive work with Ponti sparked her creativity to include furnishings and design illustrations published in both periodicals. Altara had the opportunity to work on the interior furnishings and decor the architect designed for ocean liners from 1948 to 1953.[32] In particular, she

Figure 12.4 Portrait of Lisa Licitra Ponti (left) and Enrichetta Ritter (right) working in the editorial office of the magazine *Domus*, located in Ponti's atelier, viale Coni Zugna 10, Milan, ca.1953. Courtesy Gio Ponti Archives.

produced *l'Allegoria del viaggiare* (Allegory of Travel), a large panel in oil on glass, for the *Conte Grande* in 1950, which she signed along with the architect.

Irene Brin, the pseudonym of Maria Vittoria Rossi, was a fashion journalist, collector, and art dealer. She probably met Ponti through Leo Longanesi, one of the most multifaceted and prolific intellectuals of the interwar period. A true talent scout, in 1937 he invited the still-young Maria Vittoria (it was Longanesi who suggested she adopt a nom de plume) to take charge of an international news column in the weekly *Omnibus*, which he had founded. During the first two years of *Stile*, Brin's witty and elegant writings appeared frequently, in perfect harmony with the ideas of "style" and good taste in art and architecture that Ponti embodied. She was featured in *Domus* through short reviews of art publications, translations, and refined commentary on fashion, for which she was compared with Cecil Beaton. She wrote about collecting, and in 1963 appeared in an extensive interview about the sophisticated and glamourous Galleria l'Obelisco, which Brin and her husband Gaspero del Corso had founded in Rome in 1946, as part of a *Domus* series on art dealers.[33]

To conclude this overview, I will focus on two architectural projects that were shaped by Ponti's conversations with two exceptional women.

In Caracas, the design of the Quinta (fifth) El Cerrito villa (1953–7) for the couple Anala and Armando Planchard marked the culmination of a moment of creative grace, one that Ponti called a "fairy tale."[34] Of the two, Ana Luisa (Anala) Braun Kerdel assumed a central role in facilitating the reciprocal understanding between them and the designer, becoming an essential participant in the intense design process that, at a certain point, led to an exchange of letters and drawings at least every other day (see Figure 12.5 and Plate 8).

To celebrate their wedding anniversary, the Plancharts moved into their new home; its inauguration took place on December 8, 1957, with Gio Ponti, his wife and his daughter Tita in attendance. Ponti personally placed a seal on what would become their new life: "After 'El Cerrito,' there will be nothing like 'El Cerrito.'"[35]

The presence of Nanda Vigo (born in Milan in 1936, with an architecture degree from Lausanne Polytechnic) in Italian art movements of the 1960s should also be highlighted.

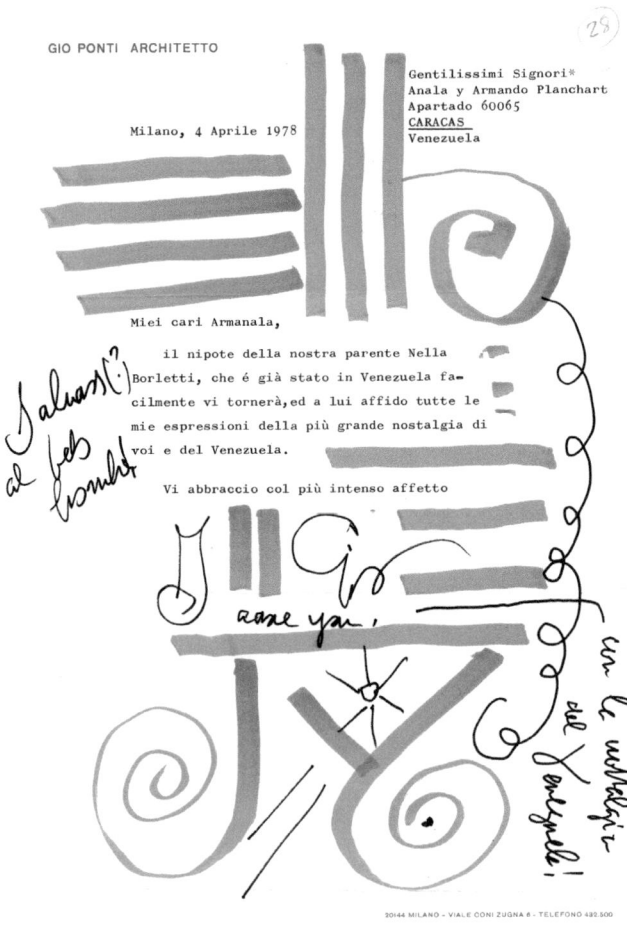

Figure 12.5 Gio Ponti, letter to Anala and Armando Planchard, Milan, April 4, 1978. Courtesy of Archivio Gio Ponti Caracas: Correspondencia.

Her work explored the conflicts and harmonies between space, light, and time in ways related to that of Lucio Fontana and Piero Manzoni. She took possession of Gio Ponti's design for the Casa Scarabeo sotto la Foglia (Beetle under the Leaf) (1965–8), which he had published but not seen realized, taking up, in her own way, his invitation to make something tangible of work.[36] Finding a site outside Vicenza and an art collector client of her own, Vigo transformed this house into a hybrid environment suspended between domestic space and a performative museum, introducing material elements from *l'architettura radicale*, such as a fur-covered spiral staircase.[37]

I will end with a reflection by Ponti on "Women and Architecture." In one of his most celebrated texts, entitled *Amate l'architettura* (Love Architecture, with 'love' written as an order to his audience), the architect inserted four bright pink pages and began by writing, "(I have learned more things from women—I am speaking of architecture—: here are three women's episodes)."[38] There are actually four episodes, which correspond to the same number of actual women whose life experiences had made him discover that there existed "an intrinsic functionality for form, beyond function." Hence there was a "danger for so many modern architects (doing without living, without any fire) . . . [while] women (senses) understand more than us men (brains): thus, the senses have a reason that Rationality does not know." In this private diary of events, thoughts, and sensations, Ponti did not omit a declaration of his appreciation for women.

On this note, we return to the image of clouds. Gio's creative cloudscape was in a very real sense composed of the women in his life. In his *Nuvole sono immagini*, the personification of the clouds as women is highly allusive. In one of his couplets, he admires the richness of women's imagination and their ability to have their "head in the clouds." His was the experience of women listening, seeking, calling, following, protecting, and being the muse. For Ponti, "clouds are angels."

Notes

I wish to thank Salvatore Licitra and Paolo Rosselli for having generously shared with me their family recollections. I am also indebted to Fulvio Irace and Hannia Gómez for their valued suggestions. I also thank Elena Tinacci, MAXXI Museum Rome, for assisting me with the consultation of books and texts by and about Gio Ponti, and Anni Pullagura from the ICA in Boston for kindly responding to my queries.

1. The drawing accompanies line 49.

2. Vanni Scheiwiller (1934–99), an art critic and publisher, was the editor of the volume, printed in 1967, in 3,000 numbered copies, by the Milanese publishing house All'Insegna del Pesce d'Oro, founded by her father. Copy 215, which I consulted, is held by the Getty Research Institute in Los Angeles, where it is part of the archive of Erich and Luise Mendelsohn, as shown by the frontispiece dedication with New Year's greetings to Louise (sic) and her daughter Esther from Giulia and Gio Ponti.

3. The exhibition, from July to December 2018, included thirty-three drawings by Lisa Licitra Ponti, displayed in a visual dialogue with a painting by her father Gio and a sculpture by Francesco Vezzoli.

4. From a letter from Ponti to Lisa, dated June 1973.

5. Lisa's recollections about this famous painting's genesis reveal the painter's personality and Ponti's family life: "Campigli was a great storyteller, a former journalist who became a painter at the suggestion of his wife, a beautiful Romanian woman named Dutza Radulesco. We lived at his place for a few months [around 1934]. He cooked in his enormous studio, ate on a ping pong table, and told us stories about his adventures during the war. During the winter we spent together, he created this incredibly measured family portrait. We were all attracted to him, to his personality, then there was a bit of distance. At a certain point he abandoned his beautiful Dutza and fell in love with a girl from Como, married her, and made her dress like his first wife, wearing sweaters and extremely heavy silver bracelets. My sister Giovanna and I wondered 'what happened? He gets a new woman then completely transforms her! What a bully!' He then found a third one and made her dress the same way. This contributed somewhat to the cooling of the relationship." See Luca Lo Pinto, "Le affinità elettive: Lisa Ponti," *Doppiozero*, September 18, 2012.

6. On the close relationships Ponti maintained with the art world and its major figures from his earliest years, see the essay by Paolo Campiglio, "Ponti, artista fra gli artisti," in *Gio Ponti. Amare l'architettura*, ed. Maristella Casciato and Fulvio Irace (Florence: MAXXI/Forma, 2019), 96–103.

7. The painting was in the living room of the house on via Brin, where the Pontis moved around 1934 after leaving their elegant fourth-story apartment in the "neoclassical" building on via Randaccio. Both buildings were designed by Ponti, who, as his nephew Salvatore Licitra has pointed out, had the good fortune to "live in four houses he himself designed." See Salvatore Licitra, "Gio Ponti: case come me," in *Gio Ponti. Amare l'architettura*, ed. Maristella Casciato and Fulvio Irace (Florence: MAXXI/Forma, 2019), 50–61. The family portrait does not include the fourth Ponti child, Giulio, born in 1937, the only one to follow in their father's footsteps and become an architect. Today the painting remains preserved in the apartment owned by Giovanna Ponti Rosselli, still occupied by her son Paolo.

8. These words and recollections are those of Giovanna Ponti Rosselli, as told to Luigi Mascheroni, "Giovanna Ponti Rosselli," *Il Giornale.it*, January 14, 2007.

9. In an unpublished interview of 2001 between architect Hannia Gómez and Anala Planchart, the wealthy client of the eponymous villa and "fairy godmother" of modern architecture in Caracas, the latter left a striking portrait of the Ponti couple: "He was a man with no interest in money. He told me that he was successful because he married very well; she was a Vimercati. That was a good family! And his much less so, he was middle-class. I replied, 'Ah, so I've found you out!' and he responded: 'She discovered me and allowed me to experiment freely, because she was an extremely intelligent woman.' She had 'elevated' him, and he was a very small man. If it was not for her, he would have gotten nowhere." In that interview, Anala made a curious reference to a little-noted detail in the history of family connections among the Borletti, who in turn were tied to descendants of the famous Parisian gold and silversmiths Christofle. Beginning continuously in 1927, they commissioned place settings and design objects from Ponti.

10. Mascheroni, "Giovanna Ponti Rosselli."

11. Born in Milan in 1922, Lisa Ponti married attorney Luigi Licitra in 1951 and was widowed early. The couple lived in the apartment on via Randaccio formerly occupied by the Ponti family. Their son Salvatore was born there and lives there still. Lisa's redesign of the home transformed the house into a *salon*, a showcase for architects, designers, and artists: "...furniture by Ponti and Mollino, decor by Fornasetti, Melotti ceramics, paintings by De Pisis, Funi, then Albers, Wirkkala glass, huge spherical lamps by Noguchi and finally, during a period of enthusiasm for contemporary art [in the late 1960s] Gilardi, Merz, Paladino, Luciano Fabro, Haring, Prini, Germanà and beyond." Licitra, "Gio Ponti: case come me," 54; Lo Pinto, "Le affinità elettive."

12. Although they may seem incompatible, *Domus* and *Casabella* were for a time managed by the same publisher, Gianni Mazzocchi, who came to Milan from his birthplace in the Marche in late 1928, where he soon became friends with Gio Ponti. The following year, Mazzocchi established l'Editoriale Domus, which continued to publish Ponti's magazine without interruption.

13. Gio Ponti, "La casa all'italiana," *Domus* (January 1928): 7; Maristella Casciato, "The 'Casa all'Italiana' and the idea of modern dwelling in fascist Italy," *Journal of Architecture* 5, no. 4 (2000): 335–53; Simona Storchi, "'La casa all'italiana': *Domus* and the Ideology of the Domestic interior in 1930s Italy," in *Beyond the Piazza: Public and Private Spaces in Modern Italian Culture*, ed. Simona Storchi (Brussels: Peter Lang, 2013), 57–75. A fuller historiography, along with a catalog of the Milanese architect's extensive and varied residential projects, is offered by Fulvio Irace in *Gio Ponti. La casa all'italiana* (Milan: Electa, 1988).

14. Massimo Martignoni, *Gli anni di Stile, 1941–1947* (Milan: Abitare Segesta, 2002).

15. For Ponti's ideas on style, see *Gio Ponti, Stile di*, ed. Cecilia Rostagni (Milan: Mondadori Electa, 2016).

16. Pagani served as the magazine's editor until June 1943, and editor-in-chief from April 1942 to June 1943. In the summer of that year, Mazzocchi invited him to co-direct *Domus* with Melchiorre Bega. He accepted on the condition of having Lina Bo as a partner. From the following January, *Domus* was issued under the signature "Pagani-Bo," and the team alternated between the editorial office's new location in Bergamo and Milan. Rostagni, *Gio Ponti, Stile di*, 8. Although not listed among the editors, Lina Bo participated in various ways in many issues. She managed issues with Pagani or even Ponti, or as a member of the "Gienlica" collective, a title constructed from the first letters of Gio Ponti, Enrico Bo, Lina Bo, and Carlo Pagani's names. She published a number of essays, mostly on houses designed with Pagani, with whom she managed the interiors section. She also produced drawings and illustrations for several articles.

17. Lisa Ponti, "'Stile' è un'isola," in Martignoni, *Gli anni di Stile*, 7.

18. Martignoni, *Gli anni di Stile*, 7.

19. Note in *Domus* 1,000, guest editor Fulvio Irace (March 2016), 8. Gio Ponti returned as director in January 1948, no. 226. With architect Mario Tedeschi and Lisa Ponti as editors. That year only six issues were published.

20. Lisa Licitra Ponti, "Penso al nome 'Daria' e alla parola 'Aria'," in *"Aria d'Italia" di Daria Guarnati. L'arte della rivista intorno al 1940*, ed. Silvia Bignami (Milan: Skira, 2008), 7.

21. Letter from Gio Ponti to Daria Guarnati, dated December 23, 1940, cited in Bignami, "Daria Guarnati e lo stile italiano," *"Aria d'Italia" di Daria Guarnati*, 13–14.

22. Ponti, quoted in Bignami *"Aria d'Italia" di Daria Guarnati*, 24.

23. Over the years, they all established connections that went beyond friendship. As Lisa recalled, "we Ponti, big and small, were all her true Italian family," in Bignami, *"Aria d'Italia" di Daria Guarnati*, 7.

24. It is worth noting that Daria Guarnati was among the first ambassadors of the Italian style in the United States, where she often traveled. Therefore, it was no surprise that she met James Plaut, who had been the co-founder of the Institute of Modern Art in Boston, renamed the Institute of Contemporary Art (ICA) in 1946. The Institute hosted the exhibition *Gio Ponti and Gyorgy Kepes* from March 6 to April 4, 1954. The press summary remarked, "Design has contributed a provocative and noteworthy chapter to the art of our day. It is therefore no surprise that the men who create today's designs display a range of capabilities that comes close to matching the complexity of a world they seek to shape. Two of these distinguished designers—Kepes of Cambridge and MIT, and Ponti of Milan—demonstrate the startling

scope of their activities in this exhibition. Essentially this is an exhibition of contrasts: Ponti's work is three-dimensional, flamboyant, and characteristically Italian, be it architecture or industrial design; Kepes' work is two dimensional, quiet in spirit, introspective, consistent in design feeling, be it photogram, photograph, exhibition design or painting." James Plaut authored the "Preface" in *Espressione di Gio Ponti*, *Aria d'Italia* (Milan: Dario Guarnati Editore, 1954), 4.

25. *Gio Ponti 1891–1979*, Seibu Museum of Art, Tokyo, 1986. The exhibition did not include an accompanying book or catalog.

26. Lisa Licitra Ponti, *Gio Ponti, l'opera* (Milan: Leonardo Editore, 1990).

27. The literature on Lina Bo Bardi is abundant. Among the most recent monographic books are Olivia De Oliveira, *Lina Bo Bardi: obra construida / Built Works* (Barcelona: Gustavo Gili, 2014); *Lina Bo Bardi 100: Brazil's Alternative Path to Modernism* (Ostfildern: Hatje Cantz, 2014); and Alessandra Criconia, Elisabeth Essïan (eds), *Lina Bo Bardi: Enseignements partagés* (Paris: Archibooks + Sautereau Éditeur, 2017).

28. Lina Bo, "Curriculum letterario," in *Lina Bo Bardi in Italia: "Quello che volevo, era avere Storia,"* exhibition catalog (Rome: Fondazione MAXXI, 2015), 34.

29. On Lina Bo and Italy, see especially Zeuler R. M. de A. Lima, *Lina Bo Bardi* (New Haven, CT: Yale University Press, 2013), and the exhibition catalog from MAXXI, 2015. Regarding collaboration between *Domus* editors and the publication of *A—Cultura della Vita*, see the tribute in *Domus* 986 (December 2014): 1–5.

30. Article in *Domus* 276–7 (December 1952): 59–66. A few years later, on an adjacent lot, Ponti designed a nine-story residential building, the eighth floor of which became his home. The building, which is accessible from via Dezza, also had access to the entrance of the shed, which occupied the space behind the condominium. Dwelling and working were magically integrated in via Dezza, which remained Ponti's headquarters until his death.

31. After the death of the magazine's legendary director, Marianne Lorenz continued in her role until 1998, a total of over thirty years at *Domus*.

32. These projects are presented in Paolo Piccione, *Gio Ponti. Le Navi. Il progetto degli interni navali 1948–1953*, intro. Lisa Licitra Ponti, Italian and English edn (Viareggio: Idea Books, 2007).

33. La Galleria L'Obelisco, located at via Sistina 146, hosted internationally prominent exhibitions and became a landmark for modern art in the capital. See *Domus* 403 (June 1963): 121–6.

34. Illustrated letter from Gio Ponti to Anala and Armando, dated August 22, 1967, cited in Hannia Gómez, *El Cerrito. La obra maestra de Gio Ponti en Caracas* (Milan: Ultreya, 2009), 235, 237.

35. "Los Arboles de Recuerdos," illustrated letter, Gio Ponti to Anala and Armando, cited in Hannia Gómez, "Villa Planchart Caracas, 1953–1957," in *Gio Ponti. Amare l'architettura*, ed. Maristella Casciato and Fulvio Irace (Florence: MAXXI/Forma, 2019), 161.

36. "Uno scarabeo sotto una foglia," *Domus* 414 (May 1964): 75–83.

37. "Una collezione in una casa," *Domus* 482 (January 1970): 68–72. By the mid-1960s, Vigo was one of the most hard-working partners at *Domus*, to which she dedicated immense investment through her work as a designer and her artistic production.

38. Gio Ponti, "Donne e architettura," in *Amate l'architettura* (Genoa: Vitali e Ghianda, 1957), 161. On Ponti as writer, see Daria Ricchi, "Scrivere l'architettura: il diario di un architetto ilanese," in *Gio Ponti. Amare l'architettura*, ed. Maristella Casciato and Fulvio Irace (Florence: MAXXI/Forma, 2019), 260–7.

CHAPTER 13

MARKING, FRAMING, AND MEASURING (IN) VITTORIO GREGOTTI'S *IL TERRITORIO DELL'ARCHITETTURA*

Chris French

A guide shepherds visitors through the low, dark interior of the Garagem Sul at the Centro Cultural de Belém (CCB) in Lisbon. An array of exhibition panels hangs from the ceiling, depicting architectural projects, histories, images, and texts brought into dialogue by architectural historian and philosopher Sébastien Marot. The exhibition, *Agriculture and Architecture: Taking the Country's Side*, is part of the 2019 Lisbon Triennale, *The Poetics of Reason*, curated by Éric Lapierre. The panels document intersections between architecture and the countryside, framing "a body of ideas or references" to "substantiate" the argument that architecture and agriculture are "complementary phases" of an "autocatalytic process" through which we engage with our built and unbuilt environment.[1] Down the long, uninterrupted wall adjacent to the array is a timeline, a "fresco … synthesizing the parallel evolutions of agriculture and architecture."[2] This timeline cuts across the open field of the array, connecting Varro's *Rerum rusticarum* (*On Agriculture*) and Vitruvius' *De architectura* to the publications of biologist Bill Mollison and environment designer David Holmgren.[3] A winding path can be discerned from the *villa suburbana* of the Roman Empire to the radical experimentation of the twentieth-century Italian *Neoavanguardia*, an evolution from architecture as an "instrument of domestication" and "symbol of a domination of the countryside" embodied by the subdivision of *pars urbana*, *rustica*, and *fructuaria* (or home, barn, and productive land) in the *villa suburbana* to the radical re-envisioning of the very notion of architecture, landscape, and city.[4]

A projection opposite the "fresco" shows Florentine group Superstudio's film *Supersurface, an Alternative Model for Life on Earth*, from 1972, in which "a network of energy and information" distributes resources. A second film follows in the loop: Andrea Branzi's *Agronica* (1995). It depicts furniture-like buildings drifting through carefully maintained agricultural landscapes, developing themes explored decades earlier by Archizoom Associati, the group founded by Branzi, Gilberto Corretti, Paolo Deganello, and Massimo Morozzi, active between 1966 and 1974. Watching the films cycle as the visiting group is guided through the array, Marot's inclusion of Branzi and Superstudio as evidence of a sustained reframing of the relationship of architecture to countryside demands attention. The "territorial integration" these thinkers proposed was predicated upon a particular attitude to landscape and city that sought to transcend the "city-countryside division," an aim closely associated with specific social (and architectural) concerns.[5] Superstudio's *Supersurface* subsumes all but the most stubborn territorial masses in its all-encompassing urban structure. Archizoom are absent from Marot's exhibition, but their key work, "No-Stop City" (1969), imagines a featureless space occupied by consumer goods and interrupted only by dominant geographical features. The countryside in these works is still marginalized, territorially reinscribed and reinscribable through the architectural figure. The logics of the *villa suburbana*, it seems, persist. But collectively, these images represent a significant investigation by the *Neoavanguardia* into urban-territorial engagement in which, despite images that are dominated by the architectural figure, the landscape became both a critical limit to and instigator of the architectural project.

In the background to these works, in several senses, is Vittorio Gregotti. The CCB was designed by Gregotti with Lisbon architect Manuel Salgado, and the same space hosted a retrospective of Gregotti's work in late 2018, centered on the theme of *The Territory of Architecture*. The early No-Stop City collages produced by Archizoom used base aerial images taken from a 1965 issue of *Edilizia Moderna* edited and arranged by Gregotti, entitled "La Forma del Territorio."[6] Gregotti was involved with the influential Gruppo 63, was curator of the Milan Triennale in 1954, and his 1966 publication *Il territorio dell'architettura*, which was revised in 2008 but has never been completely translated into English, "revealed new and previously largely unexplored horizons to the world of architectural theory and practice" which would be developed by the groups of the 1970s.[7] Like those who would follow, Gregotti's theoretical and built works responded to what he perceived as a changing relationship between agriculture and the city in Italy in the second half of the twentieth century, one in which "rural culture" was urbanized and ways of thinking about the rural had come to "reflect an urban condition."[8] His projects sought to reinterpret landscape through a "critical alteration of the relations between architecture, the city, and the form of the territory" following Friedrich Ratzel's description of "anthropogeography," which stated that the world could no longer be considered natural as it was already indelibly marked by human action.[9] Gregotti, like Archizoom, is absent from Marot's exhibition, but for architecture and the countryside to be reconnected and rethought, and to trace the specific inflection which the Italian neo-avant-garde might offer to this rethinking as Marot's exhibition invites, this chapter explores a reading of three different aspects of Gregotti's "critical alteration" established in *Il territorio dell'architettura* and made evident by two of Gregotti's built works: the processes of marking, framing, and measuring architecture and landscape.[10] To understand the complex intertwining of phenomenology and critical rationalism in Gregotti's work, one must begin with stone and a stone: the stone of the CCB and the mountains around Palermo, and a mythical stone which, Gregotti claims, is found at the very beginnings of all architecture.

Outside Garagem Sul, black basalt and white limestone *calçada* paving sketches patterns in the canyons between the stone facades of the CCB. Lioz limestone cladding, split into coursed bands—sometimes stacked, sometimes staggered—and punctuated by dark vents, covers all visible vertical surfaces, only broken by large apertures filled with white, square windows (see Figure 3.1 and Plate 3). The stone cladding follows a module, a 7.5 m grid to which "everything had to conform" so as to enable a "subliminal reading of a pre-established order."[11] This modularity, described in the breaks in the stone skin,

Figure 13.1 Marking: Lioz limestone cladding, Centro Cultural de Belém, Lisbon. Photograph ©
Maria Mitsoula. Reproduced with permission.

measures the building, setting sizes and underscoring "the public and civic nature of the
urban microsystem" of the CCB.[12] It declares constructional and organizational logics,
but also associations with the large retaining and defensive walls that structure Lisbon,
the adjacent San Jeronimos Monastery, and the Torre de Belem at the mouth of the
Tagus. These associations enabled Gregotti to claim an understanding of the specific
Portuguese socio-material history embodied by this stone which differentiated the
winning competition scheme from other competitors. Arguably, however, Portugal also
understood Gregotti. Since the 1940s, the magazine *Arquitectura* had been publishing
texts from *Casabella* written by Gregotti's mentor, Ernesto N. Rogers.[13] The continuity
that Rogers had promoted in *Casabella* between *preesistenze ambientali* (environmental
pre-existences) and architecture, and between history and situation, would develop in
Gregotti's work (reframed in Gregotti as *ambiente totale*, the "total environment"). In
1968, Gregotti participated in the Pequeno Congresso de Vitória with Álvaro Siza.
Recognizing similarities in their work, this meeting prompted Gregotti to publish a
series of articles in Italy on Siza's work.[14] Gregotti's CCB therefore materializes a
conceptual oscillation between Italy and Portugal: ideas established in Italy were
published and developed in Portugal, and subsequently re-presented in Italy through
Gregotti's introductions to Siza, only to return to Lisbon in the form of the CCB.

This oscillation exemplifies one of the challenges in describing Gregotti's work: his
theorization engages the specificities of a local situation but through a generalizing
approach, one that calls as much on Nietzsche's aphorisms and Heidegger's notion of

dwelling as the rationalism of the Italian interwar architects whom Gregotti cited as influences. At the CCB, Gregotti invoked Nietzsche. "Stone," he declared, is "more stony than it used to be;" it becomes "a value in itself that form has the duty to display."[15] Between the three stone-clad modules (the Conference Center, Performing Arts Center, and Exhibition Center were constructed; a further two modules for a hotel and equipment zone remain unbuilt), stone gardens appear. Landscape architect João Gomes da Silva's scheme sought to "make the stone stand out as an element of unity between the buildings and the gardens."[16] Stone, here, is certainly "stony," and the CCB exemplary of Gregotti's double-articulation of material. He writes, "Material refers to a particular type of material, while *materials* designates everything that is used in the realization of architecture … not only stone, wood, or earth but also climate, history, geography, acquired knowledge, and desires."[17] The stone of the CCB is both a material and *material*, a register of a complex socio-spatial history and a material thing, emerging "directly from the ground" of Lisbon.[18]

But there is another reason for Gregotti's use of stone, and for the allusion to the walls which shape the topography of Lisbon in the form of the CCB. As Kenneth Frampton describes, developing a position established by Gregotti, constructing such significant earthworks embodies "a cosmogonic transformation" of a site, a generation of a world through transformation.[19] The placing of a stone in Gregotti's thinking represents the beginnings of architecture. "Before a support was transformed into a column," Gregotti wrote in the article "Territory and Architecture" in 1976, "man put stone on the ground in order to recognize place in the midst of the unknown universe and thereby measure and modify it."[20] This first architectural gesture, the placement of this stone as the precursor to the siting of a building, allowed human consciousness to be reconciled with the unknown expanse of the landscape. Gregotti repeated the claim in 1983, this time directly addressing his lifelong friend Joseph Rykwert:

> The origin of architecture is not the primitive hut or the cave of the mythical Adam's "House in Paradise." Before transforming a support into a column, a roof into a tympanum, before placing a stone on stone, man placed a stone on the ground to recognize site in the midst of an unknown universe, in order to take account of it and modify it.[21]

This description has become imprinted in the architectural imagination. The Geographical Urbanism symposium organized by Nikos Katsikis as part of the 2015 Milan EXPO Belle Arti takes this act as its starting premise.[22] Manon Mollard cites the same address as Frampton in the introduction to the February 2020 issue of the *Architectural Review*, using Gregotti's description of this "primordial tectonic act" as an opening to consider architecture's relationship with soil. In an account of the "megaform" offered in 1999, Frampton again calls on this original architectural act of placing a stone to describe the making of architecture as the generation of a "microcosms."[23] Together, these invocations demonstrate a continuing interest in Gregotti's theorization, and as Frampton's revisionist history (his words) suggests, Gregotti's description has come to underpin a "unifying environmental trope" in twentieth-century architecture, namely a return to "a time when the prime object of architecture was not the proliferation of freestanding objects but rather the marking of ground."[24]

Gregotti proposes two methods for enacting such a marking, the first by mimesis, the second by measure, by "restless division: putting up a wall, building an enclosure … producing a densely articulated interior." Through such divisions, "a simple exterior will thus appear as a measure of the larger environment's complexity." Material, the stone of the wall and the desire to separate, marks ground, gives form to an environment through measure. Ground becomes no longer "a thing of nature," but something "more earthly and more abstract," alluding to "a nature which is historically transformed."[25] Accompanying the transcript to Frampton's lecture is an image of a model of Gregotti's project for the University of Calabria, designed in 1973. The building—a "slender 3km-long bridge" spanning hills and valleys—enacts such a measuring and marking. The roofline maintains a continuous level, allowing building heights to vary only "in response to the rise and fall of the ground plane."[26] The "expansive geographic dimension" (Frampton) of the megaform and the "measure of the larger environment's complexity" (Gregotti) are captured in the linear form of the bridge. Its units give form to the undulations of environment. However, it is an earlier university project developed shortly after the publication of *Il territorio dell'architettura* which more completely encapsulates the thinking evident in Calabria.[27] The University of Calabria project would not have been possible, Gregotti claimed, without the Science and Technology Buildings at the University of Palermo, designed with renowned Italian rationalist Gino Pollini in 1969. These buildings exemplify Gregotti's description of the anthropogeographic landscape as a product of human thought and action, and architecture as measure and modifier of that landscape.

In a lecture given in 1984, Gregotti announced that the University of Palermo project was "the first practical application of [his] theory about the design of the large landscape … [and] the importance of the context in the foundation of design."[28] He illustrated this lecture with an image of the exterior of the campus buildings, captioned "University of Palermo. As Example of Today's Italian Rationalism." The image is a close-up of one of the columns which subdivide the entrances to the courtyards and organize the programme. A beam punctuated with regular square penetrations is silhouetted against the cerulean-blue Sicilian sky. In the background, a two-storey pre-cast concrete wall limits our field of view, enclosing the courtyard. This 3.5 m thick wall, and its counterpart immediately opposite, flank and connect the buildings, providing services and circulation spaces. Standing inside one of these "simple and quiet" embankment walls, and looking through the small square apertures visible in the image, the spacing of the two walls and the arrangement of these windows are such that the city is hidden from view behind the concrete surface of the wall opposite.[29] The wall forms a constructed horizon, breached only by the peaks of the surrounding Madonie mountains, and the visual inflexibility of the concrete walls (what Pierluigi Nicolin refers to as the "hard tone" of the building) begins to speak not only to the "mortality and hardness" of Palermo's Arab-Norman architecture but also to the insistent presence of the geology of Sicily.[30] Grouped in rows of eight, these small windows present a sequence of similar constructed images of landscape. Moving through the embankment walls each window reveals a modification made by a visual reframing of the landscape.[31] The city appears and disappears. The mountains slide along the horizon. The landscape in the distance is imaged in relation to the architecture. As Guido Morpurgo observes, a "direct relationship with geography" is established by the "contrast between natural and artificial profiles … a counterpoint between the project and the landscape," the line of the wall set against the undulations of the hills (see Figures 13.2 and 13.3).[32]

This modification reframes our relationship with the landscape. By concealing the city and bringing the mountains into visual dialogue with the walls the mountains are brought close. The rippled surface of the concrete panels bleeds into the stone of the mountains, the exposed stone aggregate extends into the quarries which provided stone for Palermo, or the striations scored into the geological bedrock. These windows also frame a material history of the city. The walls conceal an area constructed during the Sack of Palermo, when vast orchards and plantations were destroyed by (largely illegal) development. In place of this new city, Gregotti establishes a visual connection with the mountains, and in place of the lost landscape he brings the material and environment of the hills into the building. The entrance terrace, the lowest of the three external terraces, is a space of exposure to harsh sun; the second creates shade through a bower of oak trees; the third incorporates a large pool for cooling and reflecting light. In keeping with Gregotti's core project tenets, a "process of modification" enacted by the building "organizes the debris contained in the context" to construct a refigured territory.[33] "The very rules of belonging" to this landscape are questioned, challenging the destructive relationship between the city and its landscape, and refuting the rapid destruction of the "golden basin" (the Conca d'Oro) of orchards around Palermo by turning to the geological time of the mountains.[34] The form of the building reframes the anthropogeographic landscape as a socially constructed (aesthetic) artifact, as "the product of the efforts of imagination and collective memory" created by a subject which "constructs as an encounter with the world."[35]

The CCB, Morpurgo suggests, finds its direct antecedent in the University of Palermo. The windows which puncture the walls of the Science and Technology buildings reappear at the CCB, small squares set within the thick stone walls with white steel frames. The 7.2m structural grid which organized Palermo expands, slightly, to a 7.5m grid in Lisbon. But more fundamentally, as Gregotti states in La città visibile (Visible City, 1993), the CCB developed ideas explored in Palermo: "in Belém, as in Palermo, the simplicity of the exterior corresponds to a great internal complexity."[36] Recalling Gregotti's description of marking, in which enclosure generates densities, while there are formal and organizational differences between these two buildings (the faceted stone blocks of the CCB are more figured than the unashamedly geometric embankment walls of the campus, streets between the five modules in Lisbon replace the terraces in Palermo, and the sealed interiors of the cultural center enclose the cloisters between the thick flanking walls), the link between the two is to be found in how—through their architecture—they refigure the relationship between architecture and its territory.

Figure 13.2 and Figure 13.3 Framing: the University of Palermo and the Madonie mountains through "earthwork" walls. Photographs © Chris French. Reproduced with permission.

Figure 13.4 Marking: prefabricated raked concrete facade panels, University of Palermo. Photograph © Chris French. Reproduced with permission.

"Architecture," Gregotti declares, "functions as a way of gauging ... landscape;" it modifies our understanding of landscape.[37] "*Modus*, modification," he writes, is intrinsically linked to measure, and to "the geometrical world of regulated things." Understanding this connection enables us to conceive of the architectural project as "a system of relations and distances, as the measurement of intervals" in time and space (rather than as a fabrication of isolated objects concerned solely with formal novelty).[38] Material and *material* mark and give measure. Measure provides the means by which we modify how we exist in our environment. The measures of the CCB are extensions of this primordial material mark making, of setting the stone and oneself in relation to a landscape (see Figure 13.1 and Plate 3).

Such an act of measuring is latent within the Italian word *paesaggio*, or countryside. "Paesaggio," Tullio Pagano notes, "derives from the Latin *pagus*, the stone planted into the soil to mark a border and identify a community."[39] This *pagus* is intrinsically double. It is both the stone which marks and the space (of community) marked out by that stone.[40] As Lyotard describes, the *pagus* is a space of discourse, where "matter offers itself up in a raw state before being tamed," a space of *compact* (*com-*, together, *pangere*, fastening) with the natural world.[41] Gregotti's architectonic *pagus*—the stone set on the ground— inscribes a border (as in Pagano) and, through the making of marks, measures. and modifications, establishes a coming-together-with the space (*paesaggio*) beyond (Lyotard), a framing of interior–exterior relations. It is in this sense that Gregotti differs from his Italian contemporaries presented in the exhibition at the CCB.

Figure 13.5 Measuring: portal windows in "earthwork" walls, University of Palermo. Photograph © Chris French. Reproduced with permission.

While Gregotti, Superstudio, and Branzi were all concerned with city-territory, for Branzi (and Archizoom) and Superstudio the integration of this territory takes a different form to the anthropogeographic intersection implicit within the *pagus*. In Archizoom's "No-Stop City" the infinite expansion of an urban figure dissolves any distinction between urbanity and countryside, addressing by negation a "distrust of the countryside and the rural" as a site of class struggle in the Marxist writings of Mario Tronti and Manfredo Tafuri.[42] By subsuming the countryside, the city as the natural site of struggle against capitalism extends ad infinitum. Archizoom, as Gregotti observed, "did not deal with the territory ... their designs flew over it – the land no longer existed. They had an abstract idea of the ground, not a concrete one."[43] Branzi, to some extent, develops this detached position. As Charles Waldheim notes, one of the main contributions of *Agronica* is that it "reanimates the long tradition of using the urban project as a social and cultural critique."[44] In Superstudio's work, architecture sought "mediation [between] rapidly changing reality and man, founding it in agriculture."[45] A cover for *Casabella* 363 (1970–1, guest edited by Branzi) provided by Superstudio depicts a mirrored rectangular prism hovering over ploughed fields, reflecting and condensing the field patterns below. The image is entitled "Reflected Architecture (The Mirror of Agriculture)," suggesting that this is a formal mediation, and that the grid of the Supersurface lacks material concerns. Instead, it forms "an energetic mesh ... divested of any figurative or referential components, including depth, physical entity, or any kind of materiality."[46] These totalizing images of an urban architecture might echo Gregotti's descriptions, but for Gregotti the project of territory is not one in which we "conceive of space as a uniform and infinite extension where no place is privileged," but something "composed of differences, discontinuities considered as value and as experience," rather than experience as a contra-indicator of value.[47]

In Garagem Sul, the film *Supersurface* is still playing nearby. A close-up shows a mountain range, a wall of stone in the distance. The camera retreats, revealing the gridded Supersurface extending into the base of the mountains. The narrator proclaims, "Look at that distant mountain. What can you see? Is that the place to go to or is it the only limit of the inhabitable?"[48] This scientific-documentary voice reverberating in Garagem Sul also echoes in Gregotti's Palermo, where the mountains form their own limit. However, these two sets of mountains represent different limits to the anthropogeographical project. In Superstudio's work they are the limit of the inhabitable. In Gregotti's work in Palermo, they represent matter in its raw state, beyond *paesaggio*, that space marked out as a site of settlement and negotiation with the world, Lyotard's space of *compact*. As in Baudelaire's *paysage*, despite Gregotti's claims that there is no nature, the *paessagio* appears here as a space separated from the natural world, not yet assimilated by the city but nevertheless part of our settlement.[49] The limits of the human occupation of the world are still recognizable and recognized.

At the end of the room the tour group has gathered around four large drawings depicting four approaches for rebinding agriculture and the city: secession, incorporation, infiltration, and negotiation. Of the four, Marot's accompanying exhibition catalog declares secession the preferred model.[50] "This is the most radical model," Marot notes, dismantling the metropolis to "enable people to tend a living landscape … of interdependent humans, plants and animals."[51] Marot's declaration makes clear a shift concealed by the movement through the hanging exhibition panels, namely that while architecture and agriculture might have twin origins, the city has taken the position of architecture in those negotiations between spaces of leisure and work (*otium* and *negotium*) that were central to the domestication of landscape beginning with the *villa suburbana*. Marot notes, "Our exhibition attempts to overthrow the well-worn, received idea that cities are the exclusive depositories of democracy … the idea of secession … describes the initiatives which attempt to free themselves from the metropolitan orbit."[52] Marot's secessionist vision, therefore, as the Supersurface, affirms a relationship between architecture and landscape in which raw landscape is still marginalized. Gregotti's project of territory, with its implicit measures and markings, appears to offer another model, not the supplanting of urbanism but modification brought about by alternative "enframings" of landscape. These modifications, made through pieces of architecture, act upon our urban-landscape relations. This, one might posit, may be the underlying reason behind recent interest in Gregotti's work suggested by his presence in *Oase*, *San Rocco*, the *Architectural Review*, and, most pertinently, Frampton's reflection on the boundary stone. This stone, Frampton claims, potentially constitutes "the core of a resistant architecture, capable of mediating our compulsive commodification of the environment," informing an architecture of the ground which directly connects us, once again, with the world.[53] But as Gregotti, following Wittgenstein, reminds us, "history … presents itself as an awareness, a terrain that we must cross to reach the structure of things, to get to touch them, but which we must leave behind when the moment comes to transform those things ourselves." Gregotti's project, as part of a reappraisal of how the countryside is made present in the work of the *Neoavanguardia*, might inform a particular understanding of our environment, a "total environment" in which "both the natural and the artificial interact at the scale of an entire territory," but in such an environment "there is," Gregotti reminds us "no nature . . . there is [only] anthropogeography."[54]

Notes

1. Sébastien Marot, "Taking the Country's Side: Common Trajectories in Agriculture and Architecture," interview by Christophe Catsaros, *Archis*, April 10, 2020, http://archis.org/volume/taking-the-countrys-side-sebastien-marot-christophe-catsaros; Sébastian Marot, *Taking the Country's Side: Agriculture and Architecture* (Barcelona: Polígrafa, 2019), 17.

2. Marot, *Taking the Country's Side*, 10.

3. Marot writes that "one of the best medieval copies of Vitruvius's *De architettura*, in the codex *Mediceus Laurentianus*, was bound together with Varro's *Rerum rusticarum* . . . Apparently, 14th century copyists still held the two disciplines as complementary aspects of the same concern . . ." Marot, *Taking the Country's Side*, 25.

4. Marot, *Taking the Country's Side*, 29.

5. Pablo Martínez Capdevilla, "The Interior City: Infinity and Concavity in the No-Stop City (1970–1971)," *Inicio* 4 (2013), 132.

6. Zeila Tesoriere, "The Territory into Architecture: Big Scale and Agriculture in Italian Architecture, 1966-1978," *AGATHÓN—International Journal of Architecture, Art and Design* 7 (2020), 59, Figure 1 and Figure 6.

7. There are a number of English translations of the earlier essay "La Forma del Territorio" from *Edilizia Moderna*, which forms the basis of the second part of *Il territorio dell'architettura*, but the book has not been translated; Alessandro Benetti, "Italia, anni Settanta. I nuovi territori dell'architettura scolastica," *Domus*, September 17, 2018, https://www.domusweb.it/it/eventi/istanbul-design-biennial/2018/09/17/italia-anni-settanta-i-nuovi-territori-dell-architettura-scolastica.html (translation by author).

8. Vittorio Gregotti, "Vittorio Gregotti in Conversation with Rolf Jenni, Christian Müller Inderbitzin and Milica Topalović," *San Rocco* 2, "The Even Covering of the Field" (Summer, 2011), 179.

9. Guido Morpurgo, *The Territory of Architecture: Gregotti & Associati, 1953–2017* (Milan: Skira Editore, 2017), 13.

10. Marot, *Taking the Country's Side*, 12, 9.

11. Nuno Grande, "Interview with Manuel Salgado, 19 December 2017," in *CCB Twenty-Five Years: Competition_Building_Landscape_Design_Collection* (Lisbon: Fundação Centro Cultural de Belém, 2018), 207.

12. Guido Morpurgo, "Belém Cultural Centre, Lisbon, 1988–1997," in *Gregotti & Associates: The Architecture of Urban Design* (New York: Rizzoli, 2008), 177.

13. See Lavinia Ann Minciacchi, "From *Casabella* to *Arquitectura*: The Italian Influence on Portuguese Post-CIAM Debate," in *Revisiting the Post-CIAM Generation: Debates, Proposals and Intellectual Framework*, Porto, April 11–13, 2019 (conference proceedings) (Porto: CEAA/ESAP–CESAP, 2019), 232–50.

14. See Nuno Correia, "Architectural Criticism, Social Debate and Portuguese Participation in the "Pequenos Congressos—1959/1968," *Revista Crítica de Ciências Sociais* 91 (2010): 41–57.

15. Vittorio Gregotti, *Architecture, Means and Ends*, trans. L. G. Cochrane (Chicago and London: University of Chicago Press, 2010), 110–11.

16. João Gomes da Silva, "Interview with Francisco Manuel Caldeira Cabral, 18 January 2018," in *CCB Twenty-Five Years: Competition_Building_Landscape_Design_Collection* (Lisbon: Fundação Centro Cultural de Belém, 2018), 210.

17. Gregotti, *Architecture, Means and Ends*, 109.

18. da Silva, "Interview with Francisco Manuel Caldeira Cabral," 210.

19. Kenneth Frampton, "The Unfinished Modern Project at the End of Modernity: Tectonic Form and the Space of Appearance," Soane Medal Lecture, November 11, 2019.

20. Vittorio Gregotti, "Territory and Architecture," in *The School of Venice*, ed. Luciano Semerani, special issue, *Architectural Design* 55, no. 5–6 (1985), 28.

21. Vittorio Gregotti, "Lecture at the New York Architectural League," section A., no.1, Montreal, February/March 1983, cited in Frampton, "The Unfinished Modern Project at the End of Modernity." Rykwert's *On Adam's House in Paradise* was published in 1972.

22. "The origin of architecture is not the primitive hut, but the making of ground to establish a cosmic order around the surrounding chaos of nature," citing the same lecture as Frampton from 1983.

23. Kenneth Frampton. *Megaform as Urban Landscape* (Ann Arbor: University of Michigan Press, 1999), 40.

24. Frampton, *Megaform as Urban Landscape*, 40.

25. Gregotti, "Territory and Architecture," 28, 30.

26. Francesco Zuddas, "The Idea of the Università," *AA Files* 75 (2017), 121.

27. Morpurgo, *Gregotti & Associates*, 173.

28. Vittorio Gregotti, "Context and Architecture," lecture, Venice, 1984, https://www.pidgeondigital.com/talks/context-architecture/play/.

29. Gregotti, "Context and Architecture."

30. Pierluigi Nicolin, "Nouvi dipartimenti di scienze all'Università di Palermo, di Gino Pollini, Vittorio Gregotti, Giuscppe Caronia," *Casabella* 394 (1974), 18. Nicolin's article is one of the few reviews of the UniPa Science and Technology buildings, published in *Casabella* under editor Mendini. Nicolin was a co-founder of Gregotti Associati, leaving in 1978, and a judge for the CCB competition in 1988.

31. Lejla Vujicic describes a similar effect at the University of Calabria, where the building "positions the observer to the world" in a manner that opens up "a multi-perspectival environment." Lejla Vujicic, "Architecture of the *longue durée*: Vittorio Gregotti's Reading of the Territory of Architecture," *arq: Architectural Research Quarterly* 19, no. 2 (2015), 172.

32. Morpurgo, *Gregotti & Associates*, 35.

33. Vittorio Gregotti, "On Modification," in *Inside Architecture*, trans. Peter Wong and Francesca Zaccheo (Cambridge, MA: MIT Press, 1996), 68.

34. Gregotti, "On Modification," 70.

35. Vittorio Gregotti, *Il territorio dell'architettura* (1966) (Milan: Giangiacomo Feltrinelli Editore, 2014), 61 (translation by author).

36. Vittorio Gregotti, *La città visibile. Frammenti di disegno della città ordinati e catalogati secondo i principî dell'architettura della modificazione contestuale* (Turin: G. Einaudi, 1993), 46; translation by author.

37. Gregotti, "Territory and Architecture," 28, 30.

38. Gregotti, "Territory and Architecture," 28.

39. Tullio Pagano, "Reclaiming Landscape," *Annali d'italianistica* 29 (2011), 402.

40. The noun form of the stative verb *pag-* to fasten, linked to the Greek πάγος, that which is fixed. The *pagus* is "the thing having been staked out."

41. Jean-François Lyotard, "Scapeland," in *The Inhuman: Reflections on Time* (1988), trans. Geoffrey Bennington and Rachel Bowlby (Cambridge: Polity Press, 1993), 186; Jean-Francois Lyotard and Jean-Loup Thébaud, *Just Gaming* (1979), trans. Wlad Godzich (Minneapolis: University of Minnesota Press, 2017), 42–3.

42. Martínez Capdevilla, "The Interior City," 132. As Martínez Capdevilla notes in "No-Stop City," the infinite extension of the city "does not imply . . . the integration of the rural world but, rather, its exclusion . . . [a] lack of interest in the agrarian that is . . . ideological."

43. Gregotti, "Vittorio Gregotti in Conversation," 182.

44. Charles Waldheim, "Notes Toward a History of Agrarian Urbanism," *Places Journal* (November 2010), https://placesjournal.org/article/history-of-agrarian-urbanism/.

45. Tesoriere, "The Territory into Architecture," 50.

46. Fernando Quesada, "Superstudio 1966–1973. From the World Without Objects to the Universal Grid," *Footprint* 8, "Defying the Avant-Garde Logic: Architecture, Populism, and Mass Culture" (Spring 2011), 30.

47. Gregotti, "Territory and Architecture," 28.

48. The Italian narration is different: "Guarda quella montagna lontana . . . cosa vedi? E' quello il luogo dove andare? O è solo il limite di abitabilità ottimale?" This translates as, "Look at that distant mountain . . . what can you see? Is that the place to go? Or is it only the limit of optimal habitability?" The difference is subtle but not insignificant.

49. Gillian Pierce observes that for Baudelaire "*paysage* . . . already implied critical difference from nature in its raw or 'undressed' state. These terms suggest artifice, a 'framing' of the natural world at the very moment of beholding . . ." See Gillian Pierce, *Scapeland: Writing the Landscape from Diderot's Salons to the Postmodern Museum* (Leiden: Brill, 2012), 24.

50. Marot declares that secession is "the only one to display an adequate measure of historical imagination . . . to take stock of the *adventure* that the present environmental predicament represents . . ." Marot, *Taking the Country's Side*, 10. In a subsequent interview, Marot is less committal: "The primary aim of this distinction is to clarify, by illustration, the varying, almost opposing discourses currently circulating about the notion of urban agriculture." Marot, interview, *Archis*, April 10, 2020.

51. Marot, *Taking the Country's Side*, 209.

52. Marot, interview, *Archis*, April 10, 2020.

53. Frampton, "The Unfinished Modern Project at the End of Modernity;" Gregotti, *Il territorio dell'architettura*, 132; my translation. See Sabini Maurizio, "Wittgenstein's Ladder: The Non-Operational Value of History in Architecture," *Journal of Architectural Education* 64, no. 2, "Beyond Precedent" (March 2011): 46–58.

54. Zuddas, "The Idea of the Università," 124; Nuno Grande, "Interview with Vittorio Gregotti, 21 November 2017," in *CCB Twenty-Five Years: Competition_Building_Landscape_Design_Collection* (Lisbon: Fundação Centro Cultural de Belém, 2018), 205.

CHAPTER 14
ALDO ROSSI, GIORGIO DE CHIRICO, AND THE ENIGMA OF TRADITION
Diane Ghirardo

Although known primarily as a painter, Giorgio de Chirico engaged in other artistic activities over the course of his life, as a sculptor, a poet, and, on at least one occasion, as the designer of a monumental fountain.[1] In 1973, for the XV Milan Triennale, de Chirico set up a grand fountain inside Sempione Park, a project that was recently restored. The fountain, named *Mysterious Baths*, drew inspiration from a series of paintings the artist completed in 1934 for Jean Cocteau's *Mythologies*.[2] The same Triennale included a section on industrial design directed by Andrea Branzi and Ettore Sottsass Jr., while the foreign section displayed works by Charles Rennie Mackintosh and images of the newly completed Sydney Opera House by Jørn Utzon. The section devoted to architecture was directed by Milanese architect Aldo Rossi, who exhibited, among other things, *La città analoga*, an image that expressed his theory of architecture and the city (Figure 14.1).[3] Nearly fifty years ago, de Chirico and Rossi crossed paths at this event, but their affinities went well beyond what was apparent on that occasion. The relation between de Chirico's art and the architecture and designs of Aldo Rossi, while superficially evident, includes depths and affinities that have been inadequately explored.

A look at some of de Chirico's earliest paintings immediately demonstrates several themes that have long been recognized as fundamental connections between their work, particularly a shared focus on evocative urban forms and spaces (see Figure 14.2). "I was the first to illustrate the metaphysics of the piazzas and cities of Italy," exulted de Chirico, because he had found "in the construction of the city, in the architectural form of the houses, the piazzas, the gardens and the landscapes, the ports, the railroad stations, the first foundation of a grand metaphysics."[4] In the years around World War I, his first compositions provoked great interest within the art world; the paintings were usually composed along the lines of Renaissance perspective, with chimneys and high towers, porticoes, and the vast spaces marked by shadows and silence. Unreal lights and clocks mark the hour, sometimes a small, slender figure or a statue appears in the background: these are the typical characteristics of de Chirico's paintings during the second decade of the twentieth century.

Between 1910 and 1919, de Chirico's metaphysical paintings might displace an object and insert it in another context, where it becomes disturbing, strange, incomprehensible. Others seemed to invite us to look at a particular object with such great intensity as to extricate it from its context, rendering it incomplete, new, and foreign. Such was the case for *The Enigma of the Oracle* (1910). De Chirico specified in 1919:

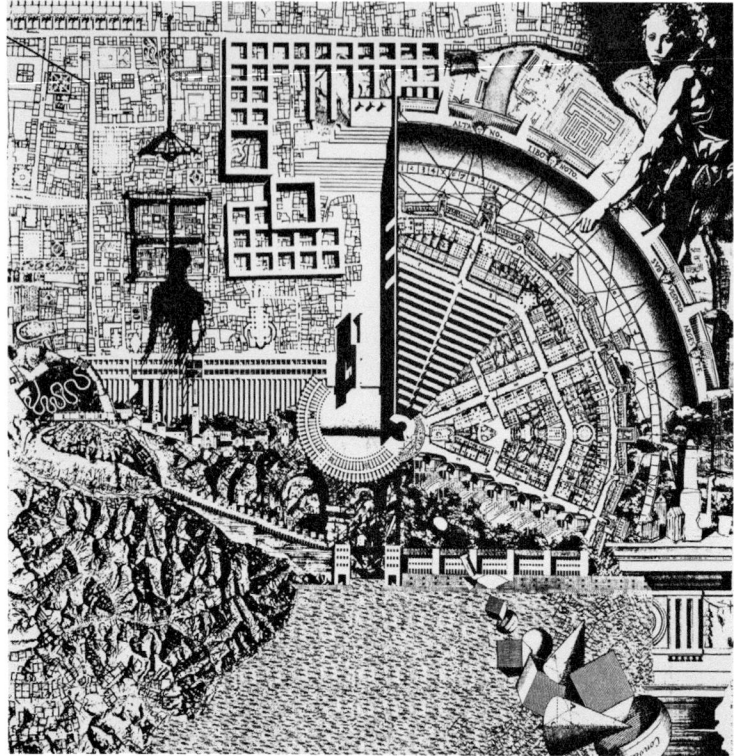

Figure 14.1 Aldo Rossi, *La città analoga*, 1981. Courtesy MAXXI Museo nazionale delle arti del XXI secolo, Roma, Collezione MAXXI Architettura, Archivio Aldo Rossi. © Eredi Aldo Rossi.

[E]verything has two aspects: one current, that which we see almost always and which people generally see. The other is the spectral, or metaphysical, that only rare individuals can see in moments of metaphysical abstraction and clairvoyance, just as some bodies shrouded in materials impenetrable to the rays of the sun only become visible under the power of artificial light.[5]

Unusually empty piazzas, silent and full of tension, trigger a vague anguish, an unusual disturbance because the apparently calm surfaces seem to hide something mysterious, even threatening, in their profundity.

Fifty years later, when Rossi began to publish his drawings and his first projects, some critics immediately saw echoes of de Chirico's paintings in his work; in fact, Rossi repeatedly and openly acknowledged his esteem for the metaphysical painter.[6] In Rossi's drawings, we often find a smokestack, chimney, or tower, not dissimilar to one of de Chirico's. In drawings for a schedule of elements, Rossi specified that in this sketch, "the form of the tower refers to that of a painting by de Chirico."[7] He also spoke of an unrealized project "born as an homage to de Chirico." In the competition for the town hall of Muggio in 1972, Rossi proposed a piazza with a statue, and wrote, "here

Figure 14.2 Giorgio de Chirico, *Il grande metafisico*, 1917. © Giorgio De Chirico/SIAE, Copyright Agency, 2021.

emblematically is a work by de Chirico." In other designs, Rossi inserted a clock similar to those often included in de Chirico's works.

Perhaps the relation between the paintings of the self-styled *pictor optimus* and Rossi's architecture seems all too obvious, yet the two also intersect in far less obvious ways. In the decade following 1919, de Chirico's designs underwent notable changes as he abandoned or reconfigured enigmatic Italian piazzas as uninhabited voids in favor of piazzas featuring gladiators, horses, and mannequins, or when he painted *The Three Graces* in 1954.[8] The artist began to make explicit references to traditional art, a turn he described as the result of a visit to the Villa Borghese gallery in Rome in 1919, when he stood stunned before a painting, perhaps Titian's 1554 work *Amor sacro e amor profano* (Sacred and Profane Love).

This harkened back to a way of learning to paint that dated to the classical era when Romans copied Greek sculptures. For de Chirico, this return to classicism was a way of learning his profession; as he wrote, "you can never know your profession fully. For me, I continually visit galleries and I study the lessons of the masters, and more than that, I often copied them, and indeed, still do."[9]

De Chirico rediscovered ancient materials and techniques, such as varnished egg temperas typical of the early Renaissance, finding them fundamental for his personal poetics. In 1928, he published his *Little Treatise on Pictorial Techniques*, a recipe book based upon his own experiments with diverse materials and ingredients, and in subsequent years he continued to experiment with his recipes.[10]

It is thus striking to see how Rossi undertook a similar journey. The project for the San Cataldo cemetery in Modena (1971) ruptured the fixed schemes that dominated the modern movement and offered something different, if difficult to define. Even today the cemetery is described by many historians as an example of a "different" architecture— that is, no longer modern but *beyond* the modern; perhaps neo-enlightenment, or neo-realist, while for others it was postmodern (see Figure 14.3 and Plate 9). Rossi's criticism of the modern movement should not have surprised because he had already published on the subject from his earliest years at university.[11] With simple, disarmingly primitive volumes in the monuments at Cuneo and Segrate, at the low-cost housing complex the Gallaratese, and at the San Cataldo cemetery, Rossi seemed to increasingly detach himself from the modern movement, opening himself to new and unexpected directions, different also from the architecture of Italian rationalism of the fascist era. This Rossi confounded critics; they did not how to explain this new architecture, even as it attracted attention and support.

Equally fascinating was the decision of Rossi to study and use ancient techniques, much as de Chirico had done. For example, in 1978, during a visit to the Modena cemetery while it was under construction, he decided to specify in greater detail some aspects of the project. He wrote in one of his *Quaderni azzuri* of trying out a revetment on the portico and the first wing: he remarked that he was specifying "a revetment in the antique manner, with brick and sand on a lime base."[12] Despite the modern appearance of the building, the reference to an "antique" treatment of the facade recalls its origins in an earlier tempo, signaling the ancient character beyond its supposedly modern qualities.

Figure 14.3 Aldo Rossi, San Cataldo cemetery, Modena, 1971. Photograph courtesy Diego Terna.

Critics' efforts to give a name to Rossi's style in his early projects saw them defining him as, among other things, a postmodern architect, which continued after the earliest projects. Instead, he *did* have ideas about how to describe his work; he always responded to critics by saying that he was not postmodern because he had never been modern; other times, with greater precision, he affirmed that "I am not post-modern; rather I am post-antique."[13] One need only review Rossi's *L'architettura della città* (*Architecture of the City*, 1966), *Scientific Autobiography* (1981), and his *Selected Writings* (1975) to grasp how fascinated he was by classical architecture, and by that of the Renaissance and especially the baroque. In his architecture he found the antique within the new because he knew that to embrace the present did not require a negation of the past.

In those early years, Rossi was one of the few architects disposed to challenge the uncontested reign of the modern movement, especially in Italy. Today it is difficult to remember that in 1971, when the cemetery competition was held, architects lived in the looming shadows of Mies van der Rohe and Le Corbusier, with his five points of modern architecture.[14] Obviously, the cemetery obeyed none of these rules: from its porticoes to the square windows to the pitched roof, everything spoke of a robustly traditional architecture, even if the modernist critics refused to recognize these elements as precisely that: traditional. Although the cemetery design divided the architectural public into ardent supporters and opponents, Rossi's drawings and the later haunting photographs of the partially completed complex became world famous. At the time, his use of color and the limpid and simple forms seemed to open to an architecture of new and unexpected possibilities. Today the projects' ties with tradition are apparent, but at the time, they were far more obscure, probably because of the abstraction of stripped and undecorated masses. In Italy, criticism focused on Rossi's presumed ideological position: for some the cemetery was a "communist" or "Marxist" project, for example.[15] Such criticism reflects common practice in Italy during the second half of the twentieth century, where a work was considered less through analysis of the design itself than as a vision refracted through one political lens or another. Ideology did not inspire, nor does it explain, this project. In any event, as in the case of de Chirico, Rossi was not the only architect to return to the origins of his art: just think of BBPR Torre Velasca in Milan, and the absurd polemics that it triggered on its completion in 1958.[16]

As we have seen, de Chirico copied the works of Renaissance masters, and Rossi did the same thing. At Berlin, Rossi's commission at Schützenstraße entailed designing a full block of apartments, shops, and offices.[17] The site had been razed to the ground by Allied bombs during World War II. Rossi drew inspiration for some parts of the complex from the surroundings, but for one section, he decided to repeat the facade of the Palazzo Farnese in Rome, whose ground floor was the work of Antonio da Sangallo the Younger, and the other floors are by Michelangelo. A painter such as de Chirico can copy for the pure joy of doing so, while an architect needs to respond to other demands: in this case, Rossi explained how his project in the first place responded to the classicizing architecture of buildings on the surrounding streets, such as the culture of the streets on Kollwitzkiez, or the celebration of the diverse autonomies as at Weberwiese.[18] He primarily thought about the typical typology of Berlin's nineteenth-century domestic architecture, the

Mietkasernen, enormous residential blocks with grand interior courtyards reached through long andrones, or entrance halls. For Rossi, the memory of these humble operations could be transformed by turning to the example of the Palazzo Farnese in Rome, in part for the simple pleasure of copying Michelangelo, but also to bind the andrones of Palazzo Farnese to those of the Mietkasernen, where the original led to splendor, the second to squalor. For the Molteni Tomb, on the other hand, Rossi instead based his design on that of Jacopo Barozzi, il Vignola, while for his last project for La Fenice in Venice, he included an homage to Palladio in the form of a wall based upon the facade of the Basilica Palladiana in Vicenza.

To anyone familiar with Rossi's work, the facade of the Scholastic Building in New York not only shows clear affinities with the adjacent buildings but features that recall other Rossi structures. Among the most prominent are the great white cylinders and the red steel beams that mark the floors. These often appear in Rossi's earlier work: the cylinder goes back to one of his first projects, the Monument to the Partisans at Segrate, and reappeared in many of his subsequent works, such as the Gallaratese, the San Saba Middle School in Trieste, the Casa Aurora in Torino. As he explained in his *Scientific Autobiography*, Rossi was struck by the white column of the never-completed palace on the Grand Canal in Venice for Duke Francesco Sforza of Milan in the middle of the fifteenth century. He inserted this element of his personal, but also historical, memory into his subsequent work, as he did with less obvious elements from the Sacri Monti of Piemonte. The red and green beams can be found at Schützenstraße in Berlin, the Linate airport in Milan, the Casa Aurora in Torino, the Fukuoka Palace, and other works. This is not the banal reproduction of elements already adopted elsewhere, nor is it an effort to restore the past. These choices by Rossi are more revisions rather than repetitions, and as he well understood, revision itself is a step forward, not a return to the past.

Rossi's respect for the traditional elements of architecture is strikingly evident in these projects. Both Rossi and de Chirico found themselves fascinated by classicism, but they arrived by different paths: for de Chirico, this derived from his encounter with the paintings of the great masters of the Italian Renaissance and baroque; for Rossi, instead, it was born from his hometown, old Milan and its classicizing architecture, but also from the lessons of Ernesto Rogers, his professor at the Milan Polytechnic, and from youthful memories of baroque churches.

The *Analogous City* image Rossi presented at the 1973 Triennale (painted by Arduino Cantàfora), demonstrates his relationship with tradition. It depicts historic buildings such as the Mole Antonelliana, the pyramid of Caio Cestio, and the Pantheon, along with some of Rossi's own projects, like the Segrate, or the Gallaratese. During this same period, Rossi began to speak about that elusive aspect of design he described as "analogous." With this term, Rossi indicated something Carl Jung described as distinct from logical thought, meaning (for Rossi) thought expressed in words, "outer directed" in that it participates in a discourse. Analogical thought, in contrast, is fantastic, archaic, unconscious, unexpressed, and virtually inexpressible through words.[19] Rossi's collage for the 1976 Venice Biennale three years later consists of fragments of Piranesi's imperial plan, traces of the Roman plan for Como, of the Parthenon, of Schinkel, Borromini, and of Rossi himself, with his Gallaratese, a coffee pot, Elba cabins, and the poet's window. In this second version of the analogous city, Rossi viewed his architectural production as the result of a creatively mysterious operation, not unlike how de Chirico described the metaphysical as the result of associations and analogies that brought forth new and strange sensations. For both, then, analogies impossible to explain with words gave birth to their poetry, without losing sight of the rules and practices of the profession.

While engaged with different materials and arguments, both devoted considerable attention to the concept of time, but with distinct emphases and theories. Time was one of the issues that most intrigued de Chirico, a preoccupation nourished by Schopenhauer, Heidegger, Kant, and above all Nietzsche. In 1910, de Chirico wrote to Fritz Gartz that he, de Chirico, was the only one to have truly understood Nietzsche, whose views were revealed in his art.[20] He wrote that "Schopenhauer and Nietzsche first taught me the meaninglessness of life and as such, that this meaninglessness could be represented."

Even though Rossi read these same philosophers, he found other writers far more intriguing, such as twentieth-century author Raymond Roussel, ancient texts by Quintilian and Livy, early Christian fathers such as St. Augustine and St. Jerome, and mystics like St. Teresa of Avila and St. John of the Cross.[21] Rossi's reflections drew in part on these texts in his personal library (architecture books remained in the office; all the others he kept at home in Milan or in his villa at Ghiffa). But his ideas also sprang from the way he viewed the world, and often from childhood experiences. His curiosity spanned from the smallest things to the largest, something a teacher at his boarding school grasped when he was in middle school. In his year-end evaluation, the priest who supervised the boys wrote of Rossi that "because [of] his exquisite sensitivity he is easily moved when faced with beauty … sometimes he allows himself to be carried away by fantasy …"[22] As Hugo of St. Victor wrote some 900 years ago, "genius acquires, memory conserves."[23] For Rossi, all was preserved in memories to be evolved and substantiated over time.

Rossi conserved many memories from his infancy, for example his visit to the colossal baroque statue of San Carlo Borromeo in Arona (known as San Carlone, or big San Carlo), when he ascended the interior stairs as if it were the Trojan Horse until he arrived at the saint's eyes and a panoramic view of Lake Maggiore, a vision he described as "like from a celestial observatory."[24] Rossi inserted part of the saint in many works, often only his hand raised in blessing, as a memory, a reference, an inspiration, a sign of continuity. He included more than San Carlone in his drawings: the statue appeared with objects recalled from the country house of his grandmother, the coffee pots, cigarettes, silverware. Along with these we find fragments of his own architecture: the Gallaratese, Segrate, San Cataldo, and yes, the towers that echo those of de Chirico.

Rossi did not view architecture as an inert product of the architect's desire to express him or herself, nor as the passive product of an ideology, but as something born within a dynamic that engages creativity and technical capacity in equal measure. The sweep of time was fundamental to Rossi's architecture; he never lost awareness of time's passage, as when he designed the copper roof of the town hall in Borgoricco, anticipating its transformative patina, or when he designed the Monument to Sandro Pertini in Milan.

There, water falls from a copper triangle with a constancy that challenges signs of time's passage evident in other parts of the project. The mulberry trees grow, lose their leaves; light filters through their branches from the light standards as the seasons change from spring, to summer, to the denuded branches of winter.

Despite his designs' visible affinities with de Chirico, Rossi understood time in a radically different way. His drawings combine a particular urban context with an appeal to his own memories, to his own past as an architect and as a man. There is no nostalgia for a lost past. In all his drawings, Rossi expressed the joy of recovered memories, re-elaborated and, in a way, relived. He approached film with the same attitude: Rossi had a habit of seeing a film many times, to better enjoy the contents rather than concentrating on the ending. The insertion of references to his earlier projects in the new ones reveals the apparently infinite capacity of his memory to reconfigure the past in ever changing ways, always fully cognizant of the fact that one cannot—or should not—want to recover it entirely. Rossi's project for the Scholastic Building in New York invites us to participate in a narration that consists not only of personal memories but also collective ones through connections deliberately sought and developed, which in turn also include reflections on his own memories. While the intellectual explains the reality of things with lucid, scientific reality, the poet transmits the meaning of things and their past and thus also the present, by means of fragments, pieces.

For Rossi, the role of fragments was suggestive; some fell into the role that they played in his drawings. It would be possible to render these fragments as such, but Rossi chose another means of conveying their expressive significance, their poetic immediacy. It came down to registering the imperfect, the fragment, the piece extrapolated from its context to be reimagined elsewhere. This is as true of his architecture as of his drawings. If his architecture seemed to reward clarity, linearity, the stereometry of pure, primitive yet timeless forms—the cube, the cylinder, the triangle—instead, it is apparent that they are realized on many registers polyphonic and complex, just as are his drawings. Only a careful study of the drawings reveals that Rossi does not propose to repeat conventional architectural forms, but the invisible and essential heart of architecture. This is perceived most meaningfully through the designs and the projects together.

The items from everyday life Rossi included in his drawings—the coffee pot, the pack of cigarettes, the Coke can, along with urban structures, plus fragments of his own architectures—were not casual choices; objects do not butt up against one another by chance (see Figure 14.4). For Rossi, a particular past registered through these precise objects, inserted in different contexts, one that was neither closed nor silent, but full of noise, of vitality, of possibilities.[25] The poet Simonides, in his reconstruction of the destroyed banquet room, demonstrated "constructive memory" by recalling how things were placed in relation to one another; in so doing he also reconstructed memory itself, as Rossi seems to do in his drawings.[26] Memory is understood as a repertoire, a mine of information and a generating force, the motor of lived experience and thus of the past itself.

In the years following World War II, when he began his studies at Milan Polytechnic, Rossi perceived Italian cities (and not only Italian cities) as suffocated by the monotony of buildings realized in the name of the international style, and he rebelled, proposing an architecture and urbanism based not on abstract scientific principles but on how people live and have lived. Rossi published *L'architettura della città* just as the international style was triumphant globally. The book was profoundly opposed to its hegemonic ideas. Rossi refused to chase after architectural fashion, just as de Chirico had refused to do in the world of art, preferring to follow his own path, not because he was stubborn or obtuse, but because he believed that one cannot accept dominant ideologies, that one must not genuflect before the dominant culture. These irreconcilable contrasts are fundamental to all his work, beginning with *L'architettura della città* and the *Scientific Autobiography*. I do not believe there is *one* explanation for all of this but rather, as in poetry, we encounter a resolution that brings us to something universal.

In Rossi's drawings there is a preoccupation with the passage of time, both chronological and atmospheric, signaled by the presence of shadows, clocks, figures in movement. While there may be a layer of melancholy that pervades his designs, this melancholy is neither tragic nor anguished, but rather one that emerges as essential. Recognizing the intrinsic significance of things, Rossi perceives their destiny from afar, along with that of human beings. But instead of battling against an inexorable fate, he accepts it, giving voice to a sense of wonder, of awe before the world, a sensation that evokes joy and pleasure. He thus manages to wrest away time's power, or at the very least destabilizes it. Such is the joy within the cube, or ossuary, at Modena, where the burial niches form rows of crosses, representing the promise of the Passion of Christ, of salvation, the primary, hopeful symbol of the cemetery itself (see Figure 14.3 and Plate 9).

The same joy infuses Rossi's drawings and writings, and especially the *Scientific Autobiography*, where he describes his affection for his drawings and the happiness he sought in his architectural projects. In the end, this joy is perceptible in his buildings, in his architecture. Consider the Modena cemetery, where the long rows of burial niches are interrupted by a regular rhythm of apertures for stairs or high windows. Here light enters, interrupting the dark corridors and conceding a relaxation to the tension. Rossi realized what de Chirico understood about the incomprehensibility of the world, but he drew very different conclusions from the painter's anguished nostalgia for an unrecoverable past. Although in Rossi's drawings and projects there is a persistent sense of our tenuous hold on reality, whether past or present, they also accept the fact that not everything can be assimilated, that it is not possible to rationalize completely. Rossi withdraws his vital force for us, as if he were the last man of the classical world, expanding toward others, toward the world, but without ever fully emerging.

Even if Rossi developed many of the same themes found in de Chirico, with fragments that flow from designs to projects and back, he readily opened new ones, as his books demonstrate. Both projects and drawings triggered, and still trigger, admiration but also criticism, from the "avant-garde" and especially "Marxists" (including those I call "Gucci communists"). He was accused of having succumbed to a merely personal poetics in the second half of his career, especially in the 1980s and 1990s, to have "sold out" in his designs for wristwatches, coffee pots, furniture, and other products; to be indifferent to the quality of construction; to no longer be a "progressive" architect once he began to incorporate elements of traditional architecture in his work.[27]

Figure 14.4 Aldo Rossi, *Il natale di Diane*, ca. 1990. © Eredi Aldo Rossi, Fondazione Aldo Rossi.

In his *Scientific Autobiography*, Rossi commented, "To what should I have aspired in my profession? Certainly, to few things, given that the grand ones were historically precluded."[28] For some critics, this demonstrated Rossi's deep melancholy and his retreat from a world of delusions in favor of a strictly internal one. Instead, his is a response to a comment of Hugo of St. Victor, when he wrote, "humility is the preliminary condition of a disciplined behavior … Why aspire to things that are so grand, when you are so little?"[29] The humility to know how much there is to learn, and the impossibility of knowing everything: fully aware of this, Rossi nonetheless affirmed the joy of producing places, spaces, buildings within or around which collective life and private life could play out. He anticipated exactly that for his mélanges of fragments built from a world of many pasts. He loved to imagine these as a stage for a future in which his architecture, his piazzas, his theaters, would not be abandoned and empty, or occupied by ghostly, inert images of a lost past, as in de Chirico's work, but alive and belonging to the people. Only when this happens, Rossi said, only then has any structure or place become architecture.

In the end, the architecture and art of Aldo Rossi do not have as their main subject architecture, nor are they epistemological or aesthetic studies; they instead embrace a moral vision of the world, his own world of specific, personal, situated memories, but our world as well. This vision of how past, present, and future might coexist provides an engine, the generating force of an art, an architecture that operates across the generations, and not only in Italy.

Notes

1. His personal autobiography is Giorgio de Chirico, *The Memoirs of Giorgio de Chirico* (New York: Perseus Books Group, 1957).

2. Jean Cocteau, *Giorgio de Chirico: Il mistero laico*, ed. Alberto Boatto (Turin: Abscondita, 2015).

3. For an introduction to Aldo Rossi, see Alberto Ferlenga, *Aldo Rossi: opera completa* (Milan: Electa 1998).

4. Magdalena Holzhey, *Giorgio de Chirico* (Cologne: Taschen, 2005), 10.

5. De Chirico, "Sull'arte metafisica," *Valori Plastici* 1, no. 4–5 (April–May 1919): 15–18.

6. Manfredo Tafuri, "The Case of Aldo Rossi," in *History of Italian Architecture, 1944–1985*, trans. Jessica Levine (Cambridge, MA: MIT Press, 1989), 135–9.

7. Aldo Rossi, *Quaderni azzurri* (Los Angeles and Milan: Electa, 1999), Book 3, January 16, 1970; for simplicity, I refer to this as *QA*, and the number of the book.

8. On de Chirico's ancient sources, see Bart Verschaffel, "The Trophy Figure in the Work of Giorgio de Chirico (and Piranesi)," *Journal of Architecture* 15, no. 3 (2010): 337–58.

9. Giorgio de Chirico, interview, *Espresso*, March 10, 1947.

10. Giorgio de Chirico, *Small Treatise on Pictorial Techniques* (*Petit Traité de technique de peinture*) (Paris: Somogy, 2001).

11. Rossi's drawing appears in Diane Yvonne Francis Ghirardo, *Aldo Rossi and the Spirit of Architecture* (New Haven, CT: Yale University Press, 2019), Figure 7.2.

12. *QA*, Book 4, Chapter 4, "The Antique Method."

13. Although Rossi made this remark often, he first theorized it in his public lecture, University of Southern California, spring 1985.

14. Charles-Edouard Jeanneret-Gris [Le Corbusier] published his "five points" in many different venues beginning in 1926. For the essay's complex history, see Werner Oeschslin and Wilfried Wang, "Les Cinq Points d'une Architecture Nouvelle," *Assemblage* 4 (October 1987): 82–93.

15. A Marxist ideology was the basis of the critique of the purists and indeed its contemporaries: Dan Graham, "Not Post-Modernism: History as Against Historicism, European Archetypal Vernacular in Relation to American Commercial Vernacular and the City as Opposed to the Individual Building.," *Artforum* (December 1981): 50–8.

16. See, for instance, Reyner Banham, "Neoliberty: The Italian Retreat from Modern Architecture," *Architectural Review* 125 (April 1959), 235.

17. Ghirardo, *Aldo Rossi and the Spirit of Architecture*, 46–50.

18. I note two residences on nearby streets: Hermann Henselmann's tower house on Weberwiese, 1951–2, and the recently restored residences on Kollwitzkiez.

19. Aldo Rossi, *QA*, Book 18, April 6, Carteggio Freud/Jung, 1818, March 2, 1910.

20. Giorgio de Chirico to Fritz Gartz, January 26, 1910, published in Gerd Roos, *De Chirico e Alberto Savinio: ricordi e documenti (Monaco, Milano, Firenze, 1906–11)* (Rome: Edizioni Bora, 1999), 422.

21. Many of these memories were found in these texts, all of which appeared throughout the *QA*.

22. Ghirardo, *Aldo Rossi and the Spirit of Architecture*, 211.

23. Hugo of St. Victor, *Didascalicon of Hugh of St. Victor* (New York: Columbia University Press, 1991), Book 3, Chapter 7.

24. Aldo Rossi, *Scientific Autobiography* (Cambridge, MA: MIT Press, 1981).

25. For an author studied by Rossi, see Maurice Halbwachs, *On Collective Memory* (Chicago: University of Chicago Press, 1992).

26. Quintiliano, *Institutio Oratorio*, trans. D. Campbell, *Greek Lyric* III (Cambridge, MA: Loeb Classical Library, 1991), 11.2.11–16, 379.

27. Diogo Seixas Lopes, *Melancholy and Architecture: On Aldo Rossi* (Zurich: Park Books, 2015), 199–200; others holding the same views include Francesco Dal Co; and Lars Lerup in a review of *A Scientific Autobiography*, in *Design Book Review* 3 (Winter 1984): 66. I have never understood what "progressive" means in architecture; I agree with Giacomo Leopardi when he wrote that "everything has been perfected from the time of Homer on, but not poetry." *Pensieri di varia filosofia e di bella letteratura*, vol. 1 (Firenze: Successori Le Monnier, 1898), 167.

28. Aldo Rossi, *Autobiografia Scientifica* (Parma: Pratiche Editrice, 1991), 27.

29. Hugh of St. Victor, *Didascalicon*, Book 3, Chapter 13.

CHAPTER 15
FURNISHING FASCIST ITALY
Ignacio G. Galán

The slogan "from the spoon to the city," originally coined by Ernesto Nathan Rogers in 1946, is conventionally taken as an appeal to architects' expanded design expertise and their ability to operate at different scales, from objects to urban environments.[1] It recalls similar expressions issued by Herman Muthesius in 1911 ("from sofa cushions to city-building"), and Max Bill's use of the same phrase in 1949, only a few years after

Figure 15.1 Collage by Lina Bo and Carlo Pagani illustrating the article "Lumen," *Stile* 10 (October 1941). Courtesy Gio Ponti Archives.

Rogers—both encapsulating a larger pursuit characteristic of the German Werkbund.[2] In spite of its diffuse origin and widespread use, Rogers's expression is often used to introduce a characteristically Italian approach to design and architectural interiors. The phrase was popularized in the 1960s and 1970s, at a time when designs produced in Italy circulated internationally through exhibitions, films, and department stores, strengthening both the country's economy and its global image. Yet Rogers introduced it in the magazine *Domus*, which he led from 1946 to 1947, in the immediate aftermath of World War II, in a country that was materially destroyed and ideologically devastated after decades of totalitarian nationalism. At stake was the identification of collective priorities: "What to do first? … What is superfluous and what is necessary?"[3] The editorial program Rogers established for *Domus* aimed to link the seemingly less consequential aesthetic properties of objects and interiors with the formation of a social body: "It is a question of forming a taste, a technique, and a morale, all directed toward the same purpose—the building of a society."[4] His approach was grounded in a humanistic approach that he emphasized in the subtitle he added to the magazine: *The House of Man* (*La casa dell'uomo*).

In spite of the popularity of this postwar slogan, Italian architects' celebrated attention to design had been shaped decades before Rogers uttered it, at the same time, in fact, that Italy underwent a process of national consolidation. Before aspiring to seamlessly design "from the spoon to the city," architects had been asked to bridge "the homeland and the chair" ("La patria e la sedia"), as conservative art critic Ugo Ojetti wrote in the pages of *Corriere della sera* in 1911, coinciding with the 50th anniversary of the Italian unification.[5] This invitation cannot be easily disentangled from the specific turn that Italian nationalism took in the following years, marked by Benito Mussolini's seizure of power in 1922. Rogers's program for the postwar Italian "domus" appealed to a "man" haunted by a figure who had pervaded the national consciousness for decades: the "Italian citizen," and the fascist program that had provided its ideological framework. The same magazine that published Rogers's agenda had previously been concerned, under the editorial direction of architect and designer Gio Ponti, with "The Italian House" ("La casa all'italiana").[6] While "Italian design" was invoked as a constitutive element of liberal subjectivity and postwar national identity, it was grounded on the fascist construction of both subjecthood and the nation. In what follows, I explore how the development of "Italian design" preceding its most popular postwar manifestations reveals how "Italy," "Italians," and a particular approach to "design" were all shaped simultaneously and in relation to each other during the fascist period.

When, in the 1970s, historian Giulio Carlo Argan approached the genesis of a self-consciously Italian design culture, he pointed to its origins in the interwar period and discussed how the investigations of this field of practice related to what he defined as "an almost theoretical problem, which is that of defining the new relationship between the object and space, the thing and the environment."[7] Argan framed those investigations in relation to the work of futurism, in which he argued that the object becomes part of space, and to *arte metafisica*, where the object does not communicate with space. For Italian designers, he argued, "[objects] define space by their very presence." This relationship was encapsulated in a term popularized in Italy between the wars:

arredamento, or "furnishing." Like its English correspondent, *arredamento* refers both to a single piece of furniture and to the ensemble of elements that furnish a unified space, an interior. It conveys a sense of tension between decoration, object design, and architectural interiors—between architecture and the applied or industrial arts—that Argan (writing elsewhere) regarded as characteristic of the modern period. In his view, in the wake of modern architecture, "everything becomes furniture; and the furniture that constitutes *arredamento* can truly be considered the most sensitive and delicate formal conclusion of architecture."[8] While the terms *decorazione* (decoration), *mobile* (furniture), and *interni* (interiors) were also used during the interwar period, the popularization of *arredamento* signaled a distinct interest within contemporary Italian culture in the material elements that construct an environment, "arranged" and "put in order" as its etymology indicates.[9]

However, beyond this so-called "theoretical problem," the approach to furnishing cultivated by architects and designers in the four decades between Ojetti's statement and Rogers's, and the shifting disciplinary emphases it signaled, were grounded in a specific historical context—one in which the relationship of objects and their environments that Argan discussed was destabilized by the increasing circulation of commodities in the market, images in the media, and populations both within the country and across boundaries, among other processes characteristic of the modern period. Furnishing and interiors were paradigmatic of these destabilizations, which manifested themselves most overtly in the disruption of regional styles and modes of living. While these destabilizations were more evident in urban centers, the interiors of the most peripheral areas of the country were just as shaken by them. In 1935, for example, Carlo Levi reported how the everyday life of southern rural households was not only connected to the images arriving from the war in Abyssinia (now Ethiopia and Eritrea) but was also "entirely American in regard to mechanical equipment as well as weights and measures." From Rome, he said "came nothing ... but the tax collector and speeches over the radio."[10] Meanwhile, the modernist developments on the peripheries of major cities like Rome were filled with the traditional furniture of many different Italian regions that had been carried there by poor, displaced populations.[11] The arrival of southern and rural migrants to Rome and the northern cities in the first decades of the century had been accompanied by a fear of cultural degeneration grounded in diverse forms of long-standing regionalist discrimination. The house was at the core of those concerns.[12]

Furnishings and interiors were not only a manifestation of the different destabilizations of the modern world, but also privileged the media through which architects hoped to respond to them. The tendency towards formal simplification and spatial ordering that broadly characterized modernist designs might be read in response to the increasingly hybrid nature of those Italian interiors pursuing the new forms of cohesion signified by *arredamento*. Moreover, following Ojetti's invitation, many architects linked this pursuit to the contemporaneous process of national consolidation. In fact, if the explorations of modernist architects and designers working at this scale considered the relationships between objects and their environments (following Argan), they also addressed the ways in which those relationships mediated the shifting links and attachments between subjects, communities, and their locations. The disjunctions ensuing from Italy's modernization and the erosion of values that was perceived to result from them stood at the core of the young nation's concerns with its own identity, which were only exacerbated by fascism. Modernist designs provided architects and designers with a referent and a medium through which to intervene in the management, articulation, and synchronization of Italian society following the fascist regime's pursuit of social control and cultural regeneration.[13]

The conception of Italian society as a reality in need of production locates the work of interwar architects and designers within a larger genealogy dating to Italy's nineteenth-century unification. In fact, the unification of the country might be understood to result from a series of conflicting (and sometimes violent) design operations—political, cultural, and economic—rather than as the result of a collective will. The popular Italian dictum characteristic of the *Risorgimento* already reflected the "designed" nature of the nation: "we have created Italy; now we have to create the Italians."[14] These words capture an understanding of the Italian state as an empty framework, one devoid of any specific content or a unified population. Significantly, this understanding functioned as an alibi for hegemonic constituencies (particularly the Piemontese aristocrats and northern industrial elites that had led the unification) in their project to supplant entrenched, usually localized and competing forms of identity with loyalty and identification with the nation. National cultural productions such as those pursued by Ojetti (including chairs, interiors, and architecture) should not be read as a cohesive manifestation of the Italian people's identity—a category that did not exist in any meaningful way—but as a project designed to stage this category's existence as a possibility and to negotiate its inclusions and exclusions. Since its inception and throughout the fascist period, the Italian nation remained an exercise in representation, "an empty simulacrum."[15]

In this genealogy, we might understand the cohesive "furnishing" of domestic interiors throughout the national borders with newly defined "Italian designs" as an intervention in the everyday life of Italians in the service of a nationalist project exacerbated by fascism. The project followed the disruption of boundaries between private and public characteristic of totalitarian regimes, putting domestic interiors to work in the service of the nation. And yet, domestic interiors were rarely transformed through the direct intervention of the fascist government. This transformation instead resulted, as often as not, from broad alliances between architects and designers and a plethora of commercial and cultural agents and national institutions that had different alliances with the regime, along with the cooperation of different media. While broadly operating to support the program of fascism, the discourse and practices of design differed from the contemporary understanding of architecture as "Arte di Stato," by which architecture was directly supported by the regime and expected to perform as its major representation.[16] Rather, the field of *arredamento* functioned as an "arena" of fascist cultural policy through which, as David Forgacs and Stephen Gundle have written, different and conflicting goals and influences were at stake and which operated in an "ambivalent" relation to international forces, following Emilio Gentile.[17] Those diverse goals and influences were negotiated by architects and designers in the material transformation of (and the images circulated for) the interiors of the nation.

The three scenes that follow illustrate the implications and complexities of what we can conceptualize as a "nation-furnishing project." They show how designers advanced this fascist ambition to "furnish" Italy while attending to the design of objects and interiors.

Scene 1

Consider the 1928 exhibitions organized by the Ente Nazionale del Dopolavoro, the regime's leisure organization, which was founded in 1925 and brought under Fascist National Party control in 1927. The fascist government used this institution to intervene directly in the market of household items for workers, simultaneously seeking to trigger consumption while promoting a culture of "modesty" that would balance individuality with a "cult of the home."[18] Rather than operating alone, the Dopolavoro worked with other institutions beyond the control of the regime to expand its reach to diverse audiences and markets, including a collaboration with the department store La Rinascente, which catered to more affluent urban constituencies.[19] Additionally, the Dopolavoro organized a series of competitions for furnishing the home between 1927 and 1929, with the hope of providing a platform that would provoke designers to match the institution's goals.[20] The largest of these competitions was set up in collaboration with the Ente nazionale per l'artigianato e le piccole industrie (an institution supporting craftsmen and small industries) and resulted in a series of exhibitions in major Italian cities. The competition asked designers, furniture makers, and commercial distributors to envision a house for workers and modest employees, and committed itself to shaping an ideal Italian family, which in the mind of the organizers would be composed of a father, a mother, and two children—smaller than the typical rural Italian households.[21]

The exhibitions included projects by a range of modernist designers, including Luigi Figini and Enrico Griffini, and displayed new aesthetic and technical trends then circulating in the country. But it also included projects submitted by manufacturers—for the exhibitions hoped to not only trigger new designs but also introduce them into the market and, ultimately, into the nation's homes. The furnishings of a small room out of cherry plywood, for example, were attributed to the firm Fratelli Suemin. Significantly, it was a whole room, consisting of several different pieces, that was offered for purchase as a set.[22] The inclusion of such submissions in the exhibition abstracted, fragmented, and recomposed "fully designed" interiors in the form of an image and a commodity, circulating beyond the location in which they were produced and valorized beyond their use.[23] And, significantly, the furnishings and interiors of private spaces were presented as an issue that exceeded the responsibility of individual inhabitants, and demanded the expertise of architects working for different institutions including Dolopavoro, the ENAPI, and La Rinascente.

These exhibitions encapsulated many of the tensions within modernist design practice and congregated together a great number of this new realm's protagonists. Similar concerns motivated other platforms, including the Exhibition of Decorative Arts, which

Questa cameretta in legno di ciliegio compensato naturale, della Ditta Fratelli Suemin, è di schietta modestia di concetto ed è una delle più piacevoli fra le cose adunate alla Mostra di Milano. È in vendita a L. 1171. (Letto, armadio, comodino, lavabo, attaccapanni).

L'ESPOSIZIONE DI MILANO DEL CONCORSO NAZIONALE PER L'AMMOBILIAMENTO ECONOMICO DELLA CASA INDETTO DALL'OPERA NAZIONALE DOPOLAVORO

PROVVIDA è stata l'iniziativa dell'Opera Naz. Dopolavoro nel bandire con l'Ente della Piccole Industrie il Concorso Nazionale per l'ammobiliamento e l'arredamento economico della casa; ben condotta è stata la organizzazione, severa e comprensiva l'opera che la Giuria, attraverso alle minori selezioni regionali — a Milano, a Firenze, a Napoli — ha compiuto; ricca di significato è stata la partecipazione particolarmente di industriali con forniture (come si vede dalle nostre illustrazioni) di spirito nettamente moderno; confortantissimo è l'interesse col quale il pubblico accompagna, anche sotto forma di sanzione materiale di acquisti, questa importante, pratica, bella manifestazione.

Riproduciamo alcune fra le più notevoli cose che sono raccolte nella Mostra Milanese, la quale compendia i risultati di tutta l'Italia settentrionale, e mentre ne segnaliamo al pubblico i risultati, esprimiamo quanto da questa manifestazione sia confortata la nostra speranza di veder nettamente convinti il pubblico e i produttori della moderna bellezza delle forme schiette semplici e pratiche.

Arch.

Accompagnamo ogni illustrazione con i prezzi di vendita, poichè questi costituiscono uno degli elementi caratteristici del Concorso e sono di obbligo dichiarati accanto agli oggetti esposti.

Figure 15.2 Wood furniture by Ditta Fratelli Suemin, featured in "Esposizione di Milano del concorso nazionale per l'ammobiliamento economico indetto dall'Opera Nazionale Dopolavoro," *Domus* 11 (November 1928). © Editoriale Domus SpA.

had been held in Monza since 1921. Initially sponsored by Guido Marangoni, that exhibition promoted the role of designers in what Marangoni conceived as a larger social project involving the creation of a "synthesis of collective taste"—a taste that would function as a substitute for regional aesthetic values at the scale of the nation and would support the increased clarity of that nation's identity and the coherence of its population.[24]

Scene 2

Specialized design media, including magazines *Domus* and *La Casa bella* (founded respectively by Ponti and Marangoni in 1928) and national newspapers such as *Corriere della sera* also contributed to this program. Marangoni presented the common impetus of these different institutions in the first issue of his magazine: "All our passionate discussions ... culminate in a single effort ... to create the new Italian house with its peculiar and typical characteristics."[25] Significantly, embedded in these arguments is an understanding of the Italian house as a structure with a specific cultural identity, as well as an assumption that this identity was not inherited, but needed to be defined. The identification of a specific "taste" for this house—one around which an Italian identity

Figure 15.3 Gastone Medin, set design for *Due cuori felici*, directed by Baldessari Negroni (1932). Included in Edoardo Persico, "L'arredamento moderno nel cinema," *La Casa bella* 59 (November 1932). Archivio fotografico della Cineteca Nazionale—Centro sperimentale di cinematografia, Rome.

might cohere—concerned architects and designers in their collaborations with these media. Both *Domus* and *La Casa bella* (which was transformed into the better-known *Casabella* under the directorship of architect Giuseppe Pagano and critic and designer Edoardo Persico) were contemporaneously concerned with gathering representations of such taste, while they also took on as their project its transformation. These editors understood that the transformation of taste allowed architects to work "with the consciousness of a polemic, not only artistic, but above all civil"—a polemic that allowed them to participate in the negotiation of the values of the nation.[26]

Beyond magazines and other print media, the expanding popularity of film became increasingly instrumental to this same goal throughout the 1930s.[27] Several critics regarded architectural interiors as a *mise-en-scène* and cinematographic interiors as real houses and used these associations to promote new designs to the Italian public. Spectators were expected to learn about new trends for the definition of the "Italian house" and, as Persico had it, the ways in which "Italians live within it."[28] Given the relevance architectural interiors had in film, furniture pieces were regarded as characters.

Take the MR chair, designed by Mies van der Rohe and included in the set designed by Gastone Medin for the film *Due cuori felici* (see Figure 15.3). Rather than consider its functional or technical qualities, Persico considered the chair in relation to the Italian population, and celebrated its design because, as he said, "it is the most similar to us . . . It resembles our sister dressed for tennis."[29] The "us" that was asked to identify with the chair was not only Persico's reader, but the inhabitant of the Italian house as broadcast through film—a house that repeatedly included these chairs despite their foreign origin. With this understanding, the design of film sets became critical in defining the inhabitants of the Italian home, but simultaneously helped shaped their other: "Have you not realized how a Liberty armchair resembles an aunt from the provinces?" Persico asked, to illustrate an undesirable model.[30] While Mies's chair was not an Italian product, it modeled Persico's vision of the (modern) Italian house through its rejection of the countryside and the south, and thus contributed to the exclusions performed in Italy by means of modernist design. Most significantly, such a design as that of Mies foregrounded those lifestyles and customs that were believed to offer ideal models for Italians (here, the cosmopolitan inhabitants of urban centers who play tennis) and, by definition, rejected others (such as those embracing the parochial values assigned to the "aunt"—a term often used derogatorily—"from the provinces"). While allegedly seeking to represent an "Italian" taste, design was thus a means for architects to assert internal hierarchies drawn along regional, ethnic, and even racially conceived lines.

Despite the diverse and often contradictory values attached to different styles, the success of modernism served to maintain the cultural hegemony of the northern cosmopolitan bourgeoisie in the construction of Italian identity.[31] Modernism thus represented a critical intervention in the debate that political theorist Antonio Gramsci termed "the Southern Question," emphasizing the dominance of Italy's northern cities over its southern rural populations (a relation that Gramsci defined as a form of "colonization"), invoking the explicitly racist ideologies then shaping the Italian nation.[32]

The design of film sets involved what architect and critic Carlo Enrico Rava defined as the "realization of a unitary and harmonic environment," with the role of the designer understood, in his words, as a "synthesizer"—a figure with the ability to formulate a meaningful whole through an integrated transformation of different material realities.[33] This was not unlike the nationalist project that modernist designers had already taken upon themselves. Design pieces traveled through screens to cinemas and spread throughout the Italian territories, participating in the coordination of the increasingly fragmented experiences of the population. Interiors real and filmed were confused with each other, and so were spaces domestic and foreign, ultimately resulting in disjointed locations that architects aimed to negotiate.

Scene 3

At the same time as architects and designers used different types of design and furniture to shape how Italians defined themselves, they also played a key role in differentiating this identity from that of other populations. This became particularly important within the context of Italian colonization. Furniture and other design artifacts were central to a growing body of knowledge that Italy developed about its colonies during the fascist era. Objects from subjugated territories were collected during ethnographic expeditions and

Figure 15.4 Salvo d'Angelo, Kitchen, featured in the "Exhibition of Colonial Equipment" at the VII Milan Triennale (1940). Archivio della Triennale di Milano. © Triennale Milano—Archivi.

later presented to the Italian public in a number of fairs and exhibitions. These events helped shape Italians' image of the colonized populations, as they allegedly illustrated their customs and framed their culture.[34] While the presentation of these objects in Italy started as early as the first colonial endeavors in the 1880s, this became a priority for the fascist regime. Exhibited dwellings from the colonized territories, shown with their furnishings and designs, confined the diverse African populations culturally and became a form of symbolic imprisonment for them.

As these expeditions and exhibitions were taking place, Italian designers simultaneously sought to participate in the project of colonization with newly defined pieces designed to accompany Italians in what Rava called the characteristically modern "adventure."[35] Consider, for example, a piece of furniture designed by Salvo d'Angelo and featured in the "Exhibition of Colonial Equipment" that Rava curated at the 1940 Milan Triennale (see Figure 15.4). Conceived as a portable kitchen, the piece was designed to be packed as a compact trunk. When opened, folding legs and panels provided work surfaces and revealed cupboards, a stove, and a sink. This kitchen allowed traveling colonizers to keep their characteristic customs and standards, while incorporating transience as a property of modern interiors. In fact, Rava's exhibition was devoted to equipment for the "nomadic" life that he deemed characteristic of colonial locations.[36] Unlike furnishings designed for use in Italy, these pieces were not identified with a specific location, but rather were defined through their capacity to circulate—given the "expansion of life horizons" that Rava understood to define the modern period.[37]

The capacity to move granted by these pieces was defined in contradistinction to the way in which Italians regarded the furnishings of the colonized populations as a form of cultural confinement. In that sense, they offered an alternative to the identity negotiations of the time. Rather than merely defining a characteristically Italian identity, they served to differentiate who was allowed to engage in the aforementioned "expansion" and who was forced to remain fixed—thus participating in the racial hierarchies and social relations that defined the Italian project of colonization. If the colonial world, according to Franz Fanon, was a "compartmentalized world," the relationship between its parts was not symmetric.[38] And while architecture was one of the privileged technologies used to sustain that compartmentalization, furniture became a tool to grant, to some, the added privilege of movement and "adventure."

*   *   *

The logics of modernist design in Italy were shaped in the struggle between two forces: on the one hand, the unfolding of characteristically modern circulatory processes, and on the other, the pursuit of stability for the "Italian home" characteristic of fascism. In the definition of Italian interiors, architects and designers brought together fragmentary and circulating furnishing elements in pursuit of new forms of cohesion. And if this was a characteristically modernist project, despite the visually distinct styles of the designs developed during this period, it is because these interiors aimed to mediate the anxieties generated by increasingly unstable relationships between subjects, communities, and their locations. This impetus must be understood in relation to the historical ambition to manage the diversity of Italy and articulate its populations, aligning the designed response to that ambition in the interwar years with the motivations of fascism.

The significance of these discourses and practices nonetheless goes beyond the specific political contingencies of the period. The case of both interwar and postwar Italy, and their interdependence, remains relevant to any understanding of how design continues to shape specific identities and different territorial articulations in a world characterized by the rise of international market transactions, electronic communication technologies, and global migration. Italy offers a paradigmatic case study for interrogating design's role in shaping spaces of residence within increasingly deterritorialized contexts and the processes of reterritorialization associated with nation building. In this consideration, design participates in what social and political theorists have called the "production of locality."[39] Aligned with the understanding of locality as something "produced," this chapter has traced design's role in the history of nation building within the cultural and political transformations of the modern world, rather than assuming that a nation (Italy) is a natural framework for the historical study of design and architecture.[40] In fact, the expression "Italian design" is a paradoxical expression because, as I have argued, design was activated in the "making" of Italians and in the "construction" of the nation. Italy was itself "designed." The oft-presented initiatives to foster an "Italian design culture" need to be instead understood as an effort to craft that culture in the first place—a project of making something specific and coherent out of the diversity characteristic of Italian regions (and their populations) and the processes of disaggregation characteristic of the modern period. This critical shift might allow us to reassess Italy's authority in the postwar culture of architecture and design by taking into account the hierarchies and exclusions that shaped both the "design of Italy" and "Italian design."

The relevance of both these processes—the dissolution of traditional identities, the fragmentation of societies, and a disembedding of social relations on the one hand, and on the other the search for different forms of identification and belonging—has only expanded in the present day. How to understand the way these pursuits are mediated by design and architecture remains a key disciplinary question.

Notes

1. Ernesto Nathan Rogers, "Ricostruzione: dall'oggetto d'uso alla città. Conferenza tenuta a Zurigo il 3 Novembre 1946 per invito dello Schweizerischer Werkbund," *Domus. La casa dell'uomo* 215 (1946): 5. In Italian, the phrase is "dal cucchiaio alla città."

2. Herman Muthesius, "Wo stehen Wir? Vortrag, gehalten auf der Jahresversammlung des Deutschen Werkbundes in Dresden 1911," in *Jahrbuch des Deutschen Werkbundes* (Jena: Eugen Diederichs, 1912), 16; Max Bill, "Die ganze Welt, vom Löffel bis zur Stadt, muß mit den sozialen Notwendigkeiten in Einklang gebracht werden," *Die gute Form, Schweizerischer Werkbund* (Winterthur: Buchdruckerei Winterthur, 1949).

3. Rogers, "Ricostruzione: dall'oggetto d'uso alla città," 3.

4. Ernesto Nathan Rogers, "Programma: Domus, la casa dell'uomo," *Domus* 205 (January 1946): 3.

5. Ugo Ojetti, "A Roma e a Torino: La patria e la sedia," *Corriere della sera* (July 7, 1911): 3. The *Corriere* was the largest national newspaper and mouthpiece of northern Italian industrialists.

6. Gio Ponti, "La casa all'italiana," *Domus* 1 (January 1928): 7. The title might also be translated as "Italianness in the house," as Maristella Casciato has suggested in "The 'Casa all'italiana' and the Idea of Modern Dwelling in Fascist Italy," *Journal of Architecture* 5, no. 4 (2000): 335. Raffaello Giolli had already used the expression "la casa italiana d'oggi" in his magazine *1927, Problemi d'arte attuale*.

7. Giulio Carlo Argan, "Ideological Development in the Thought and Imagery of Italian Design," in *Italy: The New Domestic Landscape. Achievements and Problems of Italian Design*, ed. Emilio Ambasz (New York: Museum of Modern Art, 1972), 369. The MoMA exhibition was a significant moment in the consolidation of an image of Italian design practices for North American audiences and beyond.

8. Giulio Carlo Argan, "Il problema dell'arredamento," in *Progetto e oggetto. Scritti sul design* (1956), ed. Claudio Gamba and Carlo Olmo (Milan: Medusa, 2003), 93–103. More recently, Alina Payne has analyzed the shift from the nineteenth-century interest in ornament to the concern with pieces of furniture as characteristic of modern architecture. See Alina Payne, *From Ornament to Object. Genealogies of Architectural Modernism* (New Haven, CT: Yale University Press, 2012).

9. The term "arredamento" comes from medieval Latin "arredare," derived from the Gothic term (ga)redan, meaning to arrange, to put in order, to take care. See *Vocabolario etimologico della lingua italiana di Ottorino Pianigiani*, http://www.etimo.it/. The use of the term expands beyond the period that I consider in this chapter, but is characteristic of it. The foundational 1902 *Esposizione Internazionale d'arte decorativa moderna* in Turin, for example, was concerned with "sets, details, and interiors" ("insiemi, dettagli, interni") rather than *arredamento*.

10. Carlo Levi, *Christ Stopped at Eboli* (New York: Straus and Company, 1947), 131–2.

11. See, for example, the documentary video describing the arrival of the inhabitants in the inauguration of the Borgata Tiburtino III, Rome. Istituto Luce.

12. See Casciato, "The 'Casa all'italiana," 349.

13. On the relationship between modernism and fascism, see, for example, Roger Griffin, "Modernity, Modernism, and Fascism. A 'Mazeway Resynthesis,'" *Modernism/Modernity* 15, no. 1 (January 2008): 9–24, and Walter L. Adamson, "Modernism and Fascism: The Politics of Culture in Italy, 1903–1922," *American Historical Review* 95, no. 2 (April 1990): 359–90.

14. Often attributed to Massimo D'Azeglio (in his central role in the process of national formation), it was introduced by Secretary of Education Ferdinando Martini. See Simonetta Sidoni and Gabriele Tuci (eds), *Fare gli italiani. Scuola e cultura nell'Italia contemporanea*, vol. 1 (Bologna: Il Mulino, 1993), 17.

15. Emilio Gentile, *Né stato né nazione. Italani senza meta* (Bari: Laterza, 2001), 97. According to Stephanie Malia, "The Risorgimento made its form, but the contents of the Italian state remain unsettled and indeterminate." See Stephanie Maila Hom, *The Beautiful Country: Tourism and the Impossible State of Destination Italy* (Toronto: University of Toronto Press), 9.

16. See Pietro Maria Bardi, "Architettura, Arte di Stato," *L'ambrosiano* (January 31, 1931), 40. See also his elaboration of the same arguments in Pietro Maria Bardi, *Rapporto sull'architettura (per Mussolini)* (Rome: Critica fascista, 1932). Many scholars have explored how the political implications of architecture throughout the period exceeded specific connections between individual architects or projects with the regime, and rather manifested in a state-wide involvement of the profession with the ideals and programs of fascism. See Diane Y. Ghirardo, "Italian Architects and Fascist Politics: An Evaluation of the Rationalists' Role in Regime

Building," *Journal of the Society of Architectural Historians* 39, no. 2 (1980): 109–27; Giorgio Ciucci, *Gli architetti e il fascismo. Architettura e città 1922–1944* (Turin: Einaudi, 1989); and Paolo Nicoloso, *Gli architetti di Mussolini. Scuole e sindacato, architetti e massoni, professori e politici negli anni del regime* (Milan: F. Angeli, 1999). Recent literature has brought increasing precision to the analysis of the diverse entanglements of modern architecture and fascism, its negotiation of vernacular sources beyond classicism and rationalism, its alliance with colonial endeavors, and its ramifications in the realm of urbanism. See Brian McLaren, *Architecture and Tourism in Italian Colonial Libya* (Seattle: University of Washington Press, 2006); Mia Fuller, *Moderns Abroad: Architecture, Cities, and Italian Imperialism* (London: Routledge, 2007); Michelangelo Sabatino, *Pride in Modesty: Modernist Architecture and the Vernacular Tradition in Italy* (Toronto: University of Toronto Press, 2010); David Rifkind, *The Battle for Modernism: Quadrante and the Politicization of Architectural Discourse in Fascist Italy* (Venice: Marsilio, 2012); and Lucy Maulsby, *Fascism, Architecture, and the Claiming of Modern Milan, 1922–43* (Toronto: University of Toronto Press, 2014).

17. David Forgacs and Stephen Gundle, *Mass Culture and Italian Society from Fascism to the Cold War* (Bloomington: Indiana University Press, 2007), 3; Emilio Gentile, "Impending Modernity: Fascism and the Ambivalent Image of the United States," *Journal of European History* 28 (1993): 7–29.

18. See Victoria De Grazia, *The Culture of Consent: Mass Organization of Leisure in Fascist Italy* (Cambridge: Cambridge University Press, 1981), 153.

19. See Elena Papadia, *La Rinascente* (Bologna: Il Mulino, 2011), 65. La Rinascente was promoted by a group of industrial and commercial leaders led by the Milanese politician and entrepreneur Senatore Borletti and was one of the key institutions concerned with the development of Italy after World War I. See also Franco Amatori, *Proprietà e direzione: La Rinascente, 1917–1969* (Milan: Franco Angeli Libri, 1989).

20. See Annalisa Avon, "La casa all'italiana," in *Storia della architettura italiana: Il primo novecento*, ed. Giorgio Ciucci and Giorgio Muratore (Milan: Electa, 2004), 165.

21. See Ferdinando Reggiori, "Il concorso nazionale per l'ammobigliamento e l'arredamento economico della casa popolare promosso dall'Opera nazionale dopolavoro e dall'Ente nazionale piccole industrie," *Architettura e arti decorative. Rivista d'arte e di storia* 8, no. 2 (1928): 497–8.

22. See "Esposizione di Milano del concorso nazionale per l'ammobiliamento economico indetto dall'Opera nazionale dopolavoro," *Domus* 11 (November 1928): 36.

23. Karl Marx's theory of value remains relevant here, in his understanding that "value is something purely social." Karl Marx, *Capital: A Critique of Political Economy* (1867) (New York: Penguin Books, 1992), 149.

24. Guido Marangoni, "Il mobile contemporaneo," *Le arti decorative* 8 (August 1925): 11–13. Marangoni founded the Monza Biennale in 1921 as a major exhibition to promote the decorative arts in the country.

25. Guido Marangoni, "Verso la nuova casa italiana," *La Casa bella* 11 (November 1928): 9–10.

26. Giuseppe Pagano, "L'internazionale cattivo gusto," *Casabella* 74 (February 1934): 39.

27. I have explored this relationship in Ignacio G. Galán, "Building Simultaneity in Fascist Italy: Film, Furniture, and the Reframing of the Nation," *Journal of the Society of Architectural Historians* 80, no. 2 (June 2021): 182–201.

28. Edoardo Persico (attributed, signed "Leader"), "Arredamento di un film," *La Casa bella* 46 (October 1931).

29. Edoardo Persico (attributed, signed "Leader"), "Una sedia," *La Casa bella* 45 (September 1931): 56.

30. Persico, "Una sedia," 56.

31. The fascist regime was extremely contradictory in its position toward the bourgeoisie, however, simultaneously embracing an anti-bourgeois sentiment and contributing to the sustenance of the bourgeoisie's cultural hegemony. On the increasing disdain for the bourgeoisie, see, for example, Mussolini's "Reform of Customs," in Benito Mussolini, "Al Consiglio Nazionale del P.N.F.," October 25, 1938, from *Popolo d'Italia*, October 26, 1938, in *Opera omnia di Benito Mussolini*, 36 vols, ed. Edoardo Susmel and Duilio Susmel (Florence: La Fenice, 1951–62), 29, 185–96.

32. Antonio Gramsci, "Some Aspects of the Southern Question" (1926), in *The Gramsci Reader: Selected Writings, 1916–1935*, ed. David Forgacs (New York: New York University Press, 2000), 171–85. On the hierarchy of city and countryside in relation to the Southern Question, see also Antonio Gramsci, "The City–Countryside Relationship during the Risorgimento and in the National Structure," in *Selections from the Prison Notebooks*, trans. and ed. Quintin Hoare and Geoffrey Nowell-Smith (London: Lawrence & Wishart, 1971), 264–82.

33. Carlo Enrico Rava, "Il gusto nel interni di film," *Stile* 2 (1941): 85.

34. Specific studies of decorative arts and crafts in the African colonies and the exhibitions that concern this article include Nicola Labanca (ed.), *L'Africa in vetrina. Storie di musei e di esposizioni coloniali in Italia* (Treviso: Pagus, 1992); Brian McLaren, "The Tripoli Trade Fair and the Representation of Italy's African Colonies," *Journal of Decorative and Propaganda Arts* 24 (2002): 170–97; Brian McLaren, "The Italian Colonial Appropriation of Indigenous North African Architecture in the 1930s," *Muqarnas: An Annual on the Visual Culture of the Islamic World* 29 (2002): 164–92; Brian McLaren, "Architecture During Wartime: The Mostra d'Oltremare and Esposizione Universale di Roma," *Architectural Theory Review* 19, no. 3 (2014): 299–318; and Sean Anderson, *Modern Architecture and its Representation in Colonial Eritrea: An In-visible Colony* (New York: Routledge, 2015), 191–242.

35. Carlo Enrico Rava, *L'attrezzatura coloniale alla VII Triennale di Milano* (Milan: Triennale di Milano, 1940), 9.

36. Rava, *L'attrezzatura coloniale alla VII Triennale di Milano*, 27.

37. Rava, *L'attrezzatura coloniale alla VII Triennale di Milano*, 9.

38. Frantz Fanon, *The Wretched of the Earth* (New York: Grove Press, 2004), 3

39. I am using the expression "production of locality" in relation to both Arjun Appadurai as well as Antonio Negri and Michael Hardt's work—both of whom use this expression with different meanings in their versions of globalization. Arjun Appadurai, "The production of locality," in *Modernity at Large: Cultural Dimensions of Globalization* (Minneapolis: University of Minnesota Press, 1996), 180–1; Antonio Negri and Michael Hardt, *Empire* (Cambridge, MA: Harvard University Press, 2000), 45.

40. Diane Ghirardo's recent history of Italian architecture is also fundamentally committed to understanding the role that architecture played in the modern period towards the construction of the Italian nation. See Diane Y. Ghirardo, *Italy: Modern Architectures in History* (London: Reaktion Books, 2013).

CHAPTER 16

THE INTERNATIONAL CALL: ITALIAN DESIGN, CULTURE, POLITICS, AND ECONOMICS AT THE 1972 MOMA EXHIBITION AND BEYOND

Silvia Micheli and Lorenzo Ciccarelli

The 1970s and 1980s witnessed an unexpected wave of interest in Italian production in fashion and graphic, architectural, urban, and industrial design, which figured in a global cultural discourse. This was the first time in the twentieth century that Italy gained international recognition for its contemporary design and architecture, and not simply for its historical patrimony. This fascination sprang only partially from built projects. A phase of exceptional design production coincided with the establishment of the "Made in Italy" campaign in the 1980s. At this point in time, architecture opened itself to interdisciplinary exchanges with fashion, industrial design, and even music on new terms. Its reach was dramatically broadened by means of such venues and media as museums, galleries, showrooms, magazines, television, political conventions, and music videos. Italy became an incubator for visionary design and creative output and a vehicle to promote a distinctive Italian lifestyle.[1] This wide-ranging initiative built on early efforts to position Italian design culture and its products firmly in the international imagination. At the same time, key actors staged strategic projects to boost Italian brands internationally. One such event, the 1972 exhibition *Italy: The New Domestic Landscape* in New York, was a product of protagonists working across Italy and in the US whose efforts greatly contributed to the global spread of Italian design.

The exhibition, staged at the Museum of Modern Art (MoMA) in New York between May 26 and September 11, 1972, represented a turning point in the launch and global exposure of mid-twentieth-century Italian design culture (see Figure 16.1). It was the first time Italian design had been promoted abroad with such an inclusive and comprehensive approach—and this in one of the most influential venues for art, design, and architecture in the world. It was an outstanding national achievement, considering that only one decade before, in 1961, the year of the foundation of the Milan Furniture Fair, the Italian furniture industry as such did not even exist.[2] The result of a strategic collaboration between MoMA, public and private sponsors from Italy, and contemporary architects and industrial designers, *The New Domestic Landscape* proved to be the museum's largest exhibition to date.[3] One critic observed that its "audacious thinking, industrialized thinking ... goes far beyond today's mobile homes and tract housing ... the results bear little or no resemblance, inside or out, to mass-produced housing as we know it in [the US]."[4]

Italy's achievements in the design, particularly, of automobiles and typewriters, had been previously celebrated by MoMA in a series of exhibitions. For instance, the Cisitalia

Figure 16.1 Installation view of the exhibition *Italy: The New Domestic Landscape*, Museum of Modern Art, New York, May 26, 1972 through September 11, 1972. Curatorial Exhibition Files, Exh#1004. Photographer Leonardo LeGrand. © MoMA (acc. no: IN1004.232), digital image © 2022, Museum of Modern Art/Scala, Florence.

car, designed by Giovanni Battista Pininfarina in 1946, was included in *Eight Automobiles*, curated by Philip Johnson and Arthur Drexler in 1951. The Lancia GT, again designed by Pininfarina, and the SIATA Daina 1400, for which he designed the bodywork, appeared in *Ten Automobiles* in the museum's garden in 1953. In 1966, Pininfarina's PF Sigma Italy 63, De Tomaso's Vallelunga (with bodywork by Ghia), and Lamborghini's P-400 Miura (with bodywork by Bertone) all featured in *The Racing Car: Toward a Rational Automobile*.[5] While these exhibitions featured a single type of object, the 1952 show *Olivetti: Design in Industry* focused on a single Italian manufacturer.[6] Even though the architecture critic Ada Louise Huxtable had, in 1954, curated the comprehensive survey *The Modern Movement in Italy: Architecture and Design*, the 1972 exhibition was the first that set out to critically discuss Italian design culture at a broader level, including its economic, societal and political implications.

Held in both the exterior and interior spaces of the museum, *The New Domestic Landscape* showcased 180 household "Objects" and twelve "Environments," which had been commissioned on the assumption that "the object is no longer conceived as an isolated entity, sufficient onto itself, but rather as an integral part of the larger natural and sociocultural environment."[7] The Objects, many of which were donated by Italian manufacturers and designers, became part of MoMA's permanent collection. They consisted of pieces of furniture, lighting fixtures, flatware, and china, all displayed on the terraces of the museum's garden. Works by more than 100 designers were chosen according to three main categories: formal and technical innovation (experimentation with fiberglass, polyurethane, reinforced polyester, polyethylene, pneumatic structures, and ABS plastic by producers like Arflex, Busnelli, Kartell, Artemide, Zanotta, and Gavina); sociocultural provocations (semantic manipulation of established sociocultural meanings in environments by Gaetano Pesce, Superstudio, Gruppo Sturm, Archizoom, Ettore Sottsass, Jr., and objects produced by Poltronova, Flos, and ABET-Print); and support for flexible patterns of domestic use and arrangement (including objects by Joe Colombo, Achille Castiglioni, Mario Bellini, Cini Boeri, and Angelo Mangiarotti and produced by Cassina, Flexform, and C&B).

Made in Italy and shipped to New York, the Environments were meant to represent two prevailing attitudes towards environmental design identified by curator Emilio Ambasz in the exhibition catalog section entitled "Design Program."[8] This included invited designers of established repute as well as a competition for designers younger than thirty-five.[9] The first of these attitudes was "Design as Postulation." This involved a commitment to design understood as a problem-solving activity, capable of formulating solutions for the natural and sociocultural milieu.[10] In this category, Ambasz placed three House Environments (by Gae Aulenti, Ettore Sottsass, Jr., and Joe Colombo) and three Mobile Environments (by Alberto Rosselli, Marco Zanuso and Richard Sapper, and Mario Bellini—see Figure 16.2). The second attitude was "Design as Commentary." This

Figure 16.2 Mario Bellini, "Kar-A-Sutra," 1972. Photograph by Studio Castelli. Courtesy Mario Bellini Architects.

profiled counter-design, chosen to emphasize the desire for a renewed philosophical discourse and for social and political involvement to bring about structural change in contemporary society.[11] In this second category, Ambasz included six Environments by Gaetano Pesce, Ugo La Pietra, Archizoom, Superstudio, Gruppo Sturm, and Enzo Mari.

The contents of the exhibition are already well known and studied: its Objects and Environments, the exhibited designers, and their various disciplinary and political orientations.[12] This chapter instead explores the exhibition through the protagonists who operated behind the scenes: the public and private institutions and sponsors that promoted and sustained the exhibition, considered in the broader framework of exchanges and transcultural influences that bound Italy to the United States during the 1970s. It unpacks the political implications of a cultural event that was unique and crucial to the global exposure of Italian design.

The impresario and the manager: Emilio Ambasz and Gianluigi Gabetti

The Argentine-born architect Emilio Ambasz was Curator of Design at MoMA's Department of Architecture and Design between 1969 and 1976; he conceived and curated *The New Domestic Landscape*. Ambasz had studied architecture at Princeton with Michael Graves and Peter Eisenman.[13] With the latter, he established a close professional relationship after graduation. Ambasz also taught at Princeton, and he became a fellow of the Institute for Architecture and Urban Studies in New York, founded by Eisenman in 1967. It was, in fact, Eisenman who suggested Ambasz to Drexler for the curatorial position at MoMA.[14]

According to Ambasz, he "started doing *Italy: The New Domestic Landscape* as a very simple-minded idea, completely ignorant of the subject matter, fascinated with Italian design and production."[15] He described his role as that of an "impresario," someone who can actively "trigger certain types of projects" by providing institutional support.[16] Ambasz selected and invited the Italian designers who conceived the twelve Environments with the conviction that the curator's position was that of "finding someone and providing him with water and making him bloom ... I felt it was quite important to bring up to a level of consciousness the ideas and the emotions which are embodied in the objects which man makes, so that the public can somehow take joy or pleasure in that, because they help reveal meanings and values of the culture."[17]

Eisenman's deep interest and expertise in modern Italian architecture may have inspired Ambasz's curiosity for Italian culture and design.[18] There is no evidence of strong links between Ambasz and Italian design culture before 1970.

Once the idea to organize the exhibition was seeded, it was necessary to establish a transatlantic network with select Italian architects, industrial designers, and historians of architecture to advance the exhibition and its catalog, as well as Italian public and private sponsors who could support these initiatives. Ambasz's initial interaction with Italian designers, industry partners, and public institutions was facilitated by the support of Thomas Czarnowski and Anna Querci. Czarnowski, one of Ambasz's classmates at

Princeton, was fluent in Italian and had "a great gift for logistics."[19] Before moving to the US, Querci had worked for Gio Ponti in the editorial team of *Domus*, the most prestigious Italian design journal.[20] It was Querci who introduced Ambasz to the Milanese circles around *Domus* and to the architects and designers who directly collaborated with the journal. Lisa Licitra Ponti, Ponti's daughter, together with publisher Inge Feltrinelli and design theorist Tomás Maldonado, guided Ambasz during his exploratory trips in Italy, and the quasi-totality of the designers involved in the exhibition were Milanese.[21]

One of the first key people Ambasz consulted in New York while organizing the exhibition was the Italian engineer and entrepreneur Gianluigi Gabetti (1924–2019), already a member of MoMA's Board of Trustees. Gabetti was a cultured man, fascinated by fine arts and architecture, and brother of the influential architect and historian Roberto Gabetti of Turin. Both Gianluigi Gabetti and his American wife Bettina, a "cherished friend" of the Museum since the 1960s, served on MoMA's Architecture and Design Committee, and were also members of its International Council.[22] In its advocacy for cultural exchange, the International Council and related International Program "worked closely with the United States government and agencies as well as foreign governments and international organizations."[23] Because of his specific role to foster connections between the Museum and foreign governments and agencies, and because of his dual identity as financier and art estimator, Gabetti was the ideal person to assist Ambasz in reaching out to Italian sponsors and perhaps, even, Italian institutional and political parties, thereby playing a discreet but fundamental role in the administrative and economic organization of the 1972 MoMA exhibition.

Indeed, Gabetti had worked with Adriano Olivetti since 1958, becoming president of the Olivetti Corporation of America, and he was behind the involvement of Louis Kahn and a very young Renzo Piano as architects for the Olivetti-Underwood building in Harrisburg, Pennsylvania.[24] In 1971, when the exhibition was in preparation, Gabetti met Gianni Agnelli, owner of the Italian car manufacturer FIAT, during a visit to MoMA.[25] Agnelli was the single most influential Italian entrepreneur of his generation; he was struck by Gabetti's professionalism and offered him a job back in Italy as a director at FIAT and general manager of IFI, a holding controlled by the Agnelli family (see Figure 16.3). Gabetti became one of the most trusted financial advisers of *L'Avvocato* (The Lawyer), as Gianni was nicknamed by the Italian press.[26]

Preserved correspondence shows that Gabetti's managerial positions, first at Olivetti and then in FIAT, facilitated the involvement of these two firms as principal sponsors of the 1972 exhibition. In a letter dated September 23, 1970, Gabetti wrote to the Manager for Cultural Activities of the Olivetti corporation, Renzo Zorzi, that he had been contacted by Ambasz to secure the participation of Olivetti in the exhibition, asking them to act as a sponsor.[27] Some of the most iconic Olivetti typewriters and objects, such as Ettore Sottsass's "Valentine" and Giorgio Soavi's "paperweight with ball," would be displayed among the Objects. Olivetti's support included funds for the production of exhibition information and documentation materials, extended to the orientation leaflets and the graphic and audio-visual information systems.[28] After Gabetti moved to FIAT, he worked towards involving the Turin-based company in the exhibition, too.[29] In a

Figure 16.3 Gianni Agnelli (standing) and Gianluigi Gabetti (third from the right) at the FIAT shareholders meeting, 1983. © Centro Storico FIAT, Turin.

document dated July 21, 1971, the FIAT management decided to contribute US$20,000 and to sponsor the Environments by Alberto Rosselli and Marco Zanuso and Richard Sapper.[30]

Italian forces on the move

A few pages in, the *New Domestic Landscape* catalog declares that the exhibition "is presented under the sponsorship of the Italian Ministry for Foreign Trade and ICE–Institute for Foreign Trade, and the Gruppo ENI."[31] This was one of the few occasions where Italian politics and industry entered a joint effort to export the gains of postwar Italian culture. It was a strategic investment by the government, which covered one-third of the show's total expenses; while ENI, one of the world's largest oil companies, matched its commitment.[32]

The exhibition was organized at an historically crucial moment for the Italian economy. In the postwar period, the Marshall Plan spurred Italy's economic reconstruction and, from the late 1950s and early 1960s, helped boost the nation's extraordinary period of economic growth and industrialization, known as the *miracolo economico* (economic miracle).[33] Historians agree on the decisive role that the opening up of international trade and exports had in Italy's economic growth during these years.[34] In this process, the ICE played a fundamental role.[35] Part of the Ministry for Foreign Trade, the Institute (founded in 1926) was charged with expanding the reach of Italian businesses and products. It had an information office in Italy, maintained offices in foreign capitals, and established an exhibition office which supported Italian participation in international promotional events, organized by the Institute or external sponsors. The ICE likely supported *The New Domestic Landscape* through the exhibition office, given its high cultural and promotional value for Italian industry and its furniture sector. While MoMA's role as a global stage for art, design, and architecture is widely recognized, less is known about its agency in promoting bilateral exchange among institutions and industries. Some of the exhibition's most high-profile contributors, like FIAT, Olivetti, Alitalia, ENI, and Pirelli, were also the most competitive Italian companies, both private and public, who looked to the American market with great interest. It was Ambasz who declared that "Emilio Cefis, former president of ENI, had a clear vision of the potential that this project might have for Italian industry."[36]

The first contacts between Ambasz and the ENI group date to June 1970, when the architect explained the exhibition's organization and aims to its board of directors. While the directors appreciated its academic and cultural aims, they were particularly attracted by the possibility of introducing ENI to the US market. This was consistent with the goal of its president, Eugenio Cefis, to improve and normalize relations with the US administration.[37] ENI leadership believed "the initiative proposed by Ambasz was very positive also from a commercial-financial point of view," recalling that David Rockefeller, whose family controlled the American oil industry, "is one of the partners of the Museum."[38] Indeed, Cefis understood that *The New Domestic Landscape* offered an opportunity to connect ENI to MoMA, granting it a double advantage: greater status and visibility in the huge US market, and the opportunity to exhibit in that market industrial objects in plastic and composite materials produced by two companies controlled by ENI: ANIC and Lanerossi. When Ambasz presented the exhibition project to the ENI board, it was not restricted to MoMA; he also anticipated travel to other major American cities, including Washington, Chicago, San Francisco, and Los Angeles, which greatly increased the interest of ENI.[39]

Once the idea of an exhibition on Italian design at MoMA was outlined, Ambasz and Drexler visited producers' workshops and showrooms, met designers, and followed the production of the environments.[40] Documents in the ENI archive indicate that Ambasz traveled to Italy three times: his first trip was from April 14 to 20, 1971; the second, July 21 to September 20, 1971; and finally from January 15 to 23, 1972, four months before the opening in New York—moving always between Rome and Milan, the two cities funding the exhibition. Ambasz's personal imprint on the selection of designers and the overall exhibition structure was substantial. ENI management tried several times to suggest architects and designers, but they conflicted with Ambasz's choices.[41] Out of twelve designers whom Ambasz included in the Environments section, only Marco Zanuso was an established professor at the Milan Polytechnic, showing the curator's intention—and MoMA's hope—to scout fresh Italian talent to launch internationally.

Charting Italian design culture: the exhibition catalog

Luca Molinari has observed that "the catalogue of *The New Domestic Landscape* had a tremendous impact in the following years in Italian and American academic circles. It was the first book which attempted to chart the cultural complexity of an emerging design culture."[42] The catalog was edited by Ambasz himself, who designed the cover, wrote the introduction, and curated both the exhibition material and the densely written section dedicated to critical and historical essays. The volume was published by MoMA in collaboration with Centro Di and was produced and printed in Florence.

The full title of the catalog is *Italy: The New Domestic Landscape; Achievements and Problems of Italian Design*. The addition of the second subtitle signals that the catalog was not intended to simply mirror the show. Instead, it aimed to add complexity to the reportage of Objects and Environments on display and provide complementary critical readings.[43] The catalog was conceived as an "autonomous object" that would perform as a business card of Italian design for a global audience. It was a rare cultural convergence among the different voices animating the 1950s and 1960s Italian design scene, brought together to present Italy abroad.

The first part of the catalog presents the Objects and Environments on display, grouped according to the categories discussed above. The second part, complementary to but independent from the first, includes a series of in-depth historico-critical essays whose contents go well beyond what was exhibited at MoMA. These essays together depict the most detailed history of Italian design to date. That this second part of the volume was financed by the Consorzio per le opere pubbliche (Public Works Consortium) and the Istituto di credito per le imprese di pubblica utilità (Bank for Public Utility Enterprises) makes clear the willingness of Italian institutions to leverage MoMA's prestige to present to the American public the widest possible panorama of the development of Italian applied arts and industrial design.[44] The second section ("Critical Articles") assumed a contextualizing role, offering a "body of criticism . . . especially with the sociocultural context of design and the historical processes that it undergoes."[45]

Ambasz was certainly aware of Vittorio Gregotti's *New Directions in Italian Architecture*, published in English in 1968.[46] This book was the first synthesis of the development of Italian architecture since the end of World War II. In his review of the book, Reyner Banham noted that Gregotti presented "Italian architecture in a deadlock of conflicting idealisms."[47] This is an ideological framework similar to that adopted by Ambasz for the MoMA exhibition, with its goal of "revealing the contradictions and conflicts underlying a feverish production of objects."[48] Ambasz invited Gregotti to contribute to the catalog, entrusting him with an essay on contemporary Italian design culture, the volume's longest and most heavily documented.[49] Its focus on the postwar period reinforces the sense that *New Directions* constituted a crucial reference for Ambasz. Gregotti also supplied a lengthy bibliography for his essay that was not included in the book (a typewritten copy was deposited in the MoMA library).[50]

After the exhibition closed it was soon evident that its commercial success was less substantial than its intellectual achievements. *The New Domestic Landscape* did not travel to other American cities as intended, limiting promotional exposure for the objects, design companies, and sponsors. In addition, the Environments were not taken up for industrial production and commercialization, and ENI declined to exercise its contractual right to purchase those projects.[51] Surprisingly, the Italian Institute of Statistics (ISTAT) reports that between 1972 and 1976—a period that covers the oil crisis—the volume of Italian exports to the United States decreased significantly; only from 1982 did they start to soar.[52]

Despite its negligible impact on the American sale of Italian objects, the 1972 MoMA show increased US interest in Italian architectural and design culture. Critically, the exhibition was extremely well-received. From the pages of the *New York Times*, Huxtable presented the exhibition as a "supershow" that "combined form and content, object and ideology," declaring it "the most important design show in 20 years."[53] A similar view was published in *New York Magazine*, Rita Reif writing that "the provocative ideas presented in the Italian show at MoMA may well make this the most exciting and controversial design and architecture exhibition seen here in many decades."[54]

A unique case

The role that the MoMA exhibition played in the worldwide promotion of Italian design culture was crucial and manifold. Firstly, the exhibition was the culmination of two decades of national domestic debate on social, ideological, and disciplinary problems in Italian design.[55] It was also the first truly successful attempt to promote Italian design culture at a global scale, triggering a wave of international interest without precedent. Over the next two decades, Italian designers dominated the international scene, with Milan and its design fair becoming the most creative epicenter for industrial design.

Finally, and just as importantly, the MoMA exhibition prompted the Italian architectural community to reconsider its national boundaries as the natural horizon of debate and to open up disciplinary conversation with foreign interlocutors. As a direct consequence of the event in New York, between 1972 and 1983, several cultural initiatives reframed Italian discourse on architecture and design within a larger international debate, including the 1973 *Architettura razionale*, a section of the XV Milan Triennale; the exhibition *'76 Europa/America* at the Venice Biennale; and the exhibition *Roma interrotta*, organized in Rome in 1978. In 1975, *L'architecture d'aujourd'hui* invited a delegation of professors from the Istituto universitario di architettura in Venice (including Manfredo Tafuri, Francesco Dal Co, Carlo Aymonino, Giorgio Ciucci, and Marco De Michelis) to write in the special issue "Italie 75" about Italian contemporary architecture and theories. Furthermore, these same historians, critics, and architects animated the Institute for Architecture and Urban Studies, as Venice and New York established a reciprocal attraction.[56] In what was perhaps its most commercial consequence, the Tea and Coffee Piazza Program was launched by the design company Alessi in 1979–83, bringing together architects and designers from US and Italy in a postmodern exercise across scales.

Figure 16.4 Installation view of the exhibition *Italy: The New Domestic Landscape*, Museum of Modern Art, New York, May 26, 1972 through September 11, 1972. Gelatin-silver print, 1' x 1½' (2.5 cm x 3.8 cm). Photographer: Leonardo LeGrand. © MoMA (acc. no.: IN1004.81), digital image © 2022, Museum of Modern Art/Scala, Florence.

This concise list of "transatlantic interactions" shows how, from 1972, global attention to Italian architecture and design increased dramatically and Italians responded incrementally to what can be described as an "international call." The inaugural Architecture Biennale in Venice in 1980 was the culmination of this process. With Paolo Portoghesi's *Strada Novissima*, Italy was ready to speak to the world directly—and not be represented by an international institution such as MoMA. While the international breadth of *Strada* is renowned, one of its sub-exhibitions, *L'oggetto banale*, co-curated by the Milanese architect and designer Alessandro Mendini (Alchimia), is less known, yet equally orchestrated to engage an international discussion. This small installation, made of restyled versions of ordinary objects available at supermarkets, focused on the potential of industrial design as a field of linguistic and conceptual experimentation. In the wake of the MoMA exhibition, Portoghesi's decision to involve Mendini in his Biennale was driven by his awareness of the increasing centrality and agency of industrial design for Italian design culture's international reputation. Notably, both Portoghesi and Mendini contributed essays to Ambasz's catalog.

Yet, in this inclusive list of cultural events that covers just over a decade, *The New Domestic Landscape* remains a unique case of political and commercial funding. None of the other initiatives organized to present Italian design internationally enjoyed the coordinated and generous support provided for the 1972 New York exhibition. The image of Italian design supremacy as a sort of "natural resource"—almost mythical—also leveraged centuries of academic tradition to support a national, commercial agenda. In 1972, the Italian-funded New York exhibition *New Domestic Landscape* was fundamentally a powerful advertising event that redesigned established ideas of artistic authority for a new era of global capitalism. Deep cultural roots helped this image be readily absorbed by an international audience, soon to be hooked by the "Made in Italy" campaign in the following decade, and for which *Italy: The New Domestic Landscape* provided a powerful trigger.

Notes

1. Grace Lees-Maffei and Kjetil Fallan (eds), *Made in Italy: Rethinking a Century of Italian Design* (New York: Bloomsbury, 2013). The authors discussed together all the critical arguments of this chapter. Micheli wrote the last three parts, while Ciccarelli wrote the first two and conducted archival research in Italy.

2. Rosario Messina, "Ninety Years in Two; As Time Goes By You Can Be Rejuvenated," in *1951–2001: Made in Italy?*, Marco Abate (ed.), exhibition catalog (Milan: Skira, 2001), 1.

3. Zoë Ryan (ed.), *As Seen: Exhibitions That Made Architecture and Design History* (New Haven, CT: Yale University Press, 2017), 48.

4. Rita Reif, "MoMA Mia, That's Some Show," *New York Magazine* 5 (1972): 40.

5. *8 Automobiles* (New York: Museum of Modern Art, 1951), 12–13; *Ten Automobiles* (New York: Museum of Modern Art, 1953), 6–7, 20–1.

6. Leo Lionni (ed.), *Olivetti: Design in Industry* (New York: Museum of Modern Art, 1952).

7. Emilio Ambasz (ed.), *Italy: The New Domestic Landscape. Achievement and Problems of Italian Design* (New York: Museum of Modern Art; Florence: Centro Di, 1972), 11.

8. Ambasz, *Italy: The New Domestic Landscape*, 139–146.

9. Ambasz, *Italy: The New Domestic Landscape*, 137. The Design Program is held at the MoMA Archives, Art and Exhibition Records 1970–1979, 1004. Ambasz, *Italy: The New Domestic Landscape*, 61. *Design Program Specific Considerations*.

10. Ambasz, *Italy: The New Domestic Landscape*, 137.

11. Ambasz, *Italy: The New Domestic Landscape*, 137.

12. Beyond the catalog, see Felicity D. Scott, "Italian Design & The New Political Landscape," in *Analyzing Ambasz*, ed. Michael Sorkin (New York: Monacelli Press, 2004), 109–56; *Emilio Ambasz: Emerging Nature* (Zurich: Lars Müller, 2017), 237–62; Alexandra Brown, "Operaismo, Architecture & Design in Ambasz's *New Domestic Landscape*: Issues of Redefinition and Refusal in 1960s Italy," *Proceedings of the Society of Architectural Historians, Australia and New Zealand* 27 (Newcastle, NSW: SAHANZ, 2010): 52–6. See also the traveling exhibition *Environments and Counter Environments: "Italy: The New Domestic Landscape"* (New York, Basel, Barcelona, Stockholm, Chicago, 2009–13), curated by Peter Lang, Luca Molinari, and Mark Wasiuta and supported by the Graham Foundation.

13. Museum of Modern Art, Oral History Program, *Interview with Emilio Ambasz by Sharon Zane*, New York, December 7, 1993, 2, https://www.moma.org/momaorg/shared/pdfs/docs/learn/archives/transcript_ambasz.pdf.

14. MoMA, *Interview with Emilio Ambasz*.

15. MoMA, *Interview with Emilio Ambasz*, 10.

16. MoMA, *Interview with Emilio Ambasz*, 10.

17. MoMA, *Interview with Emilio Ambasz*, 11.

18. "Interview with Peter Eisenman. The Last Grand Tourist: Travels with Colin Rowe," *Perspecta* 34 (2003): 132–8.

19. The authors in conversation with Emilio Ambasz.

20. The authors in conversation with Emilio Ambasz.

21. Ambasz, *Italy: The New Domestic Landscape*, 15.

22. "Gianluigi Gabetti—Obituary," *New York Times*, May 15, 2019, https://www.legacy.com/obituaries/nytimes/obituary.aspx?n=gianluigi-gabetti&pid=192885250.

23. MoMA Archives (New York), International Council and International Program Records, *Historical Note*, https://www.moma.org/research-and-learning/archives/finding-aids/ICIP_SeriesIB_VIb.html#series6.

24. Lorenzo Ciccarelli, "Philadelphia Connections in Renzo Piano's Formative Years: Robert Le Ricolais and Louis I. Kahn," *Construction History* 2 (2016): 201–22.

25. Aldo Cazzullo, "Gianluigi Gabetti: Io da dattilografo ad Agnelli attraverso Mattioli e Olivetti. Portai Marchionne alla Fiat," *Corriere della sera*, February 24, 2018.

26. Jennifer Clark, *Mondo Agnelli: Fiat, Chrysler, and the Power of a Dynasty* (New York: Wiley, 2011), 27.

27. Associazione Archivio Storico Olivetti (Ivrea), Centro Culturale Olivetti Milano, Grandi esposizioni, folder 19, file 98, "The New Domestic Landscape_01."

28. Associazione Archivio Storico Olivetti (Ivrea), Centro Culturale Olivetti Milano, Grandi esposizioni, folder 19, file 99, "The New Domestic Landscape_02."

29. Centro Storico Fiat (Turin), Fondo Camerana, ITCSFPIC010 1969–1975, "Corrispondenza e documentazione relativa alla mostra 'New Italian Landscape' presso MoMA New York."

30. "Corrispondenza 'New Italian Landscape.'" See also Ambasz, *Italy: The New Domestic Landscape*, 180–99.

31. Ambasz, *Italy: The New Domestic Landscape*, 5.

32. The total exhibition cost was estimated at $310,423, of which the Italian government paid $100,000, ENI another $100,000, and MoMA $110,423. See ENI Archive (Rome), Archivio Documentale, Relazioni Esterne, Coordinamento e controllo pubblicità, 3022, box 169, "Italia: il nuovo paesaggio domestico," July 30, 1970. A private MoMA document reported that the contribution of the Italian government "was agreed upon by the Director of Promotion of the Ministry of Foreign Commerce, at a meeting held on July 7, 1971, in the Italian Embassy in Washington." See Associazione Archivio Storico Olivetti (Ivrea), Centro Culturale Olivetti Milano, Grandi esposizioni, folder 19, file 98, "The New Domestic Landscape_01."

33. Paolo Scrivano, *Building Transatlantic Italy: Architectural Dialogues with Postwar America* (London: Routledge, 2013).

34. Giulio Sapelli, *Storia economica dell'Italia contemporanea* (Milan: Bruno Mondadori, 1997); Augusto Graziani, *Lo sviluppo dell'economia italiana. Dalla ricostruzione alla moneta unica* (Turin: Bollati Boringhieri, 1998). See also Robert Lumley and Zygmunt Baranski (eds), *Culture and Conflicts in Postwar Italy* (Basingstoke: Macmillan 1990).

35. Sara Nocentini, *L'ICE dalla ricostruzione ai primi anni Settanta. Appunti per una ricerca storica*, https://www.ice.it/it/sites/default/files/inline-files/Rapporto%20Ice%202007%20-%20Nocentini.pdf.

36. Ambasz, *Italy: The New Domestic Landscape*, 13.

37. Diego Cuzzi, *Breve storia dell'ENI. Da Cefis a Girotti* (Bari: De Donato, 1975).

38. ENI Archive (Rome), Archivio Documentale, Relazioni Esterne, Coordinamento e controllo pubblicità, 3022, box 169, "Appunto per il dottor Bianco," August 5, 1970.

39. ENI Archive (Rome), Archivio Documentale, Relazioni Esterne, Coordinamento e controllo pubblicità, 3022, box 169, "Appunto per il dottor Cefis," June 24, 1970.

40. MoMA, *Interview with Emilio Ambasz*, 28.

41. ENI Archive (Rome), Archivio Documentale, Relazioni Esterne, Coordinamento e controllo pubblicità, 3022, box 169, "Appunto per il dottor Bianchedi," January 4, 1972.

42. Luca Molinari, "Emilio Ambasz: The new domestic landscape exhibition at MoMA, New York NY, USA, 1972," http://radical-pedagogies.com/search-cases/a01-new-domestic-landscape-exhibition-moma/.

43. Gülru Mutlu Tunca, "A Historical Project: Doubling INDL Exhibition Catalogue," *METU Journal of the Faculty of Architecture* 2 (2013), 203.

44. Ambasz, *Italy: The New Domestic Landscape*, 8.

45. Ambasz, *Italy: The New Domestic Landscape*, 343.

46. Vittorio Gregotti, *New Directions in Italian Architecture* (London: Studio Vista, 1968).

47. Reyner Banham, review of *New Directions in Italian Architecture*, by Vittorio Gregotti, *Art Bulletin* 52, no. 3 (1970): 344–6.

48. Ambasz, *Italy: The New Domestic Landscape*, 12.

49. Vittorio Gregotti, "Italian Design 1945–1971," in Ambasz, *Italy: The New Domestic Landscape*, 315–40. Gregotti published the Italian version of the catalog essay in "I.D. Story. Italian Design 1945–1972," part 1, 2, and 3, *Casabella* 370, 371, 372 (1972): 42–50; 42–50; 34–40, resp.

50. Ambasz, *Italy: The New Domestic Landscape*, 340.

51. ENI Archive (Rome), Archivio Documentale, Relazioni Esterne, Coordinamento e controllo pubblicità, 3022, box 169, "Diritto di prelazione per l'acquisto dei progetti degli ambienti esposti al MoMA," July 28, 1972.

52. Natale Renato Fazio, *La ricostruzione storica delle statistiche del commercio con l'estero per gli anni 1970–1990*, 38–40, https://www.istat.it/it/files//2018/07/2006_6-1.pdf.

53. Ada Louise Huxtable, "Italian Design Show Appraised—Ambiguous but Beautiful," *New York Times*, May 26, 1972, 43.

54. Reif, "MOMA Mia, That's Some Show," 41.

55. Paolo Fossati, *Il design in Italia, 1945–1972* (Turin: Einaudi, 1972).

56. See Joan Ockman, "Venice and New York," *Casabella* 619–620, "Il progetto storico di Manfredo Tafuri" (1995): 57.

CHAPTER 17

APPROPRIATING ALDO ROSSI: THE DISPLACED AFTERLIFE OF *L'ARCHITETTURA DELLA CITTÀ* IN CHINA

Dijia Chen

The Italian architect and theorist Aldo Rossi was first introduced to China during the late 1980s as part of the nation's sudden exposure to postmodern architectural theories after the opening-up policy enacted by Deng Xiaoping.[1] Over the past three decades, Rossi's writings, buildings, designs, and drawings have received extensive attention in the Chinese academic community, where they were passionately studied long after the western world entered a period of inattention that spanned from Rossi's death to his more recent critical recuperation.[2] Within Rossi's oeuvre, *L'architettura della città* has been the primary focus of Chinese architects, while his other books and articles are seldom mentioned and never translated. Scholars have based their work on the English translation published by MIT in 1982, the 1992 Taiwanese edition translated from the French, and the mainland Chinese translation of the English version, published in 2006. Due to the ambiguity of Rossian terminology and the difficulty of transplanting western concepts into the Chinese language, the title of the book and specific terms are translated and explained in different ways by various authors, even today.

This chapter focuses on the first generation of commentary on Rossi in the major Chinese architecture journals, dating from the late 1980s. According to Lawrence Venuti, translated texts are always intertexts bound up with other texts, where "a disjunction between the foreign and translated texts, a proliferation of linguistic and cultural differences that are at once interpretive and interrogative" inevitably exists.[3] Intertextuality prevents the introduction and translation of foreign works from being a straightforward communication. It complicates the process of interpretation but simultaneously opens up spaces for the production of new knowledge through an adaptive absorption in the receptor's context. This consideration of the case of Rossi, therefore, scrutinizes the historiographical process through the following perspectives: the selection of the original texts; the process of translation, or the decontextualization and recontextualization of texts; and interpretation of the translated texts in the receptor's linguistic, temporal, and cultural setting. By examining the main lines of the introduction, translation, and appropriation of Rossi's typological and urban theories in China, this study unpacks the reasons behind the specific attention *L'architettura della città* garnered in China, considering how localized interpretations and appropriations appeared with specific intentions, and how the recontextualized theories of Aldo Rossi influence architecture and urban design in that country today.

The 1980s marked an extremely active period of cultural and academic development in China. After ten years of silence across the humanities due to the Cultural Revolution, scholars demonstrated unprecedented academic enthusiasm following the introduction of Deng Xiaoping's opening-up policy.[4] A widespread urge to "keep up" with its western counterparts led to the introduction, translation, and publication of a number of recent foreign works for a Chinese readership. Among the myriad historical trends at the time, two were crucial to the introduction of Aldo Rossi and his *L'architettura della città*.

One prerequisite for the specific form of Rossi's reception was the "cultural fever" in western linguistics and semiotics during the mid-to-late 1980s. Before China was open, its literature was haunted by the Soviet social modernist model. Western philosophy, on the other hand, was considered decadent and "petty-bourgeois" in nature. The "linguistic turn" of the twentieth century, culminating in the postmodern turn of the 1960s and 1970s, caught Chinese scholars' attention right after the end of the Cultural Revolution in the late 1970s. Framed as an era of "Enlightenment" in China, the 1980s saw scholars, writers, and artists struggling against the centralized and ideologized cultural production of the pre-reform period.[5] The western theories circulating at the time, therefore, were taken up as intellectual instruments for ideological emancipation.

Several features of the fervor for semiotics are particularly relevant to the introduction of *L'architettura della città*. First, as is noted by Yiheng Zhao, in the 1980s, Chinese semiotics was not distinguished from structuralism, a phenomenon that affected a wide array of disciplines, including architecture, and hence the introduction and interpretation of Rossian theory.[6] Second, from the outset, semiotics scholarship in China followed patterns found elsewhere in being fundamentally interdisciplinary, covering a broad range of fields in the humanities, including literature, poetry, art, film, and theater studies.[7] The fact that linguistic and semiotic methods were highly operable in many disciplines was crucial to the appropriation of Rossi in China. Third, from the 1990s, many studies turned to the specificity of Chinese characters, the only living non-phonetic written language in the world, and through this bridged Asian and western semiotics studies. The cultural confidence aroused by the study of Chinese characters of this moment was later reflected in the appropriation of Rossi, as we will see.

Another major prerequisite for Rossi's introduction was the reflection on modernization and cultural traditions among the architectural community in the 1980s. In China, the development of modern architecture struggled through three waves of foreign influence: the beaux-arts tradition imported during the 1920s by the first generation of Chinese architects educated in the United States; the socialist realism borrowed from the Soviet Union in the 1950s and which dominated Chinese architecture for three decades; and the postmodern theories that rushed into China in the late 1970s and early 1980s. The discussion over the so-called "National Form" (*minzu xingshi*) started during the 1950s with the slogan "socialist content with national forms." Despite the vagueness of the motto in practice, Soviet architects established a vivid model for Chinese architects to follow, with buildings decorated with functionless minarets, colonnades, and gables.[8] Based on the eclectic approaches developed in the beaux-arts tradition, designers mixed fragmented traditional Chinese architectural elements on the facade of the buildings to produce "national forms" (see Figure 17.1). Thus, the introduction of postmodernism to China in the late 1970s did not cause much obvious

Figure 17.1 Funeral of Sun-Yat Sen, Nanjing, June 1, 1929, with Mausoleum in the background. Historic Collection/Alamy Stock Photo.

change in the realm of architectural and urban design. Without a robust theoretical armature, postmodern approaches were rendered superficial and commercialized, with great emphasis on formal operations and metaphoric decorations. Reconciling beaux-arts traditions and postmodern advocacy, Chinese architects developed the so-called European continental styles (*oulufeng*) which flooded the property market with hybrid pastiches of modern and classical traditions.

In this context, the introduction of Aldo Rossi and his urban theories offered a form of resistance to the speedy modernization process and the stylistic historicism proliferating into the 1980s (see Figure 17.2). Long affected by the precepts and practices of social modernism, architectural production and urbanism in China privileged uniformity and grandeur over humanistic, cultural, and contextual considerations. The socialist movements razed towns and villages with millennial histories and produced buildings that did not conform with local conventions or existing fabrics. Under these circumstances, the younger generation, which had a better understanding of the latest consequences of semiotics fever and a stronger urge to engage with western architectural theory, sought more fundamental ways to incorporate cultural traditions into modern design beyond facade iconography. The typology theory and "analogous city" proposed by Rossi, therefore, provided them with legitimized theoretical tools and design ideas. Academic journals, overseas students, and young professors formed the pioneering

Figure 17.2 Jianghan Road, Wuhan. Imaginechina Limited/Alamy Stock Photo.

frontier for the introduction and explanation of postmodern theories. Yet, as is noted by Zhao, the hasty consumption of foreign texts in the 1980s focused more on practical application rather than in-depth comprehension.[9] Due to limited language skills and contextual differences (and as was the case elsewhere, on different terms), the reading of Rossi also suffered misinterpretation and deviation.[10]

The first Chinese version of *L'architettura della città* did not come out until 1992. Before Zhiming Shi's translation was published, knowledge of Rossi depended primarily on those Chinese students studying overseas or working directly in English and other foreign languages. As early as 1986, Lifang Wang, a graduate student at Tsinghua University, roughly introduced the basic ideas of Rossi's typological theory, emphasizing his architectural operations in reconciling contemporary design and traditional Italian urban space. The paper exemplified the initial emphasis on Rossi's semiotic interpretation of urban artifacts as a connection between the past and the present.[11] It is worth noting that the only references in Wang's paper are to two papers written by the Malawi-born architect and critic Peter Buchanan and published in *Architectural Review*.[12] The article, therefore, was more a summary of Buchanan's critiques rather than the author's own judgment of Rossi based on primary material.

In the subsequent years, several young professors and graduate students studying overseas published more detailed and thorough studies on Rossi. Kening Shen, a student at the University of California, Berkeley, wrote a lengthy paper in 1988 introducing typology and the Rossian notion of the analogous city, and discussed how Rossi's design works embodied his theories.[13] It was the first time Rossian theory was discussed by a

Chinese scholar within the larger framework of Italian rationalism. *L'architettura della città* was first introduced in Shen's paper. He translated the title of the book as "Urban/ City Architecture" (*chengshi jianzhu*), the same translation as Zhiming Shi's 1992 version.[14] The vagueness of the original Italian title—literally *The Architecture of the City*—was transplanted with a corresponding ambiguity created by the Chinese language, since "urban" as an adjective and "city" as a noun are the same word in Chinese (*chengshi*), and the title can be read either as "City and Architecture" or "Urban Architecture."[15] Neither the translator or the readers seemed to be certain about the meaning of the title.

Following Shen's paper, Qingyun Ma, a graduate student at the University of Pennsylvania, thoroughly introduced the evolution and the application of architectural typology for the first time, including its origin in eighteenth-century natural history and its introduction to architectural discourse by French predecessors to the Italian rationalists.[16] This history of typology and the connection to structural linguistics borrowed from Alan Colquhoun remained the core themes of subsequent research of the 1990s, reflecting how semiotics and linguistic theories permeated western architectural theory for much of that decade.[17] Meanwhile, since the English edition of *The Architecture of the City* was referred to as the primary source for most scholars, their analyses are inevitably colored by Peter Eisenman's reading of Rossi in that translation's introduction, in which he sees architectural forms as "texts."[18]

Ma's work demonstrated a tendency to apply Rossian theories to China's urban reality, finding that "the typological strategy combines logic with intuitiveness, in which the former suppresses but does not smother the latter. This operation, for the first time, allows architects to wander through historical materials without getting lost."[19] In the meantime, thoughts on interpreting the "Chinese style" through semiotics were proposed by other young scholars like Bingren Xiang, who considered the so-called "national form" to be a stable, latent language system, the application of which excluded superficial transplantation of decorations and fragmented elements.[20] Xiang's view was very close to the Rossian notion of typology. Building on their interpretations, studies from the 1990s and early 2000s related more to the realities of China's urban development and architectural design. Shen's 1991 study tested the incorporation of the traditional Beijing courtyard (*siheyuan*) as an architectural type for contemporary design.[21] Pei Zhu, a young lecturer at Tsinghua University, explicitly summarizes typology and the analogical city as "two major theories in Rossi's genre" that could be applicable to China in terms of abstracting cultural elements through collective memories, in order to "break through the superficial 'coat' of ancient Chinese architecture."[22] An urban planner, Dong Jing, also proposed steps for an "urban planning with Chinese characteristics" based on typology and the analogous city, appropriating the Rossian theories in a highly instrumental way.[23] The gradual turn to the operability of Rossian theories for China's urban development reflected scholars' urge to explore urban modernization without abandoning the typological features of Chinese cities. In this regard, Rossi's works were repeatedly referenced since both Italian and Chinese cities evolved through a long history and rich civilization. While Rossi's Italian contemporaries were seldom translated or mentioned in China's academic community, Chinese scholars used Rossi's work, with its solutions for Italian cities, to reflect upon their own cultural legacy. This sense of dealing with a similarly venerable built heritage gave Rossi's ideas more authority than those of US or northern European urban theorists.

Whether due to historical inertia or a lack of material, *L'architettura della città* remains the only book by Rossi actively studied by Chinese architects during the early twenty-first century. Rossi's other major written work, *A Scientific Autobiography*, was not mentioned in scholarship until 2013, and has not yet been translated.[24] The overwhelming interest in *L'architettura della città* reflects the fact that the focus on Aldo Rossi in Chinese academia has been deeply rooted in the dilemmas of urban development, design methods, and formal principles during the late 1980s and early 1990s, when scholars were seeking out western theories to solve local problems. Rossi's *Autobiography*, on the other hand, exemplified a more personal narrative and was less instrumental for China's urban conditions at the time. Meanwhile, the consistent interest in the same book also reflects how scholars may easily follow each other's works due to the absence of primary sources and adequate language skills. The history of the introduction of Rossi's works also demonstrates how the first generation of interpreters can establish which writings receive privileged status in the field, creating a hierarchy between different works by the same author. Consequently, *L'architettura della città*, as the first of Rossi's books to be introduced—and the first of his generation of Italian thinkers—became the only thoroughly studied work in Rossi's genre.[25] The academic community remained preoccupied with it even after the social context that had made it resonate with readers when it first arrived in China had changed drastically.

Additionally, most studies still privileged semiotics as the primary interpretive framework through which to approach Rossi's work. Lijun Wang and Yigang Peng, even more radically, further claimed city and architecture completely as "texts":

> Rossi's practice derives from his artistic theories. He believes that architecture and the city are the result of analogical formal operations regardless of function. Therefore, he reads city and architecture like *texts*. The author is absent, and the additional information are [sic] merely auxiliary. *Text* is everything.[26]

Although Rossian theory does concern linguistics and texts, these are not the primary features in his understanding of the complex assemblage of urban artifacts. The Chinese adaptation of Rossi's works are clearly deprived of political, economic, and social implications. Wang Shu, the first and (so far) sole Chinese Pritzker laureate, took this tendency to an extreme in his dissertation. Although as an unpublished work it had little direct impact, the dissertation exemplified a highly individualized interpretation of Aldo Rossi, which was further expressed through Wang's design practice (see Figures. 17.3, 17.4, and Plate 10).

Wang completed his dissertation, "Fictionalizing City," in 2000. His reading of Rossi is deeply embedded in the post-1980s semiotic fever and depends on an extensive quotation of structuralist and poststructuralist linguistic and semiotic works, including those of Ferdinand de Saussure, Claude Lévi-Strauss, Roland Barthes, and Noam Chomsky. He

Figures 17.3 and 17.4 Wang Shu, Youth Center, Haining, completed 1990. Photographs © Cole Roskam.

referenced all these philosophical works, however, in Chinese translation. His reading of Aldo Rossi was based on Shi Zhiming's Taiwanese version of *L'architettura della città*, which was translated from the French edition. Although the theories he read are inevitably colored by the Chinese translators' ideas, Wang does not seem to care much about "accuracy," since the dissertation is laid out in an atypical structure, with sixty parallel sections instead of chapters, and none of the citation notes meet contemporary academic standards.[27]

Wang's dissertation opens with an abstract clarifying that the author aims to "talk about the language of the city itself in a structural language," referring to *L'architettura della città*, to break away from linear time and to revive the "dead" historical legacy into active anthropological facts.[28] The author highlights at the beginning that, "although Saussure's linguistic principles only appeared in the prologue of *L'architettura della città*, they are, in fact, the fundamental and principal guidelines that run through the entire book," privileging structural linguistics as Rossi's "theoretical foundation."[29] Chapters discussing politics, economics, and land policy in Rossi's original book are selectively neglected in Wang's dissertation. By singling out the semiotic dimensions of Rossi's urban theory, Wang was able to decouple urban studies thoroughly from any sort of function:

> Type, instead of particular buildings, is the unit of the total *fait urbain* ... The relationship between type and function is arbitrary, and therefore random.[30] So type has *nothing* to do with actual functions ... The essential and structural distinction in the city lies in typological divides. The architecture in the city can only be understood through type.[31]

While Rossi does talk about the autonomy of architectural forms from function, his theory in no way implies that functional considerations are entirely irrelevant to form. For Rossi, the autonomy of form manifests in its consistency in the face of functional shifts. It should be noted that the "function" dismissed by Wang was the "ideologized functionalism" deeply imbedded in the historical conditions in 1990s China.[32] Far from the "functionalism" of the western modernist tradition, "ideologized functionalism" articulates the optimal, efficient, and economical construction model practiced by the state-owned design institutes in China that tramples on the legacies of ancient villages, ignores environmental damage, and pursues speedy modernization rather than design quality. Searching for something stable amidst social turmoil and ideological drifts, Wang celebrates "architectural typologies in a linguistic sense" as the locus of "the value of the city," criticizing the "so-called practicality which shifts with the ideology and customs of the society."[33] By depoliticizing and recontextualizing *l'architettura della città*, Wang instrumentalizes Rossian theory against urban developments of the 1980s and 1990s in China. As observed by Liu Dongyang, Wang's dissertation aims to distance itself from the pragmatism that emphasizes efficiency over quality, the organism that emphasizes totality over contingency, and the historicism that pursues familiar symbolism over cultural tradition.[34] Wang's interpretation of Rossi, therefore, was less faithful to Rossi himself, rather serving as a vehicle for an intergenerational challenge.

Extending the linguistic research into the semiotic potential of Chinese characters then also in vogue in China, Wang proposed a highly creative, individual interpretation of Rossi's typological theory: understanding the Chinese city through Chinese characters. In his dissertation, Wang states that "Rossi insists that types stay intact, just like Chinese characters that cannot be dismantled at random."[35] Indeed, Rossi argues that types are immutable, or at least relatively stable elements of the urban fabric, because they coalesce history and collective memory. Building on Rossi's theory, Wang compares architectural type to Chinese characters that have gone through history with typological stability, arguing that, like the composition of characters, type cannot be changed at the will of any individuals; it constitutes a link with history. Although this argument risks the simplification of typologies, which entertain a more abstract, latent, and structural nature, it links typology to the pressing concerns in Wang's own theoretical system. After incrementally individualizing his personal "version" of Rossi's urban theories, Wang developed a straightforward way of understanding cities and implementing design from the ancient Chinese texts and characters. As he elaborates in the later part of his dissertation:

> There is a simple and direct relationship between language and things. Each character is both an idea and an image. Characters are diagrams that resemble things in a way and can be read both conceptually and visually. Imagination may lead them into three-dimensional realms. Therefore, I believe that a city like Suzhou can be built on the basis of a plan that derives from an ancient score of *Three Stanzas of Plum Blossoms* (Meihua Sannong). In fact, as linguistic signs absent meaning, they are themselves static, identifiable figures that resemble what I call "the empty theaters."[36]

From the quotation above, it is obvious that Wang has grasped the graphic potential of the non-phonetic Chinese characters, which serve both as "an idea and an image," to read the relationship between urban space and artefacts accordingly. The diagrammatic properties of Chinese characters to generate urban forms are further unleashed when Wang applies the six principles that formulate Chinese characters in *Explaining Graphs and Analyzing Characters* (*shuowen jiezi*), an ancient Chinese dictionary from the Han Dynasty, to construct spatial relationships. For instance, the "hieroglyphic" (*xiangxing*) in the Chinese language coincides with the spatial permeation between two artefacts that are not physically adjacent to each other. They can interact within the city from a distance like an object and a mirror.[37]

While Wang's recontextualization deviates substantially from Rossi's original ideas, it constitutes a highly localized, personalized interpretation that is integrated with Chinese reality and history, and thus forms the foundation of Wang's own architectural theory and design practice. Consequently, Rossian urban theories continue to survive vibrantly and productively in Wang's acclaimed architectural works. As described by Liu, the site Wang constructs functions like a "spatial fiction," with a series of courtyards, gaps, gateways, and platforms whispering in dialogue with each other without the interruption of the visitors, or so to speak, the intruders.[38] Wang's works break free from the prevailing historicism and the blind functionalism that haunted the overall architectural production in China during recent decades. It is through his reading of Rossi that he developed a theoretical basis for a unique practice that articulates a symbolic connection with Chinese culture. Other young scholars, including Qingyun Ma and Pei Zhu who studied and wrote about Rossi, were also able to turn theory into practice and contribute to the improvement of high quality, locally produced designs as part of the first generation of contemporary Chinese architects to receive international recognition. These early readings of Rossi's ideas continue to shape China's urban and architectural scene today.

Zhao observes how the adaption of western theories in China usually "neglects the details for general understandings," since these ideas are usually "taken when useful without the need to examine the origins strictly."[39] The introduction and interpretation of Rossi from 1986 to the early 2000s served, above all, the immediate needs of a national architectural culture in a moment of change. Since the early 2000s, however, with the gradual decline of semiotic fever and the rise of independent Chinese architects in the global design market who operate beyond strictly national forces, the social and cultural context that necessitated the localization of Aldo Rossi faded away. With the publication of the mainland Chinese version of *The Architecture of the City*, translated by Shijun Huang from the English version in 2006, a new wave of interest in Rossi emerged, focusing primarily on the strict deciphering of the original texts, the original theory, and the architect himself. The importation of western academic methods also allowed for the systematic study of his main concepts. The mainland Chinese version, titled *Chengshi jianzhu xue* (The Study/Theory of Urban/City Architecture), conveys a tendency to theorize Rossian urban studies as a field or a discipline, compared to the Taiwanese version, *Chengshi jianzhu* (Urban/City Architecture). The meaning of both Chinese titles suffers from ambiguity, and neither is universally agreed upon among scholars. Several papers published in China during the 2000s stuck to the Taiwanese translation, indicating widespread doubt about the mainland Chinese title.[40] The two papers written by Liu, published in 2013, mention the dual meaning of "architettura" both as "urban artefacts and the process in which the city is constructed," making an effort to explain the original meaning of Rossi's own title.[41] The dispute revolving around the most accurate translation of the title for Chinese readers remains unresolved.

Another term important to Rossi's uptake in China is "fatti urbani," a phrase translated into "urban artefact" in the English version. Based on the translator's note, Tong explains that "urban artefact" not only refers to the physical parts of urban objects, but also involves their historical, geographical, and structural aspects, as well as the general experience of living in the city.[42] It is those lived experiences through which "fatti urbani" can be understood. Liu also addresses the notion of "fact" in "fatti urbani" as a concept that involves both objects and events.[43] In 2009, Yang and Dai discussed the French term "fait urbain," reached through the Taiwanese translation, which implies "man-made *facts* that represent the organizational conditions of the city."[44] These discussions have removed Rossi from the stereotypical framework of typology, and no longer force an attempt to integrate Rossi's theory with Chinese urban reality. The repeated, refined readings of Rossi after the 2000s, to a certain extent, are also underlined by the "intercultural hierarchies" to be found between the major and the minor translations of the same book.[45] The desire to seek the original ideas of the original author in the original language reflects the relatively disadvantaged status of the second-hand or even third-hand translations of the work, even if the latter prove to be better orientated to the improvement of local conditions. But, as argued by Gideon Toury, "a translation never gives back the source text itself, only a mediated form of it, a representation, and the mediation register norms or values in the receiving culture."[46] Translated works can never fully realize the originals, but they are productive as generators of knowledge with meanings inscribed in the receptor's cultural and linguistic situations.

The ambiguity of Rossi's terms and the complexity and intuitiveness of his theories together open up the possibility of multiple readings in their translation. Despite the linguistic differences between Chinese and the languages through which Rossi's work was received, this complexity is one of the main reasons why his ideas have been interpreted and adapted with such flexibility in China. In the last forty years, *L'architettura della città* has been translated into over thirty languages and published across the world. Different versions of Rossi's urban theories have taken hold in different temporal and geographical settings, and their interpretation continues to generate discussion and controversy. Within the wider studies of this book, the study of its life in China is merely the tip of the iceberg. As Rossi himself says in the introduction to the American edition, "like a painting, a building, or a novel, a book becomes a collective artifact; anyone can modify it in his own way, the author notwithstanding."[47] It is the adaptive, productive, and generative afterlife of *L'architettura della città* that keeps Rossi's theories alive, well beyond the place and time in which they were conceived.

Notes

1. This essay chapter expands on a paper I first wrote in 2017, which was published in Chinese in a volume I co-edited. See: Dijia Chen, ""The Acceptance of *L'Architettura della città* in China,"", in *Neighborhood Paradigm: Urbanism in the Perspective of Technology and Culture* (*linli fanshi: jishu yu wenhua shiye zhong de chengshi jianzhu xue*), eds. Tan Zheng, Jiawei Jiang & Dijia Chen (Shanghai: Tongji University Press, 2021), 53–68.

2. For example, *Aldo Rossi: The Architect and the Cities* (March 10–October 17, 2021), a major retrospective at MAXXI analyses the extraordinary theoretical and practical contributions of an "unusual architect" in the reconstruction of Berlin and ongoing debates about Barcelona. See https://www.maxxi.art/en/events/aldo-rossi-larchitetto-e-le-citta/.

3. Lawrence Venuti, "Translation, Intertextuality, Interpretation," *Romance Studies* 27, no. 3 (2009): 157.

4. The opening-up policy, sometimes referred to as "the Chinese economic reform" or "reform and opening-up," marked the beginning of the so-called "socialist market economy" in 1978. The enactment of the opening-up policy not only aimed for a market-oriented economy, but also gradually reformed the centralized planning, encouraged cultural diversity, and stimulated exchanges with the Western world.

5. Xuedian Wang, "How Was the 80s 'Reconstructed'?—A Brief Commentary on a Number of Related Theories," *Open Era* 6 (2009): 44–58.

6. Yiheng Zhao, "Semiotics as a Formal Cultural Theory: Forty Years of Development in China," *Cultural Critiques* 6 (2018): 146–55.

7. Relevant works include An Heju's *Semiotics and Literary Creation* (1985), Hu Miaosheng's *Introduction to the Semiotics of Theatre Performance* (1986), Xu Zengmin's *Film Symbols and Semiotics* (1986), Li Yousteen's *An Overview of Film Semiotics* (1986), and Zhou Xiaofeng's *Misty Poetry and Art Laws: For Modern Times* (1986). See also Zhao, "Semiotics as Formal Cultural Theory."

8. Denong Zou, "Lessons from Two Introductions of Foreign Architectural Theory—From 'National Form' to 'Postmodern Architecture,'" *Architectural Journal* 11 (1989): 47–50.

9. Yiheng Zhao, "The Fate of Semiotics in China," *Semiotica* 184 (2011): 278.

10. The reception of Aldo Rossi among Anglophone architects followed a similar arc, since the 1980 translation of *L'architettura della città* aroused confusion for many. See Mary Louise Lobsinger, "The New Urban Scale in Italy: On Aldo Rossi's *L'architettura della città*," *Journal of Architectural Education* 59, no. 3 (2006): 28–38.

11. Lifang Wang, "Italian Rationalist Architect Aldo Rossi," *Architect* 1 (1986): 34–5.

12. Peter Buchanan, "Aldo Rossi: Silent Monuments," *Architectural Review* 172 (1982): 48–54; Peter Buchanan, "Oh Rats! Rationalism and Modernism," *Architectural Review* 173 (1983): 19–21.

13. Kening Shen, "Italian Architect Aldo Rossi," *World Architecture* 6 (1988): 50–7.

14. Shen, "Italian Architect Aldo Rossi," 50.

15. The Italian title can indicate both the architecture of one particular city or all cities. In addition, the term "architecture" also can be perceived as the structuring characteristics of urban organizations.

16. These include Marc-Antoine Laugier, J. C. Quatremère de Quincy, Jacques-François Blondel, and Jean-Nicolas-Louis Durand, as well as their twentieth-century successors Rafael Moneo, Philip Steadman, and Carlo Aymonino. Qingyun Ma, "The Concept of Type and Architectural Typology," *Architect* 38 (1990): 14–32.

17. Alan Colquhoun, "Typology and Design Method," *Perspecta* (1969): 71–4. Kening Shen's "Typology in Design" in 1991, Pei Zhu's "Typology and Aldo Rossi" in 1992, and Dong Jing, "Aldo Rossi's Theory about the Architecture of the City and the Construction of Urban Characteristics," *Planners* 2 (1999): 104, all borrowed content from Ma's essay in similar ways.

18. Peter Eisenman's introduction, "The House of Memory: The Texts of Analogue," emphasizes the autonomy of architectural form as "texts," which in a way deviates from Rossi's original ideas. See Aldo Rossi, *The Architecture of the City*, trans. Diane Ghirardo and Joan Ockman (Cambridge, MA: MIT Press, 1982).

19. Ma, "The Concept of Type," 31.

20. Bingren Xiang, "Revisiting Semiotics and Architectural Design," *Time + Architecture* 2 (1988): 13–14.

21. Shen, "Typology in Design," 66.

22. Pei Zhu, "Typology and Aldo Rossi," *Architectural Journal* 5 (1992), 32, 38.

23. Dong, "Aldo Rossi's Theory about the Architecture of the City," 104.

24. Dongyang Liu, "An Intellectual Project by Wang Shu: What He Learned from Aldo Rossi's L'architettura della città," *Journal of the National Academy of Art* 34 (August 2013): 105–15.

25. Of Rossi's Italian contemporaries, Vittorio Gregotti was not studied much overall. Manfredo Tafuri was introduced around 2007–8 as a representative of postwar architectural criticism. To date, no studies have established which foreign authors were most read by Chinese architects during this period, a good topic for future research.

26. Wang Lijun and Peng Yigang, "Typology Design Methods and Architectural Form of the Constitution," *Journal of Architecture* 8 (2001), 42.

27. All Wang's notes merely listed the author and the title of the book. No page number is included.

28. The dissertation is not translated into English. See Wang Shu, "Fictionalizing City" (Ph.D. diss., Tongji University, 2000).

29. Wang, "Fictionalizing City," 4.

30. Here I use the French translation of *fatto urbano*, "*fait urbain*," following Wang's use of the Taiwanese phrase translated from the French edition.

31. Wang, "Fictionalizing City," 12.

32. Wang, "Fictionalizing City," 28.

33. Wang, "Fictionalizing City," 67.

34. Liu, "An Intellectual Project by Wang Shu."

35. Wang, "Fictionalizing City," 2.

36. Wang, "Fictionalizing City," 141.

37. Wang, "Fictionalizing City," 141.

38. Liu, "An Intellectual Project by Wang Shu," 29.

39. Zhao, "Semiotics as Formal Cultural Theory," 148.

40. See Kening Shen, "Revisiting Typology," *Architect* 12 (2006): 5–19; Ming Tong, "Rossi and *The Architecture of the City*," *Architect* 10 (2007): 26–41; Jian Yang and Zhizhong Dai, "Reduce to Type: Reading *L'architettura della città* by Aldo Rossi," *New Architecture* 1 (2009): 119–23.

41. See Liu, "An Intellectual Project by Wang Shu," 20; Dongyang Liu, "Notes on City (13): Fatti Urbani: a Différance in both Architectural Text and Texture Between Aldo Rossi and Wang Shu," *Architect* 161 (2013): 20–31.

42. Aldo Rossi, *The Architecture of the City*, rev. edn, intro. Peter Eisenman (Cambridge, MA: MIT Press, 1984), 22.

43. Liu, "Fatti Urbani," 21.

44. Yang and Dai, "Reduce to Type," 119.

45. Lawrence Venuti, "World Literature and Translation Studies," in *The Routledge Companion to World Literature*, ed. Theo D'haen, David Damrosch, and Djelal Kadir (London: Routledge, 2011), 203.

46. Gideon Toury, *Descriptive Translation Studies and Beyond*, rev. edn (Amsterdam: John Benjamins Publishing, 2012).

47. Rossi, *The Architecture of the City*, 13.

CHAPTER 18
FROM THE UNIVERSAL TO THE PARTICULAR: ROBIN BOYD AND THE POSITIONING OF ITALY IN POSTWAR ARCHITECTURAL CRITICISM

Philip Goad

On the title page to Part 3 of his 1960 book, *The Australian Ugliness*, Melbourne architect and critic Robin Boyd placed a man in a business suit and a homburg hat at the center of Leonardo Da Vinci's famous drawing of the Vitruvian Man—a man's body fixed in the center of a superimposed circle and square (see Figure 18.1).[1]

The image introduced the book's next chapter, "The Pursuit of Pleasingness," a reflection on current tendencies in architecture towards a new sensualism and the decade-long investigation into the universal laws of proportion. This invocation of

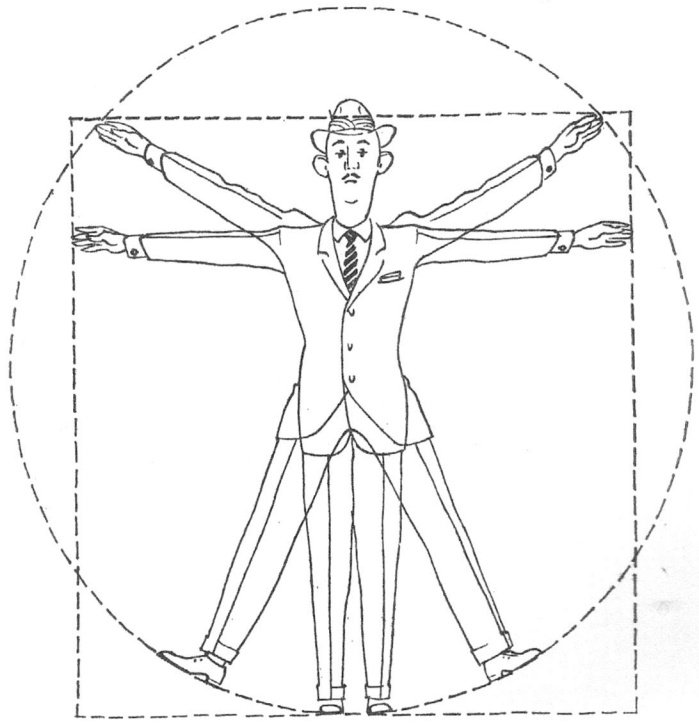

Figure 18.1 Cover page to Part 3 of Robin Boyd, *The Australian Ugliness* (Melbourne: Cheshire, 1960). Drawing by Robin Boyd. © Estate of Robin Boyd, courtesy Robin Boyd Foundation.

Renaissance theory in a book ostensibly about contemporary Australian architecture invites larger questions about the presence of Italy in Boyd's architectural writing. Between 1951 and his early death in 1971 at age fifty-two, just when he had brought Italian architect Giancarlo De Carlo to Australia to speak, Robin Boyd was Australia's sole international voice of architectural critique. His design criticism and book reviews featured in British and US journals, and he was widely respected, as were his books on Kenzo Tange (1962) and contemporary Japanese architecture (1968). But, from the perspective of the discipline's global periphery, what did engagement with Italy mean to Boyd? How was Italy positioned within Boyd's critique of contemporary architecture? Was it typical of a broader model according to which postwar critics from outside Italy appreciated contemporary Italian architecture? Furthermore, how was Boyd's engagement with Italian topics operative for other concerns or agendas, especially his own larger project of promoting Australian architecture and positioning himself as an authoritative global voice?

On February 19, 1952, Boyd, then Director of the Royal Victorian Institute of Architects Small Homes Service, wrote in his weekly newspaper column about "The Italian Influence," describing "a peaceful and pleasant invasion by Italy in the field of ideas in design of domestic products" into Melbourne's then provincial retail and architectural scene.[2] He observed three Italian arrivals: first, a series of four prototype prefabricated timber houses built in suburban East Preston; second (incorrectly), the 1950 introduction to Australia of the "Hardoy" chair, which Boyd claimed was Italian in origin but was in fact Argentinian-designed; and third, a collection of Arteluce light fittings sold locally by photographer Athol Shmith.[3] These lamps with their distinctive spindly steel supports and cone-shaped reflectors were designed by architect Vittoriano Viganò for his friend and Arteluce owner Gino Sarfatti.

This blend of design glamour, factual inaccuracy, and interest in mass production was typical of Australian architects' understandings of Italian design in 1952. Boyd was not unusual in being relatively ill-equipped on matters of contemporary Italian architecture and design. By contrast, Australian industrial designers were much better informed: Melbourne-based Clement Meadmore was a committed Italophile and had his steel-rod furniture designs published in *Domus*. When Sydney designer Gordon Andrews worked in London between 1949 and 1953, he designed trade exhibitions and showrooms for Olivetti at Kingsway, Berkeley Square, Watford, Leicester, and Nottingham, as well as, on his return to Australia, Olivetti's Sydney showroom (1956). Contemporary Italian design also came to Australia when young Milanese architect Enrico Taglietti curated the design exhibition *Italy at David Jones* (1955) at a national department store chain in Sydney and stayed on, carving out a long and distinguished career in architecture in Canberra.[4] Remarkably, Taglietti's architecture and his debt to Bruno Zevi never drew Boyd's attention despite its prominence and significance for the national capital.

Over the next ten years, Boyd's knowledge of Italian architecture, past and present, came largely filtered: through his reading of British and American journals, primarily the *Architectural Review* (*AR*) and *Architectural Forum* (especially in articles by Colin Rowe and Reyner Banham), and the 1952 Tiranti edition of Rudolf Wittkower's *Architectural*

Principles in the Age of Humanism (1949).[5] As Henry Millon, Alina Payne, Francesco Benelli, and others have observed, the British preoccupation with Wittkower's discussion of proportions in the early 1950s was framed as the parallel to Le Corbusier's *Modulor* (1950), both symptomatic of a postwar search for modernism's legitimation through history and the existential certainty of the human body.[6] In 1972, Millon quoted Boyd's 1965 pronouncement in *The Puzzle of Architecture* that Wittkower's book was "required reading in most architectural schools in the period after World War II."[7] Banham invoked Wittkower to support his formulation of the New Brutalism in 1955, and the Smithsons publicly rejected Wittkowerian geometry as "an ad hoc device" by the mid-1950s. This kept Wittkower front and center in the British discourse, which Boyd absorbed. But the motivations driving his own use of Wittkower and description of Italian Renaissance attempts to relate proportion to the human body in 1957 were very different from those of Banham and the Smithsons.

In August 1956, Boyd took up a year-long position as Visiting Bemis Professor at the Massachusetts Institute of Technology (MIT) in Cambridge, Massachusetts. Aside from minimal teaching duties, the chief task Boyd set for himself was to reflect upon contemporary American architecture. He read widely, visited many architects and buildings, and began writing. It was during this stay that he published an article on "pleasingness," an excerpt from a book manuscript that Boyd had begun with the formidable title of "While Architecture Lasts: Proposals for a Revival and a Code of Criticism of Modern Architecture."[8] Using quotations and images of Leonardo Da Vinci's and Cesare Cesariano's 1521 renditions of the Vitruvian Man taken from Wittkower's book, Boyd highlighted that these two "universal men" and those of Fra Giovanni Giocondo and Francesco Giorgi "were contained precisely within the perfect geometric form of a circle."[9] He then considered Le Corbusier's *Modulor*, outlining its rationale but ultimately finding fault with Le Corbusier's admission that an architect was free to depart from it as occasion demanded.[10] Boyd's point was the contradictory nature of the contemporary fondness for mathematical formulas for beauty through a revival of proportional systems. Significantly, his article on pleasingness post-dated *Divina Proporzione*, the IX Milan Triennale of 1951, where Wittkower and Le Corbusier's ideas were pitted against each other, and set the scene for British and European discussions on proportion during the 1950s. Notably, Boyd's article predated the infamous debate on whether proportional systems made good design easier at London's RIBA on June 18, 1957, when Peter Smithson declared the whole discussion ten years too late.[11] At the same time, the incongruity of Boyd's academic dissection of proportion in the pages of *Progressive Architecture* opposite an advertisement for Westinghouse (with the tagline "Architectural Beauty is More than Skin Deep") was striking. Boyd injected a theoretical discussion more typical of the British *AR* into a generally more pragmatic US discourse. His next article, "Decoration Rides Again" in *Architectural Record* (September 1957), was better directed towards an American readership. Its focus was on recent architectural tendencies that followed Boyd's definitions of applied, insinuated, and invited decoration, the main offender and target of Boyd's concern being the perforated screens of Edward Durell Stone's US Embassy in New Delhi.[12]

The common thread underpinning these articles was Boyd's identification of a splintering of aesthetic practice that was transatlantic as well as ideological. His October 1958 "Engineering of Excitement" article for *AR* highlighted the global phenomenon of "shape" architecture, where he agreed with Italian architect Eugenio Montuori's statement that "the mess is complete." Boyd had borrowed this quote from Bruno Zevi's 1956 contribution to *Architectural Forum*, where, in withering style, Zevi had critiqued Eero Saarinen's Kresge Auditorium and Kresge Chapel at MIT.[13] Boyd, while concerned at the ethics of this new shape architecture, was heartened by "the salutary effect of reviving spirited criticism of individual works and a more searching examination of the present position of architecture." To illustrate this, he placed Pier Luigi Nervi's condemnation of the structural illogic of Saarinen's dome (another quotation borrowed from Zevi's 1955 article) against Sibyl Moholy-Nagy's "contempt for unmitigated technique," when she asked the chilling question, "Who would be so rude and demand a view of the *exterior* of a Nervi hall?"[14] For Boyd, Nervi's work was the standard-bearer of the purity of an engineer's approach to shape architecture, illustrated in the article by Nervi's conference hall for UNESCO and CNIT Exhibition Hall, both in Paris. Boyd then considered Saarinen's "shape" buildings, ultimately warning that if "lapses of logic like the Modulor" were vain attempts to devise formulas for beauty, one should also be wary of the delusion that the new shape architecture was "leading to new realms of architectural beauty."[15] For Boyd, this article's Italian references played distinct strategic roles: they included critics whose positions he endorsed and designers whose work he praised, all in service of his larger aesthetic assessments.

Taken together, these articles show Boyd constructing his arguments of 1957 and 1958 from close readings of *AR* and *Architectural Forum*, which both regularly featured contemporary Italian buildings, issues, and historic sources. For *AR*, this seemed a special preoccupation. The same issue featuring "Engineering of Excitement" included four other articles about Italy: Georgina Masson's article, "Italia Nostra," on the eponymous organization formed to protect urban heritage; "The Exploring Eye: Death of a Monument" on the collapse of the campanile in Venice's Piazza San Marco; a mini-review of Studio Valle's tower block in Trieste; and in the regular Marginalia section, a piece titled "Tornare ai Tempi Felici" (and almost certainly written by Reyner Banham), which was a catty put-down of works by Gae Aulenti, Vittorio Gregotti, Meneghotti & Stoppino, and Gabetti & Associates (sic), and their defense by Aldo Rossi.

By contrast, *Architectural Forum* reviewed individual buildings but without elaborate commentary, such as their feature on G. A. Bernasconi, A. Fiocchi, and Marcello Nizzoli's Olivetti office building in Milan in October 1955 and, more significantly, in March 1959, the first publication outside Italy of Vittoriano Viganò's Istituto Marchiondi located on the outskirts of Milan (1955–7).[16] It was this building that Boyd chose to include in his next article for *Architectural Forum* in July 1959, entitled "Has success spoiled modern architecture?" There, Boyd focused on what he saw as contemporary architecture's abandonment of early modern functionalism in favor of a shared search for "pleasing effect." He wrote, "Present-day architecture . . . is moving toward theism, without concern for a moral code but sustained by a blinding faith in the unerring rightness and self-justification of one god: Beauty."[17]

Boyd's central focus was the contemporary American preoccupation with formalism, surface elaboration, and academicism. He invoked Mies van der Rohe, Eero Saarinen, and Edward Durell Stone ("I'm a fall guy for beauty" quoted Boyd), and took aim at an individualistic architecture culture, where "everyone would like to be a one-man avant garde." The article concluded with photographs of "six different interpretations of 'beauty'": Minoru Yamasaki's Wayne University (1958); John Johansen's US Embassy in Dublin (1958); Mies van der Rohe's Crown Hall, IIT (1955); Frank Lloyd Wright's unbuilt Arizona State Capitol (1957); Eero Saarinen's "search for form" at the Yale Hockey Rink at New Haven (1958); and Viganò's "brutalist use of raw concrete" at the Istituto Marchiondi (1958) (see Figures 18.2 and 18.3).

It is not clear who put together these six examples of "beauty"—Boyd, editor Douglas Haskell, or his assistant Peter Blake—but the images were drawn from *Forum*'s own photographic holdings and the inclusion of Viganò's building cannot be accidental. It is the only non-US-designed building in the selection and, situated graphically at top right, one might speculate it being held up as a beacon of hope or suggested choice or preference for future direction.[18]

The insertion, however modest and without elaboration, of the Istituto Marchiondi into English-speaking discourse was a first. While the building had been published in Italy and France well beforehand, the inclusion twice in *Architectural Forum* (in March 1959 and by Boyd in July 1959) predated Banham's brief discussion of the building in the

Figure 18.2 Vittoriano Viganò, Istituto Marchiondi Spagliardi, Baggio, Milan, 1954–8, view of the boarders' block and fire escape seen from the northwest. RIBA Collections.

Figure 18.3 Vittoriano Viganò, Istituto Marchiondi Spagliardi, Baggio, Milan, 1954–8, close-up of the fire escape of the boarders' block. RIBA Collections.

RIBA Journal, and its larger feature in the *Architectural Review*, both in May 1961, and its eventual celebration by Banham in *The New Brutalism* in 1966.[19]

In that same month, May 1961, Boyd participated in a survey conducted by Ernesto Rogers, editor of *Casabella*, which anchored the journal's special issue on the previous fifteen years of Italian architecture (see Figure 18.4).[20] Joining an extensive list of domestic contributors, including Vittorio Gregotti, Paolo Portoghesi, Giancarlo De Carlo, and Aldo Rossi, and non-Italians Max Bill, Douglas Haskell, and J. M. Richards, Boyd (the only figure from outside Europe and North America) answered "Six Questions on Italian Architecture." The article provided lengthy statements in Italian, with brief and selective summaries of responses in English. In Boyd's case, the editors translated his emphasis on the importance of British contributions to postwar architectural theory and his warning that it was a time for criticism and research rather than manifestoes.

Boyd's complete written responses, however, reveal a fuller knowledge of the contemporary Italian scene. In response to the question regarding which works best represented the recent evolution of Italian architecture, he chose two: Nervi's Palazzo

Figure 18.4 Cover of *Casabella continuità* 251 (May 1961), special issue devoted to "Fifteen Years of Italian Architecture." Mondadori/Electa/Marco Covi.

dello Sport in Rome (1956–7) and Gio Ponti's Pirelli Tower in Milan (with Nervi; 1956–8).[21] His choices were diplomatic and orthodox, avoiding the "polemical prize fights" stirred by Banham two years earlier. On the second question, as to whether there had been a break in the international front of modern architecture and if new classifications were to be applied to Italian architecture (a none-too-subtle allusion to Banham's Neoliberty labels), Boyd agreed, but did not name individuals or cast doubt on "experiments [that] are ugly for our eyes." He supported any search for "a complete realism of construction, with purity of form and simplicity of language, and with respect for the place, of environmental and human conditions."[22]

Casabella's third question went to the heart of the matter, asking correspondents to identify "revivals and deviations from the mainstream of the modern movement of which Italy has been accused" found outside Italy. This time Boyd did name names: of "revivalism," he pointed to Minoru Yamasaki's work "that is very close to humour, and almost a joke." Of "deviations," he made the caveat that if an orthodoxy was defined as the line from the Crystal Palace to the Seagram Building, then "the Italian works are undoubtedly very deviating and counter-current and often ugly." He then compared three buildings: Gropius & Meyer's Fagus Factory, the Seagram Building, and the Istituto Marchiondi (which he called "decidedly deviationist"). He found Seagram "too refined and full of pretension" in its facade and of Marchiondi, that it was "so unfriendly and even oppressive for the difficult boys who are destined to occupy it." In effect, Boyd acknowledged and then criticized two apogees of contemporary American and Italian architecture culture but left the Fagus Factory, a pioneering statement of modern architecture, intact. And Boyd, not content to leave it there, countered his own argument, saying "even when [a] middle way has to be identified, there will always be deviations, which I prefer, however, to individual interpretations."[23] This may not have been what Rogers and his Italian colleagues wanted to hear but nevertheless, by implication, Boyd sided with Marchiondi in preference of the culprits of "infantile regression" identified by Banham in his by then notorious article "Neoliberty: The Italian Retreat from Modern Architecture" in April 1959.[24] Boyd appeared to have effectively removed himself from a battle that was not his own. And yet, for *Casabella*'s fifth question, which asked who had made the most important contributions to architectural criticism in recent years, Boyd pointed to the British (and by implication to Reyner Banham), who "are the most patient, expressive, experienced and open-minded critics, and some of their definitions—such as Neo Liberty or Brutalism—frame with almost photographic precision current movements that could otherwise remain vague for years . . ."[25] This was clearly not what *Casabella* wanted to hear. While the editors published Boyd's words in full in Italian, telling domestic readers that the UK critics were better, they redacted their appearance in English, pointedly denying English readers the satisfaction of Boyd's affirmation.

The responses of the two other English-speaking correspondents confirm Boyd's largely Anglophone viewpoint. Haskell, editor of *Architectural Forum*, expressed high regard for Viganò's Marchiondi but focused largely on Louis Kahn's work as the harbinger of the future.[26] Richards, editor of the *Architectural Review*, charged with the most delicate task, was generous and diplomatic at first, identifying a string of significant

Italian buildings, but then launched into a strong defense of Banham's position, admittedly without his junior editor's passion, arguing with the same intensity that the Italians were essentially wasting their time in "taking up such an esoteric and limited idiom."[27]

Just two months later, in July 1961, in *Harper's Magazine*, in his article entitled "The New Vision in Architecture," Boyd joined the definition game so enjoyed by his British colleagues. Written for the American lay reader, he identified a shift in contemporary architecture since 1955, when "suddenly every important building wanted to have a monolithic idea."[28] He categorized contemporary (largely American) architecture into simplified formal sets like "the suitcase and the bunch of grapes" and "twinship and circle," once more invoking Wittkower, by whom "partial responsibility for the present rash of circles must be accepted," while excusing Nervi, who works "without a trace of mysticism and strictly within rational engineering principles." He opted for "singleness out of confusion," signaling Le Corbusier's La Tourette and Louis Kahn's Richards Medical Research Building as buildings that draw "an effect of singleness out of complexity," suggesting that Kahn's building offers "the most immediate hope to the future of the monolithic movement" before declaiming that it lacked any "visionary quality." Boyd concluded that "it is important for the monolithic movement to have hope—to look ahead and not over its shoulder, to remain on the upgrade."[29]

By "over its shoulder," Boyd was referring, by implication, not just to works by Yamasaki, Durell Stone, and Philip Johnson, but also to the Italians, whom he grouped with the Americans as "Romantics"—as opposed to the British and Japanese "Realists"—in a 1962 interview.[30] In short, in the end he shared Banham's disdain for recent experiments by Italian architects. Most significantly, Boyd had reached a point that permitted him to make distinctive yet authoritative judgments. Not wanting to be a mere offshoot of British or US criticism, he nevertheless remained dependent on their discourse for both content and platform.

After 1962, Boyd's published pronouncements on Italy were minimal. He reiterated his comments on Wittkower and the circle in his 1965 book, *The Puzzle of Architecture* (to which Henry Millon had referred), but otherwise his international attentions had shifted to contemporary Japanese architecture, world expositions, and contributing reviews of Australian buildings to international journals.[31] In 1967, for example, as Australian editor for *World Architecture* 4, he wrote on Canberra along with Hely, Bell & Horne's cluster housing project, St John's Village, Glebe (1966) in Sydney.[32] When published, Boyd would see his article placed alongside prominent coverage of Giancarlo De Carlo's University College at Urbino, where clusters of buildings celebrated informal human interaction in a pedestrian-scale urban setting. Nor could he have ignored the addition of Aldo van Eyck's words, abridged from *Zodiac*: "should the reader wonder what a relative, open and non-Euclidean concept of architecture is all about, De Carlo's masterpiece in Urbino will, I am sure, make it quite clear."[33]

One might conclude that Boyd's role was marginal or, at the very least, that he typified a prevailing position on Italian architecture that had been largely determined by the British and American architectural press—that is, if the question is what Boyd thought of contemporary Italian architecture in the 1950s and 1960s. But this is not the case, as it certainly was not for Manfredo Tafuri in 1968. Boyd was a key player in the triangulation of criticism that existed between Great Britain, America, and Italy between 1956 and 1967, particularly one created by critics writing for *Architectural Review*, *Architectural Forum* and *Casabella*, a focus of Tafuri's attention. He was not interested in Boyd's writings on Italian architecture per se, but rather in Boyd's attempts, in *The Puzzle of Architecture*, to chart contemporary modern architecture between 1950 and 1962 and identify a crisis.[34] In *Theories and History of Architecture*, Tafuri located Boyd as being symptomatic of a group of British and American critics—like Stephen W. Jacobs, Stanford Anderson, and Reyner Banham—who were committed to an "anti-historicist" tradition and yet, at the same time, forced to defend the pioneering efforts of the modern masters by resorting to the very techniques of history (which those revolutionary architects denied) in order to criticize works of contemporary architecture.[35] At the same time, Tafuri acknowledged that Boyd had clearly defined three phases in the Modern Movement: an orthodox phase (pre-World War II), Counter-Revolution, and a Third Phase—"a recovery of the original values of the Modern Movement, enriched by the positive contributions of the Counter-Revolution." He noted that "though rather simplistic, Boyd's historiographic view exemplifies very well the myths of English and American culture in relation to the objective crisis of modern architecture."[36]

Tafuri was not apportioning blame, but rather emphasizing Boyd's practice as typical of a larger critical phenomenon: critics had become historians by default (and not good ones at that), and they did not recognize this, or the limits of their discipline. Furthermore, the widespread adoption by Boyd, American critics, and architects like Saarinen, Stone, Rudolph, and Yamasaki of terms such as "significant form," "imageability," and "figurability" pointed to the influence of theorists like Clive Bell, Roger Fry, and, importantly, Susanne Langer, and their focus on the significant value of images, leading Tafuri to ultimately warn against Robert Venturi's instrumental "compositive" methods.[37] What Tafuri objected to was the uncritical search for ways of establishing a language or syntax for modern architecture, a search for a way to read it and apply it rather than, as Tafuri would prefer it, "a pitiless scrutiny of the meanings underlying apparently 'innocent' forms and choices."[38] For Tafuri, the historian's task was clear: "Beyond all this, the task of history is the recovery, as far as possible, of the original functions and ideologies that, in the course of time, define and delimit the role and meaning of architecture."[39]

My sense is that Boyd, ultimately, would have agreed. Trying, as an architect, to single-handedly carve out a space for architectural criticism as a practice from the peripheral setting of Australia, Boyd never positioned himself exclusively as an academic historian or as a career critic. Tafuri wrongly assumed that he was. But Boyd was neither a Reyner Banham nor a Vincent Scully; he was an architect who wrote, part of a cohort of practicing architects who waded into authorship in the years before a critical moment (*c.* 1968) when architectural theory came to be defined as an academic discipline occupied by full-time scholars.

In 1970, Boyd established a series of international lectures in Melbourne, choosing each speaker and each lecture to be published as a small book under the imprint of The Melbourne Architectural Papers. The first two lectures were given by J. M. Richards followed by Peter Blake, editors of the *Architectural Review* and *Architectural Forum*, the two journals that provided Boyd's knowledge of contemporary Italian architecture, which he retransmitted through critique.[40] Boyd did not live to hear the third lecture or read the book that resulted. He died on October 16, 1971, and, two days later, on the evening of the day of his funeral, Italian architect Giancarlo de Carlo delivered "An Architecture of Participation," the text of which was published as the small book of the same title in 1972 (see Figure 18.4).[41]

As the blurb on the back of the book states, "Giancarlo De Carlo completes a triangle"—England-America-Italy—clearly the same one where Boyd saw the major axes of discourse. That same text, republished in *Perspecta* in 1980, brought Giancarlo De Carlo back into the international spotlight as a paean of participatory design and a champion of an architecture of the particular over the universal. The essay has been quoted and venerated ever since.[42] Boyd's invitation had prompted the Italian to put his thoughts down on paper. It is highly likely that Boyd invited De Carlo because his work, along with that of Australian-Canadian architect John Andrews, was used by Peter Blake in his oration the year before to illustrate the response to the "third force"—"the open-ended brief, the instruction that only change is certain."[43] Boyd's "completion of the

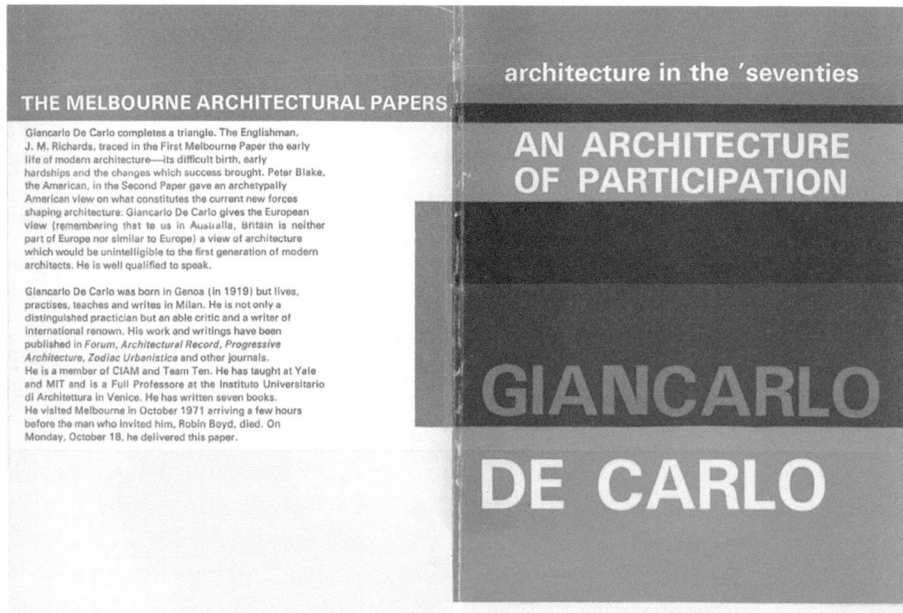

Figure 18.5 Cover of Giancarlo De Carlo, *An Architecture of Participation*, Architecture in the Seventies: Melbourne Architectural Papers (South Melbourne, Victoria: Royal Australian Institute of Architects Victorian Chapter, 1972). Australian Institute of Architects.

triangle" meant that he had made a major contribution to mapping architecture's shift from the universal to the particular.

Boyd's decade of engagement with Italian topics, critics, buildings, and publications from 1952 until 1962 was strategic. He mapped contemporary architecture's "main conversation" in that period with the aim of participating and positioning himself as an important voice, domestically and globally. His detached, engaged, only semi-marginal position (Anglophone but neither fully British or American) gave him critical perspective across the "England-America-Italy triangle." In many respects, he was less interested in the intrinsic value of each culture's contribution than in his understanding of their combined disciplinary hold on contemporary postwar discourse. As such, by 1971, he had not only developed an authoritative voice internationally on Australia and Japan—speaking on his own terms, thus challenging the "triangle"—but also, with his invitation to Giancarlo De Carlo, he revisited the "England-America-Italy triangle," reinvested its influence globally, and brought it directly and conclusively to Australian shores.

Notes

1. Robin Boyd, *The Australian Ugliness* (Melbourne: Cheshire, 1960), 155.

2. Robin Boyd, "The Italian Influence," *The Age* (February 19, 1952): 7.

3. "£1,000,000 Home Investment Plan," *The Age* (February 1, 1952): 4.

4. Enrico Taglietti, "An Italian Exhibition in Australia," *Domus* 311 (1955): 50; Ken Charlton, Bronwen Jones, and Paola Favaro, *The Contribution of Enrico Taglietti to Canberra's Architecture* (Canberra: RAIA ACT Chapter, 2007).

5. Rudolph Wittkower, *Architectural Principles in the Age of Humanism* (1949) (London: Tiranti, 1952).

6. Henry A. Millon Millon, "Rudolph Wittkower, *Architectural Principles in the Age of Humanism*: Its Influence on the Development and Interpretation of Modern Architecture," *Journal of the Society of Architectural Historians* 31, no. 2 (May 1972): 83–91; Alina Payne, "Rudolph Wittkower and Architectural Principles in the Age of Modernism," *Journal of the Society of Architectural Historians* 53, no. 3 (September 1994): 322–42; and Francesco Benelli, "Rudolph Wittkower versus Le Corbusier: A Matter of Proportion," *Architectural Histories* 3, no. 1 (2015): 1–11.

7. Millon, "Rudolph Wittkower," 83.

8. R. Boyd, "The Search for Pleasingness," *Progressive Architecture* 38, no. 4 (April 1957): 193–205. This article was expanded in the chapter "The Pursuit of Pleasingness" in Boyd's *The Australian Ugliness*, 157–206.

9. Boyd, "The Search for Pleasingness," 193.

10. Boyd used the American-published version of Le Corbusier, *The Modulor* (Cambridge, MA: Harvard University Press, 1954).

11. Peter Smithson, quoted in "Report of a Debate on the Motion 'that Systems of Proportions Make Good Design Easier and Bad Design More Difficult,'" *RIBA Journal* 64 (1957): 460–1.

12. Robin Boyd, "Decoration Rides Again," *Architectural Record* 22, no. 3 (September 1957): 183–6.

13. See "Three Critics Discuss MIT's New Buildings," *Architectural Forum* 104, no. 3 (March 1956): 156–7, 174, 178, 182.

14. Robin Boyd, "Engineering of Excitement," *Architectural Review* 124, no. 742 (November 1958), 296.

15. Boyd, "Engineering of Excitement," 308.

16. "Precise Headquarters for a Manufacturer," *Architectural Forum* 103, no. 4 (October 1955): 125–8; "Abroad: A Continuing Review of International Building—Milanese Boy's Town," *Architectural Forum* 110, no. 3 (March 1959): 223–5. The building appeared earlier in the Italian press. See Renato Pedio, "Brutalism in the Form of Architecture: The New Marchiondi Institute in Milan," *L'architettura* 40 (February 1959): 683–4.

17. Robin Boyd, "Has Success Spoiled Modern Architecture?" *Architectural Forum* 111, no. 7 (July 1959): 99–103, esp. 100.

18. Boyd's July 1959 article was followed by G. M. Kallmann, "The 'Action Architecture' of a New Generation," *Architectural Forum* 111, no. 10 (October 1959): 132–7, 244, where the editors suggested that instead of Boyd's call for "repentance and return to the early faith," that Kallmann find "the beginning of a new, serious avant-garde." Italian architects identified as participating in "action architecture" were Franco Albini and Franca Helg.

19. "Institution à Milan," *L'architecture d'aujourd'hui* 63 (December 1955–January 1956); "An Institute for Three Hundred Boys," *Domus* 318 (May 1956); "Italie: Institut Marchiondi a Baggio, Milan," *L'architecture d'aujourd'hui* 72 (June–July 1957); "Institut Marchiondi, Baggio, Milan, Italie," *L'architecture d'aujourd'hui* 81 (December 1958–January 1959); and Pedio, "Brutalism in the Form of Architecture"; Reyner Banham, "The History of the Immediate Future," *RIBA Journal* 68, no. 7 (May 1961): 250–7, 269; "Psychiatric Institute in Milan," *Architectural Review* 129, no. 771 (May 1961): 304–7; Reyner Banham, *The New Brutalism: Ethic or Aesthetic?* (New York: Reinhold, 1966), 127–8.

20. *Casabella Continuita* 251 (May 1961), special issue, "Quindici anni di architettura italiana" (Fifteen Years of Italian Architecture).

21. Robin Boyd, "Risposta alla domanda 1," *Casabella continuità* 251 (May 1961): 8.

22. Robin Boyd, "Risposta alla domanda 2," *Casabella continuità* 251 (May 1961): 8.

23. Robin Boyd, "Risposta alla domanda 3," *Casabella continuità* 251 (May 1961): 9.

24. Reyner Banham, "Neoliberty: The Italian Retreat from Modern Architecture," *Architectural Review* 125, no. 747 (April 1959): 231–5.

25. Robin Boyd, "Risposta alla domanda 5," *Casabella continuità* 251 (May 1961): 9.

26. Douglas Haskell, "Risposta alla domanda 1," *Casabella continuità* 251 (May 1961): 21.

27. J. M. Richards, "Risposta alla domanda 2," *Casabella continuità* 251 (May 1961): 28.

28. Robin Boyd, "The New Vision in Architecture," *Harper's Magazine* 223, no. 1334 (July 1961): 75.

29. Boyd, "The New Vision in Architecture," 80–1.

30. Robin Boyd, interview with Hazel de Berg, 1962, Hazel de Berg Collection, National Library of Australia, https://trove.nla.gov.au/work/19233570.

31. Robin Boyd, *The Puzzle of Architecture* (Melbourne: Melbourne University Press, 1965), 81–93.

32. Robin Boyd, "Canberra" and "St John's Village, Glebe (Hely, Bell & Horne)," in *World Architecture*, vol. 4, ed. John Donat (New York: Viking Press, 1967), 202–9.

33. Aldo van Eyck, "Van Eyck on De Carlo and Urbino," in *World Architecture*, vol. 4, ed. John Donat (New York: Viking Press, 1967), 50.

34. Manfredo Tafuri, *Theories and History of Architecture* (1968), 4th edn, trans. Giorgio Verrecchia (London: Granada, 1980), 65, 102, 125, 138, 139, 212, 225.

35. Tafuri, *Theories and History of Architecture*, 13, 65.

36. Tafuri, *Theories and History of Architecture*, 225.

37. Tafuri, *Theories and History of Architecture*, 212–13.

38. Tafuri, *Theories and History of Architecture*, 214.

39. Tafuri, *Theories and History of Architecture*, 228.

40. J. M. Richards, *A Critic's View* (South Melbourne: RAIA Victorian Chapter, 1971); and Peter Blake, *The New Forces* (Melbourne: RAIA Victorian Chapter, 1971).

41. Giancarlo De Carlo, *An Architecture of Participation* (South Melbourne: RAIA Victorian Chapter, 1972).

42. Giancarlo De Carlo, "An Architecture of Participation," *Perspecta* 17 (1980): 74–9.

43. David Saunders, review of *The Melbourne Architectural Papers: An Architecture of Participation*, *Architecture in Australia* (August 1972): 453.

CHAPTER 19
UNEXPECTED PEDAGOGIES:
HENRY HORNBOSTEL IN ITALY, 1893
Francesca Torello

Temperament

The more we travel together Alfred & myself, the more our dif[ferent] temperament shows itself. We harmonize well but look at things entirely different. Alfred always with enthusiasm and literary interest but not so much of an appreciation of form and reading of details and new ideas. He seems to find interest in looking at shops and other similar points of interest but I do not care for them and never really am conscious of the people & their peculiarities but always look for Architecture impressions & form. Colour and effects of mass, forgetting detail in most cases (but not the Architecture ones), while Alfred dwells on detail and after does not appreciate the entire effect and if so only after the details have been exhausted. It was so at school and now—we can help each other out <u>if Alfred only would forget the girls</u>.

Genoa, Wednesday, March 1, 1893

Henry Hornbostel's journal of European travel in the spring of 1893 offers a rare and original viewpoint on Americans in Italy at the turn of the century. It is also a discipline-specific narrative: the journal of a beaux-arts architect in training, creatively engaging with the pulsating core of the classical tradition.[1]

Hornbostel's work has received little critical attention, despite the fact that in the first decades of the twentieth century he was an architect of national relevance. His firm won consequential national competitions and he designed noteworthy public and private buildings—many, but not all, in Pittsburgh, a city he helped shape during its era of greatest growth.[2] In 1893, at the time of his Italian stay, Hornbostel was a young man of ambition, having recently graduated top of his class from Columbia University. He would enter the Ecole des Beaux-Arts the next fall, one of a crop of brilliant American architects that traveled to Paris to add European polish to their privileged American education.[3]

Hornbostel was traveling with classmate and future professional partner Alfred Raymond.[4] Like many other Americans crossing the Atlantic in this era, the two still saw themselves as Grand Tourists, having a clear understanding of the privilege implied in the opportunity to travel.[5] Yet the experience of Americans in Europe after the Civil War was very different from what we have been accustomed to think of as the Grand Tour. Mass travel had substituted the heroic individual journey of a century before, turning most travelers into tourists.[6] In Italy in particular, large groups of expatriates could be found in most cities, so the young Americans spent most of their time with compatriots, speaking their own language, and only rarely had contact with the locals. Hornbostel's Italy is strangely devoid of Italians—or "others" of any kind. It is instead an American, upper-middle-class social space, for which the Eternal City offers a theatrical backdrop: "In the evening after having visited the Calvins with the Annesleys we fitted up our room and retired late talking over our stay. Luck and many friends so far" (Rome, Saturday, March 18, 1893).[7]

When real, if relatively minor, travel difficulties arose—as when shipping trunks were lost between Naples and Rome and the young travelers were stranded without a change of clothes or money for a few days—they turned to the network of American expats, keeping their spirits high and waiting for their fellow travelers to invite them to dinner.[8]

The well-honed turn-of-the-century travel infrastructure (from Cook's agencies to travelers' checks) and the tendency of itineraries towards uniformity made real discovery unlikely, so it became necessary to find adventure where one could: in bike rides *fuori porta*, in feasts and celebrations (such as the Catholic piety and pomp of the *Settimana Santa*), or in a few intense and fleeting moments of appreciation of beauty, whether in architectural or in human form. As part of the tight circle of Americans, however, the two had access to experiences that would seem otherwise out of reach:

We ... next visited Mr. [Moses] Ezekiel a sculptor who received us pleasantly showed us his Columbus and other studies (Christ, Bust of Hotchkiss and the Queen[,] Judith and Columbus), also sleeping figure of Mrs. White for Cornell College and other studies. His studio was under a vault of Rom. bath (Dioclet.).

Rome, Wednesday, March 22, 1893

The adventure of the mind, to be found in the discovery of new buildings and in the exploration of ideas, replaced the practical challenges and occasional hardships of travel in the previous century. Thorough preparation (studying "photographs at college," college lectures, and Baedekers' travel guides) made Italy, and Rome in particular, a schoolbook of art and architecture, for the most part conforming to expectations and reiterating the canon, as is particularly evident in the journal's indifferent listing of sculptures seen in museums, "so much of it that one becomes tired of it all." Sites had to be visited, in part, one could say, in homage to that preparation and in fulfillment of the promise and privilege of travel. The beginning of the journal entry for Genoa seems to confirm this: "I did not look at Genoa much in a serious light as we will be there again and study what there is to study" (Genoa, Wednesday, March 1, 1893). As a document, the journal reinforces a nuanced reading of a generation's reception of Italian architecture. It clearly shows the two Americans fluctuating between admiration for the canon—and the desire to see what they are expected to see—and an effort to look beyond it, in part in search of architectural novelty, but also to attain in their experience the uniqueness that the modern travel conditions had already negated.

One of the most striking features of Hornbostel's journal is the pervasiveness of American culture and even a sense of superiority that is typically not present in American travel writing before the Civil War.[9] Events and buildings, from the firework displays at

Coney Island to recently built New York City skyscrapers, become the familiar reference points to which Italian and European sites are compared, with no concern for the obvious chronological and cultural awkwardness that ensues. Significantly, the journey is undertaken in 1893, the same year of "the White City," the World's Columbian Exposition in Chicago, the first triumphant foray of the United States into worldwide architectural visibility. Hornbostel visited Chicago (and presumably the exposition buildings, not yet open) just a few months before his departure for Europe.[10] The faux world of the Fair becomes the touchstone against which he weighed his real-world travel experiences:

> We all admired the strangeness of the city appearing very much in colour and perspective like the scenes of [popular Coney Island attraction] Pains Fireworks … The city [Gibraltar] became more & more visible and as it did so we saw the details, there were few straight walled houses, all of stucco and painted yellow some blue and few red. Mostly two stories and roof gardens. From the near distance they looked very much like the buildings of the Chicago World's Fair—like (State buildings).

Tangiers, Tuesday, February 14, 1893

In contrast, the journal is almost completely devoid of references to the Greek and Roman world. Hornbostel's familiarity with European literature and history seems limited, and the Italian sites do not evoke much for him at all. In contrast, for travelers just one generation earlier, everything from well-known works of art to the landscape itself was enlivened by a complex web of associations to literature and poetry, myths, and historical narratives. This middle-class American traveler at the end of the nineteenth century gives an impression of efficiency and at times a rather superficial, if diligent, approach to culture—a stark contrast to the indolent milords from a century earlier, with their almost unlimited resources of time and money and their deep familiarity with classical culture. Of course, since the journal was written for his own use, Hornbostel had little reason to impress, yet it is clear that his enthusiasms were elicited by the new, the modern, the technologically advanced, and in this sense Italy in 1893 had little to offer a New Yorker.

It is all the more striking, then, to witness how Hornbostel's attitude changes when it is focused on architecture. He becomes a sophisticated and clearly self-assured critic, curious and attentive to every minute detail. Contemporaneous with the creation of the Society of Beaux-Arts Architects in the United States and preceding by just one year the founding of what would become the American Academy in Rome, his journal offers a compelling private counterpoint to the institutional construction of Italian architecture. We can see how the tension between embracing and escaping from the canon plays out between institutional and individual experience, offering a window onto the interests and aesthetic predilections of a generation of architects. The account is a personal one, but it nonetheless offers clear insight into what a young American architect at the end of the nineteenth century was actually seeing and learning in Italy—and from the past. For example, the question of variation in ornament seems to elicit from Hornbostel a critical note toward his own schooling:

The most [fragments] are Roman and Greek and the bits of ornament … were so beautifully designed and varied that the idea of regularity and repetition so often thought of Greek ornament—it is not so. Its ornament and motives were all alike but still magnificently different & subtle.

Rome, Capitoline Museums, Monday, March 29, 1893

At the American Academy in Rome, Charles McKim would soon define a tightly controlled program of study, based on the strictest possible interpretation of the classicist tradition, which would hold sway well into the twentieth century[11] In contrast, Hornbostel's "self-guided" itinerary shows the complex and layered effects of unscripted Italian travel: the surprise in realizing how the direct encounter and observation complicates aesthetic judgment, the uncertain reactions towards buildings that associate ugliness with magnificence or simplicity with refinement, and the affinities and echoes between architecture and landscape that can only be understood in situ.

The positive readings of the marks left on buildings by the passing of time and human activity seem particularly remarkable, as they lead to the appreciation for architectures of impure, heterogeneous temporalities. Hornbostel reports rather blandly on the antiquities of Rome. His entry on the Pantheon barely mentions the dome, the Fora entry is titled "walk," and his disdain for "all this dead and never living Roman Temples Architecture" contrasts with the rapt attention he directs instead to mosaic work, early Christian architecture, and the irregular patterns of stone decay brought about by time. Palermo incites great enthusiasm, and observations on its architecture include brief mentions of Ruskin and Richardson, two towering figures of the previous generation and among the very few people Hornbostel names directly:

We decided to walk about town looking at all the old buildings and to our surprise we discovered so much of value and interest this own note-book was soon filled. It was as if mining and discovering gold at every step.

The detail color and general richness is so Spanish and the originality of the composition of windows and doors most astonishing.

Italian Gothic

Some of the early Gothic with Classic composition and of what we call Italian Gothic was simply beautiful and one immediately agreed with Ruskin that it was more beautiful than the later Renaissance.

All this work … has Moorish influence and is therefore so rich in surface decoration.

This work has so great a (or greater) claim that much else was forgotten but it depended so much upon its colour and state of decay for its beauty that the style was thought practical for northern climate but the English showed that it is not.

(But American Richardson showed its beauty if harmonized with F. Romanesque. It could be used for private country houses or mansions but must have the colour and material to affect it.

Palermo, Wednesday, March 15, 1893

An austere, American sense of religious decorum and respect for popular devotion could in part explain Horbostel's admiration for smaller, lesser-known Roman churches, such as Santa Croce in Gerusalemme, Santa Prassede, and Santo Stefano Rotondo:

Alfred sketched some other views and together we also visited the circular Church of St. Stefano. This was a most curious and effective plan and was very interesting for its frescoes of all the terrible sufferings of the Martyr. ... Its entrance very picturesque.

Rome, Tuesday, March 28, 1893

Santa Maria Nova (Santa Francesca Romana) appears, "with its colored crosses and glass decoration, a veritable gem. The tower to me seems of more interest and beauty than all that later Classic style and has more grace than that very fine tower of the Capitol by Michel Angelo ..." (Rome, Saturday, March 25, 1893).

In contrast, Catholic pomp is often lambasted ("The distributing of the blessed olive branches was as little religious as anything could be") as is its baroque staging.[12] Bernini is defined as "a trifle boring" and "too stucco-like," his "two colonnades are very clumsy but impressive," while Saint Peter's Basilica should have been realized as Michelangelo had designed it:

The Rococo of the 3 first bays is very disturbing and one can notice the simpler style after passing those bays. Oh how great this all would have been or could be if the walls were simple and the ceiling etc. mosaic similar to the churches in Palermo. As it is the Rococo is terribly disturbing. The coloring of the dome etc. is so much better and finer than the rest that it stands out more pure and dignified.

Rome, Palm Sunday, March 26, 1893

Moral judgment, aesthetic preference, and the taste of the treasure hunt all seem to combine in the great excitement for Santa Pudenziana (which Hornbostel calls "Prudenciana" throughout his journal):

We next walked towards St. Maggiore Maria [sic] and hunted up a small church we noticed the other day while driving home from the Lateran.

We found it and "such a church". It was a delight to see its colour proportion and design all so charming and living, full of vigor sparkle and interest. Its design of Early Christian character with details, though not according to the classic principles were full of life and a certain snap the Roman ornament did not obtain.

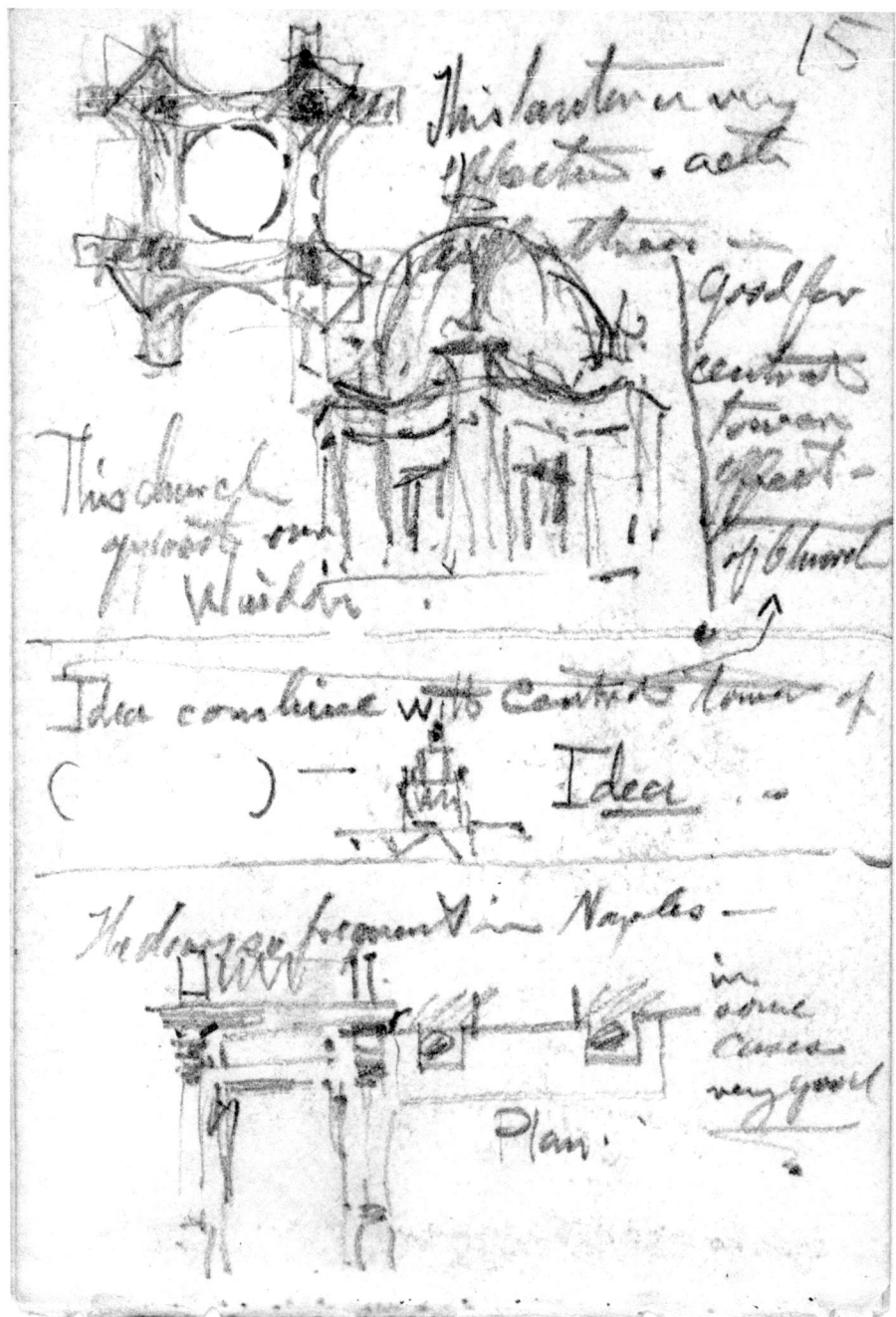

Figure 19.1 Henry Hornbostel, travel sketchbook, page 15, 1893 (Rome). Courtesy of Carnegie Mellon University Architecture Archives.

The tower well fitting to the entire and the picturesque position approach and grouping gave it all a certain cleanness which made one feel happy and delighted and pleased. The banded stone work gives it interest and beauty and the mosaic that richness so pleasant and substantial as compared with all that Rococo seen in other churches. It gave me an impulse to work up this style and also showed me that McKim Mead and White's church in N.Y. was not what it could have been. Carrere and Hastings have adopted somewhat this style in their little church front [in] uptown New York.

Interior

We entered and behold a most impressive mass. The people were all of the lower class and as devotional as possible. The interior was a simple barrel vault decorated with escutcheons and penetrated by some vaults. The screen on the side of the altar was especially interesting being designed in simple Early Renaissance style so very subtle in perspective that it looked beautiful in its simplicity. As for the service it was the first one in Rome that did not aggravate me.

(I must obtain Photo of this Church)

Rome, Friday, March 31, 1893

... I finally obtained [a photograph of] the façade and returned home as happy as a child with this treasure I thought no one else had ever seen before.

Rome, Saturday, April 1, 1893

Hornbostel is explicit that one goal of his stay is to collect material to inspire his future professional practice. He took his own photographs and purchased many others, spending time observing them and using them as a starting point to rework the design of buildings:

Photographs

I started for my favorite store and selected several more. The beauty of the environments of Rome were disclosed to me and I must see them by all means.

Rome, Saturday, March 25, 1893

Architecture

As for Architecture, I have noted points of interest in my note-book and with the assistance of photographs I will be able to benefit greatly ...

Rome, Friday, March 24, 1893

"Being a student" meant having a specific interest, typically not shared by other travelers, whom he called "sight-seers." It also meant partaking in "artistic" activities, such as sketching and making watercolors. Hornbostel's sketchbook, in addition to the journal, allows us to chart points of interest and details to which he was drawn. We can almost track his gaze while he travels, as he eagerly, even voraciously, observes and learns; we can practically follow his hand as he sketches; and observe him as he absorbs architectural precedent. These two documents combined provide insight into his sophisticated approach to historical buildings, the method and the process of learning, assimilating, and elaborating creatively on the past—inseparable steps for which the architecture of Italy is extraordinary source and material:

> Alfred has not as yet comprehended the actual secret of design and in talking hints and sketches does not generally strike the right subjects or ideas. All this study and actual contact with so much beauty has given me a confidence and standard of beauty and correctness that makes me feel perfectly happy and the more so because I am going to improve and see more beauty in the future.
>
> *Rome, Saturday, April 1, 1893*

The journal evidences an approach to history and culture rooted in architectural practice and categorically different from that of the historian, the art historian, or the literary traveler. Hornbostel's relationship with history and precedent is uninhibited and unconstrained. A skilled and sophisticated observer, he quickly processes examples and precedent in search of successful solutions and effects, in some cases even noticing good solutions to specific problems in buildings that do not impress him in their entirety. His eyes are constantly zooming in and out of the picture, noticing. The most original and valuable feature of his journal is its use throughout of brief notes titled "Ideas," indicating how lessons learned and details observed on site in Italy can be applied in "modern designs." These notes give us a direct glimpse into the inner workings of an architect's creative process and explicitly document connections and reverberations that historians must usually infer.

Arch of Constantine

Here the difference of the Early Roman and the Early Christian carving is well pictured. In fact it is the first bit of Christian carving possessed. (The ornament is all so undercut that it looks like Byzantine incision work. Very effective.)

Idea: This effect could be obtained in Terra Cotta for small ornament and interior works.

Baedekers has all other points of interest.

Rome, Thursday, March 25, 1893

Historical buildings are a great reservoir of ideas from which the young architect can freely pick what works and makes the best effect—including the architecture of his own time, significantly absent from Italy even though it appears in other parts of the journal.

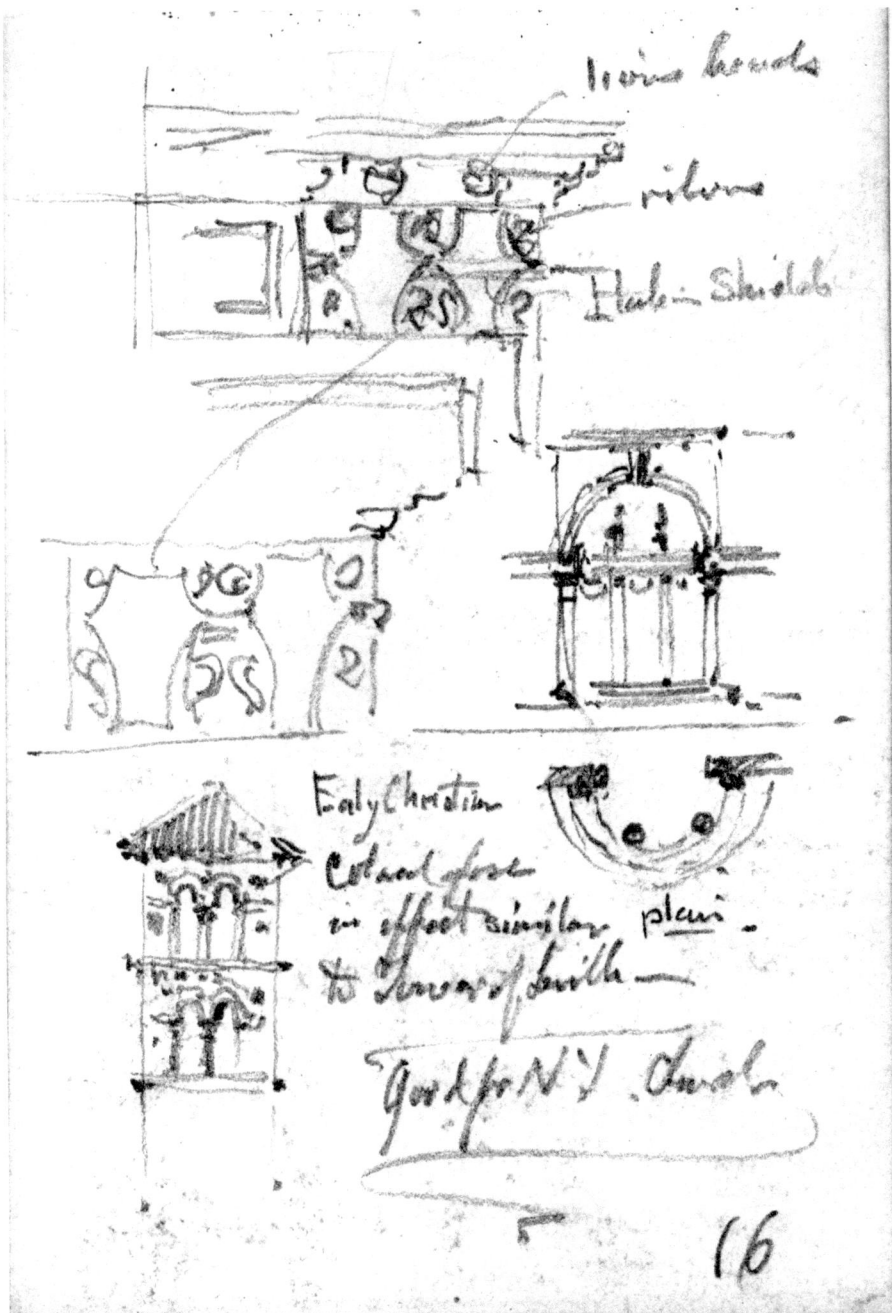

Figure 19.2 Henry Hornbostel, travel sketchbook, page 16, 1893 (Rome). Courtesy of Carnegie Mellon University Architecture Archives.

Hornbostel had absorbed his schooling and the perspective of his teachers (Alfred D. F. Hamlin is mentioned, as is William Ware).[13] Yet his approach was creative and barely concerned with the categories of the historians, to whose eyes the young architect's approach seems naive, as these entries on a book concept demonstrate:

> If I could only write and express all my ideas in good language I could hand a very interesting Architecture book to Prof. Ware about my little theories and ideas so far discovered and formed.
>
> *Rome, Thursday, March 25, 1893*

The Book

Alfred returned and together we walked to the restaurant talking about publishing some books on Early Christian Architecture and making it a book in Kirby's style [perhaps that of Henry P. Kirby] with reason[s] why and a treatise of design and history. This idea seems not bad, but it requires care and study because drawing or publishing such a book has an element of conceit or assumption about it not often favorably received.

> *Rome, Saturday, April 1, 1893*[14]

The long-term impact of Italian travel is as captivating a topic as it is a complicated one to measure and evaluate. For Hornbostel, the outcome of the travel experience would not be a book. Instead, those references became subtly interwoven in the work of his long and still seldom discussed professional practice. More strikingly, they became part of his activity as an educator.

His engagement with the Carnegie Technical Schools (renamed Carnegie Institute of Technology in 1912, now Carnegie Mellon University) began with the design of the campus masterplan, for which he won a national competition in 1904. The Department of Architecture was created immediately thereafter, with Hornbostel as its founder and first professor. In 1911, he served as Dean of the School of Applied Design (now College of Fine Arts), and when given the opportunity to design a building to house the school, he relied on his own experience of travel to do so. Completed in 1916, the College of Fine Arts is a building for the arts designed as a travel surrogate and an immersive didactic experience.[15]

A fully-fledged work of art in its beaux-arts flamboyance, and a collection of works of art in reproduction, it is a form of architectural pedagogy through curation, in which historical models are shown rather than told. Its architecture is a mediatic canvas to support its didactic content, drawing deep, rich connections with the visual culture and pedagogy of the early twentieth century—but also with clear precedents from the Roman Renaissance, most importantly Villa Madama.[16]

The College of Fine Arts incorporates and makes visual and spatial the imagery of travel guides and travel preparation books, transforming into a pedagogical tool Hornbostel's own mediated preparation. Visual references in murals, inlaid floor plans and three-dimensional details embedded in the building's own layout educated the working-class students of an industrial city's technical school, offering an alternative to the direct exposure to art and culture through world travel, which may have been, for them, out of reach (see Figure 19.3).

Many elements of the building's design recall the high points of the architect's own Italian journey. These include the prominent place of Michelangelo's plan for Saint Peter's Basilica, inlaid right at the entrance of the building: "For the greatness and sublime grandeur is first noticed when one reaches the entrance that should have been at the beginning of one of the 4 equal arms of the Greek cross" (Rome, Palm Sunday, March 26, 1893). For Hornbostel, Michelangelo represented the artist's creative genius, as he had for Louis Sullivan a generation earlier. Giving him such prominence in an academic building seems a daring move at a time when the American Academy in Rome still considered Michelangelo's work an unsuitable model for its residents.

The inventive solutions for the vaulting might have been inspired by what Hornbostel saw in Palermo: "Idea. This mosaic work gave me an impulse to use it and the thought that it could be used with great effect on the ceilings of classic vaulting and that the classic composition and details could be enhanced and made to harmonize with it in good way" (Palermo, Wednesday, March 15, 1893). Even the experience of seeing the busts of great architects in the Capitoline Museums in Rome seems to find its way in the murals of the Great Hall (see Figure 19.4 and Plate 4): "The Busts of Bramante & Vignola Palladio and M. A [Michel Angelo] were also very interesting and I will always remember their features" (Rome, Palm Sunday, March 26, 1893).

Hornbostel knew from experience that for an architect, learning from travel means something quite different than learning from a book or a photograph. Direct encounter is uniquely consequential for architecture, as it includes the material, spatial, and immersive quality of buildings. The College of Fine Arts marked the opportunity to synthetize many of the lessons learned in Europe and to transmit them to the next generations: from the realization of the mediatic power of buildings, to the deeper, layered architectural pedagogies made possible by travel and direct, embodied experiential learning.

He approached the Italian travel experience as a mark of prestige and a required step in his education, expecting to enrich a bookish, at times tedious approach to the architecture of the past and to "study what there is to study," as he noted on his arrival in Genoa. Once on site, Italy became a milieu of layered, complex architectural encounters and an entry point into a rich, animated experience of history, a reservoir of solutions and ideas in which discoveries and adventures of the mind were not only still possible but readily accessed with a short detour. Hornbostel's direct, immersive experience of landscapes and architectures of the past became the catalyst for the carving of a deeply personal path from the raw mass of locations, documents, and notions, which informed his own ideas about education and the legacy he chose to transmit to the next generations of architects. The relevance of his Italian travel transcended its scripted, controlled role as an element in his beaux-arts training, and extended long after that system's demise.[17] This longevity is at least partially explained by the Italian environment's power to foster, somewhat furtively, an insightful, dialectic relationship with history and the lesson of creative freedom.

Figure 19.3 College of Fine Arts, Carnegie Mellon University, Pittsburgh Great Hall. Portion of the ceiling mural, inlaid floor plan, and plaster cast portal framing the entrance to the Office of the Dean. Photograph by Pablo Garcia, used with permission.

Figure 19.4 College of Fine Arts, Carnegie Mellon University, Pittsburgh (USA). Detail of mural in the Great Hall. Henry Hornbostel, architect; James Monroe Hewlett, muralist, 1914-15. Creative Commons CC0 Universal Public Domain Dedication.

Notes

1. Henry Hornbostel's (1867–1961) travel journal and sketchbook are preserved in the Carnegie Mellon University Architecture Archives, and their publication is in preparation. Martin Aurand, Principal Librarian and Archivist Emeritus, generously supported my research, sharing his archive expertise, institutional memory, and insight on Hornbostel and his work in many conversations.

2. The only dedicated volumes are Walter C. Kidney, *Henry Hornbostel: An Architect's Master Touch* (Pittsburgh, PA: Pittsburgh History & Landmarks Foundation, Roberts Rinehart Publishers, 2002), and Charles Loren Rosenblum, "The Architecture of Henry Hornbostel: Progressive and Traditional Design in the American Beaux-Arts Movement" (Ph.D. diss., University of Virginia, 2009). On Pittsburgh in this era, a useful early reference is Francis G. Couvares, *The Remaking of Pittsburgh. Class and Culture in an Industrializing City, 1877–1919* (Albany: State University of New York Press, 1984).

3. On the Ecole des Beaux-arts, the essential source is Arthur Drexler (ed.), *The Architecture of the Ecole des Beaux-Arts* (New York: Museum of Modern Art; Cambridge, MA: MIT Press, 1977). See also Jean Paul Carlhian and Margot Ellis, *Americans in Paris: Foundations of America's Architectural Gilded Age: Architecture Students at the École des Beaux-Arts, 1846–1946* (New York: Rizzoli, 2014).

4. Alfred Raymond graduated at Yale in 1888, then studied architecture with Hornbostel, first at Columbia and later at the Ecole des Beaux-arts. He died in 1901. Memorial publication at Columbia University Library.

5. This resonates with the observations of Susan Schulten about the *National Geographic*, founded in 1888: "The *Geographic* would serve the mass-market tastes of the twentieth century through a yellow bordered monthly that radiated nineteenth century cultivation and privilege." Susan Schulten, *The Geographical Imagination in America, 1880–1950* (Chicago: University of Chicago Press, 2001), 154.

6. For further reading on the Grand Tour and its popular, turn-of-the-century transformation, see James Buzard, *The Beaten Track: European Tourism, Literature, and the Ways to "Culture," 1800–1918* (Oxford: Oxford University Press, 1993); Lynne Withey, *Grand Tours and Cook's Tours: A History of Leisure Travel, 1750–1915* (New York: William Morrow & Co., 1997); Jeffrey Alan Melton, *Mark Twain, Travel books, and Tourism: The Tide of a Great Popular Movement* (Tuscaloosa: University of Alabama Press, 2002); Nicholas T. Parsons, *Worth the Detour: A History of the Guidebook* (Stroud: Sutton Publishing, 2007).

7. Compare William W. Stowe, *Going Abroad: European Travel in Nineteenth-Century American Culture* (Princeton, NJ: Princeton University Press 1994).

8. These invitations were a financial lifeline. Hornbostel notes, "the amount of saving I do is astonishing for I have to last until my trunk comes from Naples" (Rome, Saturday, March 25, 1893).

9. This occurs alongside campaigns to substitute the classic European Tour for American destinations, mostly in the West, emphasizing the United States' natural and geological wonders as a replacement for history and art. Margareth Schaffer, *See America First: Tourism and National Identity, 1880–1940* (Washington, DC: Smithsonian Books, 2001).

10. While the Fair was not yet open to the public when Hornbostel was in Chicago, he certainly visited it during construction, as he worked for a number of famous New York architecture firms involved in the project (including McKim, Mead and White) between his graduation from Columbia in 1891 and his departure for Europe in the spring of 1893.

11. Lucia and Alan Valentine, *The American Academy in Rome, 1894–1969* (Charlottesville: University of Virginia Press, 1973); Fikret Yegül, *Gentlemen of Instinct and Breeding: Architecture at the American Academy in Rome, 1894–1940* (Oxford: Oxford University Press, 1991).

12. William L. Vance, "The Sidelong Glance: Victorian Americans and Baroque Rome," *New England Quarterly* 58, no. 4 (December 1985): 501–32.

13. On early US architecture schools, see Richard Oliver (ed.), *The Making of an Architect, 1881–1981: Columbia University in the City of New York* (New York: Rizzoli, 1981); Gwendolyn Wright, *The History of History in American Schools of Architecture, 1865–1975* (New York: Temple Hoyne Buell Center for the Study of American Architecture and Princeton Architectural Press, 1990); Joan Ockman and Rebecca Williamson (eds), *Architecture School: Three Centuries of Educating Architects in North America* (Cambridge, MA: MIT Press; Washington, DC: Association of Collegiate Schools of Architecture, 2012).

14. Kenneth Hafertepe and James F. O'Gorman, *American Architects and their Books, 1840–1915* (Amherst: University of Massachusetts Press, 2007). Kirby was famous for his perspectival drawings. Hornbostel would become known at the Ecole des Beaux-Arts as "l'homme perspective."

15. Dietrich Neumann, "Instead of the Grand Tour: Travel Replacements in the Nineteenth Century," *Perspecta* 41 (2008): 47–53.

16. See, for instance, Yvonne Elet, *Architectural Invention in Renaissance Rome: Artists, Humanists, and the Planning of Raphael's Villa Madama* (Cambridge: Cambridge University Press, 2018).

17. On the American Academy's reframing of the Rome Prize in architecture away from beaux-arts practice, see Denise Costanzo, "'A Truly Liberal Orientation': Laurance Roberts, Modern Architecture, and the Postwar American Academy in Rome," *Journal of the Society of Architectural Historians* 74, no. 2 (June 2015): 223–47.

CHAPTER 20
ITALIAN ROOTS IN LATIN AMERICAN ARCHITECTURAL HISTORY
Daniela Ortiz dos Santos

With the resourcefulness of someone who is rich, handsome, and well-educated, Mr. Ray Smith, associate editor of the leading North American architectural magazine *Progressive Architecture*, presents an overview of the architecture in South America ... [He] paternalistically advises South American architects not to copy the "international industrialized" architecture of the developed countries, but to be inspired by the Indigenous huts, the "*ranchitos*" and the "favelas" of the poor, as befits underdeveloped architects who operate in an underdeveloped continent ... Based on a mistake (we did not want to think of [his] bad faith), the author of the inquiry, in disguised contempt for Corbusian "plastic-formalist" positions ... explicitly exposes the conviction that true architecture is North American, based in industrial mass production, which young Latin American architects "still" cannot access, because of the underdevelopment of the country and of themselves.

Lina Bo Bardi, "Na América do Sul," 1967[1]

The title leaves no doubt as to the focus of this chapter; it deals with Italian vestiges in Latin American architectural historiography. It contributes to the study of Italian-speaking actors and their transnational social capital in embedding the use and acceptance of "Latin America" as a label for architectural histories of the region.[2] But which Latin America shall we speak of and refer to? And how to interpret the bitter yet lucid statements such as the one above from Italian-born and educated Brazilian architect Lina Bo Bardi? Fervently reacting to an article in *Progressive Architecture*, Lina (as we Brazilian scholars call her) called on readers to challenge generalizations and stereotypes; however, in doing so, she adopted a set of borrowed terms (long fostered in Italian architectural discourse) that carry problematic baggage, beginning with South America and Latin America.[3] Her choice to use both is significant. If Lina's sense of herself as "Latin American" sounds clear in 1967, this was not a natural part of her identity, but constructed and negotiated. The fact that "South America" appears throughout Lina's published writings from the 1940s on, while "Latin America" first appears among them in the mid-1960s, illustrates something of this problem.

It is likewise invoked in the pages of *Módulo*, the magazine Oscar Niemeyer founded in 1955, which became an instrumental platform for the promotion of his own projects and ideas alongside those of his social and intellectual circles. In the journal's bilingual articles (English and Portuguese), the term Latin America did not necessarily include Brazil.[4] Instead, it referred to work and projects from neighboring countries. Furthermore, Niemeyer's idea of "Brazilian architecture" itself crossed national borders to include his own overseas projects. One article, from 1976-7, presents Niemeyer's projects for a mosque in Algiers and his Mondadori headquarters outside Milan, alongside his Government Palace in Brasília and a building developed in collaboration with Pier Luigi Nervi, as examples of a "national" architecture.[5]

In the turbulent years of the 1960s and 1970s, the expression Latin America arguably acquired new complexity. Not only was it popularized and adopted by a growing number of intellectuals from the region—including Lina and Niemeyer—but international and transnational organizations also began to cultivate, through their conventions and structures, a series of practices that strengthened the institutional and legal framework to sustain a Latin American integration movement.[6] The year 1966 was pivotal: in that year, UNESCO (United Nations Educational, Scientific and Cultural Organization) initiated a major interdisciplinary study on Latin American cultures in which Italian-speaking scholars would play central roles. It also marked the creation of the Istituto Italo-Latinoamericano (Italian-Latin American Institute, or IILA). Based in Rome, this institution connected the Italian government to those of "Latin American republics" to facilitate "collaboration in the cultural, scientific, economic, technical and social" sectors. If the primary aim of the IILA was to promote political integration to help the region counterbalance US influence, it also produced academic and intellectual communities that generated complex, contentious debates through events and publications on the nature of Latin America and its constituent cultures. A growing circle of authors have demonstrated the idea of Latin America as a contradictory and unstable historical construct.[7] That architects from the region came to identify themselves as Latin Americans across the long 1970s is in part due to the influence of a few seminal publications and events, with three Italian-born figures—Roberto Segre, Paolo Gasparini, and Graziano Gasparini—at the center of a complex web of people and knowledge circulating between Europe and the Americas.[8]

Latin America from within

The 1966 UNESCO Resolution 3324 of Paris and the report it generated in 1969 record the project's funding along with plans for training, creation, and the dissemination of knowledge of so-called "other cultures"—including "their" architecture and town planning.[9] The Latin American study invited experts to examine the region's literature and art, resulting (in part) in a collection of essays and recorded interviews where "leading Latin American architects could express their points of view."[10] The essays were later published in Spanish in 1975 as *América Latina en su arquitectura*.[11] Both the Spanish edition of this work and its later English counterpart (*Latin America and its Architecture*, 1980) were organized by theme and method, including scales of urban and rural territory, rather than by regional or national boundaries.[12] A supplementary volume was published in Spanish as *Panorámica de la arquitectura latinoamericana* (1977) and in English as *The Changing Shape of Latin America* (1979)—in the latter case before the substantial publication had itself been realized.[13] It included a series of interviews, organized by country, and an impressive photographic survey. Together, these pioneering books aimed to analyze the architectural culture of the whole region of "Latin America": Central and South America and the Caribbean. They included various regional voices and views, and were sponsored not by a university or a governmental consortium, but by an international organization of growing prominence that depended for its funding on leading economies.

In this far-reaching research project, with its numerous publications, figures bridging Italy and the region under study played crucial roles. Particular attention may be given to two of its various editors: Roberto Segre for *Latin America in its Architecture*; and Paolo Gasparini, responsible for the visual portion of the volume *Panorámica*, or *Changing Shape*. In 1972, during the years in which he worked as a UNESCO photographer, Gasparini had already published *Para verte mejor, América Latina*. Segre and Gasparini shared some common experiences: both were native Italian speakers who experienced "voluntary" displacement to the Caribbean in their youth, witnessed the early years of Revolutionary Cuba, and pursued collective projects as a way to explore new readings of Latin American architecture. The reception of these sponsored publication projects, though, followed very different trajectories. Segre's collection, *América Latina*, circulated among architectural critics in the late 1970s and early 1980s, while Gasparini's books, particularly *Para verte mejor*, reached a far wider audience. His photographs depicting social injustice and the problems created by capitalism became prized as works of art, making the book a collector's item that featured in important museum collections in Europe and the Americas.

Of all these publications, Segre's edited volume *América Latina* is the least glamorous but most puzzling. A thirty-page closing essay by Segre himself challenged the "dominant cultural paradigm" shaping existing discourse on his subject and adopted an ideological stance in promoting social participation and collective labor.[14] This essay was his debut in debates about Latin America. He echoed a rising and influential group of mostly leftist intellectuals leading UNESCO programs and cultural studies organizations, boldly endorsing the Latin American Integration Movement, which UNESCO promoted in the 1960s and 1970s. Segre's written narrative and Gasparini's visual narrative together constructed an experience of the rural and urban realities of the region that was socially situated, culturally embodied, and overtly political. However, what makes it more complicated and even paradoxical is that they helped nurture the perception that this movement was produced within the region itself, as an alternative to the dominant western view of Latin America in the Cold War years.

In this respect, Segre's collection is even more significant. His future-oriented propositions and perspectives ignored the contradictions and controversies around the category "Latin America," as he later acknowledged.[15] He and his contributors had complicated relationships with the region. A glance at the authors' biographical statements in both the Spanish and English editions indicates that the voices producing an analysis "from within the region" were largely products of transnational and transatlantic displacement, either before or during the project. This intellectual migration is tied directly to the acceptance of Latin American architecture as a critical category.[16]

In 1975, Latin America was still a category found in narratives produced "outside" the region. The text of *América Latina en su arquitectura* reveals a tension, even a contradiction, between discourse and embodiment. Moreover, instead of departing from the ambiguity and complexity of Latin America, the overall discourse recalled by Segre elected a different set of aspects based on a Marxist class theory for the analysis of the roots, everyday collective practices, and meaning of Latin American architecture with a perspective towards the future.

When the book project was launched at a Buenos Aires meeting, the thirty-five-year-old Segre was newly appointed as chair of architectural history at the University of Havana, and was already internationally prominent for his writings on architecture in Revolutionary Cuba.[17] Fluent in both Spanish and Italian, and a dual citizen of Argentina and Italy, which facilitated transatlantic travel, study, and exchanges, Segre enjoyed a highly privileged view of the cultures and contexts in which he circulated.[18] Additionally, Segre was in Havana at a fertile time for the production, discussion, and dissemination of an architectural culture intersecting closely with Italian politics, particularly among left-wing intellectuals, students, and publishers. His work on the Revolutionary Cuban architectural experience was spotted by the new, booming Venetian publishing house Marsilio.[19] Five years before his *América Latina* appeared, the Italian edition of Segre's *Cuba* had already been published, following less than two years after its original Spanish edition. Besides being the first thorough study of the island's post-revolutionary architectural culture, Segre's book offered extensive original visual documentation, making it especially valuable for international scholarship.[20]

While Segre's Spanish-language books (all produced by publishers based in the Americas) were widely read and became references across the western hemisphere, his Italian writings, instead, penetrated the European academic sphere across the long 1970s. His *Architettura e territorio nell'America Latina* (co-written with Rafael López Rangel, and involving Vittorio Gregotti and Tomás Maldonado of the Politecnico di Milano) was published by Electa in 1982, directly addressing a European readership.[21] While Segre's writings on Cuban architecture catapulted him to international prominence and reverberated among leftist students, intellectuals, and publishers, his involvement in the UNESCO project from 1969 cemented his place as an authoritative scholar on the larger topic of "Latin America." Segre's engagement with this sponsored project marked his initial encounter with the theories and debates on Latin America, beyond the specific case of Cuba, and allowed a pivot in his intellectual career, as he later recognized, that opened doors to wider network of actors, institutions, and funding agencies. His work on Revolutionary Cuba and modern architecture from the end of the 1960s emphasized concepts like the "Third World." By 1975, when the UNESCO report was first published, "Latin America" had come to occupy greater space and prominence in his writing. For Segre, it was a fertile field to develop a theoretical framework in which Latin America operated as a method, a body of disciplinary knowledge, and a platform for studying and repositioning architecture and environmental and urban cultures on local and global scales alike.

Figure 20.1 Roberto Segre, *Gráfica urbana*, Havana, 1969, Graphics Department of the Commission on Revolutionary Views. Courtesy Concepción R. Pedrosa Morgado de Segre.

Figure 20.2 Roberto Segre, partial view of the José Martí district complex, Santiago de Cuba, 1964–7. Courtesy Concepción R. Pedrosa Morgado de Segre.

Baroque quarrels

América Latina en su arquitectura became more than a publication, establishing platforms for sharing knowledge, projects, and positions, and generating many further collaborative projects, transnational efforts, and research visits among its contributors.[22] However, along with the UIA congress in Buenos Aires in 1969, a series of events prior and parallel to the UNESCO collection agitated both networks and debates on Latin American architecture. These were organized by the Centro de Investigaciones Históricas y Estéticas (CIHE), a research cluster based in the School of Architecture of the Central University of Venezuela, founded in 1964 by Carlos Raúl Villanueva and Graziano Gasparini. Caracas during these years was in the spotlight because of Villanueva's design for the university campus, circulated widely in books and magazines (including a monograph in English by Sibyl Moholy-Nagy). A resident of Caracas since 1948 and a professor there since 1958, Gasparini transformed the school's research and education. Besides teaching modern architecture, the school became a place to explore research methods in architectural history. Under Gasparini's editorship, the CIHE bulletin (*Boletín del CIHE*) from 1964 until 1980 featured experimental research, conference proceedings, and debates from over one hundred contributors from institutions across the Americas and Europe. It served as an important channel for Spanish-language discussion and for the dissemination of studies on Latin American architectural and urban history and on the baroque (Gasparini's own interest) in particular.[23]

The journal's first issue presented the results of a survey among a dozen academics on the significance of "Spanish-American" baroque architecture, including established scholars such as Diego Angulo Íñiguez of Spain and Sidney D. Markman and George Kubler from the US. Gasparini's analysis highlighted a "disparity [among Íñiguez, Kubler, and Gasparini] in orientation, focus and [critical] interpretation."[24] Some contributors like Carlos Maldonado equated baroque architecture in the Spanish Americas with its expressions elsewhere, while others argued the opposite. Kubler, for example, did not believe in the "existence of a Latin American 'baroque' architecture," and insisted that "none [of its regional examples] should be confused with the baroque architecture we know in Italy and central Europe."[25] This debate permeated the two-dozen issues edited by Gasparini. While many of these conversations took place in print only, others began in conferences. One symposium hosted by the CIHE in October 1967 to discuss the "situation" of Latin American architectural historiography appeared in a special issue of April 1968. Its participants included Kubler, along with Paolo Portoghesi and Leonardo Benevolo, as well as Moholy-Nagy, the only woman who spoke.

Apart from a memorable image capturing Portoghesi in a moment of boredom during the journey, all other photographs by the brothers Gasparini suggest an intense if congenial gathering. More significant than the specific details of the conference debate was their connection to others that took place in Rome thirteen years later. This is because the Caracas event's main themes (baroque architecture in Latin America), methods (contesting nationalist and stylistic labeling), and driving questions (is it conceptually coherent to talk about a Latin American, or an Iberian-American baroque?) were equally central to the debates that took place in 1980 in the Italian capital.[26]

In April of that year, Rome followed Caracas as stage for the *Simposio internazionale sul barocco latinoamericano*. Organized and promoted by the IILA, six-dozen scholars gathered in a four-day discussion and attended the opening of an eponymous exhibition, which included a film screening session and a special light-and-music installation. This major event (both the exhibition and symposium) received funding from the IILA and UNESCO, as well as institutional support and cooperation from the twenty-one nations represented. Its opening was a political and cultural event attended by Italian President Alessandro (Sandro) Pertini, ambassadors and other representatives of IILA member countries, and the Italian community of baroque scholars. The resulting catalog (1980) and conference proceedings (published in two volumes, in 1982 and 1984) are products of concerted institutional, political, and intellectual efforts to assert the significance of the region's artistic and built cultures of the seventeenth and eighteenth centuries, but also to process their Italian "origins".[27] The essays thus reveal competing notions of a Latin American baroque. The catalog's introduction by IILA General Secretary Carlo Perrone Capano calls the Rome event "unprecedented," even as Paolo Portoghesi's essay restated much of his argument from the CIHE symposium's 1967 proceedings.[28]

Despite a general agreement on the need to investigate, discuss, and disseminate the artistic and architectural expressions of the seventeenth- and eighteenth-century

Americas, participants like Ramón Gutiérrez believed that an "interpretative crisis" around the idea of an "American baroque" had been exposed.[29] A great deal of effort was made to discuss these different agendas, although no definitive solutions were reached. Indeed, despite the editors' considerable efforts, the symposium proceedings revealed a prevailing sense of confusion and an absence of common ground among the seventy-three lectures originally delivered in Rome in Spanish, Portuguese, French, and Italian, and from which three-dozen short essays were published. The catalog, instead, offered a coherent, coordinated narrative. It provided a great variety of architectural and artistic examples, largely unknown to the general European public. It begins with seven brief essays followed by abundant (mostly unpublished) photographs of sculptures, church facades, gates, window frames, monastery patios, and frescoes on vaulted ceilings, mostly drawn from the contributors' personal collections. The essays immediately pose the question of "which Latin American Baroque" is under discussion. Does it belong to the Americas as a whole? Would a study on just the Spanish Americas be more appropriate? Or, better, the "Iberian-Americas"? Graziano Gasparini, Damián Bayón, Leopoldo Zea, and Francisco Curt Lange stress Latin America in their titles, while Portoghesi describes an "American" contribution to the baroque.[30] Miguel Batllori uses "Iberian-Americas," and Erwin Walter Palm refers to the Spanish Americas. These terms stem from different points of departure and ideological and methodological agendas. Despite this complexity, the second part of this generously illustrated catalog lacks detailed descriptions or contextual analysis of what it shows. It instead offers an accessible, uncontroversial narrative on both the baroque and the concept of Latin America.

Although the baroque operated as a vehicle for revisiting Latin American art and architecture as a category, both were topics of controversy and dispute. While authors such as Portoghesi and Ramón Gutiérrez adopted "American Baroque" as a methodological instrument, others like Erwin Walter Palm claimed it was impossible to define an "urban Baroque in Latin America."[31]

Throughout the symposium's debates on baroque architecture in the Americas, Gasparini cultivated the idea of Latin America, less for its historical accuracy than for an ideological reason: to promote production of a Latin American history from within. In this sense, he and Segre shared a common ambition. Gasparini's controversial positions were less about categorization than the type of narratives constructed. In his papers in the *CIHE Bulletin*, in his UNESCO book, and IILA publications, Gasparini consistently rejected the idea that the baroque architecture of Latin America was directly linked to the baroque experience of Spain and the Iberian Peninsula. The issue, for him, was that the dominant narratives produced in Spain excluded alternative explanations based on other modes of communication, circulation of people, and knowledge exchange. He insisted on revisiting the subject's historiography and incorporation of new sources. Gasparini thereby linked the baroque architecture in Latin American with Italian treaties, techniques, and construction knowledge brought to the Americas by Jesuits, whose specialized education came from Venice. For Gasparini, Venice and Paris were the "real" centers of "knowledge transfer," leaving Madrid as a secondary source. His thesis conflicted with established views about Spanish colonial history; it was not easily accepted by the scholarly world, as he himself recognized, and remains a minority position.[32] For Italy, this exchange provided a claim to influence on Latin American culture; for Latin Americans, emphasis on extra-Iberian sources was a way to assert independence from established histories of colonial influence.

Conclusion

If today architects generally identify Latin American architecture as a relatively coherent expression, as Lina Bo Bardi began doing in the late 1960s, we should keep in mind its embedded theoretical conflicts, ideological frictions, and competing visions. The construction, circulation, and consumption of the category "Latin America" in both popular and scholarly literature had numerous authors with complex histories and agendas. The involvement of organizations, scholars, photographers, and events with direct ties to Italy highlights some of its ambiguities, and its intense political and cultural valences, with perennial calls for a Latin American integration movement operating amidst Cold War geopolitical tensions and left-wing and reactionary interests on both sides of the Atlantic. While these projects across the long 1970s helped legitimize the phrase "Latin America" on a global scale, they were also products of a period when the idea of Latin America in architecture (recent or remote) was contradictory, ideologically charged, and in dispute. As this conflict went beyond mainstream academic discourse and languages into international communication, its various footholds in Italy and Italian-language circles played an important and heretofore overlooked role in the transatlantic circulation and absorption of a basic and still questionable idea: that the architecture of nations as diverse as Mexico, Cuba, Venezuela, Brazil, and Argentina can be discussed as a unified phenomenon.

Notes

1. Lina Bo Bardi criticizes the stance in C. Ray Smith, "In South America: After Corbu, What's Happening?" *Progressive Architecture* 47 (September 1966): 141–61. See Lina Bo Bardi, "Na América do Sul: após Le Corbusier, o que está acontecendo?" *Mirante das Artes* (São Paulo) 1 (January–February 1967): 10–11 (translation by author).

2. As in, for instance, Clelia Pozzi, "Latin America Made in Italy," *ABE Journal* 5 (2017), http://journals.openedition.org/abe/10798—even if this article treats "Latin America" as a neutral term.

3. Without attempting to diminish the complexity of the notion of "Latin America," it seems useful to note that the term is an invention and a convention. Originating in the nineteenth century, it first appears in French to specify the non-English speaking areas of the American continent. In the early twentieth century, heated debates on pan-Americanism and Latin-Americanism included a wider circle of participants, including an increasing number of English-speaking voices, whose narratives served as a theoretical basis for the US policy agenda for the continent. South America, in contrast, has a much less complex meaning, and is here treated as a geographical region, the southern subcontinent of the Americas. See, for

example, Leslie Bethell's seminal *The Cambridge History of Latin America*, 12 vols (Cambridge: Cambridge University Press, 1985–2008).

4. Mário Barata's report on the 1963 art biennial of São Paulo illustrates Brazilian intellectuals' inconsistent identifications with Latin America. See Mário Barata, "Latin America, including Brazil, at the VII Biennial," *Módulo* 35–36 (October–December 1963): 31–7.

5. Oscar Niemeyer, "Considerações sobre a Arquitetura Brasileira," *Módulo* 44 (December 1976–January 1977): 34–41.

6. The intersection of international organizations and intellectual migration has been useful to an ongoing project that explores Latin America as a category and the architectural historiography of the region during the Cold War era. Some of the reflections presented here derive from investigations carried out at the Center for Critical Studies in Architecture of the Goethe University Frankfurt.

7. Seminal publications on Latin American architectural historiography include Ramón Gutiérrez, *Arquitectura y urbanismo en Iberoamérica* (Madrid: Ediciones Cátedra, 1984); Jorge Francisco Liernur, *Escritos de arquitectura del siglo XX en América Latina* (Madrid: Tanais, 2002); Marina Waisman, *El interior de la historia: historiografía arquitectónica para uso de Latinoamericanos* (Bogotá: ESCALA, 1990); Silvia Arango, "Una historiografía latinoamericana reciente sobre arquitectura y ciudad," *Year 20*, special issue, *Diseño en Síntesis* 40–41 (2009): 32–43; Patricio Del Real and Helen Gyger (eds), *Latin American Modern Architectures: Ambiguous Territories* (New York: Routledge, 2013); and Barry Bergdoll, Carlos Eduardo Dias Comas, Jorge Francisco Liernur, and Patricio Del Real, *Latin America in Construction: Architecture 1955–1980* (New York: Museum of Modern Art, 2015).

8. Milan-born Roberto Segre (1934–2013) studied architecture in Buenos Aires and taught architectural history at Havana following the Cuban Revolution. In the early 1990s he moved to Rio de Janeiro, launched a research cluster on urban history and digital representation, and led Docomomo Brazil. One of the most important photographers of architecture in Latin America, Gorizia-born Paolo Gasparini (b. 1934) moved to Venezuela in 1954 and was commissioned by UNESCO in 1967 to conduct photographic projects in the region. His brother Graziano (1924–2019) studied in Venice and collaborated with Carlo Scarpa before moving to Caracas in 1948. He was a scholar of baroque architecture and its historiography and an architect specializing in the preservation and conservation of historic buildings.

9. UNESCO, *Report of the Director General on the Activities of the organization in 1969. Communicated to Member States and the Executive Board in accordance with Article VI, 3.b of the Constitution* (Paris: UNESCO, 1970), 181, https://unesdoc.unesco.org/.

10. The expert meeting in Buenos Aires was held in conjunction with the 10th International Union of Architects Congress, which was headed by César Férnandez Moreno, editor-in-chief of the UNESCO Latin American collections, and attended by more than 3,000 people. See Federico A. Urgate, "10th UIA Congress Procedure," in *Review of the International Union of Architects* 58-59-60 (December 1969): 24–6. Known participants include Francisco Bullrich, Amancio Williams, Graziano Gasparini, Roberto Segre, and Carlos Raúl Villanueva. In the *UNESCO Bulletin* (March 1972), Moreno claimed that Latin America was "witnessing a veritable 'Cultural Explosion.'" Signed up to coordinate an ambitious study project within the UNESCO program on Latin American cultures, Moreno played an important role in the outcome of the study, which appeared in the collection *América Latina en su cultura* among various platforms, communication channels, and records either produced or sponsored by UNESCO. The meeting ended with a recommendation for Francisco Bullrich, given his publication record on this issue, to act as rapporteur and editor of the book project on architecture and town planning, to appear in Spanish first, with a subsequent volume in English. Despite Bullrich's appointment as rapporteur to the UNESCO experts meeting (the

committee in Buenos Aires had recommended him for this job), the task was later given to one of the youngest scholars of the group, Roberto Segre.

11. Roberto Segre (ed.), *América Latina en su arquitectura* (Paris: UNESCO; Mexico City: Siglo XXI Editores, 1975). Among contributors to Segre's book, Jorge Enrique Hardoy and Diego Robles Rivas had been involved in international organizations engaged not only in architectural interests, but also in design and environmental and urban studies. See Ramón Gutiérrez, "Jorge Enrique Hardoy: su aporte a la história urbana de América Latina," *EURE* 21, no. 2 (April 1995): 9–15; Jorge E. Hardoy (ed.), *Urbanization in Latin America: Approaches and Issues* (New York: Anchor Books, 1975); Arturo Almandoz, "Urban Planning and Historiography in Latin America," *Progress in Planning* 65 (2006): 81–123; James Fathers and Gui Bonsiepe, "Peripheral Vision: An Interview with Gui Bonsiepe Charting a Lifetime of Commitment to Design Empowerment," *Design Issues* 19, no. 4 (2003): 44–56.

12. Roberto Segre and Fernando Kusnetzoff (eds), *Latin America in its Architecture*, trans. Edith Grossman Holmes (New York: Holmes & Meier, 1980). Bullrich, Robles Rivas, and Hardoy contributed to the Spanish edition, but their papers did not appear in the English version.

13. Damián Bayón and Paolo Gasparini, *Panorámica de la arquitectura latinoamericana* (Barcelona: Blume-UNESCO, 1977), and *The Changing Shape of Latin American Architecture: Conversations with Ten Leading Architects*, trans. Galen D. Greaser (Chichester: Wiley, 1979).

14. Roberto Segre, "Comunicación y participación social," in *América Latina en su arquitectura*, ed. Roberto Segre (Paris: UNESCO; Mexico City: Siglo XXI Editores, 1975), 269–99.

15. Roberto Segre, *América latina fim do milênio: raízes e perspectivas de sua arquitetura* (São Paulo: Nobel, 1991), 12–18.

16. Among the thirteen authors of the book's more expansive Spanish edition, four were heavily involved with Italian-speaking architectural communities: Enrico Tedeschi and Gui Bonsiepe, in addition to Segre and Paolo Gasparini's brother, Graziano.

17. Roberto Segre, *La arquitectura de la revolución cubana* (Montevideo: Universidad de la República, Facultad de arquitectura, 1968), and *Diez años de arquitectura en Cuba revolucionaria* (Havana: Ediciones Unión, 1970).

18. Segre's autobiography is a useful source; see Roberto Segre, "The Meaning of Italian Culture in the Latin American Architecture Historiography. An Autobiographical Essay," *Cadernos PROARQ* 19 (December 2012): 290–318.

19. Roberto Segre, *Cuba, l'architettura della rivoluzione* (Padua: Marsilio, 1970). Marsilio's publications, which included Giancarlo de Carlo's *Urbino* (1966) and Aldo Rossi's *L'architettura della città* (1966), went beyond Italian circles and were read in schools and institutions across Europe. See Antonio Labalestra, "La cultura comunista e la 'formazione del nuovo architetto' negli anni Sessanta. Alcune considerazioni a margine di uno scritto inedito di Aldo Rossi," *Quaderni di architettura e design* 2 (2019): 53–73.

20. Consider Banham's review of the Italian edition: "Segre's book needs attentive reading not because of obscurity but because of its strangeness and it's well worth refurbishing your Italian to follow Segre's argument." Reyner Banham, review of *Cuba, Official Architecture and Planning* 34, no. 6 (1971): 467–8.

21. Roberto Segre and Rafael López Rangel (eds), *Architettura e territorio nell'America Latina* (Milan: Electa, 1982), 8. Segre's introduction to *Tendencias arquitectónicas y caos urbano en América Latina* (Mexico City: Gustavo Gilli, 1986) noted that *Architettura e territorio nell'America Latina* was indeed addressed to a European audience.

22. Two important initiatives beyond Segre and López Rangel's books deserve attention: (1) Graziano Gasparini's bulletins of the *Centro de Investigaciones Históricas y Estéticas*

275

(University of Venezuela), which published articles by Jorge Hardoy (1969) and Segre (1972); and (2) the lecture series on industrial design Segre and Fernando Salinas hosted in Havana in 1972, having as guests Tomás Maldonado, then professor at Milan; Gui Bonsieppe, then head of the *Cybersyn* in Chile; Claude Schnaidt, then lecturer at the Unité pédagogique d'architecture in Paris; Martin Kelm, then director of the Central Office of Design of the German Democratic Republic; and Yuri Soloviev, director of the government-sponsored USSR Research Institute of Industrial Design VNIITE. See Silvia Fernández, "The Origins of Design Education in Latin America: From the Hfg in Ulm to Globalization," *Design Issues* 22, no. 1 (2006): 3–19.

23. Notable contributors to the *Boletín del CIHE* include Sibyl Moholy-Nagy, George Kubler, Erwin Walter Palm, Sylvio de Vasconcellos, Fernando Chueca Goitia, Leonardo Benevolo, Paolo Portoghesi, Damián Bayón, Teresa Gisbert, Carmen Aranovich, Jorge E. Hardoy, Enrique del Moral, Roberto Segre, Marina Waisman, and Ramón Gutièrrez. The *Boletín del CIHE* is available in the digital collections of the University of Venezuela Press, www.edicionesfau.com.

24. Graziano Gasparini, "Encuesta sobre la significación de la arquitectura barroca hispanoamericana," *Boletín del CIHE* 1 (January 1964), 42.

25. Gasparini, "Encuesta sobre la significación de la arquitectura barroca hispanoamericana," 12.

26. José de Nordenflycht Concha, "Roma 1980: barroco local en contexto global," *La otra dirección. Percezione dell'arte latinoamericana in Italia*, special issue, *Quaderni culturali IILA* 1 (November 2018): 61–70.

27. *Barocco Latino Americano* (Rome: Istituto Italo-Latino Americano, 1980); and Vittorio Minardi (ed.), *Atti Simposio internazionale sul Barocco Latino Americano, organizzato dall'IILA sotto gli auspici dell'UNESCO*, 2 vols (Rome: Istituto Italo-Latino Americano, 1982, 1984).

28. Carlo Perrone Capano, preface to *Barocco Latino Americano*, 9. In the same volume, see Paolo Portoghesi, "Il contributo Americano allo sviluppo dell'architettura barocca," 11–13, and Paolo Portoghesi, "La contribución Americana al desarrollo de la arquitectura barroca," *Boletín del CIHE* 9 (April 1968): 137–46. Appointed as chief curator of the show in Rome, Portoghesi was at the same time directing the first Venice Architecture Biennale, "The Presence of the Past." On the latter, see Léa-Catherine Szacka, *Exhibiting the Postmodern: The 1980 Venice Architecture Biennale* (Venice: Marsilio, 2016); and Silvia Micheli, "Between History and Design: The Baroque Legacy in the Work of Paolo Portoghesi," in *The Baroque in Architectural Culture, 1880–1980*, ed. Andrew Leach, John Macarthur, and Maarten Delbeke (Farnham: Ashgate, 2015), 195–210.

29. Ramón Gutièrrez, "Repensando o Barroco americano," *Vitruvius* 2 (December 2001), https://vitruvius.com.br/revistas/read/arquitextos/02.019/819.

30. In "Il contributo americano allo sviluppo dell'architettura barocca," Portoghesi explores the baroque as a form of "operative criticism" of architectural culture. The text is almost entirely based on the much earlier essay (published in Spanish as "La contribución Americana al desarrollo de la arquitectura barroca"). See Paolo Portoghesi, "Il contributo americano allo sviluppo dell'architettura barocca," in *Atti Simposio internazionale sul Barocco Latino Americano, organizzato dall'IILA sotto gli auspici dell'UNESCO*, vol. 1, ed. Vittorio Minardi (Rome: Istituto Italo-Latino Americano, 1982), 275–84.

31. Erwin Walter Palm, "Urbanismo barocco en América Latina?" in *Atti Simposio internazionale sul Barocco Latino Americano, organizzato dall'IILA sotto gli auspici dell'UNESCO*, vol. 1, ed. Vittorio Minardi (Rome: Istituto Italo-Latino Americano, 1982), 215–220.

32. See Graziano Gasparini, "Análisis crítico de la historiografía arquitectónica del barroco en América," *Boletín del CIHE* 7 (April 1967): 9–29; *América, barroco y arquitectura* (Caracas: Ernesto Armitano, 1972); "The Present Significance of the Architecture of the Past," in *Latin America in its Architecture*, trans. Edith Grossman Holmes, ed. Roberto Segre and Fernando Kusnetzoff (New York: Holmes & Meier, 1980), 77–103; and "La arquitectura barroca latinoamerican: una persuasiva retórica provincial," in *Atti Simposio internazionale sul Barocco Latino Americano, organizzato dall'IILA sotto gli auspici dell'UNESCO*, vol. 1, ed. Vittorio Minardi (Rome: Istituto Italo-Latino Americano, 1982), 387–98.

INDEX

Places are in Italy unless stated otherwise. Illustrations are shown in *italic* figures.

A—Cultura della Vita 157–8
abstract approach to architecture 48–51
academicism 2, 4
aesthetic experience 41, 42, 43, 48
agency 129
Agnelli, Gianni 211, *212*
agriculture 165
air conditioning 119–20
Alberti, Leon Battista
    concinnitas 98
    De re aedificatoria 81–3, *82–3*
    disegno of 84
    family exile and return to Florence 70–2, 76
    forms 44
    lineamenta of 84
    models 87, 88
    Palazzo Rucellai, Florence 73, *74*
    rediscovery of 86
Albini, Franco 16
Algarotti, Francesco 55, 57, 59
Altara, Edina 158–9
Ambasz, Emilio 209–11, 213, 214
American Academy in Rome 44, 139, 147, 252, 259
Americans in Italy *see* Hornbostel, Henry
anachronism 75
analogical thought 185–6
anatomy *see* human body
Andrews, Gordon 236
anthropogeography 166, 169, 170, 174, 175
ANY 28, 32
architect, the 19, 84, *85*, 85
    see also intellectual, Italian architect as (1920–80)
architectural criticism
    doubling 32
    England-America-Italy triangle 243, 244–5
    ideology and 184
    of Rossi 188
    of shape architecture 238
    spatial interpretation of Zevi 45–6, *47*, 48
    Wölfflinian style 49–50
architectural education 123–5
    see also universities
Architectural Forum 238–9
architectural historiography 41–51, 221, 243
    Wölfflin and the psychology of art 41–2

architectural orders 57–8, 81
architectural practice 57
    see also models and modelling
Architectural Record 237
Architectural Review 20, 49, 50, 168, 238, 240
architectural schools 22
    see also education; universities
architecture as a profession 4, 84–6, 91–2
architecture, beginning of 167–9
Archizoom, "No-Stop City" 166, 173
Argan, Giulio Carlo 194, 195
Aria d'Italia 155–6
Aristotelianism 127–30, 133
Arquitectura 167
arredamento 195
art history 41
arte metafisica 179–80, *181*, 194
Assemblage 28, 35, 36
Associazione per l'architettura organica
    (APAO) 17, 19
Atlantic Alliance 103
Australia, perspective from *see* Boyd, Robin
automobiles 207–8

B of the Bang 90, *90*; Pl. 2
backyards, entry by 28–31
Banham, Reyner
    and functionalism 60, 61
    on Gregotti 214
    on Istituto Marchiondi Spagliardi, Baggio
      239–40
    Neoliberty article 241
    polemic with Rogers 20
    on Wittkower 49, 237
Bardi, Pietro Maria 157
    Quadrante 16
    Rapporto sull'architettura (1931) 12
baroque architecture
    Latin American 271–3
    Rossi and 185, 186
    Venturi and 139–40, *140*, 141, *142*, 147
Bartoli, Cosimo 82
BBPR
    Torre Velasca 20, *21*, 55
    Val d'Aosta 16

Index

beams and cylinders 185
beauty 238–9
beaux-arts 2, 4, 222–3
Bellezza 158
Benevolo, Leonardo 24
Berenson, Bernard 42, 46
Bergren, Ann 35, 36
Berlin, Germany 184
Bernstein, Phil 90
Biermann, Veronica 82
BIM 86, 87, 90
Biondo, Flavio 74
Blake, Peter 244
Bo Bardi, Lina 157–8, 265
body *see* human body
Boletín del CIHE 270–1
Bontempelli, Massimo 16
Bottoni, Piero 96–7
boundary stones 172, 174
Bousquet, Antoine 88
Boyd, Robin 235–45
    1950s Italian design in Australia 236
    on beauty 238–40, *239*
    on decoration 237
    England-America-Italy criticism triangle 243,
      244–5
    on Italian architecture 240–1
    later publications 242
    lecture series 244
    "The New Vision in Architecture" 242
    on "pleasingness" 237
    on shape architecture 238
    Wittkower, influence of 236–7
Branzi, Andrea, *Agronica* 165, 173
Bredekamp, Horst 87
Bretis, Herwig 90–1
bridge 169
Brin, Irene 159
Brunelleschi, Filippo *70*, 70–2, 76, 87
Buchanan, Peter 224
Budapest, Hungary 109–10, 112, *113*, 114, *115*
Building Information Modeling (BIM) 86, 87, 90
building waste 125–6, 130–3, *131–2*

Campigli, Massimo, *La famiglia dell'architetto* 152,
    153
Cardoso Llach, Daniel 90
Carnegie Mellon University, Pittsburgh 258–9,
    260–1; *Pl. 4*
Carpo, Mario 82, 86
cars 207–8
Casa bella/Casabella
    articles published in Portugal 167
    continuity and 11
    foundation of 12
    functionalism 59

IAUS special issue 29–30, *30*
    interiors 199, *199*, 200
    Oppositions and 28
    rationalism and 14
    review of Italian architecture (1961) 240–2
    scope 16, 19, 20
    Superstudio cover 173
Casa Scarabeo sotto la Foglia, nr. Vicenza 161
Cefis, Eugenio 213
Centro Cultural de Belém (CCB), Lisbon, Portugal
    165–7, *167*, 170, 174; *Pl. 3*
Centro de Investigaciones Históricas y Estéticas
    (CIHE), Venezuela 270–1
Certosa, Padula 140, *140*
chair *199*, 200
Chicago, Illinois, USA 251
China 221–30
    application of Rossian theories 225–9, *227*; *Pl.*
      10
    knowledge of Rossi before translation 224–5
    semiotics in China 222, 225, 228–9
    translation of Rossi 225, 229–30
    urban architecture in China 222–4, *223*
Chinese characters 228–9
Chioggia 31
Choay, Françoise 69
churches 42, 252–3, 255
circular economy 126
City of the European Recovery Program (exhibition,
    1950) 103–4, *104*
Clark, Kenneth 48
classicism, return to 182, 184, 185
clichés 147
climate and architecture 109–21
    air conditioning 119–20
    apartment block, Rome *111*, 112
    comfort zone 118–19
    cultural resonance of design 117
    cyclical approach to 120–1
    formalism 116
    globalization of the international style 114–15
    historical events 117–18
    "House Reversed," Budapest 112, *113*, 114
    Olgyay brothers 109–10, 112, 116, 118, *119*,
      120
    Stühmer Chocolate Factory, nr. Budapest 114,
      115
    value, assignment of 116–17
clouds 151, *151*, 161
coastal architecture 138
College of Fine Arts, Carnegie Mellon University
    258–9, *260–1*; *Pl. 4*
colonization *201*, 201–2
columns 57–8
comfort zone 118–19
Como, Casa del Fascio 14

computational art 90
computational models 88–91
Comunità 17
conception 127
concetto 127
concinnitas 98
concrete 123–4
conferences 95, 98, 271
Congrès Internationaux d'Architecture Moderne
    (CIAM) 55, 61
continuity 11, 17, 19, 167
Corsignano *see* Pienza
Cosenza, Luigi 138
countryside 165–6, 172, 173, 174
criticism *see* architectural criticism
Cuba 268
cylinders and beams 185
Czarnowski, Thomas 210–11

D'Angelo, Salvo *201*, 202
Danti, Vincenzo, *Trattato delle perfette proporzioni*
    129
Davidson, Cynthia 32
De Carlo, Giancarlo 19, 244
De Chirico, Giorgio 179–80, *181*, 182, 186
De Finetti, Giuseppe 14
De Golyer, Everett 139
Deamer, Peggy 36
deconstruction 126, 131
design culture 194, 203
design method *see* climate and architecture
designing 84
digital turn 83, 86, 88–9
Diotallevi, Irenio *15*, 16
disegno 4, 84, 86, 126–7
domestic architecture 184–5
    see also housing; *Italy: The New Domestic
        Landscape* (MoMA, 1972)
domestic interiors *see* interiors
Domus
    content 154
    foundation of 12
    headquarters 158
    interiors 194, 199, 200
    Irene Brin and 159
    and *Italy: The New Domestic Landscape*
        (exhibition, 1972) 211
    Lina Bo and 157
    Lisa Ponti and 155
    Marianne Lorenz and 158
    Ponti and 14, 19
Donetti, Dario 82
Dorfles, Gillo 97
doubling of Venice 31–2, 34, 36–7
drawing 84
Duce/Il Duce *see* Mussolini, Benito

Due cuori felici (film, 1932) *199*, 200
Dunn, James Clement 103

Early Christian architecture 252–3
Edilizia Moderna 20, 166
education 123–5
    see also universities
Eisenman, Peter 31, 51, 116, 210
El Cerrito villa, Caracas, Venezuela 160
Ellis, William 30–1
empathetic response 43–4
Ente Nazionale del Dopolavoro 197, *198*, 199
entries *see* backyards, entry by
environment *see* climate and architecture
Environments 209–10
European Recovery Program 103–4, *104*
Evans, Robin 86
exhibitions
    Agriculture and Architecture (2019) 165, 174
    City of the European Recovery Program (1950)
        103–4, *104*
    by Huxtable 145
    interiors 197, *198*, 199, *201*, 201–2
    Italy: The New Domestic Landscape (MoMA,
        1972) 207–17
    Milan Triennales 96–7, 179, 185
    Studi sulle proporzioni (1951) 95–105
exile 70, 71–2, 72–3
experiential subjectivity 42–3, 46, 51
experimental construction projects 17

facades 73, *73–4*, 112, 114–15, 166, 184, 185
fascism 11–14, 16, 194–203
Febvre, Lucien 76–7
Feltrinelli, Inge 211
FIAT 14, 211–12
film *199*, 200, 201
Florence
    cathedral cupola *70*, 70–2, 76, 87
    fortification drawings 44, *45*
    Palazzo Rucellai 73, *74*
    railway station 14
Forgacs, David 196
form and matter *128*, 128
"form follows function" 43, 58
formalism 116
fountain 179
framing 170, *171*, 172
Frampton, Kenneth 168, 169, 174
Frascari, Marco 64, 88
"from the spoon to the city" 193–4
function and form 43–4, 55
function and representation 55, 57–8, 61–2, 64
functionalism 55–65
    architectural practice 57
    art historians on 58–9, 61–2

cause and effect 62
in China 227–8
determinism and 43
eighteenth century Italian scholars 55
function and representation/form 55, 57–8,
    61–2, 64
"function," introduction of the term 55
"Functional City" congress (1933) 61
materials 57
rationalism and 59–61
recent interpretations 64
semiotics of architecture 64
Furlan, Francesco 82
furnishing 195
furniture 197, *198*, 199, *201*, 202
futurism 194

Gabetti, Gianluigi 211, *212*
Gardella, Ignazio 16
Gasparini, Graziano 270–1, *272–3*
Gasparini, Paolo 267
Gengaro, Maria Louisa 59
Ghent University, Belgium 123–4
Giedion, Sigfried 13, *13*, 99
Giovannoni, Giuseppe 16
glass 115
globalization, of international style 114–15
Gnecchi-Ruscone, Francesco 95, 101, *102*
Gramsci, Antonio 200
Grand Tour 31, 249
Greenough, Horatio 58
Gregotti, Vittorio 166
    anthropogeography 166, 169, 170, 174
    architecture, beginning of 167–9
    Centro Cultural de Belém (CCB), Lisbon 166–7,
        167, 170; *Pl. 3*
    Italy: The New Domestic Landscape (exhibition,
        1972), essay 214
    marking of ground 169
    measuring 172
    modern movement and 19–20, 24
    New Directions in Italian Architecture 214
    territory 173–4
    University of Calabria, bridge 169
    University of Palermo 169–70, *171–3*, 174
Gruppo ENI 212, 213
Gruppo 7 59
Gruppo Toscano 14
Guarnati, Daria 155, *156*, 156, 157
Gundle, Stephen 196

Haishi project design 32–4, *33–4*; *Pl. 1*
Hang-Qin Island, China 32–4, *33–4*; *Pl. 1*
harmony 98–101
Harper's Magazine 242
Haskell, Douglas 241

Hauck, Anthony 86
Havana, Cuba 268
Hays, K. Michael 28
Heatherwick Studios *90*, 90; *Pl. 2*
Hight, Christopher 85
hill towns 35
Hirdina, Heinz 84
    see also Latin American architectural
        historiography
Hoffmann, Josef 138
Hook New Town, England 31
Hornbostel, Henry 249–61
    American culture, reference to 250–1
    book, ideas for 258
    classical culture and architecture, response to
        251–2
    Early Christian architecture, appreciation of
        252–3
    Ideas of 256
    photographs as source material 255
    Rome 253, *254*, 255–6
    sketches by *254*, 255–6, *257*
    tourism 249–50
    work, impact of travel on 258–9, *260–1*;
        Pl. 4
Horton Plaza, San Diego, California 35
"House Reversed," Budapest 112, *113*, 114
housing
    Budapest, Hungary 112, *113*, 114
    Milan *15*, 16, 17
    Rome *111*, 112
Hughes, Francesca 89
human body 99, 101, 102, 104–6, 124, 129–30
humanism 194
Hungary *see* Budapest, Hungary
Hunt, John Dixon 27–8
Huxtable, Ada Louise 145, 208, 215

ICE–Institute for Foreign Trade 212–13
identity 196, 199–200
image act 87
immigrants 147
INA-Casa 19, 22, *23*
Institute of Architecture and Urban Studies (IAUS)
    28, 30–1
Institute of Contemporary Art (ICA), Boston,
    USA 157
intellectual, Italian architect as (1920–1980) 11–24
    experimental construction projects 17–19, *18*
    fascism, architecture under 11–14, 16
    intellectuals and universities 22, 24
    neorealism and organic architecture 17
    political life 23–4
    Rogers and the modern movement 19–20
    Samonà and urban planning 20–2
intellectual objectivity 48–9, 51

interiors 193–203
    arredamento 195
    colonization, context of *201*, 201–2
    destabilizations 195
    exhibitions 197, *198*, 199
    fascism, influence of 196
    flexibility of *111*, 112
    identity 196
    Italian design 194, 203
    media, role of *199*, 199–201
    nation building 196, 203
International Laboratory for Architecture and
    Urban Design (ILA&UD) 27, 28–9, *29*
interpretation of architecture 43–4, 45–6, 55, 57–8,
    61–2, 64
intertextuality 221
Isozaki, Arata 32–4, *33–4*; *Pl. 1*
Istituto Italo-Latinoamericano (IILA) 266, 271
Istituto universitario di architettura di Venezia
    (IUAV) 20–2, 28, 46, 48
Italianness 27–8, 31, 33, 34, 35, 147
    see also Venice
Italy, and architecture 3–4, 5–7
Italy: The New Domestic Landscape (MoMA, 1972)
    207–17
    Ambasz, the curator and impresario 210, 213, 214
    catalog 214
    Environments 209–10
    impact and consequences 214–17
    industrial support 213
    Italian contacts 210–11
    Objects 208–9
    political support 212–13
    previous exhibitions 207–8
    reviews 215
    sponsors 211–12

Jameson, Fredric 28, 36
Janus 31, 32
Jarzombek, Mark 41
Jefferson, Thomas 58
Jerde, Jon *35*, 35–6
Jing, Dong 225
journals 12, 17, 19, 20
    see also Casa bella/Casabella; Domus; Stile
        A—Cultura della Vita, ANY, Architectural
        Forum, Architectural Record, Architectural
        Review, Assemblage, Arquitectura, Bolet.n
        del CIHE, Bellezza, Comunità, Harpers
        Magazine, L'architecture d'aujourd'hui,
        Metron, Oppositions, Perspecta, Progressive
        Architecture, Spazio, Urbanistica
Jung, Carl 185

Kahn, Louis 138, 242
Kaufmann, Edgar, Jr. 62

Kaufmann, Emil 55, 61–2
Koolhaas, Rem 69
Kowalski, Piotr 112
Krautheimer, Richard 140
Kubler, George 271

Lang, Susanne 84
L'architecture d'aujourd'hui 215
L'architettura, cronache e storia 19
Latin American architectural historiography
    265–73
    CIHE, Venezuela 270–1
    definition of Latin America 265–6
    Segre and Latin America 267–8, *269–70*, 272
    "Spanish-American" baroque architecture
        271–3
    study of Latin America 266–7
Le Corbusier
    functionalism and rationalism 59–61
    Le Modulor 95, 101, *102*, 237
    Vers une architecture (1923) *1*, 1–3, 59
    Villa Stein 49, *50*
Levi, Carlo 195
Libera, Adalberto 16
liberty *see* Neo-Liberty
lichens 36
Limone sul Garda 118, *119*
lineamenta 84
linguistic turn 222
Lisbon Triennale (2019) *see* Centro Cultural de
    Belém (CCB)
Liu, Dongyang 228, 229, 230
Lodoli, Carlo 55, *56*, 57, 58, 59, 61–2, 64
L'oggetto banale 216
Lombardo, Ivan Matteo 95–6, 98, 103
Longanesi, Leo 159
Lorenz, Marianne 158
L'Orme, Philibert de, *Premier Tome de L'Architecture*
    85, 85
Lyotard, Jean-François 172

Ma, Qingyun 225
magazines 158
    see also journals
Magnel, Gustave 123–4
Mahr, Bernd 89
Maldonado, Tomás 211
mannerism 50–1
manuscripts 101–2, 103
Marangoni, Guido 199
marble *see* terrazzo floors
Marescotti, Franco *15*, 16
marking of ground 169, 170
Marot, Sébastien 165, 174
Marsh, Andrew 120
Marshall, George 103

Index

Marzoli, Carla 95, 97–8, 99–100
Massachusetts Institute of Technology (MIT) 110, 237
materiality 123, 127
materials 57
    see also concrete; deconstruction
Mattè-Trucco, Giacomo, FIAT factory, Turin 14
matter and form 128, *128*
Maxwell, Robert 50–1
McKim, Charles 252
Meadmore, Clement 236
measuring 169, 172
media see film; journals; magazines
Medin, Gastone *199*, 200
Mediterranean architecture 138
Memmo, Andrea 55, 58
memories/memory 186, 187
Mendini, Alessandro 216
Metron 17
Michelangelo 44, *45*, 46, *47*, 127, 253, 259
Michelet, Jules 76
Michelucci, Giuseppe 14
Mies van der Rohe, Ludwig *199*, 200
Milan
    fascism, architecture under 14, 16
    housing *15*, 16, 17
    Istituto Marchiondi Spagliardi, Baggio 238, *239*, 239–40, 241
    Torre Velasca 20, *21*, 55
Milan Triennale VIII 96–7
Milan Triennale IX see Studi sulle proporzioni (Studies on Proportion) (exhibition, 1951)
Milan Triennale XV 179, 185
Milano verde project 16
Milizia, Francesco 55, 57–8, 62
Millon, Henry 237
Mitrović, Branko 84, 86
models and modelling 86–91
Modena 182, *183*, 184; *Pl. 9*
Modern Architecture (exhibition, 1932) 145
modern movement 19–20, 24
Modern Movement in Italy (exhibition, 1954) 145, 208
Módulo 265–6
Molinari, Luca 214
Mollard, Manon 168
Moneo, Rafael 48
Montuori, Eugenio 238
Moretti, Luigi 16, 46, *47*
Morpurgo, Guido 170
mountains 170, *171*, 174
Movimento italiano per l'architettura razionale (MIAR) 12, 59
Movimento studi d'architettura (MSA) 17
Mud Island, Memphis, Tennessee, USA *35*, 35–6
Muggio 180, 182

Muratori, Saverio 16
Museum of Modern Art (MoMA), New York, USA
    automobile exhibitions 207–8
    Italy: The New Domestic Landscape (exhibition, 1972) see Italy: The New Domestic Landscape (MoMA, 1972)
    Modern Movement in Italy (exhibition, 1954) 145, 208
    typewriter exhibition 208
Mussolini, Benito 12–14
Muzio, Giovanni 14

Naples 139, 140–1, *142–4*, 145, 146, 147
nation building 196, 203
Neo-Liberty 20, 241
Neoavanguardia 165, 166
Neoplatonism 126
neorealism 17
Nervi, Pier Luigi 145
new mannerism 50–1
new towns 31
Niemeyer, Oscar 265–6
Nietzsche, Friedrich 167–8, 186
Novecento movement 14

Objects 208–9
Oechslin, Werner 87
Ojetti, Ugo 194
Olgyay, Aladar and Victor 109–10, 112, 116
    apartment block, Rome *111*, 112
    comfort zone and 118–19
    "House Reversed," Budapest 112, *113*, 114
    lemon house epiphany 118, *119*
    return to ideas of 120
    Stühmer Chocolate Factory, nr. Budapest 114, *115*
    The Work of Architects Olgyay + Olgyay 110
Olivetti 211, 236
Olivetti, Adriano 16, 17
Omnibus 159
Oppenheimer, Nat 90
Oppositions 28, 32
orders see architectural orders
organic architecture 17

Pacioli, Luca, *De divina proportione* 98, 99, 102, 105
Padula *140*, 140
paesaggio 172, 174
Pagani, Carlo 157
Pagano, Giuseppe 14, *15*, 16
Pagano, Tullio 172
pagus 172, 173
Palanti, Giancarlo 114
Palazzo Farnese, Rome 184–5
Palazzo Piccolomini, Pienza *73*, 73–4, *75*; *Pl. 5*

Palazzo Rucellai, Florence 73, *74*
Palermo, Sicily 252–3, 259
Palladio, Ándrea 44
    Villa Foscari 49, *50*
Palm, Erwin Walter 272
Panofsky, Erwin 127
Parcell, Stephen 84
pedagogy 46, 258
    see also education; universities
Peng, Yigang 226
Pérez-Gómez, Alberto 64
Persico, Eduardo 16, 200
Perspecta 44
perspective 86
philosophy 222
photographs *140*, 141, *142–4*, 255, 267
physical sensation 42–3
Piacentini, Marcello 16
piazzas 141, 145
Piccinato, Luigi 14, 16, *23*
Piccolomini, Enea Silvio 72–5
Pienza 72–5, *73*, *75*; *Pl. 5*
Pininfarina, Giovanni Battista 207–8
Piranesi, Giovanni Battista 2
Pius II, Pope 72–5, 76
place-making 27
Planchart, Anala and Armando 160, *160*; *Pl. 8*
Platonism 48
Plaut, James Sachs 156
political life 23–4
Pollini, Gino 169
polyurethane 131, *131*
Ponti family portrait 152, *153*, 153
Ponti, Gio 151–61
    architectural designs 160, 161
    Aria d'Italia 155–6
    Bellezza 158
    biography 157
    Domus 14, 154, 155, 158
    family 152–4, *153*
    ICA exhibition 157
    Milan Triennale VIII 100
    Nuvole sono immagini 151, 151
    Stile 154–5
    women and 152, 157–61
Ponti, Giovanna 152–3
Ponti, Letizia (Tita) 153
Ponti, Lisa Licitra 211
    biography of Ponti 157
    cloud drawing 151
    and Enrichetta Ritter 158, *159*
    family background 153
    journals and 154, 155, 156
portable kitchen *201*, 202
Portoghesi, Paolo 216, 271
Portugal *see* Centro Cultural de Belém (CCB)

precision to uncertainty 81–92
    architecture as a profession 84–6, 91–2
    De re aedificatoria 81–3, *82–3*
    models and modelling 86–91
    rediscovery of Alberti 86
Princeton University, USA 110
printing 81–2, *82*
Progressive Architecture 237
proof of method 87
propaganda 103–4
proportional systems 101–2, 237
proportions *see Studi sulle proporzioni* (Studies on
    Proportion) (exhibition, 1951)

Quaderni di Domus 157
Quadrante 16
Quaroni, Ludovico 16, 19
    Tiburtino neighborhood 17–19, *18*
Querci, Anna 210–11

Ragghianti, Carlo 59
Raggruppamento architetti moderni italiani
    (RAMI) 12
rationalism 12–14, 59–60
Rava, Carlo Enrico 201, 202
Raymond, Alfred 249
reasoning 57
regionalism 17–18
Reif, Rita 215
Renaissance architecture, approaches to
    41–51
    abstract approach to architecture 48–51
    empathetic response to 43–4
    influence on 20th century 28, 69
    physical sensation and 42–3
    spatial interpretation of 46, *47*
Renaissance churches 42
Renaissance as rebirth and return 69–77
    exiles return *70*, 70–5, *73–5*; *Pl. 5*
    influence on 20th century 69
    life and rebirth 75–7
    tyranny of 77
revivalism 241
Richards, J. M. 241–2
Richardson, Henry Hobson 253
Ridolfi, Mario 16
    Tiburtino neighborhood 17–19, *18*
Rigoristi 58, 64
Rittel, Horst 89
Ritter, Enrichetta 158, *159*
Rogers, Ernesto N.
    Casabella 11, 19, 20, 167
    Domus 194
    modern movement and 19–20
    "from the spoon to the city" 193–4
    see also BBPR

Rome
apartment block *111*, 112
churches 253, 255
City of the European Recovery Program
(exhibition, 1950) 103–4, *104*
Colosseum 57–8
fascism, architecture under 16
journal accounts of Henry Hornbostel 253, *254*,
255–6
the lesson of *1*, 1–3, 4
Pantheon 57
Porta del Popolo 57–8
post-war period 17
Saint Peter's Basilica 255, 259, *260*
Simposio internazionale sul barocco
latinoamericano (1980) 271–2
Tiburtino neighborhood 17–19, *18*
Venturi in 138–9
Victor Olgyay in 110
Rossellino, Bernardo 73, *73*, *75*; *Pl. 5*
Rossi, Aldo 179–89, 221–30
application of Rossian theories in China 225–9,
227; *Pl. 10*
classicism, return to 182, 184, 185
criticism of 188
cylinders and beams 185
De Chirico, esteem for 180
drawings, fragments in 187, *189*
humility 189
knowledge of Rossi in China 224–5
La città analoga 179, *180*, 185–6
L'architettura della città 55, 62, *63*, 64, 188
L'architettura della città in China 221, 225, 226,
227, 230
memories/memory 186, 187
San Carlo Borromeo statue 186
San Cataldo cemetery, Modena 182, *183*, 184,
188; *Pl. 9*
Scholastic Building, New York 185, 187
Schützenstraße, Berlin 184–5
Scientific Autobiography 185, 188, 189, 226
time and 186–7, 188
translation of Rossi 225, 229–30
Rotor 125–6, 130–3, *131–2*
Rowe, Colin 31, 49–51, *50*
Royal Hungarian Technology University 109–10
Rudofsky, Bernard 138
rural architecture 17–18
see also countryside
Ruskin, John 252
Rykwert, Joseph 55, 62, 168

salvage, architectural 126, 131
Samonà, Giuseppe 16, 20–2, *23*
San Carlo Borromeo statue, Arona 186
San Cataldo cemetery, Modena 182, *183*, 184, 188; *Pl. 9*

San Diego, California, USA 35
Sartoris, Alberto 14
Gli elementi dell'architettura funzionale 59–60, *60*
Schlosser, Julius von, *Die Kunstliteratur* 58–9
Scholastic Building, New York, USA 185, 187
Schützenstraße, Berlin, Germany 184–5
Scott, Geoffrey, *The Architecture of Humanism* 42–3,
44, 46, 51
Scully, Vincent 43–4, *45*
Segre, Roberto 267–8, *269–70*
América Latina en su arquitectura 267–8
semiotics in China 222, 225, 228–9
semiotics of architecture 64, 225
shape architecture 238
shells 32
Shen, Kening 224–5
shopping centers 35
Shu, Wang 226–9, *227*; *Pl. 10*
sight-seeing 249–50
Simmel, Georg 4–5
Siza, Álvaro 167
Smith, George E. Kidder 145
Italy Builds: Its Modern Architecture and Native
Inheritance 145–6
Smithson, Alison and Peter 237
Italian Thoughts 27, 28, 36
Smithson, Peter 28–9, 32, 34, 36, 48–9, 55
solar radiation, mitigation of 110, 112, *113*, 114–15,
115
southern Italy *see* Naples
Southern Question 137, 200
"Spanish-American" baroque architecture 271
spatial interpretation of architecture 45–6, *47*, 48
Spazio 46
staircases 140, *140*, 141, *142–4*; *Pl. 7*
Stengers, Isabelle 117
stereotypes 147
Stile 154–5, 157, 158, 159
Stokes, Adrian 36
stone 166–7, *170*; *Pl. 3*
stone, placing a 167–8, 172, 174
Strada Novissima, Venice Biennale (1980) 216
Studi sulle proporzioni (Studies on Proportion)
(exhibition, 1951) 95–105, *96*; *Pl. 6*
conference 95, 98
exhibition 95, 101–2, *102*, 104–6, *105*
harmony 98–101
human body 99, 101, 102, 104–6
organizational structure 97, 100
political background 95–7, 100–1, 103
program and title 98, 100
propaganda 103–4
Stühmer Chocolate Factory, nr. Budapest 114, *115*
Sullivan, Louis 43, 58
Superstudio, *Supersurface, an Alternative Model for*
Life on Earth 165–6, 173, 174

Tafuri, Manfredo 4, 31, 32, 36, 69, 243
Taglietti, Enrico 236
taste 199–200
Terragni, Giuseppe, Casa del Fascio, Como 14
terrazzo floors 130, *130*
territory 165, 173–4
Tiburtino neighborhood 17–19, *18*
time 133–4, 186–7, 188
time, architecture outside of 75
Tong, Ming 230
tourism 249–50
Toury, Gideon 230
transcoding 28, 36
translation 221, 225, 229–30
travel diary 249–58
Turin, fascism, architecture under 14
Tuscan Aristotelianism and deconstruction
        123–34
    agency 129
    anatomy and proportions 129–30
    architectural education 123–5
    concetto 127
    disegno 126–7
    matter and form *128*, 128
    terrazzo floors *130*, 130
    time 133–4
    Tuscan Aristotelianism 127–30, 133
    waste materials, use of 125–6, 130–3, *131–2*
two-foldedness *see* doubling of Venice
typesetting *see* printing
typology 225, 228

uncertainty *see* precision to uncertainty
UNESCO 266–7
UNESCO Headquarters, Paris 112
unification of Italy 137, 196
United States 35–6, 103, 145–6, 147, 185
    see also Italy: The New Domestic Landscape
    (MoMA, 1972)
Universale di Architettura 46
universities 22, 24
University of Calabria 169
University of Palermo 169–70, *171–3*, 174
urban planning *15*, 16, 17, 21–2
Urbanistica 17

Varchi, Benedetto 125, 127, 129
Venezuela 270
Venice 20–2, 27–37
    backyards, entry by 28–31
    doubling of 31–2, 34, 36–7
    Haishi project design 32–4, *33–4*; *Pl. 1*
    Italianness of 27–8
    mud and lichens of 36
    shells of 32
    theatricality of 34–5

United States, work of Jerde in *35*, 35–6
    Water-Biennale Park *29*, 29
Venice Biennale (1980) 216
Venturi, Robert 138–41, *140*, *142–4*, 145, 147–8
    Complexity and Contradiction in Architecture
        141, 147
Venturi, Robert, Sr. and Vanna 147
Venuti, Lawrence 221
vernacular architecture 137–8
Vidler, Anthony 43
Viganò, Vittoriano, Istituto Marchiondi Spagliardi,
    Baggio, Milan 238, *239*, 239–40, 241
Vigo, Nanda 160–1
    Casa Scarabeo sotto la Foglia, nr. Vicenza 161
Villa Foscari, near Venice 49
Villa Planchart, Caracas, Venezuela 160
Villa Stein, Garches, France 49
Vimercati Ponti, Giulia 152–3
Visconti, Lucchino, *Ossessione* (film, 1943) 17
Vitruvian Man 99, 235, *235*, 237
Vittorini, Elio, *Conversazione in Sicilia* 17

Waldheim, Charles 173
Wang, Lifang 224
Wang, Lijun 226
waste materials, use of 125–6, 130–3, *131–2*
Watson, Donald 114
Weaver, William 139
Wendler, Reinhard 89
windows 169–70, *171–3*
Witt, Andrew 86
Wittkower, Rudolf
    Architectural Principles in the Age of Humanism
        48–9, 51, 236–7
    harmony 98–9
    proportions 102
    rationalism and 61
Wölfflin, Heinrich 41–2
workflows 90–1
World's Columbian Exposition (1893) 251

Xiang, Bingren 225

Yamasaki, Minoru 241

Zevi, Bruno 157
    influence of 48, 238
    journals 19
    organic architecture 17
    Quaroni, clashes with 19
    spatial interpretation of architecture 45–6, *47*, 48
    university 24
Zhao, Yiheng 222, 229
Zhu, Pei 225
Zhuhai City, China 33
Zuccari, Federico 126–7